The World and Literature
of the
Old Testament

The World and ... of th... Old Testament

John T. Willis
Editor

שְׁמַע יִשְׂרָאֵל יְהוָה
אֱלֹהֵינוּ יְהוָה אֶחָד׃

COLLEGE PRESS PUBLISHING COMPANY

Joplin, Missouri

LIBRARY OF CONGRESS CATALOG CARD NUMBER 78-52454

STANDARD BOOK NUMBER 0-89900-058-4

PRINTED IN U.S.A.

Acknowledgment

This commentary is based on the text of the Revised Standard Version of the Bible, copyrighted 1946, 1952, 1971, and 1973 by the Division of Christian Education, National Council of Churches, and used by permission.

5 4 3 2 1

Contents

Introduction

The fundamental presupposition lying behind all OT literature is that the God of Israel (Yahweh) is continually at work throughout nature and all nations to accomplish his purposes. Thus the various books of the OT record great events in nature, Israelite history, and world history and give a theological interpretation of the meaning or meanings of those events. Man can use various scientific tools to understand and reconstruct historical facts, but there is no way by a scientific method to verify or disprove the accuracy of theological interpretation by the various biblical authors. This must be accepted by faith or rejected by unbelief. The Christian accepts the theological proposition that "all scripture [here meaning the OT] is inspired by God and profitable for teaching, for reproof, for correction, and for training in righteousness" (2 Tim. 3:16).

The OT (like the New) is not a book of dogmatic theology; i.e., it is not arranged along the lines of great theological concepts, such as God, man, Christ, the church, ethics, and eschatology. There is good reason for this. God cannot be limited to any set of abstract, religious declarations deduced from Scripture by his creature man. Man cannot anticipate how God will behave in any given situation. God is not programmed to act according to any logical human system. He is God! And he acts as he wills as each new situation arises. The biblical writers do not speculate on God's nature; they record his mighty acts and declare their relevance to their own audiences. Thus all biblical texts are tied to the historical situation in which they were originally produced. The task of the commentator is twofold: (1) to reconstruct the historical situation in which a divine word was delivered, a divine act was performed, or a book was written; and (2) to explain the divine message that the author of that book intended for his audience.

A modern commentary is forced to deal with many matters that would have been unnecessary for those to whom the various books of the Bible were first addressed. They knew firsthand the author or authors, the historical setting, the language (Hebrew, Aramaic, or Greek), the emphases the author(s) intended, the location of sites mentioned in the text (geography), the lay of the land (topography), the meaning of various customs and practices (both secular and religious), kinds of dwellings, articles of clothing, etc.

Modern man, however, is not in such an advantageous position. Hebrew, Aramaic, and Greek seem far away and long ago. The average English-speaking Christian must depend on British and American translations prepared by biblical scholars. Customs, dress, modes of travel, dwellings, types of animals and birds, etc., mentioned in the Bible are strange to modern man and must be learned by careful study often involving a number of disciplines. These and many other considerations make it necessary for the biblical text to be explained either orally in classes, sermons, or study situations, or in writing, as in commentaries, introductions, and special studies. Essentially there is no difference between a Bible class teacher explaining a biblical passage orally to a class and a commentator explaining that same passage in writing to any who would care to read his comments. Whether this is done in oral or written form, it is done by fallible men with imperfect knowledge and can always be corrected or improved. It is with this conviction and in the spirit of a dedicated search for truth that the *Bible Study Texbook Series* is designed.

A careful study of the Bible is indispensable to one who seriously believes that it contains the word of God. He who holds such a conviction approaches the text in a spirit of humility, sincerely desiring to understand its meaning. He tries diligently to rid himself of preconceived ideas and strives to open his mind and heart to allow the various inspired writers to say what they really intended to their original audiences and not what he would like for them to have said. Thus he never reaches the place where his mind is closed to possible interpretations different from those to which he has already been exposed. In fact, he welcomes new light on any passage. After all, if his interpretation is correct, he will not be afraid to examine any position, because his correct understanding can reveal the inadequacies of other views. If he is incorrect and is honestly searching for truth, he will be glad to abandon wrong understandings for more correct ones. It would be impossible to grow intellectually or spiritually (as 2 Pet. 3:18 admonishes) if one did not have to re-examine his earlier views and attitudes again and again and frequently change them. The contributors to the present commentary series offer their *present understanding* of the biblical text (which in each case is based on many years of careful and prayerful preparation and study) and pray for greater insight as the years come and go.

Although the commentators in the *Bible Study Textbook Series* are scholars in their own right, they are charged to write for the average church member and not for other biblical scholars. Hebrew, Aramaic, and Greek words and phrases, words and phrases in other foreign languages, technical scholarly terminology, allusions to other works, and footnotes are used very sparingly, and then proper explanations are given. A list of abbreviations appears at the beginning of each volume.

Commentaries can deal with a variety of issues. This series will concentrate on explaining the biblical text in its original context (exegesis). Responsible application to the reader's own life (hermeneutics) must proceed from that point.

But before one undertakes a study of any single OT book, it is helpful to get a panoramic picture of the historical periods lying behind OT literature, of the ways this literature came into existence, and of the kinds of literature involved. This introductory volume is designed to aid the reader toward these ends.

John T. Willis

I

Rewarding Bible Study

John T. Willis

If the Bible contains God's message to man, man's most important task is to interpret the various books of the Bible as their authors intended for them to be understood. The Bible is not written in a special "Holy Spirit language." If it were, man could not understand it unless God gave him the key for decoding that language or a miraculous, superhuman wisdom that would enable him to comprehend it. In other words, God communicated with men in languages they already knew and were using. Thus, in interpreting the biblical text, it is essential to use the same method and tools that are used in approaching other types of literature. This is not to imply that the Bible is not unique among the world's literature. It simply affirms that man must strive to ascertain and employ a responsible method of study if he wishes to understand the Scriptures correctly.

One's approach to the Bible, as well as the method he uses to try to understand it, is governed partially by his view of inspiration. The Bible claims to be inspired of God (2 Tim. 3:16). There is no way to prove or disprove this claim absolutely, although arguments have been advanced on both sides of the issue. It must be accepted by faith or rejected by unbelief. The contributors to the *Bible Study Textbook Series* believe this claim.

Now this faith in itself demands that one go to *the Bible itself* to learn *how* God did this. Man is in no position to *dictate to God how* he must have done it. Texts like Luke 1:1-4, John 20:30-31, 1 Kings 11:41, and many others show that at least much of the time *God did not dictate* words *mechanically* to men who wrote the Bible as an employer would dictate a letter to his secretary. Rather, the various biblical authors wrote to people with real needs and problems in living situations. They were personally involved in the lives of their readers and often told them how they felt about them. When Paul says to his brethren in Colossae, "I want you to know how greatly I strive for you, and for those in Laodicea, and for all who have not seen my face" (Col. 2:1), he is relating *his own* feelings, and not words that God is forcing him to say by mechanical dictation. A warm, intimate, personal relationship usually existed between biblical authors and their audiences.

The Holy Spirit superintended the writing of the various biblical books. As Luke did research in preparation for writing his gospel to Theophilus, as he scrutinized the narratives in his possession and the oral reports that he had received, God superintended his work so that those things he selected were the most relevant to the needs of his audience and so that he presented them in the most suitable fashion for that audience. But Luke still used oral and written sources and did research in preparing his gospel. Perhaps a theoretical example would best demonstrate the point. If some early Christian preacher related to Luke Jesus' parable of the prodigal son, and if he did so accurately with proper emphasis and meaning, there would be no point in God *dictating* this story to Luke *mechanically*. And when Luke himself declares he gained his information through reading earlier narratives and through hearing oral reports of eyewitnesses and ministers of the word (Luke 1:1-4), it would be a denial of God's inspiration of Luke to argue that God dictated it to him.

It would be presumptuous to think that any person or group could construct a method for studying the Bible that would be flawless or that would stand the test of all archeological, linguistic, and literary discoveries that present and future generations of scholars will make. This chapter suggests certain principles that are generally recognized as basic in understanding a biblical passage. The various books of the Bible contain the message of God delivered to man on different occasions over a period of approximately one thousand three hundred years. That message was always relevant to the intended audience, even when it announced events in the distant future. The first task of the commentator is to ascertain the way an author (or authors) of a biblical book intended to speak to the needs of the audience to whom his (or their) book was addressed. This puts one in a position to evaluate modern problems and needs and to apply the message of the Bible to contemporary situations.

The Panoramic View

It is basic to a correct understanding of any biblical text that the modern reader not lose sight of the larger picture in which an event occurred, a statement was made, or a book was written. The author (or authors) of each book of the Bible wrote for a specific audience that had its own peculiar set of needs and problems, and his intention was to speak to those needs and problems in a meaningful way. The apostle John said to his readers: "Now Jesus did many other signs in the presence of the disciples, which are not written in this book, but these are written that you [this shows John had a particular audience in mind] may believe that Jesus is the Christ, the Son of God, and that believing you may have life in his name" (John 20:30-31). It is possible for one to know well the intricate details of the events in the life of Jesus that John relates without understanding *why* John related *these events* in the manner that he did for *his audience*. It is one thing to know the details of a historical event (or a sequence of events). It is quite another thing to understand the *religious purpose* the writer had in mind (his theology) in relating that event to *his* readers. And to fail to understand the writer's theology is to miss the basic purpose of the Bible.

There are three indispensable tools that the serious student must repeatedly consult to keep the panoramic view of the various books of the Bible in mind. One is competent *introductions* to the OT. These works treat the date, authorship, structure, and purpose of the various OT books. Without these matters fixed in mind, one is not in good position to do an exegesis of a specific text in a book. Major recent introductions include: O. Eissfeldt, *The Old Testament: An Introduction* (New York: Harper and Row, 1965); G. Fohrer, *Introduction to the Old Testament* (Nashville: Abingdon, 1968); and R. K. Harrison, *Introduction to the Old Testament* (Grand Rapids, Mich.: Wm. B. Eerdmans Publishing Company, 1971).

A second indispensable tool is good works on OT *history*. It is not adequate to understand the details of a historical event. One must also see the complex combination of people and circumstances that led up to and produced that event, and in turn other events to which it ultimately pointed. Important histories of Israel are: J. Bright, *A History of Israel* (2d ed. Philadelphia: Westminster Press, 1972); and M. Noth, *The History of Israel* (2d ed. London: Adam & Charles Black, 1965).

A third essential is studies of OT *theology*. Because of the various personalities, periods, and circumstances connected with the writing of the biblical books, each book (or group of books) has its own theological terms and emphases. Different authors may use the same words in different ways because of their theological interests. Major recent OT works in this area include: W. Eichrodt, *Theology of the Old Testament,* 2 vols. (Philadelphia: Westminster Press, 1965); G. von Rad, *Old Testament Theology*, 2 vols. (London: Oliver and Boyd, 1962 and 1965); and H. Ringgren, *Israelite Religion* (Philadelphia: Fortress Press, 1966).

Generally speaking, the modern reader finds it easier to apply these principles to Paul's letters than to other biblical writings. One reason for this is that Paul wrote within a relatively brief period of time, was not recording or interpreting the meaning of a lengthy period of history, and spoke directly to the immediate needs and problems of his readers. But many biblical books differ sharply from Paul's letters on these points. It would be a serious mistake, for example, to approach 1 and 2 Kings in the same way as Paul's letters.

Much biblical literature that records historical events is the end product of a long process. First, the event itself actually occurred. Second, that event or a portion of that event was preserved in the memory of an eyewitness or participant or in writing. Third, this was handed down orally or in writing from generation to generation. Finally, a biblical writer (under divine guidance) *selected* events or portions of events that had been handed down to him as he recounted past events for his audience. This selection was governed by the needs and problems of his audience and by the message that he intended to convey to them (John 20: 30-31; 21:25).

Writers of Scripture often claim that this is the way in which they wrote their books. Luke explains to Theophilus that he was not an eyewitness of the events in the life of Jesus that he was recording, but that he had gleaned information from reading "narratives" written by "many" authors prior to the writing of the gospel of Luke (Luke 1:1), and from hearing or talking to people who were "eyewitnesses" of the events or who had preached about events in the life of Jesus ("ministers of the word") (Luke 1:2). Luke further declares that he did not take at face value everything that he had read or heard but did careful research to make sure that what he wrote Theophilus was correct (Luke 1:3). He states that his purpose is that "you [Theophilus—note that Luke had a specific audience in mind] may know the truth concerning the things of which you have been informed" (Luke 1:4). Each event recorded in this gospel must be interpreted in light of this stated purpose else it may be misinterpreted.

The two books of Kings cover a period of approximately four hundred years (from the death of David ca. 961 B. C. [1 Kings 2:10] to the elevation of Jehoiachin of Judah in Babylon by Evil-Merodach or Amel-Marduk ca. 561 B. C. [2 Kings 25:27-30]). Obviously, a book cannot have been written earlier than the latest event recorded in that book.

Thus, 1 and 2 Kings did not exist in their present final form earlier than 561 B. C., and they could have been completed much later than this time. Yet, frequently the reader is invited to consult sources used in preparing 1 and 2 Kings if he wishes to learn additional information: "the book of the acts of Solomon" (1 Kings 11:41), "the Book of the Chronicles of the Kings of Israel"(1 Kings 14:19; 15:31; etc.) and "the Book of the Chronicles of the Kings of Judah" (1 Kings 14:29; 15:7; 2 Kings 14:18; etc.). Since this author could not have been an eyewitness of much of the information related in his book, he had to depend on earlier sources handed down to him. It is both interesting and important to understand the events he selects and includes in his work, and the sources from which they came to him. But it is of primary importance to understand the needs and problems of the people for whom he wrote and the purpose he had in mind in writing. A detailed knowledge of the historical events related in 1 and 2 Kings is insufficient if one does not gain an understanding of the purpose the author had in mind in relating these events. (For a more detailed discussion of the making of biblical books, see Ch. 7.)

One gets insights into the needs and problems of recipients of a biblical book and into the author's purpose by weaving together the various statements in that book. For example, from Paul's admonitions in 1 Corinthians, it is possible to reconstruct a reasonably clear picture of the situation in the church at Corinth when he wrote this letter. Recurring words, expressions, or ideas and an author's own summary of events provide clues to his thought. Before recounting details about specific judges that delivered Israel from foreign oppressors during their early years in the land of Canaan, the author of the book of Judges gives his own summary of this whole era (Judg. 2:11-23). He emphasizes that it was characterized by four religious features: (a) Israel *apostatized* from God by serving the Baals (vss. 11-13, 17, 19); (b) God *punished* them for this by sending enemy nations to oppress them (vss. 14-15, 20-23); (c) Israel "cried to the Lord"or *repented* and returned to his service (vs. 18); (d) God *delivered* them from their foes by raising up a judge to save them (vss. 16, 18). Then, as he rehearses the story of the major judges, he follows this same four-point pattern:

Judge	Apostasy	Punishment	Repentance	Deliverance
Othniel	3:7	3:8	3:9	3:9
Ehud	3:12	3:12	3:15	3:15
Deborah	4:1	4:2	4:3	4:4ff.
Gideon	6:1	6:1	6:6-7	6:7ff.
Jephthah	10:6	10:7	10:10	11:1ff.
Samson	13:1	13:1	X	13:2ff.

This recurring theological pattern is hardly accidental. The author of the book of Judges is trying to show the original readers of his work that when God's people forsake the Lord for other gods, they are punished; but when they repent and return to him, he delivers them from their enemies.

In attempting to comprehend an author's purpose, it is important to determine whether he approves or disapproves the words or actions of people in his account. Sometimes the author makes this clear by his own statements or by the way he relates an event. For instance, when Samson asked his father and mother for permission to marry a Philistine woman of Timnah, they rebuked him for wanting to marry a foreigner (Judg. 14:2-3). But the author of the book of Judges tells his reader: "His father and mother did not know that it was from the Lord; for he was seeking an occasion against the Philistines" (vs. 4). This writer approves Samson's desire to marry a Philistine woman, because this provides a situation in which Samson can carry out God's will to begin to deliver Israel from the Philistines. (See 13:5.) Frequently it is very hard to determine whether a biblical author approved or disapproved the words or actions of his subjects. For example, it is not clear whether the author of the book of Genesis condoned or condemned Jacob for forcing Esau to sell him his birthright before allowing him to eat some of the red pottage he had prepared (Gen. 25:29-34).

Determining the religious thrust or theology of any biblical context is an art that perhaps no man ever masters completely. It demands that one put himself wholly into the situation. He must understand the historical situation that gave birth to a biblical book (or set of books). But more than this, he must try to capture the intentions and feelings of the biblical author and his audience. He must seek to understand how that author expected his audience to respond to his work and what responses he hoped to achieve in writing as he did. Frequently some things an author did not say are as significant as the things he did say; or the attitude in which he wrote is just as important as what he wrote; or the order in which he presented his thoughts reflects his emphasis more than any one of those thoughts in isolation. (See Ch. 9 for a presentation of the major emphases in OT theology.)

FROM THE LARGER
TO THE SMALLER CONTEXT

It is essential to a correct understanding of the Bible to begin with a whole book in its larger historical and theological setting and then move to the smaller subdivisions, paragraphs, verses, lines, and words in that book. Here again competent OT introductions and theologies are indispensable. After determining the major theological emphases in a book, it is necessary to determine the extent of each subdivision and paragraph in that book. For example, the famous passage on love in 1 Corinthians 13:4-7 is part of chapters 12–14, as Paul's recurring introductory phrase "Now concerning" (12:1) and the subject matter demonstrate. It is also part and parcel of the entire book of 1 Corinthians. If one studies these verses apart from their larger contexts, it is possible that he will miss the emphasis Paul had in mind.

In chapters 12–14, Paul is discussing the problem involving tongue speakers and prophets in the Corinthian church; throughout the book of 1 Corinthians he is endeavoring to build bridges between brethren who envy one another and brethren that feel superior to their fellows. The commentator must try to understand how Paul intended for the admonitions in 13:4-7 to speak to the immediate situation involving tongue speakers and prophets and to the more general problem of envy and arrogance, but also how these admonitions fit together with the rest of this book to convey a relevant divine message to his Corinthian brethren. Only then is one in a position to decide how the message in these verses applies to situations in the modern church and world. If one isolates 13:4-7 from chapters 12–14, or chapters 12–14 from the spirit and message of the whole book, he runs the risk of misunderstanding the passage itself. At the same time, of course, the way in which one determines the larger theological thrust of a book is by carefully doing exegeses of the different passages in that book.

THE HISTORICAL SETTING

In order to interpret a passage correctly, it is necessary to understand the historical setting in which an oracle was delivered, or a conversation was held, or a song was composed, or a narrative was written, or a book was completed. The more information one can accumulate concerning the speaker, the audience, the place, events leading up to what is recorded in the text, and results of what is said or done, the more likely he is to understand the passage correctly. Concrete illustrations emphasize the importance of these considerations.

The speaker. John 9:31 says, "We know that God does not listen to sinners." This passage has been used to argue that God does not answer a person's prayers if he is not a Christian. But the *speaker* here is the blind man that Jesus healed at the pool of Siloam. (See vss. 1, 6-7, 13, 24, 30.) "We" refers to the blind man and the Pharisees. This statement shows that in the days of Jesus one group of Pharisees believed that any Jew who was not a Pharisee (or at least a supporter of the Pharisees' position) was a "sinner" and that God would not answer his prayers. The Pharisees contended that since Jesus was not a Pharisee or a supporter of the Pharisees' position, he was a "sinner" (vss. 16, 24). It is in response to this that the blind man speaks in verse 31. He reasons that he could not have been healed unless Jesus had asked God to heal him, and since he did heal him, God must have listened to Jesus— because "we know that God does not listen to sinners." Since God listened to Jesus, he cannot be a sinner, as the Pharisees insist. This verse does not mean that God does not answer a person's prayers if he is not a Christian. For one thing, the speaker (the blind man) is *not speaking authoritatively* like Moses at Sinai or Paul on the Areopagus but is simply stating the view of the Pharisees and their sympathizers. Not everything that is said by everyone in the Bible is the word of God to man. It is important that this be kept in mind if one is to determine what portions of the Bible express the views of Satan (as Gen. 3:1, 4; Matt. 4:3, 6, 9), the opinions of men (as the words of Peter in Matt. 16:22), or views contrary to those of an inspired writer, quoted by him for the sake of refutation (Col. 2:21). Second, the context of John 9:31 makes it clear that the author of this book opposes the position of the Pharisees on this point. Third, other passages in the NT teach that God does answer prayers of people who are seeking him, even though they are not yet Christians (Acts 9:11; 10:1-4).

The audience. The Lord says through the prophet Ezekiel, "When I open your graves, and raise you from your graves, . . . I will put my Spirit within you, and you shall live" (Ezek. 37:13-14). Some have interpreted these words to refer to the resurrection from the dead in the last day. However, the people to whom the Lord is speaking here (his audience) are not individuals who had died physically. The context shows that they were very much alive physically when the Lord spoke these words, for they were the Jews who had been carried into Babylonian exile in 587 b. c. Now they were cumbered with despondency; they had lost all hope (vs. 11). The Lord addresses himself to *that* problem. He compares their feeling of hopelessness with *death*. Then he promises that they will return to Palestine by using the figure of enlivening the dead (vss. 12-14). If one takes seriously the audience, he cannot interpret Ezekiel 37:1-14 to refer to the resurrection from physical death in the last day.

Factual details of an event. The more factual information one can glean and reconstruct of a historical situation lying behind an event, a conversation, a message, or a song preserved in a biblical passage, the more likely he is to understand that passage correctly. Reconstructing the historical background of a text usually requires a great deal of research. A case in point is Isaiah 1:7-8. This text comes from a time when the country of Judah lay desolate, the cities of Judah had been burned with fire, a foreign army ("aliens") had devastated the land, and the "daughter of Zion" (Jerusalem) was left like a besieged city. The only event that fits all these details in Isaiah's lifetime is Sennacherib's invasion of Judah and Jerusalem in 701 B. C.

However, in order to get a proper picture of this event, it is necessary to examine a number of primary sources: 2 Kings 18–20; 2 Chronicles 29–32; Isaiah 36–39; the Annals of Sennacherib (which are available in English translation in J. B. Pritchard, ed., *Ancient Near Eastern Texts* [3d ed., Princeton: Princeton University Press, 1969], pp. 287-88; D. W. Thomas, ed., *Documents from Old Testament Times* [New York: Harper & Row, 1961], pp. 64–70); other passages in the book of Isaiah that may come from the same time period or that shed further light on Hezekiah's reign, as Isaiah 10:5-32; 17:12-14; 28–33; relevant passages from Isaiah's contemporary Micah, as Micah 1:8-16; 3:9-12; 4:8–5:6; Jeremiah 26:16-19; and possibly certain psalms, as Psalm 83 (which specifically mentions Assyria in vs. 8).

It is also important to become acquainted with the views of specialists on Hezekiah's reign. A wide variety of literature is available in this area. For the sake of illustration, representative types of studies may be listed:

(1) Commentaries: e.g., Otto Kaiser, *Isaiah 1–12. The Old Testament Library* (London: SCM Press Ltd., 1972).

(2) Histories of Israel: J. Bright, *A History of Israel* (2d ed., Philadelphia: Westminster Press, 1972), pp. 277-308.

(3) Bible dictionaries: H. B. MacLean, "Hezekiah," *The Interpreter's Dictionary of the Bible,* vol. 2 (Nashville: Abingdon Press, 1962), pp. 598-600.

(4) Bible atlases and other works on archeology: G. E. Wright and F. V. Filson, *The Westminster Historical Atlas to the Bible* (2d ed., Philadelphia: Westminster Press, 1956), pp. 54-55, 73.

(5) Articles in scholarly journals: S. H. Horn, "Did

Sennacherib Campaign Once or Twice against Hezekiah?"
Andrews University Seminary Studies 4 (1966), pp. 1-28;
J. B. Geyer, "2 Kings 18:14-16 and the Annals of
Sennacherib," *Vetus Testamentum* 21 (1971), pp. 604-606.

(6) Special studies: Brevard S. Childs, *Isaiah and the
Assyrian Crisis* (London: SCM Press, 1967).

A vast amount of literature is available on almost any
biblical text or subject, not only in English, but also in many
foreign languages. Only very rarely (if ever) is it true that
one has read *everything* on any biblical passage or problem.
There is always information to which the commentator has
not yet been exposed, and thus his interpretations must be
offered in a spirit of humility and as views subject to change
as new discoveries are made and new information is
learned. He who is serious about discovering what actually
happened historically and about learning God's message in
that situation is eager to read all he can on the subject and
to abandon incorrect impressions or beliefs for more accurate ones, both intellectual and spiritual.

In order to get a better understanding of many historical
events recorded in the Bible, it is necessary to consult
reliable maps. One should learn the locations of cities,
mountains, rivers, valleys, and lakes in relationship to each
other, and distances between various places (geography).
He should also fix in mind the lay of the land, so that he will
know whether a locality is *down* in a valley or *up* on a hill,
the features of the surrounding terrain, etc. (topography).
Y. Aharoni and M. Avi-Yonah, *The Macmillan Bible Atlas*
(New York: The Macmillan Co., 1968), offer excellent aids
along these lines.

In many biblical stories, it is important to learn as much
as possible about clothing worn by various groups of people
or nations, kinds of equipment used in warfare, different
sorts of money, secular and sacred buildings with their fur-
niture, agricultural implements, types of animals and plants,
means of transportation, political and economic practices,
etc. The five-volume work edited by M. Avi-Yonah and
A. Malamat, *Illustrated World of the Bible Library*
(Jerusalem: The International Publishing Co. Ltd., 1958), is

very illuminating in these matters. (For an outline of Old Testament history, see Chs. 4 and 5.)

LANGUAGE

Meaning of words. It is basic to a study of any literature to understand the meaning of words used in the text. One must be extremely careful to discover the meaning that the biblical writer or speaker had in mind and avoid superimposing his own definition on a word. This is very difficult and requires much work and self-discipline.

In addition to the difficulty of translating Hebrew, Aramaic, and Greek into the best possible English equivalents, three matters pose serious problems for English readers. First, modern English-speaking people often use words found in the Bible but attach a different meaning to them from what was intended by the biblical writer. One example is the use of the word "soul" (Hebrew *nephesh*; Greek *psyche*). The average twentieth-century man in the English-speaking world uses "soul" for the inner part of *man* that will live *eternally*. However, many passages where this word appears will not allow this meaning, and even the KJV avoids translating the original words by "soul" in a number of places. According to the Hebrew of Genesis 1:20 God said, "Let the waters bring forth swarms of living *souls*" (KJV, "the moving creature"); and in Genesis 1:24 God said, "Let the earth bring forth living *souls* (KJV, "the living creature") according to their kinds." Biblically speaking, then, fish and beasts have *souls* just as man does. Now since this word cannot mean the inner part of *fish* or *beasts* that will live eternally, biblically speaking it is not clear that the word "soul" is what distinguishes man from other creatures of God. "Soul" usually denotes the whole living being or life itself. For example, when 1 Samuel 18:1, 3 says that Jonathan loved David "as his own *soul*," it means that Jonathan loved David as *himself*. When Paul tells the Thessalonians, "we were ready to share with you not only the gospel of God but also our own *souls*" (1 Thess. 2:8, see the KJV and the ASV), he means that he and Silas and

Timothy were willing to share *themselves* with them (see the RSV and NEB).

Second, frequently words have changed their meaning in the course of the development of the English language. A word that had one meaning when the KJV was published in Great Britain in 1611 may have an entirely different meaning in America today. One example is "treasures" (Hebrew *'otseroth*) in the KJV of Job 38:22:

> Hast thou entered into the *treasures* of the snow,
> Or hast thou seen the *treasures* of the hail?

Three to four centuries ago, the word "treasure" meant not only wealth or riches, but also a place where treasures were stored. *The Oxford English Dictionary,* vol. 9 (Oxford: At the Clarendon Press, 1933), p. 305, cites several examples of this usage of "treasure" in English literature from the fourteenth to the sixteenth centuries A.D. To be sure, the Hebrew word *'otseroth* can mean wealth (Isa. 2:7; 30:6; Jer. 15:13), but frequently it means places where wealth and other things are stored up (1 Kings 7:51; 15:18; 2 Kings 12:18; Jer. 38:11; Ezek. 28:4). The context of Job 38:22 demands this latter meaning. In verses 19 and 24, the Lord asks Job if he knows where light dwells; in verse 19, he asks him if he knows where darkness lives; in verse 24, he asks him if he knows where the east wind is kept until God is ready to scatter it on the earth; and in verse 22, he asks him if he knows where snow and hail are stored up until God is ready to use them. God is not asking Job if he has "examined" the "riches" that *come out of* the snow, but if he has "entered into" the "treasuries or storehouses" *out of which snow comes.* Deuteronomy 28:12 speaks of *rain* coming out of God's "good treasury the heavens"; Jeremiah 10:13; 51:16; and Psalm 135:7 say God brings forth the *wind* from his "storehouses"; Psalm 33:7 declares that God puts the *deeps* in "storehouses"; and, following the same basic figure of these verses, Job 38:22 presupposes that God keeps *snow* and *hail* stored up in heavenly treasuries or storehouses.

Now since "treasures" meant "treasuries or storehouses"

in 1611, the Anglican and Puritan scholars who translated the KJV correctly chose "treasures" to translate the Hebrew *'otseroth*. However, since "treasures" has now come to mean primarily "wealth or riches" and since this is not what God intended in the words recorded in Job 38:22, it has become necessary to translate *'otseroth* by "treasuries" (ASV), "storehouses" (RSV), "storehouse or arsenal" (NEB), and the like, to convey the correct thought to English-speaking readers living in the twentieth century. The issue here is not which English version is truest to the original Hebrew. They are all accurate, and they all say the same thing. The only thing that would make them *appear* to differ in the modern reader's mind is that the word "treasures" does not mean the same thing to the average man today that it did 350 years ago. Because the English language has changed, more recent translations have been forced to use different words from those found in earlier versions in order to avoid conveying an incorrect idea of the meaning of the original to modern man. (A complete list of passages using *'otseroth*, with the meaning of this noun in each passage, is given in F. Brown, S. R. Driver, and C. A. Briggs, *A Hebrew and English Lexicon of the Old Testament* [Oxford: At the Clarendon Press, 1968], pp. 69-70.)

Another English word whose meaning has changed since the publication of the KJV in 1611 is "simplicity" in 2 Corinthians 11:3—"But I fear, lest by any means, as the serpent beguiled Eve through his subtlety, so your minds should be corrupted from the *simplicity* that is in Christ." Occasionally, modern man uses this passage to show that the *Bible* is "simple" (i.e., "easy to understand"). If this is true, it contradicts passages like 2 Peter 3:15-16:

> And account that the longsuffering of our Lord is salvation; even as our beloved brother Paul also according to the wisdom given unto him hath written unto you; as also in all his epistles, speaking in them of these things; in which are some things *hard to be understood*, which they that are unlearned and unstable wrest, as they do also the other Scriptures, unto their own destruction.
>
> (KJV)

But there is no contradiction here, because in 2 Corinthians 11:3 (a) Paul is not talking about the Bible, but about the devotion of the Corinthian brethren; and (b) in 1611 "simplicity" in a context like this did not mean "easy to understand," but "sincerity." The average man understood *sim*plicity" to be the opposite of "*dup*licity," "hypocrisy," "dishonesty," or "infidelity." *The Oxford English Dictionary,* vol. 9 (Oxford: At the Clarendon Press, 1933), p. 66, provides examples of this meaning in English literature from the sixteenth through the nineteenth centuries. The Greek word here is *haplótēs.* All Greek scholars agree that it means "singleness, sincerity, honesty, fidelity." So in 2 Corinthians 11:3 Paul is expressing his fear that Satan will cause Christ's bride (here the Corinthian church) to become unfaithful to her betrothed. (See also vs. 2.) The word "simplicity" conveyed this idea to the average man when the KJV and ASV were published, but in more recent translations it has become necessary to use "sincere devotion" (RSV) or "single-hearted devotion" (NEB) to render the original correctly for modern man, because the generally accepted meaning of "simplicity" has changed as the English language has developed.

Third, the same word does not necessarily have the same meaning everywhere it appears in Scripture. An example of this is the word "heaven." According to Genesis 1, "heaven" stands over against "earth" (vs. 1), God makes a firmament to separate the waters above from the waters below and calls it "heaven" (vss. 6-8), he creates the sun, moon, and stars and sets them in this firmament of (called) "heaven" (vss. 14-15, 17), and he makes birds to fly above the earth across the firmament of (called) "heaven" (vs. 20). Clearly "heaven" here means the sky or the atmospheric space above the earth. But the apostle Peter tells Christians, "we have been born anew . . . to an inheritance which is imperishable, undefiled, and unfading, kept in *heaven* for you" (1 Pet. 1:3-4). Here "heaven" does not mean the sky, but the eternal home of God's people.

It is indeed important to interpret scripture by scripture. But this does not mean that it is correct methodologically to transfer the meaning of a word in one context to other contexts that use the same word. Instead, the first responsibility of a Bible student is to seek to understand a word in its own context, for it is possible that it may have a meaning there which it has nowhere else in Scripture. For various reasons, a particular author may choose a particular word (which is commonly used in different senses elsewhere) to convey his theological emphasis. For example, Paul uses "the Lord" almost exclusively of Jesus Christ.

Meaning of expressions. Man uses not only words but also phrases to express his thoughts. Frequently words that mean one thing when they are used in isolation have an entirely different meaning in a stereotyped expression. A case in point is the contemporary American expression "You are pulling my leg." One would arrive at a very amusing interpretation of this phrase if he analyzed each word instead of looking at the whole expression. "You are pulling my leg" does not mean "You are exerting a force on my limb so as to cause motion toward you," but "You are teasing me." Similarly, the Bible contains many phrases that must be understood as idiomatic or stereotyped expressions if one is to interpret them correctly.

Several OT passages contain the phrase "He slept with his fathers." To "sleep" means to fall into a natural and temporary diminution of feeling and thought, and "father" means a male parent. Yet the expression "He slept with his fathers" does not mean "He fell into a natural and temporary diminution of feeling and thought with his male parents." It simply means "He died." This is clear from the context, because after a person "sleeps with his fathers," he is "buried" (1 Kings 2:10; 11:43, 14:31). It is also clear from synonymous expressions used with this phrase. God says to David, "When *your days are fulfilled* and *you lie down with your fathers,* I will raise up your offspring after you" (2 Sam. 7:12). According to 1 Kings 11:21, "Hadad heard in Egypt that David *slept with his fathers* and that Joab the commander of the army *was dead.*" "When *David's time to die* drew near," he said to Solomon his son, "I am about to *go the way of all the earth*" (1 Kings 2:1-2); a few verses later the text says, "Then David *slept with his fathers*" (vs. 10). The Lord said to King Josiah, "I will *gather you to your fathers,* and *you shall be gathered to your grave* in peace" (2 Kings 22:20). All these passages show that the expression "to sleep with one's fathers" means "to die."

A proper understanding of this principle partly explains why it is impossible to translate many passages in the Bible literally. If scholars did this, not only would numerous lines sound strange, but they would be unintelligible to modern man. One example is 2 Samuel 5:4. Translated literally, the original Hebrew says, "A son of thirty year David in to reign him, forty year he reigned." No English version translates this verse literally. If one did, it would be wrong. The task of biblical translators is to transfer the *ideas* of the Bible into corresponding modern ideas, and not to translate each word slavishly into a corresponding English word. Thus the translators of the KJV in 1611 wisely avoided a literal translation of 2 Samuel 5:4 and produced a good correct English sentence: "David was thirty years old when he began to reign, and he reigned forty years." More recent versions have adopted this same policy. All English versions of the Bible have their strengths and weaknesses, and therefore one should examine all of them as he seeks to understand God's word. A careful study of the RSV shows that it is a most accurate translation. (Unless otherwise noted, this version is quoted in the *Bible Study Textbook Series*.)

Figurative language and linguistic peculiarities. A major problem God has in communicating his message to man is couching divine attitudes, thoughts, and imperatives in understandable, challenging, relevant, memorable human language. He bridges the communication gap by beginning with concepts man already understands and using them as avenues for conveying his will. Thus the Bible is full of allegories, parables, figures, and other types of linguistic peculiarities. If one is to interpret the biblical text correctly, it is essential that he determine whether the original writer or speaker *intended* for his words to be taken literally or figuratively. Sometimes the Bible specifically states that a certain paragraph is allegorical or parabolic: Paul says his remarks on Sarah and Hagar compose "an allegory" (Gal. 4:24—applying to 4:21-5:1); and Matthew states that Jesus' story of the sower who planted seed on different types of soil was a "parable" (Matt. 13:3, 18—applying to 13:3-9, 18-23). In other instances, it is clear from the nature of the statement itself that a biblical text is intended to be taken figuratively. Problems arise for the reader when the biblical writer or speaker does not state specifically whether he *intends* to be relating historical facts or whether he *intends* to be telling an allegory or parable or using a figure. In passages or books where this is not clear, it is necessary to admit that a dogmatic conclusion cannot be reached. Here it may be helpful to note and illustrate various kinds of figures used in Scripture.

Hyperbole is intentional exaggeration used for the sake of emphasis. When a hunter says, "I missed that deer a mile," everyone knows that he does not mean this literally, but that he is exaggerating to show disgust because he missed his game. On one occasion Jesus said: "It is easier for a camel to go through the eye of a needle than for a rich man to enter the kingdom of God" (Matt. 19:24). Some take this statement literally and then try to explain it by claiming that "the needle's eye" was a small gate through which a camel could not pass unless all his load was taken off his back. But there is no evidence for such a fanciful interpretation. Jesus is simply using hyperbole. He means that the possession of great wealth makes it very difficult for man to put his trust wholly in God. In Obadiah 4, the Lord speaks of Edom setting her nest among the stars. Obviously this is not intended to be taken literally, but is a hyperbole used to emphasize Edom's arrogance.

A *simile* is a comparison using "like" or "as" and clearly indicates a figure. One psalmist says, "*As* a hart longs for flowing streams, so longs my soul for thee, O God" (Ps. 42:1). Clearly his point is that man's yearning for refreshing strength from God is like a thirsty deer's desire for fresh water. A *metaphor* is a comparison not using "like" or "as." A psalmist says: "We are . . . the sheep of his (God's) pasture" (Ps. 100:3). This cannot mean that human beings are *really* sheep, or imply that God is *really* a shepherd that brings sheep to a literal pasture. Rather, it suggests that God's relationship to his people is similar in a number of ways to a shepherd's relationship to his sheep.

Metonymy is the use of one word for another with which it is closely associated. When a guest says to a woman who has prepared the meal he is eating, "You set a good *table*," everyone knows that he means, "You prepare good *food*." He uses the word "table" because it is closely connected with "food" that is set on the table. Paul writes: "As often

as you eat this bread and *drink the cup*, you proclaim the
Lord's death until he comes" (1 Cor. 11:26). But it is
obvious that he does not really mean for Christians to drink
the cup (i.e., the container), but the *wine* contained in the
cup.

Synecdoche is a figure of speech in which part of an
object is used for the whole object or the whole is used for a
part. When Paul says, "How beautiful are the *feet* of those
who preach good news" (Rom. 10:15, quoting Isa. 52:7),
both the context and common sense show that he has in
mind the whole person, and not just his feet. God promises
Abraham, "Your descendants shall possess the *gate* of their
enemies" (Gen. 22:17); similarly, Jesus promises Peter,
"The *gates* of Hades shall not prevail against it"
(Matt. 16:18). In both cases the "gate" is used as a symbol
for the whole city or kingdom.

Irony and *sarcasm* are methods of expression in which a
speaker or writer means exactly the opposite of what he
says. If a child rushes into the house covered with dirt and
mud and his mother says, "Billy, you look beautiful,"
everyone realizes she is being sarcastic and means the
opposite of what she actually says. When Job says to his
three friends, "No doubt you are the people, and wisdom
will die with you" (Job 12:2), there can be no question that
he means they are very imperceptive and unwise. And when
Elijah says mockingly to the prophets of Baal, "Cry aloud
(i.e., to Baal), for he is a god" (1 Kings 18:27), he really
means, "You can yell as loudly as you like, but you are
wasting your time, because Baal is a nonexistent figment of
your imagination and not a god."

Litotes is the use of an understatement in order to
increase the effect. The psalmist declares, "A broken and
contrite heart, O God, thou wilt not despise" (Ps. 51:17).
But it is clear that he is not concerned with God's not
despising his penitent heart, but with his enthusiastically
welcoming it.

Personification is speaking of an object or an abstract
concept as if it were a person. First Chronicles 16:33 says
that trees will sing for joy, and in Psalm 98:8 the poet

summons the floods to clap their hands. Proverbs 9:1-6 depicts wisdom as a woman who prepares a sumptuous banquet and invites all men to come into her house and eat of her food.

A *euphemism* is the substitution of an inoffensive expression for one that might be offensive. The KJV of 1 Samuel 24:3 (following the Hebrew text literally) says that Saul went into the cave "to cover his feet." This is a Hebrew idiom meaning "to have a bowel movement" (see also Judg. 3:24), not "to take a nap," as the casual reader might think. The "running issue" (KJV), "issue" (ASV), or "discharge" (RSV, NEB) from a man's body described in Leviticus 15:2, 3, and 19 is probably gonorrhea, a contagious inflammatory disease of the genitourinary tract affecting the male's urethra.

In order to speak of God in language that man can understand, it is necessary to speak of him as if he were a man (*anthropomorphism*) with human passions (*anthropopathism*). Such language is always inadequate because it cannot describe God as he is in the absolute, but only in accommodative language. Many problems have arisen because men take anthropomorphic statements literally. If God warns certain people that he will do something and then does not do it because they repent, the Bible says that God "repented" (Jon. 3:9; 4:2). This is not to be taken literally. Rather, the Bible is using language common to men to convey a great truth concerning God (viz., he is compassionate and forgiving). To pursue the meaning beyond this is to go beyond the intention of biblical writers.

Aposiopesis is the sudden breaking off of a thought before it is completed. Several examples of this phenomenon appear in the OT, and it is important to recognize this for correct interpretation. When Moses prayed to the Lord in behalf of Israel, he cried: "But now, if thou wilt forgive their sin—and if not, blot me, I pray thee, out of thy book which thou hast written" (Exod. 32:32; see also Gen. 3:22-23).

Hendiadys is the use of two words occurring together or joined by "and" to express one idea. The phrase translated "my rock and my salvation" in Psalm 62:2, 6 appears to be a hendiadys meaning "my rock of salvation" or "my mountain of triumph."

Merismus is the expression of a totality by using the two extremes in a class. The expression "good and evil" in 2 Samuel 14:17 means "all things that are on the earth," as the parallel line in verse 20 shows. "Man and beast" in Psalm 36:6 is a comprehensive term meaning all God's creatures.

Any time the word "of" occurs in an expression, one must decide whether the author intended for the word after "of" to be the subject (*subjective genitive*) or the object (*objective genitive*) of the word before "of." This must be decided in each context on the basis of context and parallel texts. The "love *of* Christ" in 2 Corinthians 5:14 must mean "Christ's love for us" (subjective genitive), and not "our love for Christ" (objective genitive), as the following line and the whole context show. The "gift *of* the Holy Spirit" in Acts 2:38 must mean "the gift which is the Holy Spirit" (subjective genitive), and not "the gift which the Holy Spirit gives" (objective genitive), because this is most natural in the context and is parallel to Acts 5:32.

Singular and plural. In many passages, a correct understanding is possible only if one rightly discovers whether a certain word is singular or plural. One problem area here is the second person pronoun. Modern American English makes no distinction between "you" (singular) and "you" (plural). But there is a distinction in the biblical languages (Hebrew, Aramaic, and Greek). In earlier stages of the English language, this distinction was made by using "thou, thine, and thee" for the singular and "ye, your, and yours" for the plural. This was part of daily speech. If a man met one person on the street he would say, "How art *thou*?"; but if he met two or more he would say, "How are *you*?" The idea that "thou" carries with it a special connotation of reverence cannot be substantiated. When Jesus says, "*Thou* blind Pharisee" (Matt. 23:26, KJV), he has no intention of showing reverence. And when he says to the devil, "Get *thee* hence, Satan" (Matt. 4:10, KJV), it would contradict the whole tenor of the paragraph and of the entire

New Testament to conclude that Jesus was showing him reverence. The word "thou" indicates the singular number and has nothing to do with showing reverence.

This understanding is crucial in interpreting a number of texts. One example is Luke 22:31-32:

> Simon, Simon, behold, Satan hath desired to have you (plural, so all the apostles), that he may sift you (plural) as wheat: But I have prayed for thee (singular, so Peter), that thy (singular) faith fail not: and when thou (singular) art converted, strengthen thy (singular) brethren (i.e., the other apostles who are weaker than you, Peter, and will depend heavily on your stronger faith).

A second problem area involving the singular and the plural is the adjective. In English it is often impossible to tell whether an adjective is singular or plural. There is a clear distinction in the biblical languages. One passage in which this distinction must be understood in order to interpret the text correctly is Hebrews 12:23, where the KJV and ASV have the expression "church of the first-born," and the RSV has "assembly of the first-born." On the basis of passages like Hebrews 1:6, a few have erroneously assumed that "first-born" in Hebrews 12:23 refers to Christ and from this conclude that the author of Hebrews had in mind "the church of Christ." The fact is that the Greek word translated "first-born" here is a genitive *plural* (*prototókōn*), and the writer means "church (or assembly) of first-born ones (people) who are (note the plural verb) enrolled in heaven." Just as the phrase "church of the Thessalonians" (1 Thess. 1:1; 2 Thess. 1:1) means the church *made up of* people who live in Thessalonica, so "church of the first-born" means the church made up of first-born people.

A third problem area involving the singular and the plural is the imperative. In the biblical languages it is easy to distinguish between a command addressed to one person and one addressed to many, but the English language frequently does not make this distinction. For example, if a man says "Go!" in English, it is impossible to tell whether he is speaking to one person or to a group. An understanding of this principle is important in interpreting Micah 6:1-2. In verse 1, "Arise" and "plead" are singular, i.e., they are addressed to *one* person: apparently the Lord is speaking to Micah here. But in verse 2, "Hear" is plural, i.e., it is addressed to a *group*: now Micah is speaking to the "mountains."

The thoughtful biblical student who does not know Hebrew, Aramaic, and Greek should use other means of finding out whether an ambiguous second person pronoun, adjective, or imperative is singular or plural. (a) He should consult as many English versions of the Bible as possible. The NEB would help one avoid an incorrect interpretation of Hebrews 12:23, for it reads, "assembly of the first-born citizens of heaven," which is an excellent translation of the meaning of the original. (b) He should consult a number of responsible commentaries written by scholars that know the biblical languages. (c) He should study competent Bible dictionaries that are devoted to word studies, such as *The Theological Dictionary of the Old Testament* and *The Theological Dictionary of the New Testament*.

Tone of voice and emphasis. Subconsciously everyone who reads the Bible hears a certain tone of voice and emphasis in many texts. Admittedly, these matters must remain subjective in numerous passages, but there are many where the original emphasis is clear from the nature of the Hebrew, Aramaic, or Greek expression, or from the context. Certain clues may be suggested here.

Many statements in the Bible are not complete sentences. They indicate excitement or an inability to express oneself adequately because of the nature of the situation, thus reflecting an air of authenticity. This is often obscured in various English translations, apparently because the translators feel that they must produce a smooth-flowing literary work. According to the Hebrew text of Amos 3:11, the Lord urgently warns Israel: "An adversary! Even round about the land!" Usually English versions obscure this urgency by reading: "An adversary there shall be even round about the land" (so KJV and ASV, similarly RSV and NEB). A similar exclamation appears in the Greek text of Acts 8:36 when the eunuch cries out: "Look, water! What is to prevent my being baptized?" His excitement is obvious. But English versions diminish this by reading, "See, here is water; what doth hinder me to be baptized?" (so KJV and ASV, similarly RSV and NEB).

In the biblical languages, the pronoun appears in the verb form itself. Therefore when a pronoun appears along with the verb, ordinarily the speaker or writer is placing emphasis on that pronoun. Gideon's reply to the men of Israel who wanted him to rule over them was, "*I* will not rule over you" (Judg. 8:23), and in the Hebrew the "I" is emphatic. It is unfortunate that translators of modern versions have not devised means to indicate when such emphases are intended in the original text.

The word order of the original text often shows where the biblical writer or speaker intended for the emphasis to be placed. When the elders of Israel urged Samuel to give God's people a king, Samuel prayed to the Lord. According to the word order of the Hebrew text, the Lord answered, "Not *thee* have they rejected, but *me* have they rejected from being king over them" (1 Sam. 8:7). The emphasis is on the words "thee" and "me."

Once again, it is important for one who does not know the biblical languages to compensate for this by reading several English translations, consulting good commentaries, and studying scholarly articles dealing with the biblical text.

CUSTOMS AND ABIDING TRUTH

Throughout the history of Christianity, followers of Christ have debated the difficult question of whether a certain biblical command was intended for Christians in all times or whether it was limited to Christians in the first-century world. No certain solution to this problem which would apply to all situations has yet been suggested. Thus serious searchers for truth must respect each other's opinions in these matters and refrain from taking dogmatic positions which are unwarranted on the basis of present knowledge of Scripture. (See Rom. 14:1-8.)

Two observations are important here. First, the study of

one biblical text after another leaves the distinct impression that what is essential to religion is not merely external acts performed correctly, but the meaning of those acts and the motives of those doing them. Fasting was a widespread practice in biblical times, but it meant different things on different occasions. Sometimes people fasted to show their grief over someone's death (1 Sam. 31:13; 1 Chron. 10:12; 2 Sam. 1:12), sometimes to express their penitence of sins they had committed (1 Sam. 7:6; 2 Sam. 12:16, 21-23; Jer. 14:12; Jon. 3:5; Matt. 6:16-18), and sometimes to reflect great concern over the seriousness of a critical situation (Neh. 1:4; Esth. 4:3, 16; Ps. 35:13; Acts 13:2-3). But Isaiah 58:1-9 declares that for God, genuine fasting is liberating the oppressed, sharing bread with the hungry, taking the homeless poor into one's house, and clothing the naked.

Second, a belief, teaching, or religious practice does not have to originate in Israel or Christianity to be central to Judaism or Christianity. Jesus declared that no commandment is greater than to love God with one's whole being and one's neighbor as himself (Mark 12:28-34). Yet God summoned man to do this long before Christ ever came to earth (see Deut. 6:4-5; Lev. 19:18). To love God and one's fellowman completely is central to Christianity, and yet this did not originate with Christianity, nor is it unique to Christianity.

TYPES OF LITERATURE

In order to interpret any piece of literature correctly, it is necessary to determine the type of literature it is and the characteristics of that type. Generally speaking, the literature found in the OT may be divided into six large groups. This chapter offers a brief introduction to each group. (A more detailed discussion is given in Ch. 6.)

Narrative. The primary means of recording history in the OT is prose narrative. The following things should be kept in mind in reading narrative material. (a) The major emphasis in relating history is religious, not preserving facts. The various biblical writers describe events for the purpose of teaching great lessons concerning God and man. Frequently an author states the theological point he wishes to make in the midst of the account he is handing on to his readers. As the writer of 2 Samuel 8 tells of David's victories over the Philistines, the Moabites, the Syrians, and the Edomites, he declares that "the Lord gave victory to David wherever he went" (vss. 6, 14). (b) Biblical writers selected those stories or parts of stories that would make the greatest impression on their readers and that would best suit their purpose in writing a book (John 20:30-31). (c) The Bible does not always present events in the exact chronological sequence that they occurred. There are many ways in which narratives can be arranged, and the Bible student should try to discover the arrangement intended by the authors of the various books.

Law codes. Most of the legal material in the OT is found in Exodus 20–31, Leviticus, Numbers 2–6, 8–10, 15, 19, 28–30, 34–36, and Deuteronomy 4–30. Many of these laws are bound together in codes, such as the Ten Commandments (Exod. 20:1-17; Deut. 5:6-21), the Book of the Covenant (Exod. 20:23–23:22; see 24:7), the Holiness Code (Lev. 17–26), etc. These laws fall into two large categories. Some are stated absolutely without any modifications, as "You shall not kill" (Exod. 20:13). Scholars call these *apodictic laws*. Others depend on the circumstances, as:

> If he (a slave) comes in single, he shall go out single; if he comes in married, then his wife shall go out with him. If his master gives him a wife and she bears him sons or daughters, the wife and her children shall be her master's and shall go out alone. . . .
> Exodus 21:3-4

Scholars call these *casuistic laws*. Unfortunately, many find biblical laws meaningless and uninspiring. If one could realize that they are people-centered, and are designed to meet the needs of men in real life situations, he would study them enthusiastically and greatly benefit from it.

Poetry. Much of the OT is in Hebrew poetry. It is a great weakness of the KJV that it is printed so modern man cannot tell what is poetry and what is prose. The serious student must consult the RSV and other modern translations to discover this. Hebrew poetry occurs in Job 3:1-42:6, Psalms, Proverbs, Lamentations, large portions of the prophetic literature, and various portions of the historical books.

The most prominent characteristic of OT poetry is parallelism, which consists of various types. Sometimes two lines say the same thing in different words, making synonymous parallelism:

Pride goes before destruction,
and a haughty spirit before a fall.

Proverbs 16:18

Sometimes the second line expresses a thought that stands in contrast to the first line, which makes antithetic parallelism:

A soft answer turns away wrath,
but a harsh word stirs up anger.

Proverbs 15:1

The OT also contains synthetic, emblematic, stairlike, and inverted parallelism.

There are also other characteristics of Hebrew poetry. Frequently the same refrain occurs several times in a poetic piece:

How are the mighty fallen.

2 Samuel 19:25, 27

Let them thank the Lord for his steadfast love,
for his wonderful works to the sons of men.

Psalm 107:8, 15, 21, 31

Many poems in the OT are acrostics, i.e., each succeeding line, verse, or group of verses begins with the next letter in the Hebrew alphabet, as Psalm 119, the description of the good wife in Proverbs 31:10-31, and Lamentations 1-4.

Prophetic. A number of literary types appear in the prophetic books. Biographical and autobiographical accounts occur in both prose and poetry. The most predominant literary type used by the prophets is a brief oracle which was originally addressed to a specific situation. The literary style of an oracle was often derived from familiar facets and customs of Israelite life. The prophets used oracles of doom to announce imminent punishment (Mic. 3:9-12) and oracles of hope to announce future deliverance (Jer. 30:18-22). They pronounced warnings and woe oracles upon God's people (Isa. 5:8-23) and foreign nations (Isa. 10:5-19; Amos 1:3–2:8) because of their sins. They used taunt songs against enemies (Isa. 37:22; Jer. 48–51) and laments or dirges over God's people (Amos 5:1-2; Ezek. 19:1-9). They assumed the role of the plaintiff's lawyer in God's lawsuit against his unfaithful people (Mic. 6:1-8; Hos. 4:1-3).

Wisdom. The fundamental literary type found in the OT wisdom literature (Job, Proverbs, Ecclesiastes, and certain Psalms) is a simple proverb, designed to teach a great lesson in memorable words. Many proverbs are couched in the form of comparisons:

> Like a madman who throws firebrands,
>   arrows, and death,
> is the man who deceives his neighbor
> and says, "I am only joking!"
> > Proverbs 26:18-19

There are many numerical proverbs in the OT, and frequently they assume that a riddle has been proposed which deserves solution (Prov. 6:16-19; 30:11-31; see Judg. 14:14, 18). Occasionally the Wise Men (see Jer. 18:18; Prov. 24:23) presented their teaching in rather long poetic pieces that dealt with the same subject throughout, as the loose woman (Prov. 5:7-23; 6:20-35) and wisdom (Prov. 8).

Apocalyptic. There are a few chapters in the OT that deal with an ideal future for God's faithful people (Isa. 24–27; Ezek . 38–39; Dan.; Zech. 9–14). Scholars call this type of material *apocalyptic*. Although there is no consensus concerning this material, a few observations can be made. These works were delivered in a time of great crisis for the purpose of encouraging God's people to stand firm in the midst of severe persecution. Their various authors used fantastic symbolism, imagery, and visions to convey their message. Evidently the meaning of this imagery was clear to the original audiences (although much of it is not clear to modern man), because these authors intended to "reveal" God's message to their hearers or readers, not to "conceal" it. It seems likely that they chose to use imagery in order to protect themselves and their audiences from persecution that would surely come if their enemies understood what they were saying. The modern reader should interpret apocalyptic pieces as God's message addressed to the writer's audience, and not as a panoramic view of human history from the writer's time to the end of the world. This is not to deny that apocalyptists spoke of the end of the world, but to emphasize that they spoke primarily for the people of their own day.

The same God who guided the production of the Bible gave man a highly complex mind. The biblical message is addressed to this mind. Therefore it is a very complex message. God expects man to use his mind to its fullest capacity in comprehending that message. This is a long and difficult process. One must give his lifetime to it. But it is extremely rewarding for the humble, growing, responsible student.

BIBLIOGRAPHY

Many kinds of books that are useful in Bible study are mentioned in the body of this article. Here only a few additional books are listed.

Essential Books for a Pastor's Library. 4th ed., Richmond, Va.: Union Theological Seminary, 1968.

Hahn, H. F. *Old Testament in Modern Research.* Philadelphia: Muhlenberg Press, 1954.

Kaiser, Otto, and W. G. Kummel. *Exegetical Method: A Student's Handbook.* Translated by E. V. N. Goetchius. New York: The Seabury Press, 1967.

Meek, T. J. *Hebrew Origins.* New York: Harper & Row, Publishers, 1960.

Nida, E. A., and C. R. Taber. *The Theory and Practice of Translation.* Leiden: E. J. Brill, 1969.

Rowley, H. H., ed. *The Old Testament and Modern Study,* reprint. Oxford: At the Clarendon Press, 1961.

II

The Canon and Text of the Old Testament

Neil R. Lightfoot

In recent years events have taken place that again and again have brought the Bible before the eye of the general public. The 1930s marked the acquisition by the British Museum of the celebrated Sinaitic Codex, which in 1859 had been "discovered" by Constantine Tischendorf in St. Catherine's Monastery at Mt. Sinai. The 1940s exhibited the remarkable Dead Sea Scrolls (more accurately described as the Judean Desert Scrolls), eventually comprising in total hundreds of Bible and Bible-related texts, a number of which antedate the standard OT text a thousand or more years. Added to such well-known events has been, from the beginning of the century down to now, the recovery of a substantial number of NT papyri from the sands of Egypt. With this new material have inevitably come new interest in and new questions on the background of the various books of the Old and New Testaments. In the limits of one chapter I will seek to sketch this background of the OT as it relates to questions of canon and text.

CANON

Terms

The word "canon" is actually a Greek word (*kanōn*) which has had many uses. Essentially the term refers to a "reed"; then to a "tool" used by a carpenter or builder. *Kanōn* was used especially for a carpenter's "level"; as such it was a straight piece of wood with a scale on it. It was also used as a scribe's "ruler." From the literal sense of "level" or "ruler," all the metaphorical senses are derived: (1) a "written law" or "rule" to distinguish right from wrong, a "rule" of life. In this sense the teachings of Jesus or the words of Scripture might be called a *kanōn*. (2) an exemplary or ideal man may be compared to a straight ruler and called a *kanōn*. (3) a rule of grammar, a rule or principle in philosophy, or, ecclesiastically, a rule of faith or a church ordinance might be termed a *kanōn*. (4) a very common use is "list," probably derived from the row of marks on a level or ruler. The Eusebian Canons, for example, are found in many manuscripts of the Gospels. They are lists in ten columns to assist the reader in locating parallel passages in the Gospels. (5) from the above, *kanōn* also refers to a list of persons eligible for office or privilege; and then to a list of people commemorated in the mass, the living and dead for whom prayers are said. To put a dead person in such a list is to *canonize* him.

Of the many different senses in which *kanōn* is used, the important one for this discussion is (4), *kanōn* in the sense of a list. When so used it denotes the list of accepted writings which were read in public worship and were regarded as having divine authority. The word *kanōn* is first used in this way by Athanasius shortly after A.D. 350.

The word "apocrypha," like "canon," has various uses. It is a Greek adjective (neuter plural) that literally means "hidden things" or "hidden (books)." In its early usage it was the practical equivalent of "esoteric" and stood for books that were to be read by the "enlightened" inner circle, books that were excluded from public use. At length "apocrypha" came to mean "heretical" and "spurious." In 367, Athanasius in his Easter Letter refers to the Scriptures as "canonical" (*kanonizomena*) as contrasted to those writings that were "apocryphal" (*apokrupha*). In modern times "apocrypha" is mostly used for the fourteen or fifteen books associated with the OT (and printed in some editions of the

English Bible) which are not found in the Hebrew canon.

The word "pseudepigrapha" (literally, "false writings") technically should denote books written with fictitious names; but practically it refers to those Jewish writings which were excluded not only from the OT canon but from the Apocrypha as well. Unlike the Apocrypha, which are represented in various manuscripts of the Septuagint (LXX) and the Latin Vulgate, the Pseudepigrapha in no way approached canonical status.

As applied to the OT, the word "canon" marks off thirty-nine books from all other books, which alone are accepted as Holy Scripture. But how did these particular books come to be acknowledged as authoritative? How was the OT canon effected, and what were the principles and criteria of canonization? What of the circumstances and persons involved in the process? The questions are *historical* in nature. They do not concern as much the origin and contents of Scripture as the general use and recognition of them.

The historical evidence on these points is somewhat scattered and sometimes even scarce. The problem is compounded because many of the books of the OT had to make their ways separately into the canon. Although this adds strength to the canonical list, the evidence on a number of books is not as abundant as the researcher would like to have. There is the difficulty also of distinguishing between what the ancients regarded as "Scripture" and what books were to them profitable for reading.

Divisions of the Canon

At an early date the Jews divided their Scriptures into three sections: the Law, the Prophets, and the Writings (or Hagiographa). The Law contains the five books of the Pentateuch: Genesis, Exodus, Leviticus, Numbers, and Deuteronomy. The Prophets include eight books that are subdivided into Former Prophets and Latter Prophets. The Former Prophets are Joshua, Judges, Samuel, and Kings; the Latter Prophets are Isaiah, Jeremiah, Ezekiel, and the Twelve (the "Minor Prophets" from Hosea to Malachi). The

Writings are eleven in number: Psalms, Proverbs, and Job (regarded as books of poetry); Song of Solomon, Ruth, Lamentations, Ecclesiastes, and Esther (known together as the Five Scrolls); Daniel, Ezra-Nehemiah (counted as one book), and Chronicles. The total number of these books is twenty-four. Some methods of reckoning (attaching Ruth to Judges and Lamentations to Jeremiah) count twenty-two books in all, the number corresponding to the twenty-two letters of the Hebrew alphabet. Whether the books are counted as twenty-four or twenty-two, it is important to remember that these books are precisely the same as the thirty-nine books of the OT found in most editions of the English Bible.

When Jesus speaks of "the law of Moses and the prophets and the psalms" as being fulfilled in him (Luke 24:44), his division of the Scriptures approximates the Jewish threefold division of the OT. But the NT also suggests a twofold division. One often reads in the NT such expressions as "the law and the prophets" (Matt. 5:17; Luke 16:16; Rom. 3:21) and "Moses and the prophets" (Luke 16:29; John 1:46; Acts 28:23). These expressions are typical Jewish ways of referring to the OT, for there is no question that at this stage the Writings formed a portion of acknowledged Scripture. "The law and the prophets," and such expressions, simply meant the OT. Parallel to NT usage is that of the Qumran community, which was located adjacent to the Dead Sea, whose writings about this time also speak of what is written in Moses and the prophets. The LXX, likewise, does not follow a threefold arrangement.

Early History of the Canon

In later Judaism the threefold division of the OT was compared to the holy places of the temple—the Law to the Holy of Holies, the Prophets to the Holy Place, and the Writings to the Temple Court. The Jewish position for long centuries has been that the Law is foremost and that the Prophets and Writings exist to explain the Law. The Prophets and Writings, to be sure, are inspired; but the Law is basic. It is convenient to approach the subject of canon in three parts. This is not to suggest, however, that it has always been this way; neither does it suggest inferiority of one part to another nor that the canonization of the various OT books necessarily took place in three separate stages.

The Law. The conception of canon preceded by many centuries the formal recognition of the canon. The ideas of inspiration and canonicity are distinct, but ultimately the idea of canonicity is derived from that of inspiration. To begin with, the Law was law for the people of Israel because God himself spoke the Ten Commandments and wrote them down (Exod. 20:1; 24:12; 32:16; 34:1; Deut. 4:13, etc.). Moses wrote down the words of the Lord spoken at Sinai (Exod. 24:4); the memorial concerning Amalek (Exod. 17:14); the journey of Israel in the desert (Num. 33:2); all the words of God's law (Deut. 31:9, 24); and the song found in Deuteronomy 32:1-43 (Deut. 31:22). Later, Joshua, Samuel, and others (Josh. 24:26; 1 Sam. 10:23; Isa. 30:8; Jer. 36:2) wrote down the commandments of the Lord. Deuteronomy specifically warns not to add to the divine commands or subtract from them (Deut. 4:2; 12:32).

These passages that note the writing down of God's commands are important. The writing down, as Schrenk says, is a mark of revelation (*Theological Dictionary of the New Testament*, vol. 1, p. 744). Further, the writing down is a witness for future generations. Exodus 40:20 relates that Moses took the "testimony" (the stone tablets containing the Ten Commandments) and placed it in the ark of the covenant for preservation. Deuteronomy 31:24-26 states that when Moses had finished writing "the words of this law in a book, to the very end," he commanded the Levites to put the book in the ark "that it may be there for a witness against you." First Samuel 10:25 says that Samuel wrote down the rights and duties of kingship in a book and "laid it before the Lord." Preservation is not tantamount to canonicity; but an authoritative writing down and a careful watch over the things written are suggestive of it.

Throughout its history Israel was bound to keep the law of Moses. To Joshua God said: "This book of the law [the law of Moses] shall not depart out of your mouth, but you shall meditate on it day and night, that you may be careful to do according to all that is written in it" (Josh. 1:8). To Solomon David said: "Be strong . . . and keep the charge of the Lord your God, walking in his ways and keeping his statutes, his commandments, his ordinances, and his testimonies, as it is written in the law of Moses . . ." (1 Kings 2:3; cf. 2 Kings 14:6; Mal. 4:4, etc.). In the time of King Josiah (621 B.C.), after "the book of the law" was found in the temple, the book was solemnly read in the hearing of the people; and both king and people pledged that they would keep the words of the covenant written in the book (2 Kings 22–23; 2 Chron. 34–35). Two hundred years later, in the time of Ezra and Nehemiah, Ezra read to all the assembled people; and the people entered into a covenant to keep the law of Moses (Neh. 8–10). The last incident is usually pointed to as the approximate time when the Pentateuch was canonized. Certainly by this time it was acknowledged, but it should be kept in mind that the recognition of the authority of the law of Moses waxed and waned over the centuries according to the vicissitudes of Israel's spiritual fortunes. When, as often, Israel experienced a depression of faith, it acknowledged no divine authority in the written books. The period of Ezra and Nehemiah, therefore, should be looked upon as a time of revival of interest in the law. It ought not be cited as evidence of a recent origin of the Pentateuch.

The Prophets. When Ezra read the law to the people, no mention is made of his having read also from the Prophets. This does not mean that at that time the divine authority of the prophets was not recognized. Indeed, Ezra, as he addresses God and speaks of Israel, says: "Many years thou didst bear with them, and didst warn them by thy Spirit through thy prophets . . ." (Neh. 9:30). Yet, so far as is known, it was not the work of Ezra and Nehemiah to gather the prophetic books together and close the prophetic canon. They could not do this because in their time true prophets were still arising among the people. It was not until some time later, when the voice of prophecy was stilled, that a final collection of the prophetic writings could be made.

The authority of the Former and Latter Prophets has practically never been disputed. The Former Prophets (Joshua, Judges, Samuel, and Kings) relate the progress of religious history. They are included in the Prophets because either they were thought to be written by prophets or they were regarded as being written under prophetic inspiration. The Latter Prophets (Isaiah, Jeremiah, Ezekiel, and the Twelve) from the first stood on their own. Their authority was associated with the individual prophets who fearlessly gave a "thus says the Lord." Their predictions of Israel's and Judah's future doom came true, and this augmented their authority. Men like Isaiah and Jeremiah wrote their prophecies down (Isa. 8:16; Jer. 36:2ff.), and men like Daniel later "perceived in the books" what had been written earlier (Dan. 9:2). Such reading and searching "in the books" suggests canonical rank for the prophetic books—Jeremiah is specifically mentioned by Daniel.

The Writings. The general term applied to this group of books indicates its heterogeneous character. The different types of books represented complicate the question of canon. It would be a mistake, however, to think that these books were not acknowledged until after the other divisions of the OT were canonized. It is well known that this is not the case for Psalms, Proverbs, and perhaps others.

Psalms is first by order of the books that compose the Writings. It is often known as "the hymnbook of the Second Temple." This designation is appropriate, although it should not be thought that the Psalms all originated after the exile. To the contrary, a large number of the Psalms are of great antiquity. Who wrote the Psalms—traditionally seventy-three are attributed to David, others to the sons of Korah, to Asaph, to Solomon, to Moses, etc.—and under what precise circumstances, is not known. The final form of the Psalms undoubtedly depends on earlier collections. Passages like Joshua 24:26 show that certain chosen persons added authoritatively in writing to "the book of the law of God." Similarly, as various writings were authoritatively added to the sacred collection, so in the compilation of the Psalms it can be assumed that an authoritative person(s) worked under divine guidance. If this analogy is correct, the same assumption applies with reference to Proverbs. Obviously, many of the proverbs are ascribed traditionally to Solomon (Prov. 10:1); other proverbs by other persons are also included. But it is important to remember that the sacred character of a later or final collection of proverbs would not have been acknowledged if the proverbs had originated with a recent compiler.

Among the Writings certain books were contested. It was necessary for the OT canon to pass through a period of trial as did the NT canon. With the NT certain books, such as the four Gospels and the epistles of Paul, from the outset seem to have been universally accepted. These books were called *Homologoumena* (Greek, *homologein,* "to agree to," "to acknowledge"). Other books, however, were for a while disputed—due to their limited circulation they were accepted in some parts of the church and rejected in other parts. These books were called *Antilegomena* (Greek, *antilegein,* "to speak against"). An impartial investigation of canon recognizes and distinguishes between these two categories. Suffice it to say that the canon of either testament is no worse or less secure because there were disputes about some books and their place in the canon.

Two books of the Writings were especially controversial, Ecclesiastes and the Song of Solomon. Discussions concerning them among the Jews were still going on in the last half of the first century and even later. Information about these discussions comes from the Mishnah, that portion of the Talmud which consists of the oral law formulated by the end of the second century A.D. The rabbis, always careful that the Holy Scriptures not be lightly handled, devised a law to the effect that sacred books communicated ceremonial uncleanness to hands that might touch them. Hands thus touching the sacred books would have to be washed; books that "defiled the hands" were the books regarded as being divinely inspired. In the Mishnah there is a treatise entitled "Hands" (Yadaim). In this the two books of Ecclesiastes and Song of Solomon are involved, for the question is whether these books "defile the hands." The Mishnah (Yadaim 3. 5) affirms specifically that both of these books are sacred. But the rival, first-century rabbinic schools of Shammai and Hillel disagreed on Ecclesiastes, the former rejecting, the latter accepting it.

The Song of Solomon, due to its subject matter, posed problems for acceptance. It is often asserted that this poetic work would have never made the canon if allegorical interpretations of it by Jews and later by Christians had not been adopted. But this is mere assertion. The Song of Solomon if interpreted literally as a poetic love song(s) is not to be disparaged unless physical love in marriage is discordant with the laws of creation. Yet the loud protest of Rabbi Akiba (second century A.D.), in the same passage of the Mishnah mentioned above, is the surest evidence that there was controversy over the Song of Solomon. Akiba said:

> God forbid! No man in Israel ever dissented about the Song of Songs, holding it not to be sacred. The whole age altogether is not worth as much as the day on which the Song of Songs was given to Israel; for all the Scriptures are holy, but the Song of Songs is the holiest of all. If there was a division, it was only over Ecclesiastes.

Limits of the Canon

Disputes about certain biblical books are not unnatural. They presuppose the existence of a basic corpus of holy writings whose limits had already been broadly fixed. It is necessary, now, to examine the extent of the OT canon. The evidence comes both from Jewish and Christian sources. In considering the latter, the evidence from the NT alone will be viewed, although much supportive evidence could be adduced from Christian materials in the early centuries of the church.

A long-established tradition associates the gathering of the canonical OT with Ezra and Nehemiah. This association naturally goes back to Ezra's reading of the law to the people (Neh. 8–10), but there are other evidences for this tradition as well.

Second Esdras (Latin title, 4 Esdras) is one of the books

of the Apocrypha. A composite work whose main portions are dated about A.D. 95, it contains a fanciful account of the origin of both the canonical and noncanonical books of the OT. Ezra is depicted in Babylon after the destruction of Jerusalem. He complains that the law of Moses has been burned, and he asks God's Spirit to come upon him to write down everything that has happened from the beginning. In response God tells Ezra to select five men who are trained to serve as secretaries and to withdraw from the people for a period of forty days. Ezra does this. The next day he drinks from a cup that is offered to him. His heart pours forth understanding; his mouth is no longer closed. The men write what is dictated to them, in characters they had never learned. The narrative continues:

> So during the forty days ninety-four books were written. And when the forty days were ended, the Most High spoke to me [Ezra], saying, Make public the twenty-four books that you wrote first and let the worthy and unworthy read them; but keep the seventy that were written last, in order to give them to the wise among your people.
>
> 2 Esdras 14:45-46

Although the story is legendary, it possesses some value. The distinction between the twenty-four books which are to be read by the "worthy" and "unworthy" and the seventy books which are for the "wise" alone points up the acknowledged difference at that time between the canonical and noncanonical works. The twenty-four books unquestionably are the same as the thirty-nine in present editions of the OT. Though a legend, the account witnesses that in the first century A.D. the Jews recognized twenty-four books as especially sacred.

Josephus likewise limits the canon. He was a priest and a Pharisee, who wrote at the close of the first century A.D. In his Against Apion he defends the Jews by arguing that they possessed an antiquity unmatched by the Greeks. It is true that Josephus is highly partisan in his presentation, and any assessment of him must take this into account. What Josephus says, nevertheless, may be taken as representative of how many Jews felt on these matters. He writes:

> It therefore naturally, or rather necessarily, follows (seeing that with us it is not open to everybody to write the records, and that there is no discrepancy in what is written; seeing that, on the contrary, the prophets alone had this privilege, obtaining their knowledge of the most remote and ancient history through the inspiration which they owed to God, and committing to writing a clear account of the events of their own time just as they occurred)—it follows that we do not possess myriads of inconsistent books, conflicting with each other. Our books, those which are justly accredited, are but twenty-two, and contain the record of all time.
>
> Of these, five are the books of Moses, comprising the laws and the traditional history from the birth of man down to the death of the lawgiver. This period falls only a little short of three thousand years. From the death of Moses until Artaxerxes, who succeeded Xerxes as king of Persia, the prophets subsequent to Moses wrote the history of the events of their own times in thirteen books. The remaining four books contain hymns to God and precepts for the conduct of human life.
>
> From Artaxerxes to our own time the complete history has been written, but has not been deemed worthy of equal credit with the earlier records, because of the failure of the exact succession of the prophets.

Josephus then goes on to expound the Jewish veneration of Scripture:

> We have given practical proof of our reverence for our own Scriptures. For, although such long ages have now passed, no one has ventured either to add, or to remove, or to alter a syllable; and it is an instinct with every Jew, from the day of his birth, to regard them as the decrees of God, to abide by them, and, if need be, cheerfully to die for them.
>
> Against Apion 1. 7-8

The citation is lengthy and is given in full because of its importance. From Josephus several conclusions may be derived.

1. The number of those books looked upon as having divine authority is carefully limited. Josephus fixes the number at twenty-two. As seen earlier, this is but another

way of counting the books in order that the number might correspond with the twenty-two letters of the Hebrew alphabet.

2. The division of these books is according to a three-part pattern—five books of Moses, thirteen books of prophets, and four books of hymns to God and principles dealing with man. But it should be noticed that this threefold division is not that of the familiar Law, Prophets, and Writings. Josephus includes all the historical books in the prophets, including Chronicles, Ezra, Nehemiah, and Esther, as well as Daniel and Job. The remaining four books, therefore, must be Psalms, Proverbs, Ecclesiastes, and the Song of Solomon; for these alone meet the requirements of his description.

3. The time covered in these books is expressly limited. Josephus believed that the canon extended from Moses to Artaxerxes (464–424 B.C.). The Jews believed that prophetic inspiration ceased with Malachi, who apparently was a contemporary of Ezra and Nehemiah. This was the period of Artaxerxes. Others indeed wrote later, but their writings are not on a par with the earlier writings. In other words, according to Josephus, the canon is closed.

4. The text of these books is sacred. No one has dared to expunge or alter it, since to every Jew these writings are "decrees of God."

Even though for Josephus the canon was closed, as seen earlier, discussions on certain books continued among some of the rabbis. By the end of the first century A.D. certain things had happened which pushed the Jews to resolve any differences they might have had on the canon. By now the glorious temple in Jerusalem had been destroyed. The Jews for several centuries had been dispersed over the known world. Increasingly it had become difficult to maintain Jerusalem as the center and focus of all religious activity. Away from Palestine, Hellenistic Jews especially became book-centered rather than temple-centered. In the meantime other writings had arisen, many of which were pseudepigraphic in character. There was, besides, a new religion that had come on the scene—Christianity. It, too, had its writings. So what were the writings that were to constitute the book?

It would be inaccurate to say that when a group of Jewish rabbis met in A.D. 90 at Jabneh or Jamnia, near Joppa on the Mediterranean Sea, they forevermore answered this question. In the first place, they had no authority to decide anything. In the second place, even if they had had authority, the issues at stake were not finally settled. It would be correct to say that the discussions and decisions (?) at Jamnia reflected general opinion at that time. The canon in reality was substantially fixed long before Jamnia. Jamnia did not admit certain books into the canon but, to speak more accurately, allowed certain books to remain.

It has already been observed that the Talmud witnesses to varying opinions on certain books. Some of the books of the OT were Antilegomena—disputed books. But the Talmud itself, based on traditions that are centuries old, unhesitatingly accepts these disputed books. In a kind of commentary on the Mishnah, called a Gemara, a rather long statement is made about the authors and editors of the OT:

> Moses wrote his own book, and the section about Balaam and Job. Joshua wrote his own book, and eight verses in the Torah. Samuel wrote his own book, and the books of Judges and Ruth. David wrote the book of Psalms at the direction of the ten elders, the first man, Melchizedek, and Abraham, and Moses, and Heman, and Jeduthun, and Asaph, and the three sons of Korah. Jeremiah wrote his own book, and the book of Kings and Lamentations. Hezekiah and his company wrote Isaiah, Proverbs, Song of Songs, and Ecclesiastes. The men of the Great Synagogue wrote Ezekiel, and the Twelve, Daniel, and the Roll of Esther. Ezra wrote his own book and the genealogies in Chronicles down to his own time.
>
> Baba Bathra 14b-15a

In this listing of the writers of the OT, two things stand out. First, the canonical books begin with Moses and go down to the time of Ezra. This agrees remarkably with the statement of Josephus. Second, though others besides the original authors have been involved in shaping or editing certain books, this work is not thought to be inconsistent with the authority inherent in them.

Other evidence on the canon, much older than that of the Talmud and of Josephus, could be cited; but evidence in the B.C. era is not as substantive or pointed as statements made in the OT itself. But one reference will be given. The book of 1 Maccabees, a well-known book of the Apocrypha written about 100 B.C., speaks several times as though it had been a long time since a prophet appeared among the people. The book relates the fierce struggles of the Jews to regain their political and religious freedom in the second century B.C. Near the close of the book, Simon Maccabeus is elected high priest, commander, and leader by the Jews. First Maccabees 14:41 says that the Jews were well pleased with this choice, that Simon was to be "governor and high priest for ever, until there should arise a faithful prophet." The latter clause should be compared with other similar statements in the book—"until there should come a prophet to show what should be done with them" and "the like whereof was not since the time that a prophet was not seen among them" (4:46; 9:27). In the centuries following Malachi, the Jews themselves recognized that they had no prophet. This is why, for example, the Wisdom of Jesus the Son of Sirach (usually known as Ecclesiasticus, written about 180 B.C.) was rejected by the Jews. The author, they reasoned, was known to live in fairly recent times, after the death of the last prophet, when the spirit of prophecy had departed from Israel.

Thus far, on the limits of the canon, Jewish sources have been considered. There are evidences also from Christian materials.

The NT evidence on the OT canon is quite strong. One type of evidence may be seen in the NT portrayal of the scribes. The scribes, it is said, did not teach with authority. They argued and interpreted and fenced in the law of Moses with their traditions, but they did not speak authoritatively. They did not disguise themselves as prophets. For them the voice of prophecy had ceased.

The NT stance is in agreement with that of the scribes, at least in so far as acknowledging the undisputed authority of the old writings. "It is written," the NT says—whatever is written is unquestionably so. Characteristically the NT speaks of the OT as "the Scripture" (John 7:38; Acts 8:32; Rom. 4:3); the use of the singular refers to Scripture as a whole. The NT also calls the OT "the Scriptures" (Matt. 21:42; John 5:39; Acts 17:11), designating together all the parts of Scripture. The Old Testament is also "the holy scriptures" (Rom. 1:2), "the sacred writings" (2 Tim. 3:15), etc. These names and titles are not studiously registered. They are the standard nomenclature of the times. Such designations mark the OT off from other books; and it is important to notice that these designations by the NT authors are never applied to the Apocrypha.

But NT designations of the OT do not tell precisely which books were regarded as canonical. The NT, however, does quote extensively from the OT; in all, from thirty-one out of thirty-nine books. The remaining eight books (Ezra, Nehemiah, Esther, Ecclesiastes, Song of Solomon, Obadiah, Nahum, Zephaniah) are not quoted simply because there was no occasion for quoting them.

Elsewhere the NT gives hints as to the contents of the canon. Jesus spoke of the time "from the blood of Abel to the blood of Zechariah, who perished between the altar and the sanctuary" (Luke 11:51; cf. Matt. 23:35), thus referring to the martyrs listed in the OT. It is to be remembered that the Hebrew Bible begins with Genesis and ends with Chronicles. Abel, of course, is the first martyr in Genesis, and Zechariah is the last martyr in 2 Chronicles. Jesus' words "from the blood of Abel to the blood of Zechariah" strongly suggest that his OT went from Genesis to 2 Chronicles, with all the other books in between.

Concerning the contents of the canon, the question is sometimes raised about NT quotations of noncanonical materials. As noticed previously, the NT never uses such designations as "scripture" or "holy scripture" for any apocryphal book. In this connection the quotations of Jude in Jude 9 and in verses 14-15 have to be considered. Jude 9 tells about the archangel Michael contending with the devil over the body of Moses. It is said that Jude here quotes from the pseudepigraphic book entitled the Assumption of Moses. But it should be said that it is not known with certainty that this is the case. The Assumption of Moses has been preserved only in fragments, and the fragments do not contain the material alluded to by Jude. On the other hand, it is possible that Jude makes mention of a traditional story that formed the basis of the apocryphal book.

Jude 14–15 gives reportedly a prophecy of Enoch, and it is true that this prophecy is found in the apocryphal book of Enoch (1 Enoch 1:9). But here several things need to be said: (1) It is possible that Jude is acquainted with this prophecy from a different source. (2) It is possible that both the book of Enoch and the book of Jude draw upon a common source of oral tradition. (3) It is probable, however, that Jude quotes directly from the book of Enoch. If so—and the form of the quotation is almost precisely in agreement with the book of Enoch—Jude does not quote Enoch as "scripture" nor does he say "it is written." When a writer cites another work, this does not mean that he necessarily regards the work as divine. Paul quotes from the heathen poets (Acts 17:28; Titus 1:12). He also names, evidently from a noncanonical source, Jannes and Jambres as magicians of Pharaoh (2 Tim. 3:8); but in doing so he does not thus sanction his source as being from God.

In summary, the witness of the NT to the OT canon is of supreme importance. The NT does not specifically spell out each book that ought to comprise the OT, yet it gives evidence that in the first century the canon of the OT was firmly established. The evidence from Jewish sources in this period is abundant and persuasive. The canon of the Hebrew Bible today includes exactly the same thirty-nine books of the OT found in most editions of the English Bible.

Qumran and the Canon

Hundreds of manuscripts, popularly known as the Dead Sea Scrolls, began to come to light in 1947 and the years following. These materials were discovered in caves located west of the Dead Sea. The vast majority of these manuscripts are connected with Qumran, a Jewish community which was situated on the northwest portion of the Dead Sea. In all, about six hundred manuscripts (most of them fragmentary) have been found near Qumran. It is believed that most of these manuscripts were taken from the Qumran library and placed in the caves for safekeeping.

Extensive archeological work has shown that the Qumran community existed in the period from the second century B.C. to the latter part of the first century A.D. These centuries, of course, are very important for the canon of the OT. Do the books of Qumran shed significant light on the canon? Is it possible to discover which books were especially treasured at Qumran?

At this point several observations need to be made. (1) The Qumran sect, which separated itself from the mainstream of Judaism in the second century B.C., does not represent normative Judaism. It would be a mistake, therefore, to take Qumran as some kind of standard by which the canon can be measured. (2) The Qumran documents include both biblical and nonbiblical texts. About 175 of the scrolls are copies of the OT in Hebrew. These include a number of copies of Deuteronomy, Psalms, Isaiah, and the Minor Prophets. Every book of the OT is represented, except Esther. The scrolls vary in length and in condition of preservation of the Bible text, from a fragmentary copy of Chronicles to practically a full-length copy of Isaiah. (3) Since the Qumran library includes both biblical and non-biblical materials, it is extremely difficult to distinguish between the books that were "Scripture" at Qumran and those that were esteemed as useful and valuable for life in the community.

With the above observations in mind, certain information about the Qumran documents may still prove helpful. There is no question that Qumran accepted the Law and the Prophets. The number and range of manuscripts on this portion of the canon attest this. Moreover, commentaries produced by the Qumran community on parts of Genesis, Isaiah, Hosea, Micah, Nahum, and Habakkuk strengthen this conclusion. Among the Writings, Psalms is conspicuously represented by some thirty manuscripts. Job and

Proverbs are likewise well represented. For Ecclesiastes, Song of Solomon, Ruth, and Lamentations, there are fragmentary manuscripts; so also for Chronicles and Ezra-Nehemiah. The only book of the Writings not directly represented is Esther. But it is difficult to say whether this is significant. The book is short; and, further, some have claimed that there are oblique allusions to Esther in other Qumran scrolls (G. W. Anderson in *The Cambridge History of the Bible,* vol. 1, p. 150).

The book of Daniel is well represented by fragments from at least eight different manuscripts. In other scrolls there are definite allusions and quotations from Daniel; some quotations are introduced by the words "as it is written in the book of the prophet Daniel." The book of Daniel, therefore, unquestionably was a part of the Qumran canon. Incidentally, the Qumran evidence on Daniel is against the additions to Daniel found in the Apocrypha (The Prayer of Azariah and the Song of the Three Young Men, Susanna, and Bel and the Dragon).

In summary, the evidence of Qumran shows that the books of the OT were not only in existence but were in extensive use in the period approximating the beginning of the Christian era. At Qumran many of these books were being commented on and quoted as "scripture." On this point the Qumran evidence supports the evidence of the NT, which is more complete. No negative evidence on the OT canon has come from the Dead Sea Scrolls.

The Apocrypha

This study of canon thus far has concerned itself mainly with the thirty-nine OT books found in most editions of the English Bible. But early editions of the English Bible, including that of the Authorized or King James Version of 1611, included the Apocrypha in separate sections. The Apocrypha, as seen earlier, includes fourteen or fifteen books (the number varies depending on whether The Letter of Jeremiah is counted separately from Baruch) not found in the Hebrew canon. The following is a list of the Apocrypha:

   1. The First Book of Esdras

2. The Second Book of Esdras
3. Tobit
4. Judith
5. The Additions to the Book of Esther
6. The Wisdom of Solomon
7. Ecclesiasticus, or the Wisdom of Jesus the Son of Sirach
8. Baruch
9. The Letter of Jeremiah
10. The Prayer of Azariah and the Song of the Three Young Men
11. Susanna
12. Bel and the Dragon
13. The Prayer of Manasseh
14. The First Book of Maccabees
15. The Second Book of Maccabees

All but three of these (1 and 2 Esdras and the Prayer of Manasseh) are considered canonical by the Roman Catholic Church. The Apocrypha is given a semicanonical status by the Church of England. It reads them "for example of life and instruction of manners," but it does not apply them "to establish any doctrines."

The Apocrypha is found entirely in Greek and Latin manuscripts, although by no means in all of them. Second Esdras, for example, is found in no Greek manuscript, and The Prayer of Manasseh is not found in all of the Greek copies. But since in the Greek manuscripts most of the Apocrypha stands side by side with the canonical books, this raises once again the question of which books ought to comprise the canon.

It is often said that the Greek or Alexandrian canon differed from the Hebrew or Palestinian canon and therefore that the Alexandrian canon included the various books of the Apocrypha. But one should guard against assertions and generalizations. It is important to notice that the number of Apocryphal books in Greek copies is not the same. The Greek copies evidence no fixed canon of the OT. It is also important to remember that the Greek copies extant are not those belonging to Alexandrian Jews but are of Christian origin. Any supposed difference between an Alexandrian and

Palestinian canon would be difficult to trace on the basis of manuscripts copied by Christian scribes. There is, in fact, little evidence to show that the conception of canon by Jews outside Palestine was different from that within Palestine.

Various reasons can be given for not according canonical status to the Apocrypha—that Christ and the apostles, so far as the evidence goes, did not accept the Apocrypha; that Josephus (apparently also Philo) rejected it; that early Christian lists did not include it, etc. But the question is not why reject the Apocrypha. The fact is that the Jews never accepted these books. The books originated after the time of Ezra, when the voice of prophecy had died out. To accept the Apocrypha as canonical, therefore, would be unthinkable for the student of history.

TEXT

The study of the text of the OT follows to some extent the pattern traced in the study of canon. Both canon and text are data of history. They concern not so much the divine but the human side of the Bible. While canon deals with the historical process involved in the collection and recognition of certain books as Scripture, text has to do with the historical process by which the Scriptures were transmitted from generation to generation.

The word "text" is used to refer to the precise wording of a document. If one speaks, for example, of the "text" of Isaiah, he has reference to the exact words (including spelling and word order) of the book of Isaiah. This in itself presents problems, for the prophet Isaiah lived 700 years B.C.; and until recently no Hebrew manuscript of the book of Isaiah was known to exist earlier than the ninth century A.D. The time gap is considerable and could only be spanned by an accurate and consistent transmission of the text over the centuries. It is necessary to assume that over a long period of time, when copies of the text were being made from previous copies and where human skills and unskills were at work in the making of these copies, scribal slips and alterations would occur in the text. It is the work of the textual critic to detect such alterations and to restore the wording of the text as far as it can be discerned from the text materials at his disposal.

Manuscripts of the Text

The oldest extant manuscripts of the Hebrew Bible are the Qumran manuscripts from the Dead Sea area. These, along with other manuscripts located in the same vicinity, are dated from about 250 B.C. to A.D. 135. These manuscripts are, of course, without dates; but evidence for their age is derived from paleographical (pertaining to the study of ancient writing) deductions and archeological investigations of the sites connected with the discovery of the manuscripts.

The manuscripts of this early period are written in well-lined columns on leather rolls, although a few have been found on papyrus sheets. The main Isaiah scroll from Qumran is made up of seventeen strips of leather sewn together, constituting a roll of more than twenty-four feet in length and more than ten inches in height. This and other scrolls were wrapped in linen cloth and placed in jars for safekeeping (cf. Jer. 32:14). The Isaiah manuscript is conveniently referred to as IQIsᵃ. (The Q indicates the region of Qumran; the number before the Q, the cave in which the manuscript was found; the abbreviation after the Q shows the contents of the manuscript; the letter suspended above the line gives the number of the manuscript. Thus IQIsᵃ stands for the first manuscript of Isaiah found in Cave 1, Qumran.)

Among the numerous biblical manuscripts of Qumran, several stand out prominently. IQIsᵃ, dated about 100 B.C., contains the whole of Isaiah, except for a few small breaks of the text due to age and wear. For all practical purposes, the text of this ancient scroll reads the same as the standardized text (called the Massoretic text [MT]) in printed Bibles. There are, to be sure, a number of divergent readings represented in it, some of which are worthwhile; but the majority of readings have to do with grammar, spelling, different forms of proper names, etc.

IQIsᵇ, which contains a substantial part of the text of Isaiah, goes back to the latter half of the first century B.C.

Its significance is due to the remarkable agreement it has with the MT. Both of these Isaiah manuscripts clearly demonstrate that the classic MT type of text was in existence in pre-Christian times; yet, interestingly, these manuscripts do not measure up to the high copying standards exhibited in medieval manuscripts of the MT.

Other Qumran manuscripts with considerable portions of the biblical text include an early copy of Exodus. This manuscript is known as 4QpaleoEx", that is, one of the many copies of Exodus from Cave 4, written in old Hebrew script known as "paleo-Hebrew." This Exodus copy is from the early part of the second century B.C. and contains some forty columns of an original fifty-seven. Two manuscripts of the books of Samuel are of special interest. One (4QSam'), from the first century B.C., has preserved in fragmentary form forty-seven of an original fifty-seven columns of 1 and 2 Samuel. The other (4QSam") dates back to the third century B.C. One Psalms manuscript (11QPs'), among many, includes forty canonical Psalms, as well as other poetic and narrative material, and several psalmlike compositions.

Manuscripts from Qumran enumerated so far are paralleled by texts from the same period discovered in the same general area near Wadi Murabba'at, at Masada, and in other places. From Masada have come such items as a scroll of Psalms 81–85, with a text identical to that of the MT; and a copy of Psalm 150 from the end of a roll, showing that the Psalms collection there terminated in the same way as in the modern Psalter. From Wadi Murabba'at has come especially a scroll of the Minor Prophets. Dated about A.D. 100, its text extends from Joel 2:26 to Zechariah 1:4, including (in traditional order) Amos, Obadiah, Jonah, Micah, Nahum, Habakkuk, Zephaniah, and Haggai. Several columns of the manuscript are wonderfully preserved; others only imperfectly. The manuscript is remarkably like the MT, having only three variant readings of any importance whatever.

Next in age to the earliest Qumran materials is the Nash Papyrus. This is a small leaf that contains the Ten Commandments and the Shema (Deut. 6:4ff.). Since it is dated about 150 B.C., its form of writing was especially important in fixing dates for the various Dead Sea Scrolls.

For the remaining manuscripts of the OT and those that shed light on its text, it is necessary to move into the Middle Ages. One manuscript in particular is the Samaritan Pentateuch, which must now be mentioned because of its claims to antiquity. The Samaritan Pentateuch is often listed with the OT versions; strictly speaking it is not a version but a form of the Pentateuchal text that reaches back into pre-Christian times. The earliest known example of this text is the Abisha Scroll, proudly kept by the small Samaritan community at Nablus in Palestine. Written in a form of the archaic script, it originated, the Samaritans claim, in the time of Joshua. But the text of the manuscript, which consists of various strands, goes no farther back than the last part of the eleventh century A.D. On the whole it can be said that the Samaritan Pentateuch presents a form of the text similar to and yet different from the MT. The Samaritan variations to a large extent have to do with spelling differences and such differences as reflect the Samaritan belief that worship should be on Mt. Gerizim instead of Jerusalem; but other differences are in agreement with the LXX form of the text instead of the MT.

Before discussion of the "model codices" of the MT, brief mention should be made of the Geniza Fragments. Toward the end of the nineteenth century, at Cairo, in the old Jewish synagogue, thousands of pieces of manuscripts were found in a room walled off from the other portion of the building. The room, called a "genizah" (Aramaic *genaz*, to hide), was a kind of storehouse for manuscripts that were no longer usable. Any manuscript that was old or incorrect, in order to prevent the misuse of something with the sacred name of God on it, was stored up and later would be given ceremonial burial.

From the Cairo Genizah have come some two hundred thousand fragments—biblical texts in Hebrew and Aramaic, Aramaic paraphrases of the text, Talmudic and liturgical texts, letters, lists, etc. These texts date mainly from the sixth to the eighth centuries A.D. They include occasional divergencies from the MT, but they are especially important for the light they cast on the transmission of the text in this period of time.

The model codices are so called because they are the prototypes of current editions of the Hebrew Bible. The Cairo Prophets, known as C, was copied by Moses ben Asher in A.D. 895. It contains both the Former and Latter Prophets and is still the property of the Karaite sect of Jews in Cairo. The Aleppo Codex, known as A, copied by Aaron ben Moses ben Asher about A.D. 930, was until recently a marvelous codex of the entire OT. In 1947, however, it was badly damaged in riots against the Jews; it was later smuggled into Israel, where now its preserved portions will be used for further editions of the Hebrew Bible. The Leningrad Codex, known as L, is a complete copy of the OT. Its notes indicate that it was copied in 1008 from manuscripts written by Aaron ben Moses ben Asher. It has served as the basis of the critical edition of the Kittel-Kahle Hebrew Bible in wide use today.

History of the Text

That few really old Hebrew manuscripts have survived does not indicate a lack of scribal activity over the centuries. To the contrary, the Jews from early times were conscious of the foibles of those who copied the Scriptures. Thus there arose schools of professional scribes (cf. 1 Chron. 2:55), men who were trained in the art of writing, who were specialists in the law, and who were the supreme guardians of the text they transmitted.

Rules were formulated for the handling of the text. Multiplication of copies by dictation was not allowed. Each scroll had to be copied directly from another scroll. Official copies used in the synagogues were derived ultimately, until A.D. 70, from a master copy in the temple. Synagogue copies were kept in a cupboard that faced toward Jerusalem, and the rolls in the cupboard were the most sacred objects in the synagogue. (For these details, see C. H. Roberts in *The Cambridge History of the Bible*, vol. 1, pp. 49-50.)

Evidence of the scrupulousness of the scribes is manifold.

When for some reason a manuscript had a letter too large or too small, the copies made from it duplicated even these features, with the result that these letters of unusual size appear today in printed editions of the Hebrew Bible. But the scribes were textual critics as well as transcribers. If, for instance, the scribe found an error in the manuscript he was copying, say a letter omitted in a word, he would insert the missing letter above the line and leave the word on the line as he had found it. If, similarly, the scribe found an extra letter in a word, he would leave the word the same but put a dot above the letter in the word which he questioned. These corrections were carried down through the manuscripts and are likewise in modern Hebrew Bibles.

The scribes made other corrections. With reference to the above, there are fifteen places in the OT where the scribes inserted dots over single letters or whole words. One example of this is Genesis 33:4, the words "and he kissed him." The dots show the doubts of the scribes over the words, but the scribes did not alter the text because the text was regarded as unalterable. On occasion the scribes felt obligated to suggest a change in the way the text should be read orally. Some words, they thought, would be inappropriate or grammatically incorrect if read publicly in the synagogues. In these cases they would suggest in the margin of the manuscripts changes that were to be followed by the reader. The reader would learn to read the text one way while the text was written another way. But everyone understood that the written text was not to be altered.

These and similar practices were of long-standing tradition among the Jews. It was the function of *Masora*—the Hebrew term for tradition—to guard the text. It was one of the functions of the scribes to count the letters and words of the text. The Hebrew word for scribes is *sopherim*, which means "counters." The scribes counted the middle verse, the middle word, and even the middle letter of a book. The middle verse of the Law is Leviticus 8:7, the middle word is in Leviticus 10:16. The middle verse of the Hebrew Bible is Jeremiah 6:7. The scribes counted the number of times a particular word or a particular form of a word occurred in a book. Lists were made up of such words, and for a long time they were retained only in the powerful memory of the ancient mind. Later they were embodied in writing to form the massive written collection of *Masora*.

The Massoretes, "the masters of the tradition," were the descendants of the earlier scribes. Active between about the sixth and tenth centuries A.D., the Massoretes are especially known for their system of vowel points and accents which they applied to the text. Up until their time, the text of the OT had been without vowels. The Massoretes feared, since Hebrew was being less and less spoken, that the true pronunciation of the consonantal text might be lost. The points they added above and below the line would serve as a safeguard against this. The Massoretes also compiled a mass of careful instructions for copyists, which were included above and below and on the margins of the manuscript page and at the end of a book. The Massoretes of Tiberias in Palestine were the most important of the Massoretes; and the ben Asher family of Tiberias, with whom several of the model codices are associated, are especially renowned. Because of the labors of the Massoretes and their extensive contributions to the preservation of the text, the standard Hebrew text today is known as "the Massoretic text."

Condition of the Text

The meticulous care and concern of the Massoretes for the text, however, could not give a text without error. Indeed, as has been seen, the Massoretes and earlier scribes were fully aware of scribal errors in the text. Some of these errors can be traced back very early, to the paleo-Hebrew script where, for example, an *n* could be easily confused with a *k*, or a *d* with a *t*. Of the later square Aramaic characters, the form of writing used in practically all of the biblical manuscripts, *d* and *r*, *h* and *ḥ*, and other letters almost identical in appearance can easily be confused. Nor were the scribes of biblical manuscripts immune from such typical scribal mistakes as transposition of consonants, writing letters once instead of twice or twice instead of once, omission due to words of similar ending or beginning.

It is clear, then, that despite precautions to the contrary, there are errors in the MT of the OT. In 2 Samuel 5:16, one of David's sons is Eliada; in 1 Chronicles 14:7 the son's name is Beeliada. The MT in Genesis 10:3-4 reads Riphath and Dodanim; in 1 Chronicles 1:6-7 Diphath and Rodanim. First Kings 4:26 reads 40,000, but 2 Chronicles 9:25 reads 4,000. First Kings 7:26 reads 2,000, but 2 Chronicles 4:5 reads 3,000. The various texts cannot all be correct. While it is true that these errors are not of much consequence, they show quite clearly that the MT sometimes is faulty.

The textual critic can go even further in detecting errors. He sees that by a different division of words in the text of Amos 6:12, the difficult MT, "Does one plough with oxen?" becomes the understandable "Does one plough the sea with oxen?" Psalm 49:11 should read "Their graves are their homes for ever," in agreement with the Greek and Syriac versions, instead of "Their inward parts are their homes for ever." The difference between "their graves" and "their inward parts" is simply whether one of the letters in the word is *b* or *r*, letters that look very much alike in the Hebrew text. Examples of this sort, where the MT in minor points needs correction, can be multiplied. This points up the value of the versions which, as far as the Bible text is concerned, are always secondary to the manuscripts in the original languages. Nevertheless, the versions do supply a great amount of information on the OT text and often come to the rescue when the textual critic is wrestling with a textual problem. The LXX text, the Latin and Syriac translations, the Aramaic paraphrases called "Targums," and others are of immense importance in recovering the text of the OT.

But how does all of this bear on the condition of the OT text? Is the text soundly based or is the text precarious? And what light, after all, is cast on the text from the Dead Sea Scrolls? Perhaps it is best to answer the last question first.

It is difficult at this time to give a full assessment of the scrolls and their impact on the entire text of the OT. Each book, in reality, has its own textual history; and, therefore, broad generalizations on the text are unwise. Some scholars now posit different text-types in the pre-Christian era. Frank M. Cross, for example, thinks that three different textual families, in Palestine, in Egypt, and presumably in Babylon, developed slowly between the fifth and first centuries B.C. (Cross, "The Contributions of the Qumran Discoveries to the Study of the Biblical Text," *Israel Exploration Quarterly* 16 (1966), 81-95). Certainly there is evidence from Qumran, from 4QSamᵃ, 4QSamᵇ, 4QpaleoExᵐ, and others, that other forms of the text existed similar to that of the LXX and of the Samaritan Pentateuch and different from that of the MT. On the other hand, it is well known that a large number of the scrolls in text-type are allied with the MT; they exhibit indeed an early MT called "Proto-Massoretic." And of the many different textual readings that have come to light in the scrolls, the MT again and again presents the superior reading.

Perhaps the best way to respond to a question on the overall condition of the text is to juxtapose two statements made by two different scholars. One statement is that of James Moffatt who, in his Introduction to his translation of the Bible, says, "Now the traditional or 'massoretic' text of the Old Testament, though of primary value, is often desperately corrupt." The other statement is that of William Barclay, ". . . we need have no fear that the Massoretic text of the Old Testament is anything but accurate" (*The Bible Companion,* William Neil, ed., p. 412). The two statements are not as hopelessly contradictory as they appear to be. While they perhaps represent different biases, they certainly reflect different perspectives. Moffatt, speaking as a translator, refers to the sticky textual problems that are sometimes presented to translators. (One doubts, however, whether the translator has the freedom to rearrange and amend the text as Moffatt does. This "freedom" is likewise engaged in too liberally in the New English Bible OT.) But Barclay's statement comes from a volume addressed to the average reader about his Bible, assuring the reader that the message of the OT still speaks clearly in the MT. Besides, the word "corrupt," as used by a textual critic, is a relative term. The textual critic is concerned with the minutiae of the text in its transmission. His task is to search for a pristine text even in matters of spelling. By and large, a late manuscript or recension of the text will be relatively "corrupt"; an earlier one relatively "pure." The general reader, unacquainted with such terminology, might be misled by the hyperbolic language sometimes used concerning textual variations.

For all practical purposes, then, the MT, upon which modern editions of the Hebrew Bible are based, is a very good text. Indeed, it needs to be emphasized that the MT is a text of extraordinary quality.

> My own studies in text criticism lead me to feel that in the books of the Old Testament all the way through Samuel the Masoretic text (not the Septuagint and not certain Qumran texts) must remain the touch-stone against which discrete variants are gauged.
>
> James A. Sanders,
> "The Dead Sea Scrolls—A Quarter Century of Study,"
> *The Biblical Archaeologist* 36 (1973):141-42

> ... the authenticity of the Massoretic text stands higher than at any time in the history of modern textual criticism, a standpoint which is based on a better assessment of the history of the Jewish transmission.
>
> Bleddyn J. Roberts,
> "The Old Testament: Manuscripts, Text and Versions,"
> *The Cambridge History of the Bible,*
> Vol. 2, Cambridge: University Press, 1969

> Many instances show, according to what has been said, that texts have suffered corruptions in the course of the centuries. But as emphasized above: it never has touched religiously, or rather theologically relevant matters. And the view more and more gains ground that the *Massoretic text* upon the whole is the best form of the text, even if versions in many single cases may have a better reading.
>
> Aage Bentzen,
> *Introduction to the Old Testament,* Vol. 1, p. 101

It is no mere antiquarian interest that seeks answers on

the canon and text of the OT. The study of canon and text investigates the grounds and sources of faith. The student, with a knowledge of these sources, is a better prepared student and a student who ought to be better equipped for life.

BIBLIOGRAPHY

Anderson, G. W. "Canonical and Non-Canonical." *The Cambridge History of the Bible* Vol. 1. P. R. Ackroyd and C. F. Evans, eds. Cambridge: University Press, 1970.

Ap-Thomas, D. R. *A Primer of Old Text Criticism.* New York: The Macmillan Co., 1957.

Cross, Frank M., Jr. *The Ancient Library of Qumran and Modern Biblical Studies.* Garden City, N.Y.: Doubleday & Co., 1961.

Filson, Floyd V. *Which Books Belong in the Bible?* Philadelphia: The Westminster Press, 1957.

Lewis, Jack P. "What Do We Mean By Jabneh?" *The Journal of Bible and Religion* 32 (1964):125-132.

Lightfoot, Neil R. *How We Got the Bible.* Austin: The Sweet Publishing Co., 1961; Grand Rapids: Baker Book House, 1963. Filmstrips published by Gospel Services, Houston, Texas.

Metzger, Bruce M. *An Introduction to the Apocrypha.* New York: Oxford University Press, 1963.

Roberts, Bleddyn J. "The Old Testament: Manuscripts, Text and Versions." *The Cambridge History of the Bible.* Vol. 2. Cambridge: University Press, 1969.

Roberts, C. H. "Books in the Graeco-Roman World and in the New Testament." *The Cambridge History of the Bible.* Vol. 1. Cambridge: University Press, 1970.

Würthwein, Ernst. *The Text of the Old Testament.* New York: The Macmillan Co., 1957.

III
Bible Archeology and Geography

Jack P. Lewis

History and geography are inseparably connected, for history is the story of how man met the challenges of his environment. Each region of the biblical world presents that challenge in distinctive ways.

A circle with a 1,500-mile radius drawn from Jerusalem would take in every people associated with the OT. The region comprises a north-south expanse comparable to that from Montreal to Nicaragua and an east-west expanse comparable to that from New York to Amarillo, Texas. The area is bounded by five seas: the Black Sea, the Caspian, the Persian Gulf, the Red Sea, and the Mediterranean. Its rivers are the Nile, the Jordan, the Litany, the Orontes, the Abana, the Tigris, and the Euphrates.

THE FERTILE CRESCENT

The Fertile Crescent is a term coined by James Breasted to designate that tillable area which has one tip at the Persian Gulf and the other in the Nile valley. Available water resources made food production possible in an area otherwise surrounded by desert regions—deserts that begin at the Atlantic, cross Arabia, and continue to the Gobi Desert of Mongolia. Water determined not only the location of settlements but also the trade routes from one center to another. One did not take the more direct route from Babylon to Jerusalem across the desert. He went up the Euphrates, crossed to what is now Aleppo, and then came down from the north via Damascus. Or he went to Mari, to Tadmor, and to Damascus.

Palestine is the land bridge between the Mesopotamian and the Nile valleys where early civilizations developed; it is also a halfway point between the Hittites in the north and the Arabians in the south. Palestine's history is determined by her position. No independent political or economic development could take place; the struggle of neighboring powers engulfed her.

MESOPOTAMIA

Mesopotamia, the name given by Polybius and Strabo to that portion of the Fertile Crescent formed by the Tigris and Euphrates valleys, designates the area that is the scene of the earliest sections of the OT, the land in which the dominating powers of Assyria and Babylon arose, and the locale of at least the early part of the Jewish exile (2 Kings 15:29; 17:6). "By the waters of Babylon . . . ," the poet said (Ps. 137). This area, all of which lies north of 30 degrees north latitude—the latitude of New Orleans—influenced Israel more than did Egypt, from the time of the monarchy to the time of Alexander the Great.

In the OT a northern sector of this Euphrates area is called Aram-Naharaim (Aram of the two rivers—Gen. 24:10; Judg. 3:8ff.), but the Greek translators used Mesopotamia for it and thereby contributed a word to our religious vocabulary. The total region today is controlled by Turkey, Syria, and Iraq, but its major portion is in Iraq. With the area open to invasion, marauding tribes descended from the mountains and took over the fields. Periodic migrations from the desert into the cultivated areas took place, but eventually the newcomers were assimilated.

The Euphrates, the longest river in western Asia, is 1,800 miles from its source to the sea. At first its descent is sharp, but in the last 1,200 miles it falls only 10 inches per mile. Formed from two tributaries, one which begins in the Armenian highlands at a lake 8,625 feet above the sea in the vicinity north-northwest of Ezerum and the other which begins at 11,500 feet elevation northwest of Diadin, the Euphrates takes life where the two join 115 miles above Samasat (ancient Samasata). Flowing first in a southwesterly direction until it cuts through the Taurus Mountains, the river reaches the Syrian plain at Samasat at an elevation of only 1,500 feet. Continuing to a point within 100 miles of the Mediterranean, and at one place 450 miles separated from the Tigris, it has descended to only 628 feet above the sea when it swings around to the southeast to empty finally into the Persian Gulf. Along the way it flows past Jerabulus, which was Carchemish, where Nebuchadnezzar II defeated Pharaoh Necho in 605 B.C. (2 Kings 24:7; Jer. 46:2ff.). Further along its western banks are the sites of Dura Europas and Mari. From Samasat to Hit is 720 miles of treeless country. At Hit the river is thirty to thirty-five feet deep and 250 yards wide and flows at four miles per hour. In this upper region the irrigable land is not more than a thousand yards wide and the surrounding area is arid. Below Hit no tributaries join the river in its 550-mile flow to the Persian Gulf. Much of the water is dissipated through evaporation. The river winds past ancient Babylon and eventually joins the Tigris at Qurna, sixty miles above Bosra, to form the Shatt-el-Arab. This last stream is 1,000 yards wide and from three to five fathoms deep. One estimate is that the two rivers (Tigris and Euphrates) lose 90 percent of their water between Qurna and Amra by dissipation into canals and lagoons. After flowing past Bosra, the Shatt-el-Arab empties into the Gulf. It is thought that in antiquity the course of the river in the lower regions may have been different and may have passed Sippar, Kish, Nippur, Erech, and Ur.

The Euphrates served as a boundary between the Assyrians and the Hittites, divided the eastern and western satrapies of the Persian Empire, later was at various times the eastern boundary of the Roman Empire, and still later was a border against the Mongols. But it was also an avenue of commerce and its banks have many sites of antiquity representing its long history.

Designated in the Bible as "the river" (Num. 22:5; Deut. 11:24) and as "the great river" (Josh. 1:4), the Euphrates is one of the four streams issuing out of Eden (Gen. 2:10-14). It is the northern boundary of the land promised Israel (Gen. 15:18; Deut. 1:7; Josh. 1:4), and it was reached by Israel during the Hebrew monarchy (2 Sam. 8:3; 10:16; 1 Kings 4:24).

The Tigris, 1,150 miles long, another of the rivers flowing out of Eden (KJV *Hiddekel*, Gen. 2:14), was the scene of one of Daniel's visions (Dan. 10:4). Beginning in Armenia (Turkey) northwest of Diarbekr, this more eastern of the two rivers leaves the mountains 250 miles from the Euphrates and flows southward past Mosul. The Tigris flows more water and is more constant than the Euphrates. Near Mosul was the location of Khorsabad, city of Sargon; and across the river from Mosul on the left bank was ancient Nineveh. Twenty miles further was Kalah (Nimrud). The Tigris is then joined on the left by the Greater Zab. This fertile triangle formed by these two rivers is known as the Assyrian Triangle. Below this junction on the west bank is Kalaat Sherqat, the site of ancient Assur. By the time the Tigris reaches Baghdad the two rivers are only twenty miles apart. The upper Tigris is navigable only to native rafts floating on inflated skins, which in flood times can cover the downstream distance from Mosul to Baghdad in three or four days. There is no upstream traffic. In the upper alluvial area the Tigris lies lower than the Euphrates so that irrigation canals run off the Euphrates and empty into the Tigris.

The climate of Mesopotamia has not significantly changed since the beginning of Sumerian times (5000 B.C.), but the soil has changed as a result of layers of sediment from the rivers and the drift of sand from the desert, which may vary from twelve to twenty-three feet in thickness. Herodotus speaks of harvests of 200 to 300-fold around Babylon in the Persian period; however, the land is not so productive today. There is a rainy season, and the rainfall is about 8 inches annually, which may be compared with 60 inches in the state of Georgia. While temperatures may drop below freezing at night in the winter, normal summer temperature is 108 degrees Fahrenheit in the shade and 120 to 140 degrees in the sun.

The rivers were capricious and often changed their courses, leaving flourishing cities to decay and abandonment. However, there has also been a salinization of the soil both from the water of the rivers and from surface groundwater. The danger of salinization is mentioned in very early texts and thereafter periodically through history. In northern areas where the water table was lower, the danger was, of course, less; but Sumerian civilization developed in the south and may well have declined under the impact of salinization.

The irrigable land of ancient Mesopotamia was more extensive than that of Egypt. In the middle Euphrates, water for irrigation was either drawn in a skin from the river and dumped into aqueducts or was raised by great water wheels. The lower valley was fertile under irrigation, but the ancient canals were continuously silting and had to be replaced with new canals. While some of the ancient canals can be traced out, not one-hundredth of the old system is now in working order.

When the rains coincided with the melting snows of the Taurus and Zagros mountains, catastrophic floods resulted, giving rise to flood stories. The Sumerian flood story has Zuisudra as its hero, but later stories named Utrahasis and Utnapishtim. The river reaches its maximum in May and its minimum at the end of November, which is exactly the opposite season for these points of the Nile. In the hot summer when most needed for irrigation, the rivers are low. The spring and summer may bring severe dust storms, removing the top of the desert and depositing it on the cultivable land. Beek argued that Woolley's alleged "silt layer" at Ur was really a dust storm deposit. It is through control of the rivers that the modern state of Iraq exists.

It has often been pointed out that climate affected religion in antiquity. The hostile environment in Mesopotamia fostered belief in gods who were as capricious and unreasonable as were the rivers.

Theories differ on the question of the receding of the coast line of the Persian Gulf. Older students assumed that the gulf once came inland almost as far as Ur and Eridu. Some ancient texts mention Eridu as a port city, but at the present time other students argue that the shore once extended further into the gulf than it does now and suggest that river traffic could be sufficient to explain the allusions to Eridu as being on the sea.

Wheat and barley grew well in ancient Mesopotamia. The total habitable area of Assyria was about 5,000 square miles. It was her need of grain from Babylon that led her to attempt to control Babylon. Her need for trade explains her westward expansion, which brought her into conflict with Egypt.

The north had stone for building, and asphalt used for joining brick and for making floors watertight could be mined at Kirkuk and Hit. Oil, so valuable today, played no role in the ancient world. The mountains in Kurdistan were still covered with trees, and the date palm of the delta goes back to at least the third millennium. Today the Mesopotamian delta has more than 18 million date palms of 350 varieties and is a center of the world's date production.

Mesopotamia is divided into regions. The lower alluvial region is Sumer (the land of Shinar in the Bible, Gen. 11:1ff.); further north is Akkad. Even as late as the Persian period Cyrus denominated himself "King of Sumer and Akkad." The Sumerian area was stoneless; buildings were made of sun-dried brick. It furnished the earliest known writing. Later the area became the heartland of Babylon.

Still further to the north is the land that became Assyria. As we have seen, its chief cities were on the Tigris River. Assyria extended itself over Babylon and then in the west eventually reached to Upper Egypt. Assyria's heartland had a more moderate climate than Sumer did.

West of Assyria between the Euphrates, the Balikh, and the Habor rivers, the Hurrian kingdom of Mitanni developed in the period between the sixteenth and fourteenth centuries. Mitanni is not mentioned in the Bible, but the

Horites, its peoples, are. Beyond Mitanni was the Hittite Empire extending into what is today Turkey.

Data are insufficient to permit the definite location of the Garden of Eden, though it is obvious that it is placed in the Tigris-Euphrates valleys. The two other rivers, Pishon and Gihon (Gen. 2:10-14), are unlocated. The beginning of music (Gen. 4:21) and of metalwork (Gen. 4:22), trades known to us from Sumerian civilization, is mentioned.

The temple towers called *ziggurats* such as that at Ur show the form of construction which has mud brick laid in asphalt with burned brick casing on the exterior, similar to that described for the tower of Babel (Gen. 11:1ff.). Remains of about thirty-five of these structures are known from various Mesopotamian sites.

The ark of Noah is said to have landed in the mountains of Ararat (Gen. 8:4), doubtless the area designated Urartu by the Assyrians. From a very early time a volcanic peak without a crater, now in Turkey near the Russian border, has been designated Mount Ararat. There is no historical record of an eruption of the volcano which formed Ararat. The mountain, covered with volcanic stone, rises 16,946 feet in a gradient of 45 to 60 percent. Its snow line is at about 14,000 thousand feet, but it is scalable, and numerous individuals reach its summit each year. The claims of sightings of remains of the ark which have been made through the centuries are numerous; however, they have no real claim to credibility.

Ur of the Chaldees, from which Abraham and his family migrated (Gen. 11:31; 15:7; Neh. 9:7; Acts 7:2), is most commonly identified with the site in the lower Euphrates valley 120 miles south of Babylon and 150 miles north of the Persian Gulf. Here J. E. Taylor found a dedicatory inscription of Nabonidus in the *ziggurat* designating the place as Ur of the Sumerians. Leonard Woolley's excavations at Ur show it to have been a center of moon worship and to have had a highly developed culture before patriarchal times. While now located fifteen miles from the Euphrates and out in the desert, Ur is thought to have once been on the river and to have had an estimated population of 250,000 people.

A migration from Ur to Haran would represent a journey of about six hundred miles. Cyrus Gordon has attempted to locate Ur in the upper Euphrates rather than in the lower region, but the effort is not convincing.

Haran is located in the Balikh valley of the middle Euphrates region between the Tigris and the Euphrates. In Abraham's day it was also a center of moon cult just as Ur was. The Mari tablets tell that the Benjamites signed a treaty with the king of Haran in the temple of Sin at Haran. The Terah family migration coming from Ur in reality took them from one shrine center to another. Today the main routes of travel have passed Haran by, and it is a quiet Turkish village off the beaten paths of civilization. Its houses—in a treeless plain—are of the mud-beehive type, many examples of which are in northern Syria. Haran is best reached in a side trip from the Turkish city of Urfa (called Edessa in late antiquity). In Abraham's day, Haran was at the intersection of major trade routes—that from Aleppo to Nineveh and that from Babylon to Asia Minor. Although excavations carried out there by D. D. Rice in 1951, 1952, and 1956 revealed the temple of Sin beneath the Islamic mosque-fortress, for all practical purposes Haran is still an unexcavated site. The large mosque is thought to be not more than a thousand years old. No tablets of Terah's day have been found at Haran, nor are there other specific traces of the patriarchs there.

It was at Haran that God made promises to Abraham (Gen. 12:1-3), and many years later the servant of Abraham came back to Aram-Naharaim to seek a wife for Isaac. Still later Jacob came there to serve Laban in exchange for his daughters Rachel and Leah. It is called the land of Aram in the Bible (Num. 23:7; Deut. 23:4; Judges 3:8; Hos. 12:12).

ARAM

We here use the name Aram for that part of the biblical world now controlled by Lebanon and Syria. Like Palestine this region has four areas: the coastal plain, the mountains, the Rift Valley, and the highlands. It extends from the

Amanus Mountains to the Ladder of Tyre, about 260 miles north to south, and 140 miles from the sea to Palmyra.

The Mediterranean coast from Turkey to Sinai extends 400 miles but in Lebanon is never more than four miles wide and is broken into short strips by promontories. Often the mountains rise almost out of the sea, and at Nahr al-Kalb (Dog River), just north of modern Beirut, they reach the sea, forming an effective barrier to passage. The plain is well-watered by the runoff from the adjoining highlands and is very fertile. The plain in places such as around Tyre has the heavy, red soil that makes for excellent cultivation. It is not extensive enough, however, to support a large population, making trade essential to existence. Major caravan routes did not connect Galilee with this area. Israel made no effort to conquer it even in the golden age of David and Solomon, and neither did Aram attempt to dominate Israel. Rather, the two allied with each other.

Extending from the Amanus Mountains on the north to the border of Israel on the south are the Lebanon Mountains, which limit communication with the interior. The major break in the mountains at Nahr el-Kebir forms the division between Lebanon and Syria; but below this point there are no passes, and traffic must go over the mountains. Peaks extend up to 11,824 feet and are snow-covered six months of the year, giving the name Lebanon (from a Semitic root meaning white) to the area. The mountains receive a great deal of rainfall. Within Lebanon they stretch 105 miles southward to a point just north of Tyre. Once forested with the famous cedars of Lebanon, the mountains are now largely bare. Only a few cedars remain in a protected grove. Hills and ravines make communication between one part of the country and the other difficult, and isolated groups find it easy to maintain their identities.

The Biqa', called "the valley of Lebanon" in the Bible (Josh. 11:17; 12:7), lying between the two mountain ranges, is in the area of Hamath 1,015 feet above the sea. The valley, however, rises to 3,770 feet elevation at Baalbek and varies in width from six to ten miles. Near Baalbek the Asi River begins and drains northward into Syria. The Litany

River begins not far away, drains southward and then turns abruptly westward to empty into the sea between Tyre and Sidon. At the plain of Ijon (1 Kings 15:20) the valley has descended to only 1,600 feet elevation. The Biqa' contains the most favorable soil in Lebanon for cultivation.

The Anti-Lebanon range rises south of Homs and extends southward to Mount Hermon and beyond. Hermon, also called Siron (Deut. 3:9; Ps. 29:6), rises to 9,383 feet and is at times visible as far south as Frank Mountain near Bethlehem. Though covered with snow in the winter and though snow patches remain in the summer, it has no true glaciers. The melting snows feed springs on all sides of the mountain and give life to the Jordan and to the Litany.

Precipitation, falling between November and March, decreases in Lebanon as one goes from north to south and from west to east. Beirut has about 31.9 inches of rain a year, but in the mountains the figure may rise to 59.7 inches. In the Biqa', however, it decreases to 24.8; and at Damascus, beyond the next range of mountains, rainfall is only 10 inches. The contrast between spring, when everything is green, and summer, when vegetation has burned, is everywhere striking.

The fig, the olive, and the vine are native to Lebanon, but it was the cedars (mentioned both in inscriptions and in the OT) which attracted ancient kings to the region (2 Kings 14:9; Ps. 29:5; Zech. 11:1-2). About four hundred of the cedars, the tallest of which is about eighty feet, remain in a grove above Bisharri.

The Lebanese area faced the sea with many anchorages along its coast, but it had a sparseness of farm land from which to feed its population. These factors made the Phoenicians a seafaring people, and it is in this role that the cities of the Lebanese coast are of interest to the Bible reader.

Byblos, despite the fact that it is not mentioned in the Bible, bequeathed its name to history in the word "Bible," for the town was named from the word the Greeks used for papyrus. The story of Wen Amon in the eleventh century tells of an Egyptian who came there to trade papyrus for cedar to make a ceremonial barge. Letters from King Zimreda of Sidon are in the Amarna collection. Sidon later felt the power of the Assyrians and still later that of the Babylonians and the Persians. A great mound of murex shells there tells of Sidon's significance in the purple industry. Sidon (the KJV also uses the spelling Zidon) is mentioned as a place from which Laish (taken by the Danites) was isolated because of the mountains (Judg. 18:7, 28). Today called Saida, the city is about twenty-five miles north of Tyre. It is mentioned as a boundary point as early as the blessing of Jacob (Gen. 49:13). Sidon's gods were among those served by the Israelites (Judg. 10:6), and Solomon had a Sidonian wife (1 Kings 11:33). Elijah spent a part of the drought at Zarephath (modern Serafand), a city belonging to Sidon, where a widow provided for him (1 Kings 17:9). Sidon is often mentioned in the oracles of the prophets, which include references to its mercantile position (Isa. 23:2-4; see also Jer. 25:22; 27:3; 47:4; Ezek. 27:8; 28:21, 22; Joel 3:4; Zech. 9:2). The Sidonians were among those furnishing cedars for temple reconstruction at the time of Zerubbabel's return from exile (Ezra 3:7).

Tyre is particularly important because of Hiram's relationship with Solomon. The city was situated on a small island and its harbor was protected by a breakwater built by Hiram. The island is connected with the mainland by an isthmus first formed by Alexander the Great but now covered with sand. Tyre is mentioned in the Amarna letters and in the Keret epic from Ugarit. Wen Amon visited it about 1100 B.C. Hiram furnished materials to David for the building of his house (2 Sam. 5:11; 1 Chron. 14:1) and then to Solomon for the temple (1 Kings 5:1; 1 Chron. 22:4; 2 Chron. 2:3-18). Tyre's king fought along with Ahab against Shalmaneser III at Qarqar in 853 B.C. Ahab married Jezebel, daughter of Ethbaal, king of Tyre and priest of Ashtart. The prophets saw the wealth and pride of Tyre as sure evidence of its approaching doom (Isa. 23:1-18; Jer. 25:22; 27:3; 47:4; Ezek. 26:2-28:18; Joel 3:4-8; Amos 1:9-10; Zech. 9:2-4). Nebuchadnezzar II besieged Tyre thirteen years before it yielded. It later came under the domination of Persia and still exported cedars and other products at the time of the reconstruction of the Jewish temple. Roman provincial administration tended to combine the entire Levant (the East) into one province, Syria. In the NT period Herod the Great did building at Tyre, Sidon, Byblos, Beirut, Tripolis, and Damascus.

Syria is first important in the OT because of the roads that cross it. One road crossed the desert from the Euphrates to Palmyra (Tadmor), proceeded to Damascus, then southward across the Jordan to Megiddo and to Egypt. Roads that hugged the line of springs at the base of the Anti-Lebanon Mountains converged on Damascus. Every road to Phoenicia had to pass through the valley of the Barada River. One could cross in this way into the Lebanese valley and follow the Orontes northward with one branch going off into the Syrian gates into Asia Minor but with the main road swinging eastward below the Taurus Mountains to the Euphrates where that river comes nearest the Mediterranean. The road then continued to the Tigris River and down to the Persian Gulf.

It is surprising that the Syrian cities are not mentioned in the migration of Abraham, for he must have passed through them. His servant Eliezer came from Damascus. The Orontes River waters northern Syria, flows past what became Antioch, and then empties into the sea. Aleppo, not on the river and not mentioned in the Bible, is older than the patriarchs. Located at the crossroads in northern Syria, it has been occupied by all the nations who passed this way. Today it is a city of about half a million.

Neither is Ebla (Tell Mardikh), lying forty-four miles south of Aleppo, mentioned in biblical narratives. This site, covering one hundred forty acres and estimated to have once had a population of 260,000, has since 1975 yielded more than 16,500 cuneiform tablets dating about 2300 B.C. and written in Sumerian and in a language now called Eblaite (or "Paleo-Canaanite), which reveal a civilization in upper Syria that was previously undreamed of. The Ebla tablets are the earliest known West Semitic texts. Ebla traded with Anatolia,

Palestine, and western Iran. In the tablets geographical names like Canaan, Hazor, Megiddo, Dor, Joppa, Lachish, Gaza, Salim (Jerusalem?), Sodom, and Gomorrah occur. Names of Canaanite deities lika Dagon, El, Asherah, and Kemosh have been identified. Preliminary reports assert that personal names like Eber, Abraham, Ishmael, Esau, David, Michael, and Micaiah are paralleled though there is no reason to connect any Eblaite figure with a biblical one. The Ebla materials offer exciting possibilities in the study of OT backgrounds.

Also in the north of Syria, near where Latakya is now, was Ugarit. Ugarit is not mentioned in the Bible, but excavations of the 1930s indicate that this place had a thriving civilization in the second millennium B.C. Ugaritic tablets reveal a city rich in trade with a religious system comparable to that denounced by the Hebrew prophets. Babylonian, Hurrian, Hittite, Aegean, and Egyptian cultures all mingled there.

Much further south the Barada (Abana) flows east from the Anti-Lebanons to water Damascus in what otherwise would be desert. Damascus, at 2,264 feet elevation, is seventy miles from the sea and 160 miles northeast of Jerusalem. The city turns from the sea to dominate the trade routes of the steppe and desert. Roads leading from Arabia, Mesopotamia, Egypt, and Asia Minor converge on her. While the site is indefensible, Damascus usually allied with her neighbors. The Barada makes the area an oasis before the river breaks up into about five streams and is absorbed in the desert eighteen miles east of Damascus. The Pharpar (2 Kings 5:12; possibly the Nahr al-A'waj) also flows eastward on the south of Damascus. Mohammed is said to have remarked on his refusal to enter the oasis that one can only go to Paradise once and that he did not wish to do so here on earth.

Damascus has never been the center of an extensive empire, though it has made continual efforts in this direction. It was a rival to Samaria and Jerusalem during the divided kingdom period, at which time an Aramaean kingdom was reigned over by the series Ben Hadad I and II,

Hadadezer, Ben Hadad III, Hazael, and Rezin. Eventually Damascus was overrun in 733 by Assyria. Today it has a population of one and a half million.

The "way of the sea," which connected Egypt with Mesopotamia, passed through Damascus and connected it with Palestine. There were constant trade contacts between the two regions. Hamath and Riblah, major cities of Syria, were located in the areas drained by the Orontes. Other Aramaean states besides Damascus were formed in North Syria: Aram Maacah, Aram Bethrehob, and Zobah.

PERSIA

Since Persia had no chronicler of its own, no native Herodotus or Xenophon to tell its story, it has remained comparatively unknown. Our information derives from the Jews and the Greeks who were the enemies of the Persians. Archeological excavation of the past generation, however, has brought Iranian cultural history to light through pottery and cuneiform inscriptions on clay and stone. Of relevance to the Bible chiefly in the exilic and postexilic ages, Persia is mentioned in the Bible in a number of late passages (2 Chron. 36:20; Esth. 1:3; Ezek. 27:10; 38:5; Dan. 8:20; 10:1, 13, 20; 11:2).

Persia proper, as distinguished from the total empire it came to control, lies east of the Tigris-Euphrates valley in the area today ruled by Iran. Located between the Persian Gulf, the Caspian Sea, and the Indus basin, Persia covers an area twice the size of Texas. On the west lie the Zagros Mountains, which have a width of 125 miles and extend northeast to southeast for 620 miles. Peaks of the range extend up to 5,570 feet. The Elburz range, stretching along the shores of the Caspian Sea with peaks up to nineteen thousand feet, forms a northern barrier, and the Makoran range on the east separates the area from Pakistan.

Called by one writer "the driest place on earth," two-thirds of the area is desert. Rainfall around Teheran ranges between 9 and 11 inches, falling only in the winter season (November to March). Between the mountains is the Iranian plateau, averaging three thousand feet in elevation. The plateau has some oases, but is chiefly cultivatable only in the areas that can be irrigated with water from the mountains. The melting snows of winter bring water. Elaborate underground channels necessary to avoid evaporation in the high temperatures are maintained today, as they doubtless have been since the beginning of history. Harvest is finished by the end of April. The hot summers with temperatures over the 100-degree mark were noted by the Greek historians, who tell of the barley popping when spread out to dry (Strabo 15.3.10).

Within the mountains are long, narrow valleys furnishing excellent pastureland. As temperatures rise in the lower valleys, herdsmen find it necessary to move their herds to upper pastures, making for a nomadic life.

Though bordered by the Caspian Sea, the Persian Gulf, and the Gulf of Oman, ancient Persia was landlocked. Unlike the Greeks, whose life came from the sea, the Persians were not a seafaring people. Commerce was overland and the significant cities lay on the trade routes. Persia was the land bridge between Mesopotamia and areas that lie further east. Limited on the north by the Caucasus Mountains, Achaemenid Persia really faced west. Here she came into conflict with the Greeks, but Athens and Sparta successfully resisted Darius and Xerxes. Darius was defeated at Marathon in 490 B.C., and Xerxes lost the naval battle off Salamis in 480. A hundred years later fortunes had reversed; Alexander swept over the East and attempted to fuse two cultures by marriages. However, the union was short lived and Rome eventually became Alexander's true heir; yet Rome never extended to Persia.

In earlier times, Elam, located on what is today the Iranian plateau, had Ecbatana as its capital (Herodotus 1. 98–100). It sat astride the most prominent trade route from east to west. Elam, as a descendant of Shem, already appears in the table of nations in Genesis 10:22; and Chedorlaomer, one of Elam's kings, participated in the raid that took Lot captive (Gen. 14:1ff.). Some of the prophets have oracles against or mention Elam (Isa. 21:2; 22:6; Jer. 25:25; 49:34-39; Ezek. 32:24; Dan. 8:2). But, in general, the world of the OT was the scene of the struggle of the powers of Mesopotamia with Egypt until the exilic age when the Medes and the Persians burst onto the scene.

The Medes are first mentioned in history by Shalmaneser III in 853 B.C. in a list of his enemies. They occupied the northern part of what is now Iran. Among the other places of exile of the northern tribes are "the cities of the Medes" (2 Kings 17:6). Isaiah 21:2 lists Media among threatening forces in his oracles. The Medes captured Assur in 614 and then joined with the Scythians and the Babylonians in the overthrow of Nineveh in 612. They then moved into the northern parts of the defeated empire as the Babylonians did into the southern part. By expanding into Asia Minor they limited Babylon on the north. During this period Persia, lying east of Babylon, was only one of the vassal states of Media. Jeremiah points to the Medes as the eventual destroyers of Babylon (Jer. 51:11).

It was the Achaemenid kings, however, who built and for two centuries maintained in one family the Persian Empire —an empire extending from the Indus River on the east to the Aegean on the west, and from the Oxus to the Nile. Isaiah 43–45 comments on Cyrus' lightninglike rise to power. Though king of Anshan (which seems to be southern Elam and especially the area around and including Susa), Cyrus set himself to overthrow Astyages, ruler of the Medes. After his troops had mutinied, Astyages himself was captured in 549 B.C., and Cyrus proceeded to Ecbatana, Astyages' capital. The new state built by Cyrus consisted of Medes and Persians; Ecbatana was now maintained as a summer residence. Cyrus describes himself as "King of Anshan; King of Persia; King of Babylon." Cyrus pushed rapidly westward. Sardis was captured in 546, Babylon in 539, and then Cyrus' successors extended themselves into Egypt in 525. Within a thirty-year span the Achaemenids had built an empire larger than any the world had seen west of China—an empire to last until the conquests of Alexander the Great in 330 B.C.

Darius I molded these diverse regions into an organized empire with roads and an efficient post system

(Herodotus 5. 52–54; Esth. 3:13). Horses were kept at each station so that a courier could have a fresh mount and set off immediately for the next station. The "King of Kings" ruled over twenty satrapies whose names Herodotus preserves (3. 89f.); Judah belonged to that region called "across the river." The world had never before known rulers of such wealth and power. The law of the Medes and Persians, not subject to the whims of rulers, kindled the imagination of the Middle East. Darius was the first of the Achaemenids to subscribe to the ideals of Zoroastrianism, but Cyrus had earlier proved tolerant, allowing the Jews and other subject peoples to rebuild their temples and to worship in their own way. Zoroastrianism's ideals of the continuous struggle between good and evil, light and darkness, was not out of harmony with such policies. The Persians allowed each country to have its own language, customs, and system of laws. The trilingual royal inscriptions represent the languages spoken by the people, but Aramaic was the language of commerce used all the way from India to the Mediterranean. Gold and silver coins called *darics* were used for exchange in the empire.

The Persians solved the problem of ruling their diverse territory and of its extremes of climate by moving their capital three times a year. In the winter it was Susa on the Euphrates side of the Zagros Mountains, in the spring it was at Persepolis, and in the summer at Ecbatana, where the increased elevation could make life bearable. Rages (Ray in the suburbs of Teheran) was not a capital but has some interest to biblical students because of its role in the book of Tobit. Of these four cities only Ecbatana and Susa are actually mentioned in the canonical books of the Bible.

Scenes from Esther (1:2; 2:5) and Nehemiah (1:1) are from Shushan (Susa), the ancient capital of Susiana (now Khuristan). Susa was 150 miles north of the Persian Gulf and was on the Mesopotamian side of the Zagros Mountains rather than on the Iranian plateau itself. The Susa plain is a bay of the Mesopotamian lowland extending far into the Zagros. Only a hundred miles from Sumer, it is really a province of Sumer, but unlike the Mesopotamian region it does not grow dates as lower Mesopotamia does; hence, though on the west of the mountains, it adheres to the plateau. Susa had roads both to Ecbatana 190 miles away and to Persepolis, 585 miles away. Its situation offered good communication with Mesopotamia and with Asia Minor. The Achaemenids built a Royal Road from Susa to Sardis.

Susa is much older than Darius; excavations reveal habitation back to 4000 B.C., but by 521 Darius had taken up residence there (Herodotus 3. 129). Buildings were made of sun-dried or of kiln-fired bricks. The palace surpassed that of Ecbatana in splendor. Darius has left behind an inscription describing the building of his palace out of materials brought from many countries. The royal buildings were destroyed by fire during the reign of Artaxerxes I (465–425 B.C.), but the site was continuously occupied until the time of the Islamic conquest. Excavations were begun in the nineteenth century on the four tells which mark the remains of Susa. Jacques de Morgan, R. de Mocquenem, and R. Girshman have all worked there. Recently a statue of Darius has been unearthed. The village of Shush, near the old site, claims to have the tomb of Daniel the prophet, venerated by the Shi'ite Muslims.

The river Ulai (Dan. 8:2, 16) has been identified with the Karun. At an earlier time the Karun had a branch that ran about two miles east of Susa. The stream is estimated to have been nine hundred feet wide and twelve to twenty feet deep. Alexander the Great is said to have sailed on it from Susa to the Persian Gulf.

The Behistun rock is a massive memorial carved on the side of a 3,800-foot peak near the village of Bisitun, from which the rock takes its name. Here alongside the main east-west road, Darius I in 516 B.C. (the year the temple in Jerusalem was restored) carved a panel 300 feet above the plain in which he depicts himself in life size treading on the neck of Gaumata, who had opposed his rise to power. Behind Gaumata is a procession of other rebel leaders roped together. An inscription in old Persian, Elamite, and Akkadian, done in cuneiform characters, tells of Darius' rise to power. The inscription was visible through the centuries, but it was not until 1835 that H. C. Rawlinson succeeded in copying it and in deciphering cuneiform. This accomplishment opened to the Western world the secrets locked in that script.

Ecbatana (today Hamadan) the ancient capital of Elam, was located on the main trade route that connected Mesopotamia and the Iranian plateau just where that route enters the plateau. It was also located on the road that came north from the Persian Gulf leading on to the Caspian Sea or to Armenia. Ecbatana was made a summer residence by Cyrus, and there in the archives during the reign of Darius I (Ezra 6:2) was found a copy of his decrees concerning the rebuilding of the temple in Jerusalem. Ecbatana was also the home of Sarah in the story of Tobit (Tobit 3:7), and the book of Judith (1:1-4) describes its fortifications. Hamadan is located on top of the ancient remains so that extensive archeological work has not been carried out, but native digging has brought to light many Achaemenid objects.

Arrian (*Anabasis* 3. 19-20) locates Rages eleven days' forced march for Alexander's army from Ecbatana. Rages, a road center, was located south of the Alburz Mountains which border the Caspian Sea. Occupied as early as 5000 B.C., Rages has left ruins which are now about five miles southeast of Teheran in an area called Ray. Tobit, who is presented as a Jewish exile in Nineveh, had once lived in Rages and had left ten talents of silver with Gabael. In the course of the story of how Tobias and Azarias journeyed to recover the money, Rages is mentioned six times (Tobit 1:14; 4:1, 20; 5:5; 6:12; 9:2).

No Western writer before Alexander the Great mentions Persepolis. Even Ctesias, the Greek physician who lived at the court of Artaxerxes II (405–358 B.C.), seems never to have heard of it. It also goes unmentioned in the Bible. Cyrus had built his capital at Pasargadae in a plain of 5,000 feet elevation. A monumental gate found there had the inscription: "I am Cyrus the king of the Achaemenid." Of his great audience hall, only a single pillar forty feet tall remains standing. Less than a mile south of it is the tomb of Cyrus. The Iranian archeological authorities have excavated the Pasargadae area since 1949.

Somewhat farther south and at a lower elevation, fifty miles from modern Shiraz, Cambyses founded Persepolis. But it was Darius (521–485 B.C.) who was its builder, and the construction was continued by Xerxes. Never really an administrative center, Persepolis was built for the glory of the Achaemenid kings. Here at the great Nowruz festival the king received the delegates and their tribute from all over the empire. They are depicted on the monumental staircase. Eventually Persepolis was burned by Alexander the Great and was never reoccupied; hence, it is quite well preserved.

Travelers such as Pietro delle Valle (ca. A.D. 1622) visited and described Persepolis, but the place remained comparatively unknown until it was finally excavated, first by the Oriental Institute of the University of Chicago, 1931–1934 and 1939 and then by the Iranians. A monumental staircase leads up to a gate-building opening onto a gigantic terrace which is 1,500 by 1,000 feet. On the platform stood the hall of 100 columns, and there Xerxes had his palace and harem, which are identified by an inscription that designates the builder. Also there is the audience hall of Darius and Xerxes. In the hillside near Persepolis are the tombs of the later Achaemenid kings. Unparalleled in the world, Persepolis reveals some of the greatness of those who built a world empire and then let the Jewish exiles return home.

THE HITTITE LAND

The Hittites are treated in the Bible as inhabitants of Palestine. Heth himself is listed as a descendant of Canaan (Gen. 10:15). Along with others, Hittites regularly appear in lists of Canaanite inhabitants (Gen. 15:19-21; Josh. 3:10). Ezekiel charges that the mother of Jerusalem was a Hittite (Ezek. 16:3). Abraham bought the cave of Machpelah from Ephron the Hittite (Gen. 23:1ff.); Esau married Hittite women (Gen. 26:34; 36:2); Uriah was a Hittite (2 Sam. 11:3); Solomon had Hittite princesses (1 Kings 11:1) and traded with the Hittites (1 Kings 10:28-29; 2 Chron. 1:17); and even at later times Hittite kings could be presumed to participate in Palestinian wars (2 Kings 7:6). The name Hittite was used loosely in antiquity. Assyrian inscriptions sometimes refer to the west as Khatti, that is, the Hittite Land. Sargon's records call the people of Ashdod Hittites. However, in this section of our study we use the term Hittite Land to designate an area that is in modern Turkey—an area that lies off the main scene of OT history. In antiquity no one power dominated the whole of Turkey. Many peoples reacted against each other. The table of nations (Gen. 10) lists the figures Lud, Meshech, Tubal, and Togarmah, whom OT scholars conjecturally assign to the Hittite area, but the Hittite empire had disappeared before the kingdom of Israel arose. Extrabiblical sources do not suggest for it an influence south of Kadesh on the Orontes.

At the height of its power between 1700–1200 B.C. the Hittite Empire extended from Mitanni on the east to the sea on the west, and from Palestine on the south to the Black Sea on the north. Its capital was Hattusha (Boghazköy), which has within this century been excavated; its thousands of recovered tablets have been deciphered with startling results. The Hittite land is cut off from the Fertile Crescent by the Taurus Mountains, part of a system that stretches in an easterly direction from Spain to China. Peaks extend up to more than ten thousand feet, are snow-capped, and form an effective barrier limiting commerce to certain passages. One such pass is the "Syrian Gates" which connects Antakya with Iskenderun in Turkey today. Here beside the modern highway which seeks a gentler slope can be seen remains of an earlier road that did dozens of U-turns as it zigzagged up the mountain.

Semites did not advance beyond the Taurus, but the peoples beyond that barrier often invaded the Fertile Crescent. The Hittites conquered Babylon about 1600 B.C. but were unable to maintain domination in this region, and the kingdom of Mitanni grew up as a buffer between the Hittites and Assyria. Egyptians and Hittites struggled for domination of Palestine, but effective campaigns of Thutmoses III at Megiddo in 1468 B.C. and of Rameses II at Kadesh on the Orontes in 1300 B.C. brought a stalemate. Rameses II and Hattusilis made a treaty of non-aggression in 1284—the first known in history. Both Egyptian and Hittite copies of this treaty have been preserved; the border between the two powers is set to the south of Kadesh in middle Syria. Eventually the Hittite Empire crumbled under the impact of the invasions of the Sea Peoples.

After the fall of Hattusha we have no records for Asia Minor proper, but Syria was ruled for a time by both Aramaean and Hittite kings. Over the years, influences from these areas may well have been felt in Palestine in the ways the Bible suggests.

Solomon's trade extended to the Hittites. On the basis of cuneiform evidence it is thought that Kue, where he acquired his horses (1 Kings 10:28; 2 Chron. 1:16-17), some of which he used for his chariots and some of which he sold, is to be located in the plain that in Roman times became Cilicia but now is in Turkey south of the Taurus range.

EGYPT

One of the earliest cultures to develop, Egyptian civilization was already 3,000 years old when Greece came into being. The life of Egypt has always been the Nile River. An ancient oracle of the god Amun said, "Egypt is the land watered by the Nile in its course; and those who dwell below the city of Elephantine and drink that river's water are Egyptians." Herodotus called Egypt "the gift of the Nile"; while an Arab general in the eighth century said of it, "All its wealth comes from the blessed river that moves through it with the dignity of a Caliph."

On the Nile today one can see the boats called *feluccas* sailing just as they are represented in the pictures in the early tombs. They float downriver with the current but go upriver with the aid of the wind. The Nile, extending 4,145 miles, is probably the world's longest river, followed by the Amazon with 4,000 miles. The Mississippi-Missouri was once taken to be the longest, but the U.S. army engineers now give its length as 3,891 miles. With some tributaries originating

6,000 feet above sea level, the Nile wanders from its source at Lake Victoria to the Mediterranean at Rosetta for 4,145 miles while covering an airline distance of 2,450 miles. It drains a vast area of northeast Africa.

Unlike the rivers in North America, the Nile flows northward. It is fed by rains in the interior of Africa where rainfall averages 50 inches a year; then the river is formed by the junction of the White Nile and the Blue Nile at Khartoum, 1,897 miles from the Mediterranean. Khartoum is 1,300 feet above sea level. The Nile is joined by its last tributary at Atbara, 200 miles below Khartoum, and then it traverses a course of 1,600 miles (40 percent of its total length) without a tributary. Below Khartoum there are six cataracts, only one of which is in Egypt proper. Within Egypt the Nile flows its course of 930 miles. Though formerly the river was navigable from the Mediterranean up to the second cataract, now the new high dam blocks navigation at Aswan. Before reaching Aswan from the south, the Nile flows through granite mountains which confine it to its bed, and then it reaches its last cataract at Aswan (Syene of the Bible; Ezek. 29:10; 30:6). However it is customary to number the cataracts from the Mediterranean so that the Aswan cataract is called the first one. It was at this point that the ancient site of Yeb (Elephantine) was located. Here, 550 miles from the Mediterranean, the Aswan dam with locks for navigation was built in 1902 in order to impound water for irrigation purposes. More recently the high dam has been constructed with Russian aid. Not only is the Nile a source of water for irrigation but, as the main traffic artery of Egypt, doubtless has discouraged the development of good road systems.

At Cairo the river is split by an island so that near the hotels it does not appear in its full width. It is actually between 550 and 990 yards wide. Twelve miles below Cairo the Nile divides into the Rosetta and Damietta branches, each of which is 146 miles long. The depth of either branch is about twenty-three feet when at full flood. The triangle formed by the watered areas of these streams makes up the Delta, a region 125 miles north to south and 115 miles wide.

At one time there were seven branches of the Nile in the Delta, but now there are networks of canals.

The rains in the mountains of Abyssinia cause an annual overflow which in turn brings rich soil from the highlands of Abyssinia and spreads it over Egypt. Unlike rivers in America that are at low water in the summer, the Nile rises in June and reaches its peak in August. The flood lasts about four months and near the beginning of October the river is back in its normal banks. At Cairo the difference between the lowest and highest water levels is twenty-six feet. Inscriptions record flood levels as early as the fourth millennium B.C. Pliny wrote, "at twelve cubits, hunger; at thirteen, sufficiency; at fourteen, joy; at fifteen, security; at sixteen, abundance." Since a minimum flood could mean drought and famine, likely the flood made the difference between the fat years and the lean years of the Bible. "To rise and sink like the Nile of Egypt" was a proverbial phrase used in Palestine (Amos 8:8; 9:5). Today the flow is regulated by dams and a series of canals, but these are not an unmixed blessing. The dams prevent the nourishing silting that once came with the floods, so that the land grows less productive. In Egypt agriculture is entirely dependent on irrigation for the average rainfall at Cairo is only 1 to 2 inches a year and at Alexandria only 8 inches. The uniformity of the Egyptian's world left its mark on his beliefs.

Egypt lies entirely south of 30 degrees north latitude (the latitude of New Orleans). It was the unification of the two regions, upper and lower Egypt, with their symbols of the lotus and the papyrus, that gave life to Egypt. The Nile valley is rarely wider than twelve miles and is bordered by steep cliffs. Ninety-nine percent of the population lives in the valley, which is only 3.5 percent of the land area of modern Egypt. The rest is desert. Egypt was never invaded from the east, west, or south, but was vulnerable from Canaan across the Sinai peninsula.

Memphis, the first capital of Egypt after the unification of upper and lower Egypt, was built by Menes (or Narmar) about 3100 B.C. Called Noph in the Hebrew Bible from its Egyptian name Men-nefer, Memphis was the capital in the

Second Dynasty when Djoser built the step pyramid nearby at Saqqara. During the Hyksos period (1750–1570 B.C.) before Avaris in the Delta was chosen, Memphis served these rulers as their center. Ptah, who was the oldest of the gods and the creator of mankind, had a temple at Memphis (Herodotus 2. 99). His symbol was the Apis Bull.

Exposed as it is, Memphis was frequently sacked by invaders such as Esarhaddon of Assyria and by the Persians. It declined after the founding of Alexandria but continued into the Christian period. Theodosius (A.D. 379–395) ordered its temples destroyed, and finally the general of Caliph Omar completed the demolition. Stones from Memphis went into the building of Old Cairo. In the OT both the prophets Jeremiah (Jer. 46:19) and Ezekiel (Ezek. 30:13) threatened Memphis with destruction.

Flinders Petrie and the staff of the University of Pennsylvania Museum have excavated monuments of this city whose name to the prophet Hosea (9:6) symbolized Egypt itself. At the site of the village Meit Rahina, about thirteen miles south of Cairo, is to be seen the alabaster sphinx of Ramses II of the Nineteenth Dynasty (ca. 1293–1225 B.C.). Two colossal statues of Ramses II were found here. One has been re-erected in the central square of the train station of Cairo. The other, lying prone on the site, has been enclosed in a specially constructed building.

Thebes, called "No" in the OT, was the chief city of upper Egypt and was its capital from the time of the expulsion of the Hyksos (ca. 1575 B.C.) to the Assyrian invasion under Ashurbanipal (ca. 661 B.C.). A Theban prince of the Eleventh Dynasty was the first to take the title "King of Upper and Lower Egypt"; and Kamose, a Theban, freed Middle Egypt from Hyksos domination. Homer speaks of "hundred-gated Thebes from which valiant men issue forth on missions of conquest." A center of worship of the god Amun, Thebes is called "No-Amon" in Nahum 3:8. It is threatened by the prophets Ezekiel (30:14-16) and Jeremiah (46:25).

The site of Thebes, 450 miles south of Cairo, is today surrounded by the ruins of temples and burial complexes, many of which have been visible throughout the centuries. The modern city of Luxor with its 30,000 population occupies only a part of the ancient site. On the east side of the Nile are Karnak and Luxor, while on the west side are the valley of the Kings, the valley of Queens, Deir el-Bahri of Queen Hatshepsut, the Qurneh temple of Seti I, the Ramesseum of Ramses II, and Medinet Habu of Ramses III. The Egyptians built their homes, since decayed, out of clay. They built their temples of limestone from the desert and of granite from Aswan. These have defied time and are most impressive.

Heliopolis, that is, "On" (Gen. 41:45, 50; 46:20; Jer. 43:13), was located nineteen miles north of ancient Memphis. It is now Tell Hisn, northeast of Cairo near the village of Metiryeh. As its name suggests, it was sacred to the Egyptian sun god, Re. Strabo (17.1.27) claims the city was laid waste by Cambyses.

The pyramids were already old when Abraham came to Egypt, but no records inform us of places he visited. The sojourn of the Israelites was in a district called Goshen (Gen. 45:10; 46:28ff.; 47:1ff., 11; Exod. 8:22; 9:29). While this name does not occur in Egyptian sources, it is thought to lie in the northeastern Delta. It was an intermediate meeting place for Joseph and his father (Gen. 46:28) when the latter came to Egypt. It likely was north of and included the Wadi Tumilat, a fertile area which connects the Nile with the Bitter Lakes. It is irrigated by a canal from the Nile. Raamses, built by the Israelites (Exod. 1:11) is possibly the location of San el-Hagar; Pithom may be Tell el-Ratabeh; and Succoth, Tell el-Maskhutah. The identifications are disputed. The buildings at Tell el-Maskhutah, built partly of bricks with straw and partly without straw, are now thought to be fortifications instead of store chambers as formerly thought. We have no specific evidence in secular history of the Israelite sojourn in Egypt.

SINAI

The Sinai peninsula, lying between the Gulf of Suez and

the Gulf of Aqaba, is a triangle with sides of 190 miles and 130 miles and a base of 150 miles. The Wadi-el-'Arish (the brook of Egypt), which drains a large segment of northern Sinai, is the natural boundary between Palestine and Sinai. From Kantara on the Suez Canal to Raphia is only 117 miles. Thutmoses III took his army from Sile in Egypt to Gaza in ten days, and later Titus did the same in five days.

Covered with sand dunes in the north and with mountains and deep canyons in the south, Sinai is a land of transit. Egyptians mined turquoise and copper in its mountains and called it the "land of mines." Even today it has supplies of manganese and oil. No doubt Bedouin have sparsely roamed its wastes from an early time, as they do today. Sinai's position made it a place one had to cross to get from Egypt to Palestine.

While there are lists of Israel's camping places (Num. 33 and Deut. 1), none of these has been definitely located. At the dividing point between Egypt and Sinai, the Red Sea comes to within 100 miles of the Mediterranean. Part of this distance is taken up by the Bitter Lakes. No markers tell where the Israelites crossed the sea, and the matter is disputed.

Some scholars have questioned that Mount Sinai is in the peninsula at all. In North Arabia there is a mountain called Jebel Hanab where the volcano of Jebel el-Badr was active in historic times. The Bedouin regard it as sacred and do not let their flocks approach it (cf. Exod. 19:23). Some have suggested that Horeb should be in this region. It would better fit with the position of Midian (of whom Jethro was a priest) which at some times is related to the mountainous area of Saudi Arabia. However, these arguments are inconclusive.

Because of the terrain, there are a limited number of possibilities of moving through Sinai. Israeli scholars tend to identify the Reed Sea (identified with the Red Sea as early as the Septuagint version) with Lake Sirbonis; they argue that the Israelites crossed the sand bar extending out into the Mediterranean and that Mount Sinai is Jebel Hallal, located about twenty-five miles west of Kadesh Barnea. However, prominent ways of crossing Sinai would include the "way of the land of the Philistines" running from what is now

Kantara to Gaza. This way was well guarded by the Egyptians and was forbidden the Israelites (Exod. 13:17). Further south is the "way of Shur," which connected the area of modern Ismalia with Beersheba. Though Hagar used this road (Gen. 16:7), the Egyptians also had fortifications here. Still further south is the "way of Mt. Seir" (Deut. 1:2), which likely corresponds to the present Pilgrim's road leading from Suez to Eilat. Finally, there is the desert road which uses the wadis in the south of the peninsula and passes near Jebel Musa, the traditional site of Mt. Sinai or Horeb (Exod. 3:1; 17:6). There are no perennial streams in Sinai, but the dry wadi beds can become a torrent when there has been a rain in the mountains. Surrounded entirely by desert, fed by no river, the Red Sea about Sinai has a temperature above 70 degrees Fahrenheit even in January.

While the claims of 7,370-foot Jebel Musa as the site of the giving of the law are solely traditional, dating back to the pilgrimage of Silvia in A.D. 388, this southern location would seem to fit the requirements of Elijah's forty-day journey from Beersheba (1 Kings 19:3-8). Tradition has identified Marah (Num. 33:8; Exod. 15:22-23) with Ain Hawrah; Elim (Exod. 15:27; Num. 33:9) with Wadi Gharandel; and Rephidim (Exod. 17:1) with the Feiran Oasis, one of the largest oases in Sinai. The Er-Raha plain has been thought a possible place for the Israelite camp during their stay at Sinai, and Edward Robinson considered Ras Safsafa at its end to be Mount Sinai. But more widely accepted is Jebel Musa, a mountain block about two miles long, one mile wide, and rising to one predominant summit. At its base Justinian built St. Catherine's monastery in the sixth century and it is still a place of pilgrimage.

Kadesh, whence the spies were sent out, where Miriam died, and where Israel must have spent a long time, is only eleven days march from Sinai (Deut. 1:2). It has been conjecturally identified with an oasis area about fifty miles southwest of Beersheba where there are four prominent springs: Ein Qadeis, Ein Qoseimah, Ein Muweilah, and Ein Qudeirat. The last of these flows forty cubic meters an hour and is the richest spring in northern Sinai.

Israel's long stay in the wilderness was a punishment for her lack of faith. While there are areas in which the tamarisk tree grows in limited quantities, and though the insect that infests it secretes a white sugarlike substance that some have identified with manna, there is not enough to support any group of people. This theory has to assume that living on manna is legendary. Some have noted that quail migrate across the peninsula at certain seasons and could have been captured by the Israelites. But these efforts should not diminish the marvel of the wilderness experience. In an area of such meager water and food resources, a body of people would have to be miraculously sustained to survive.

PALESTINE

Palestine takes its name from the Philistines, who were late invaders on its scene and who occupied only a portion of its area. The early Egyptians called it "the land of the sand dwellers," but another early name is Canaan (Gen. 11:31). This name is first attested in the tablets from Alalakh. It may be connected with "trade" or "commerce," since the root word indicates a trader or merchant (Job 41:6; Prov. 31:24; Zech. 14:21). Another theory is that Canaan meant "land of the purple." The Greeks then called it Phoenicia from the Greek word meaning "purple," hence Canaanite and Phoenician mean the same thing. Reference is, of course, to the purple dye that was produced along the Phoenician coast.

The Palestinian landscape makes the main lines of communication to run north and south, either along the sea coast, along the backbone mountain ridge, through the Jordan valley, or through Transjordan. The backbone mountain ridge is broken at the Jezreel valley. Armies could pass through the coastal plain without bothering the mountain; consequently, the mountains and the Jordan valley developed civilizations influenced by, yet isolated from, Egypt and Mesopotamia.

Covering about ten thousand square miles, small when

compared with the United States, Palestine lies between 31 and 35.15 degrees north latitude and is about the size of the state of Vermont. From Dan to Eilat is 250 miles; from Dan to Beersheba only 150; from Akko to the Sea of Galilee is twenty-eight miles; and from Gaza to the Dead Sea is forty-five miles. Samaria and Jerusalem were only thirty-five airline miles apart. None of the world's greatest cities lie within Palestine's borders. Jerusalem lies at 31.45 degrees north latitude, roughly comparable to that of Savannah, Georgia, and Jackson, Mississippi. Palestine's climate, though varied, is in general to be compared with that of southern California.

Despite its small size, the land is divided into distinct areas so that one can hardly go ten miles without being in a new landscape. Beginning at the sea, one has ascended to 2,500 feet when he reaches Jerusalem twenty-five miles away. At Jericho he has descended to 1,200 feet below sea level though he is only seventeen miles from Jerusalem, and at Amman, twenty-five miles further, he has ascended to 3,000 feet above the sea; but in the whole journey he has covered only seventy-two airline miles. From Hebron to the moun tains of Moab is only thirty-six miles airline.

The Jordan with its deep gorge tended to divide the countries on either bank. In fact, Palestine's broken landscape made it a land of separate tribes: Canaanites, Perizzites, Ammonites, Kenizzites, Hittites, etc. The Tell el-Amarna letters reflect an area divided into innumerable city states. In such a broken land a revolution can occur without affecting those only a few miles away. Laish was only fifty-five miles from Sidon and only forty miles from Damascus, yet it was isolated from them (Judg. 18:7). Palestine has five distinct areas: the coastal plain, the central mountain range, the Rift Valley, the Transjordan region, and the Negeb to the south. The climate varies according to these regions.

Except for limited areas Palestine was too hilly for irrigation and was entirely dependent upon rainfall. The rain came from the west off the sea; the east wind brought dryness and oppressiveness. The area with rain sufficient for cultivation on the eastern Mediterranean coast is seldom more than one hundred miles wide. Moses described it as "a land of hills and valleys, which drinks water by the rain from heaven, a land which the Lord your God cares for; the eyes of the Lord your God are always upon it, from the beginning of the year to the end of the year" (Deut. 11:11-12).

The modern consensus is that there has been no appreciable decrease in rainfall in the past 6,000 years. The lowering of the water table is due to overcultivation, to deforestation, and to the destruction of vegetation by man and his flocks.

Rain is the most uncertain factor in Palestine. The line between the desert and the tillable land moves back and forth depending on the year. Drought is frequent and Jeremiah describes one with graphic pathos (Jer. 14:2-6). Though Jerusalem has 24 to 26 inches of rain a year—the same annual rainfall as London—it comes in four months of the year. South of Hebron rain drops to 12 inches, Jericho has only 4 inches a year, the Dead Sea only 2 inches, and Elath less than half an inch. There is the hot dry summer from May to September when no rain falls. The cooler air of the night makes for morning mist in the hills that quickly disappears (Hos. 6:4; 13:3; Job 7:9). Wind blows off the sea in the afternoon and can be used to blow away the chaff in threshing (Ps. 1:4). There is heavy dew, which helps plants survive in the summer drought (cf. Judg. 6:36-40; Ps. 133:3).

There is a transitional period for six weeks both in the fall and in the spring when the wind must blow either from the east or the south (cf. Isa. 27:8; Jer. 4:11), bringing great discomfort and often damage to plants if it is spring.

Then the rain comes from November to March. At first it is spotty (cf. Amos 4:7-8). The "early rain" is from November to February, slacking off into the "latter rain"—showers —in March and April (cf. Deut. 11:14; Joel 2:23). There are about fifty rainy days a year, then "the winter is past, the rain is over and gone" (Song of Sol. 2:11). Thunder is common (cf. Ps. 29), and hail (Isa. 28:2; Hag. 2:17) may fall. Snow is not unusual in the mountains in the winter and may stay around four or five days. An 18-inch snowfall at Jerusalem in 1967 was particularly damaging to trees and power lines. Water must be stored in the rainy season in cisterns unless a city happens to be near one of the continuously flowing springs (cf. Jer. 2:13). Plants bloom in February and March; then after March the summer burn sets in.

The rocks of Palestine are flint, limestone, chalk, basalt, and sandstone. Building stone and clay of different sorts for pottery-making are abundant. The current barrenness of the hills is due to erosion. Though naturally a forest region that had to be cleared (Josh. 17:18), the trees were cut, the land grazed over, and ruin resulted. Earthquakes are most frequent in the Jordan valley. One destroyed the Qumran community in 31 B.C., and that of 1927 at Jericho was severe.

Israel colonized only where wheat, olives, and grapes grew. Wheat and barley furnished bread, olives grew in abundance furnishing oil, and grapes furnished wine (Isa. 5:1-7; 2 Chron. 2:15). Grapes, figs, and carobs furnished sugar. Walnuts, pomegranates, dates, melons, leeks, and garlic were grown. The almond grew and blossomed white in the spring (Jer. 1:11-12). Again in the words of Moses:

> A land of brooks of water, of fountains and springs, flowing forth in valleys and hills, a land of wheat and barley, of vines and fig trees and pomegranates, a land of olive trees and honey, a land in which you will eat bread without scarcity, in which you will lack nothing, a land whose stones are iron, and out of whose hills you can dig copper. And you shall eat and be full, and you shall bless the Lord your God for the good land he has given you.
>
> Deuteronomy 8:7-10

In contrast with these crops, the orange groves, the prickly pear, the fields of tomatoes, and the eucalyptus trees along the roads today are not native to the land.

The coastal plain. Now rich, fertile, farming country, the coastal plain was never occupied by the Israelite people in OT times. One has called attention to the fact that the boundaries between the Arabs and the Israelis in 1948–1967 roughly corresponded to that between the Philistines, whose chariots of iron could maneuver in the plain, and the Israelites, who held the hills. The sand dunes along the sea often made the plain unsuitable for passage, clogged the rivers, and made swamps. The "way of the sea" (Isa. 9:1 [in Hebrew 8:20]), which crossed into the plain at Megiddo, hugged the hills to avoid these problems. Later the Romans bridged the streams and the road could go nearer the coast. The coastal plain, warmed by the sea, has frost only once in about twenty years.

North of Mount Carmel is the Zebulun valley, through which the Qishon empties into the sea. Continuing to the north is the Acco valley, which terminates at Rosh Ha-Niqra (the Ladder of Tyre) where the valley is two and three-fifths miles wide. Rosh Ha-Niqra is the division point between Lebanon and Israel. Twelve miles long and five wide, this plain has over 28 inches of rain a year and has abundant springs. Its soil is the deep red soil that makes for excellent cultivation. It was the area claimed by the tribe of Asher, but the plain was marshy and the settlements were back along the mountain. Acco was not taken by the Israelites at the conquest (Judg. 1:31). Acco was the port of this region, but now the port has shifted across the bay and Haifa, the third largest city of Israel, thrives on its commerce. Haifa is not a biblical city.

Carmel juts out into the sea, leaving a pass only 200 yards wide along the coast which was easily defended. The steep slopes of Carmel make an effective barrier, but the view from the summit is breathtaking. Here was the scene of Elijah's conflict with the prophets of Baal (1 Kings 18:20ff.). Caves in the mountain were occupied by men back to the Stone Age. Just below Carmel, the valley opens into a narrow plain twenty miles long and up to a mile and a half wide. On this shore was Dor, one of the ports of the OT period mentioned in the adventures of Wen Amon. The plain has deep, red soil.

The Sharon plain begins at Mount Carmel and extends thirty-four miles to the Yarkon River. In the north the plain is about two miles wide, but it widens to twelve miles at Joppa; further south the coastal plain widens to thirty miles in the Philistine area. It has rolling hills that rise up to three hundred feet. Known in poetic appeals to its fertility in the OT, the plain grew the flower called the rose of Sharon, which is thought to be a narcissus variety. Parts of the plain were once forested. The Sharon has 20 to 24 inches of rainfall a year and practically no frost. Perennial streams flowed through it, though today their water is otherwise utilized. The Sharon is the only part of the coastal plain the Israelites effectively possessed. The OT refers to it six times.

The Judean coast extending from the Yarkon River to the Nahal Lachish has sand dunes stretching inland five miles in the south, but further inland there is red sand and then the heavy red soil. In the north the Ras el 'Ain spring furnishes abundant water, giving life to the Yarkon River, which empties into the sea north of Tel Aviv. The twenty-mile long Yarkon is a perennial stream. The ancient town of Joppa, older than the Israelite conquest, lay in this area of the coastal plain.

The Philistine plain extends for about forty-seven miles down to the River of Egypt (the Wadi-el-'Arish), which is the natural boundary between Palestine and Sinai. This Wadi is 210 miles south of the mouth of the Litany and 117 miles below Rosh Ha-Niqra. The rolling hills of Philistia extend to an elevation of 250 feet. From the sand dunes to the foothills is a strip five to ten miles wide.

Into this area came the major Philistine migration after the "Sea Peoples" had been blocked by Ramses III in Egypt about 1170 B.C. They established city states, with Gaza, Ashkelon, Ashdod, Ekron, and Gath the chief centers. The "way of the sea" traversed this region, and these cities dominated this road, one of the oldest in the world. On it the armies of Egypt and of Mesopotamia passed and repassed. Philistia was open to diseases from Egypt (Deut. 7:15). The prophets speak of Philistia with pity as a prospective victim of the invasion forces that also brought Israel down—in fact, the whole area is open to invasion (cf. 2 Kings 19:9). It was good for growing grain; its streams carry water only after the winter rains, but rain averages 14 to 20 inches and there are also wells. Around Gaza there are abundant springs, making for beautiful orchards. Gaza lies three miles inland but it was the terminus for trade routes from South Arabia. Of the Philistine cities, only Ashkelon is on the sea.

Unlike Greece, where the people by nature are destined to travel the sea, Palestine is on a lee shore with prevailing winds from the southwest. There are no good anchorages south of Mount Carmel, and the sea current is northward parallel to the coast. These factors helped determine that its people are not seafarers. A symbol of raging against the Lord (Isa. 17:12, 13), the sea is a barrier (Num. 34:6), and Jonah is the only OT character who is said to have taken a journey on it. Invaders did not come from the sea until after they had already captured the land. None of the Mediterranean islands are visible from Israel, but the OT does mention Cyprus, Rhodes, Crete, and a few others. Josephus said of the Jews, "Well, ours is not a maritime country, neither commerce nor intercourse which it promotes with the outside world has any attraction for us. We devote ourselves to the cultivation of the productive country with which we are blessed" (*Against Apion* 1. 12).

The mountains. The mountain area of Palestine may be considered in the regions of Galilee, Samaria, and Judea as one proceeds from north to south. These regions are the central focal point of biblical interest.

Galilee (meaning "circle") is about fifty-five miles from north to south and twenty-five to thirty miles east to west. It was in some periods surrounded by heathen (cf. Isa. 9:1 [8:23, MT]). The Jezreel valley (called Esdraelon by the Greeks) is drained in the west by the Kishon River, which overflowed and mired down Sisera's chariots (Judg. 5:21). It flows through a narrow pass, crosses the plain of Acco, and empties into the Mediterranean. A swamp through which the "way of the sea" crossed on a basalt ridge, today the valley of Jezreel, with the swamps drained, is among the best farm land of the country. In this valley Megiddo guarded the pass through the Carmel range. Ahab's palace was at Jezreel, and it was here that the tragedy of Naboth took place (1 Kings 21:1; cf. 2 Kings 9:30; 10:11). The largest valley in Israel, Jezreel is bordered on the south by the Carmel, the Samaria, and the Gilboa mountains. The plain of Jezreel was the scene of such major OT events as Gideon's exploits (Judg. 6:33; 7:1) and Saul's defeat by the

Philistines (1 Sam. 28:3ff.). In each case Israel was on the slopes of Mount Gilboa to the south, and Midian and the Philistines, respectively, to the north on the slopes of Moreh. The valley divides around the Hill of Moreh, and in the northern wing of the valley Mount Tabor rises in isolation to 1,500 feet above the valley, making it a distinctive part of the landscape. It was here that Barak gathered his forces (Judg. 4:6). Reaching a watershed elevation of only about 230 feet at Jenin, the Jezreel valley slopes off to Bethshan at 200 feet below sea level and then on to the Jordan valley, making one of the natural east-west thoroughfares of the country.

Upper Galilee, surrounded by hills that extend up to four thousand feet, belonged to Naphtali. Though well-wooded and fertile, this area was off the center of the OT story. Lower Galilee, made up of valleys and hills which range up to one thousand eight hundred feet, was the possession of Zebulun and Asher. The valleys are oriented in an east-west direction, and passage parallel to the ridges is relatively easy. Israel at first experienced difficulty in taking the area from the Canaanites, leaving the northernmost tribes cut off from the rest of the tribes (Judg. 1:27); hence there were battles here in the days of Deborah (Judg. 4–5), again after the Philistine victory at Aphek (1 Sam. 4:1ff.), and later at the time of Saul (1 Sam. 29:1; 31:1ff.).

Mount Carmel extends from the sea in a southeasterly direction for thirteen miles to the Samaria mountains. Rising sharply to 2,000 feet, it made an effective barrier, and its four passes are of great strategic importance. They are at Yokneam, Megiddo, Taanak, and Jenin (Engannim; cf. 2 Kings 9:27, "ascent of Gur"). Thutmoses III reported, "The capture of Megiddo is as the capture of a thousand towns." Solomon fortified it (1 Kings 9:15), and Josiah died there in a vain attempt to block Pharaoh Necho (2 Kings 23:29). The pass at Jenin opens into the Dothan valley and then leads into the heartland of Samaria.

The Joseph tribes—Ephraim and Manasseh—had the mountainous strip for about forty-five miles south from the Jezreel valley. It was a region more accessible from the coastal plain than was the territory of Judah and hence more

often invaded. Its mountains have more abundant vegetation than Judah. The cities of Manasseh were Shechem,
Tirzah, Samaria, and Dothan.

Tirzah, seven miles east of Shechem, served as the capital of
Israel from Jeroboam I to Omri. However, one of the natural
east-west crossings of the country ascends the mountains
from the Damiya bridge area (near biblical Adam) up the Wadi
Fari'a past Tirzah, passes between Mount Ebal and Mount
Gerizim and then descends to the sea by a gentle slope. Hence
Tirzah was vulnerable to Israel's enemy, Aram.

The most famous of all the mountains of Samaria are Mount
Gerizim (2,840 ft.) and Mount Ebal (3,080 ft.), between which
lay Shechem, in the narrow pass that is oriented east and west
(Deut. 27:12-13). Abraham first came to Shechem when he
entered the country (Gen. 12:6); later Joshua brought Israel
there for the reading of the law (Josh. 8:30-35).

Ephraim's mountains are about twenty miles wide and
reach from Geba almost to Shechem. Its cities were Bethel
and Shiloh. Bethel is only ten miles north of Jerusalem.
Ephraim had the heart of the country, and its name could
designate the entire northern kingdom (Isa. 11:13; Hos. 6:4).
The mountain ridge has been compared with the skeleton of
a fish with a central ridge from which other ridges reach out
from northeast to southeast. Passage is possible along the
watershed on the backbone ridge, but a few miles on either
side one would be going continuously uphill and downhill
over high ridges and down into deep valleys.

In Benjamite territory between Bethel on the north and
Jerusalem on the south were some of the most important
cities like Gibeah, Michmash, Mizpah, Anathoth, and
Ramah. The area is approachable from the Jordan valley
through a wadi and also from the sea through the valley of
Aijalon. Here from the west the ascent of Beth-horon gave
easy access to the highlands. There was no natural boundary between Judah and Benjamin; hence, the limits were not
exactly defined. However there was a shift in agriculture
from olive culture to vine culture. From Bethel to Beersheba is
only fifty-five miles.

The territory of Judah was only twenty to thirty miles

wide. Its eastern part is on the lee of the mountains, receives little rain, is treeless, and is made up of gorges and canyons. Tending to be wilderness, it is called Jeshimon (Num. 21:20, KJV; 1 Sam. 23:24) or the wilderness of Judah (Josh. 15:61). It was suitable as a refuge of fugitives but also offered defense from invasion from this direction. The desert extends almost to the watershed road on the mountains.

Hebron, the highest city in Judah at 3,300 feet elevation, controlled the road from the Shephelah (see below) to Engedi on the Dead Sea. Here at Hebron, Abraham received promises from God, and here he and Sarah were buried. David reigned from Hebron before he was accepted by Israel. David's ancestral home, Bethlehem, is fifteen miles farther north, but it only came to prominence through him and then later through the birth of Jesus.

Jerusalem came under Israelite domination only after David captured it from the Jebusites, but he made it the capital of his kingdom—doubtless a fortunate political choice since it lay on the border between the north and the south. Surrounded by higher mountains and built on a promontory, it was enclosed on the east by the Kidron valley and on the south by the valley of the sons of Hinnom. Its natural water supply was on the west slope of the Kidron. Enrogel was near the junction of the two valleys. Jerusalem has frost twenty to sixty nights a year; has snow in the winter occasionally measuring 18 inches; and has an average August temperature of 75.2 degrees.

The Shephelah. The west slope of the mountains of Judah is divided into two terraces, one below the other. The term Shephelah (lowland) designates these hills south of the Aijalon valley which form an intermediate zone separating the mountains from the Philistine plain. Furthermore, a north-south valley intervenes between the hills of the Shephelah and the mountain itself, making an effective moat. Since it was disputed territory between Israel and the Philistines, many of their encounters took place on the eastern border of the Shephelah. David eventually broke the Philistine power in the area.

From north to south through this region there are significant valleys. The valley of Aijalon is the site of Joshua's battle with the kings. It offers the best approach from the sea to Jerusalem. The valley of Sorek, in which are Zorah, Eshtaol, and Beth-shemesh, is the scene of the Samson stories and of those of the captivity of the ark. The valley of Elah is the scene of David's fight with Goliath.

A series of fortresses guarded this natural approach to Jerusalem: Debir, Lachish, Libnah, Azekah, Makkedah, Beth-shemesh, and Gezer. Joshua carried a campaign through the valley of Aijalon (Josh. 10:10-12) after he had conquered the first cities in the central mountain area. The Philistines invaded through the valley to Michmash in Saul's day. Gezer, one of its most prominent sites, was not taken at the time of Joshua (Judg. 1:29), but it was later taken by Pharaoh and given to Solomon's wife as a dowry (1 Kings 9:16-17).

The Rift Valley. The single most distinctive feature of the Palestinian landscape is the Rift Valley (often called the Ghor), through which the Jordan river flows. Resulting from a geological fault, the rift begins in southern Turkey, runs between the Lebanon and Anti-Lebanon mountains, crosses the length of Palestine, and continues into central Africa in the general region of Nairobi, Kenya. In the Lebanon area where the valley is well above sea level, it is called the *Biqa'*. With an abundance of water, it is an excellent farming region for grains and fruits. Within it lie such sites as Hamath and Baalbek. At the south of Lebanon the rift is blocked by a basalt dam and the Litany River, which drains it, turns abruptly westward to empty into the sea. The basalt also formed an effective barrier to north-south travel in antiquity and today is the boundary between Israel and Lebanon.

Guarded on the north in ancient times by Abel beth-maacah and by Dan, the rift has flowing through it the three streams fed by the melting snows of Mt. Hermon, making up the sources of the Jordan River. Beginning on the east side there is the Banias River surfacing in abundant springs from a cave. For the ancients, the springs made Banias (Caesarea Philippi) a spot sacred to the god Pan.

After flowing for about two miles, the water thunders over a fall into a deep canyon as it continues its way toward Galilee. A second stream, the Leddan, breaks out in springs at Tell Dan, flows four miles, and then joins the Banias. A third is the Hasbani, which flows off from the west side of Mt. Hermon and then after twenty-four miles joins the other two just south of their confluence. A fourth river, the Bareighit, not rising from Mt. Hermon, drains the west side of the valley and empties into the Hasbani just before that stream joins the Jordan.

In ancient times these streams, after flowing seven miles, formed the swamps of Lake Huleh. The lake was 230 feet above sea level and about two by three miles in size with a depth of six to sixteen feet. The Huleh basin is about nine by three miles, roughly triangular with the base on the north. Its swamps grew the papyrus plants, valuable in antiquity for making writing material. The state of Israel has now drained the Huleh valley and turned it into exceedingly prosperous fishponds and farms. However, it is rumored that Israel, confronted with the progressive salinization of Lake Galilee, is making plans to reconstitute the lake as a filtering place for water of the Jordan system.

Leaving Lake Huleh, the river flows two miles to what is now known as the Daughters of Jacob bridge—the only practical crossing of the river above Galilee. An unidentified tell at the river's edge remains from some ancient guard post on the trunk way from Damascus to Egypt, over which traffic moved from the dawn of history. Farther back in the valley stood Hazor, one of the most impressive sites in all of Palestine, a place conquered by Joshua (Josh. 11:10ff.) to give Israel control of the northern area. Ten miles below Lake Huleh, after dropping rapidly through a basalt gorge out into a delta of about one mile width, the Jordan enters the Sea of Galilee.

Lake Galilee, also called Chinnereth and Tiberias, is thirteen miles long and eight miles wide in a pear shape. It is 690 feet below sea level and about 160 feet deep. There are many underground streams flowing into it. The area of Tiberias had hot mineral springs. While the lake abounds with fish, some of the springs are saline, making the water unsuited for continuous irrigation. The state of Israel has sealed off some of these by channeling them into aqueducts running along the side of the lake. The water of the lake, varying from green to blue, at times is mirror calm, but at other times pitches up in white caps. The lake is shut in on all sides by hills which rise above sea level. The plain of Gennesaret lies on its northwest shore. Today Galilee, though a tourist haven, has a rustic atmosphere and is bounded only by Tiberias and by the kibbutz farming communities. But in NT times nine towns lined its shores —places like Capernaum, Chorazin, Bethsaida (Julias), Magdala, Tiberias, Dalmanutha, and Greek cities of Gerasa and Gadara.

The airline distance from Lake Galilee to the Dead Sea is sixty-five miles, but the Jordan twists to three times that length in its descent. The average fall is nine feet to the mile. About twenty-five miles south of Galilee the rift narrows and then varies from three to fourteen miles in width. South of its narrow point the valley becomes much drier and is divided into three levels. There is the Ghor, then the badlands that are deeply eroded and unsuited for any use, and finally the Zor (or thicket), which is also called "the pride of the Jordan." This last area is about 150 feet below the Ghor level and from 200 yards to one mile wide. The area floods at times (Josh. 3:15). The lions once found there have long since disappeared.

These regions make the Rift Valley a natural boundary between peoples. The Ghor contains many antiquity sites. Nelson Glueck reported seventy for which no ancient name is known. The river itself varies from 90 to 100 feet in average width and from three to ten feet in average depth. There are at least six fords where the river can be waded. The water is a muddy brown.

Five miles after the Jordan leaves Galilee, it is joined on the east by the Yarmuk, which drains the Golan Heights and forms the modern boundary between Jordan and Syria. Unmentioned in the Bible, the Yarmuk has cut a deep canyon and flows an equal quantity of water with the Jordan to the point at which they join. Fifteen miles north of the Dead Sea, the Jabbok (Nahr-es-Zerqa), which rises near Amman and flows for fifty miles with a drop of fifty feet to the mile, joins the Jordan. Its valley has many tells not mentioned in the Bible. It formed the boundary of Amman, and it was the site of Jacob's wrestling with the angel (Gen.32:22-29). From its western side the River Jordan is fed by the Wadi Fari'a, which flows down from springs in the area of ancient Tirzah. This wadi's valley furnishes one of the east-west passages through the country. It joins the Jordan in the area of Damiya (Adam).

The exact site of the crossing of the Jordan by the Israelites at the conquest is unknown. Adam, at which the waters of the Jordan were cut off, is at Damiya.

Near Jericho the Jordan valley widens out to about fourteen miles. Jericho is an oasis formed by the abundant waters of Elisha's fountain, which breaks out at the foot of the tell of the ancient city. There are also other springs in the area such as Ain Duk, and from at least Roman times water has been brought down from the mountain in aqueducts in the Wadi Qelt. These waters are all absorbed in Jericho's gardens rather than actually feeding the Jordan. The water, together with Jericho's semitropical climate, makes the area especially delightful for growing palm trees, melons, vegetables, and citrus fruits.

The Dead Sea (called the Salt Sea in the OT—Gen. 14:3; Num. 34:3, 12; Deut. 3:17; Josh. 3:16; 12:3; 15:2, 5; 18:19 —and not mentioned in the NT) is 104 miles south of Banias, where the Jordan begins. It is fifty-three miles long and ten miles wide. The surface of the sea is 1,242 feet below sea level and the water at the northeast end is 1,320 feet deep, making this rift the lowest spot on earth. The sea has no outlet. The water is a bluish green and contains 30 percent solids—five times that of regular sea water. The sea is a great deposit of chlorides of magnesium, sodium, calcium, and potassium, and there are also magnesium bromides. The crystallized minerals along the shore form lovely patterns on rocks and sticks. The sea has been a source of salt from an early time; the Bible speaks of "Salt

City" (Josh. 15:62). The countries of Jordan and Israel are now exploiting this mineral treasure. While there is no life in the sea, animal and vegetable life are to be found on its shores. The hills rise to two thousand five hundred feet above the water on the west bank and to three thousand on the east. Rainfall in this area averages 2 inches a year.

While passage is not possible along the east shore of the sea, there are hot springs at Chalorae, to which Herod the Great came for bathing during his illness. The rivers Arnon (Mojib) and Zered (Zerqa) enter the sea from the east. Part way down the sea the Lisan peninsula extends nine miles into the sea, reaching to within two miles of the west shore. Here the water has a depth of fifteen feet, but in ancient times one could wade across. The Lisan itself is watered by five streams and becomes a broad, fertile plain on the east. Just to the east, Paul Lapp excavated Bab edh-Dhra', which contains an Early Bronze Age cemetery.

There are several sites on the west shore. Ein Feshka, near the north end, had a settlement in the seventh and eighth centuries B.C. The Qumran community flourished about two miles north of this spring in the first century B.C. Farther down the west shore, the oasis of Engedi (1 Sam. 23:29; Song of Sol. 1:14) breaks the barren monotony. Then ten miles farther south, back from the shore on an isolated peak, is the fortress of Masada. Near the southern end of the sea there is a salt mountain 650 feet high and more than five miles in length. This formation is popularly called "Lot's wife" in memory of the biblical story (cf. Gen. 19:26). At the south end of the sea there is a salt plain extending eight miles, upon which the sea encroaches in times of flooding.

From the Dead Sea southward the rift is known as the Arabah. After thirty miles the floor rises to the sea level, and then at Jebel er-Rishe it reaches 630 feet above the sea. From that point on, the rift is at times no more than six miles wide. The Arabah finally terminates at Aqaba-Eilat, 100 miles south of the Dead Sea. Ezion Geber was the name of the port in Solomon's time. It is on the gulf which is one of the arms of the Red Sea.

Transjordan. The area east of the Jordan was traversed from Damascus to Aqaba by the "King's Highway" (Num. 21:22), which was used by the four invading kings in Abraham's day (Gen. 14). Later it was used by the Israelites at the time of their wilderness journey (Num. 21:27-30) and a list of towns along it is given. The highway descended from the plateau through the Wadi 'l Yātim to Aqaba, whence in antiquity one could continue to Egypt.

This plateau area east of Jordan, homeland of the tribes of Reuben, Gad, and the half-tribe of Manasseh, is cut into regions by deep canyons made by the rivers that drain its highlands into the Jordan or the Dead Sea. However, more influential than the canyons were the boundaries determining how men made their living. Wheat was grown in Bashan, vines in Gilead, and sheep in Ammon and Moab. Edom relied on trade and on her copper mines.

The area averages two thousand feet in elevation and slopes off in the east from the tillable land to the desert. On the north the eastern region is the Hauron; the central, the Bashan; and the western part is the Golan Heights overlooking the Sea of Galilee. This district, beginning at the foot of Hermon, is thirty-five miles from north to south on the west and fifty miles on the east. Because of its rising elevation it receives rain to push the desert back eighty miles east of the Rift Valley—125 miles from the Mediterranean. Annual rainfall varies from 12 to 24 inches and is usually adequate for farming, but years of plenty are sometimes followed by years of drought. Aphek (Fiq) and Edrei (Der'a) are in this region. The Bashan was open to Syrian attack on the north, but it is bounded on the south by the Yarmuk River. The Yarmuk, while named in Pliny's *Natural History*, is not mentioned in the Bible; but it flows as much water as the Jordan at their confluence. The area's basalt rocks give evidence of earlier volcanic action. Its rich soil was once wooded and its cattle and its oak trees draw attention in the Bible (Amos 4:1; Isa. 2:13; Ps. 22:12). The description is particularly suitable for upper Golan. Though rainfall is limited, it grows rich crops of grain in the southern area.

Gilead is the area between the Yarmuk and the Jabbok

rivers, a distance of thirty-five miles, and a width of settlement of thirty to forty miles from the river Jordan. It is made up of high ridges which average two thousand feet above the sea, with some of its peaks reaching up to three thousand feet, in contrast to the Jordan, which is 800 feet below sea level in this area. Gilead, Succoth, Penuel, Jabesh-gilead and Ramoth-gilead were its cities. Rainfall in this region averages 28 to 32 inches. The area was forested (Jer. 22:6-7) and balm from its trees was famous (Jer. 8:22; 46:11). The area was always in close contact with western Palestine; in the conquest it was assigned to the tribes of Gad and Manasseh.

South of the Jabbok the country becomes a treeless plain, which was the area of the kingdom of Sihon, the Ammonites, and Edom. The Moab plateau is twenty to thirty miles wide and eighty miles north and south. Its highest peak is 4,056 feet above sea level, while the Dead Sea, five miles away, is 1,300 feet below sea level. Deep canyons like that of the Wadi Mojib (Nahal Arnon), whose canyon is 1,700 feet deep and two miles broad at the top, cut through the plateau. The area receives more rain than the Judean hills, and in the Book of Ruth Bethlehemites migrated there in times of famine. The area is particularly suitable for sheep (2 Kings 3:4-5).

In this area lay the cities of Kir-hareseth (Kerak, a chief military stronghold), Aroer, Dhibon, Madeba, and Heshbon, and nearby is the traditional Mount Nebo (cf. Deut. 32:49), 3,631 feet in elevation, overlooking the lower Jordan valley and the north end of the Dead Sea. There is no clear boundary between the areas of Moab and Ammon. Tophel, Dibon, Heshbon, and Madeba have almost the names they had in Bible times.

Within the upper basin of the Jabbok was Rabbath Ammon, now the city of Amman with over two hundred thousand population. The Jabbok, rising sixty miles east of the Jordan, descends to below sea level seven miles from the Jordan, while the plateau to the north and south is 2,000 feet above the sea. This river was the site of Jacob's struggles with the angel.

The area of Edom extends from the Wadi Hesi (Brook

Zered, Num. 21:12), 100 miles to the Gulf of Aqaba. This area is about twenty miles wide and slopes off into the desert. In the south, peaks slightly exceed five thousand feet. Reddish granite (Edom, that is, "red," may be connected with the color of the stones of the area) alternates with a multitude of other hues. In the Bible the area is also called Mount Seir. In the central area lay Petra, whose inhabitants cut its stone cliffs into buildings. This Edomite stronghold is likely Sela (Obad. 3). While the south is devoid of rainfall, in the north the western slopes receive 16 to 20 inches of precipitation, often in the form of snow in the winter, making farming possible. The area had copper workings at Feinon (Punon, cf. Num. 33:42-43); it was once wooded, but the Turks deforested it to get fuel for the railroad in World War I. Its cities included Teman (Tawilan) in the south and Bozrah (Buseira) in the north.

Through this region passed the King's Highway (Num. 20:17; 21:22). The people made their living by some farming but chiefly by mining copper, trade, and taxes on the caravans that used their road.

BIBLIOGRAPHY

Surveys

Aharoni, Yohanan. *The Land of the Bible*. London: Burns & Oates, 1966.

Baly, Denis. *The Geography of the Bible*. New York: Harper & Brothers, 1957.

Baly, Denis, and A. D. Tushingham, *Atlas of the Biblical World*. New York: World Publishing Company, 1971.

Orni, Efraim, and Elisha Efrat. *Geography of Israel*. 2d rev. ed. Jerusalem: Israel Program for Scientific Translations. 1966.

Smith, George Adam. *Historical Geography of the Holy Land*. 25th ed. London: Hodder and Stoughton, 1931.

Atlases

Aharoni, Yohanan, and Michael Avi-Yonah. *The Macmillan Bible Atlas*. London: Collier-Macmillan Limited, 1968.

Beek, Martin A. *Atlas of Mesopotamia*. Translated by D. R. Welsh. London: Thomas Nelson and Sons, 1962.

May, H. G., ed. *Oxford Bible Atlas*. Oxford: Oxford Universtiy Press, 1962.

Wright, G. E., and F. V. Filson. *The Westminster Historical Atlas of the Bible*. Rev. ed. Philadelphia: The Westminster Press, 1956.

IV
History of
Old Testament Times, Part I

From Abraham to Solomon

John T. Willis

Any researcher who has attempted to reconstruct the
history of the ancient Near Eastern world during the period
covered by the movements and individuals mentioned in the
text of the OT realizes his inadequacy for the task. Archeological and linguistic discoveries are being made continually, and
their results are being published in a large number of journals
and books in various modern languages. It is impossible to
stay abreast of the latest find and to assimilate its significance
for a better comprehension of the world of the Bible.
Undoubtedly some (if not many) of the observations offered in
the present chapter will be out of date by the time the present
volume is published. Yet this is to be expected in a field as rich
and exciting as that of the biblical world.

FROM THE PATRIARCHS TO THE EXODUS (2000–1290 B.C.)

The World of Abraham, Isaac, and Jacob (2000–1720 B.C.)

Mesopotamia. Since Abram and his family migrated from Ur
(in southern Mesopotamia) to Haran (in northern Mesopotamia) and thence to Palestine (Gen. 11:31–12:3; Josh. 24:2-3;

Neh. 9:7-8; Acts 7:2-4), it seems logical to begin a survey of ancient history with observations concerning important information about Mesopotamia. At the beginning of the Middle Bronze Age (2050–1950 B.C.), Ur-Nammu initiated the Third Dynasty of Ur (2060–1950 B.C.). His reign was characterized by the erection of fine buildings and much literary activity. His law code is the oldest known. In spite of his efforts to revive the ancient Sumerian culture (2800–2360 B.C.), its destiny was sealed, the Sumerian language fast gave way to Akkadian, and Semites were gaining the upper hand.

The OT Amorites (Gen. 14:13; 15:21; etc.), Semitic invaders from the Arabian Desert whom the Mesopotamians called "Westerners," swept into the Fertile Crescent and by 1700 B.C. controlled the main cities from Syria to Babylon. A power struggle emerged among Assyria, Mari, and Babylon. For a brief period (1750–1730 B.C.) Assyria held the upper hand.

Then Mari gained control of the major portion of the land (1730–1700 B.C.). Its most outstanding king was Zimri-Lim, who had a magnificent palace covering over fifteen acres and containing almost three hundred rooms. In excavations at Mari from 1933 to 1939 under A. Parrot and from 1951 to 1956 under other archeologists, approximately twenty thousand cuneiform tablets have been unearthed. Around five thousand of these were written to Zimri-Lim by kings, officials, and common people throughout the region from Syria to Mesopotamia. Two letters sent to Zimri-Lim have to do with prophetic oracles in the name of the god Adad or Hadad of Aleppo, which contain many elements that call to mind utterances by OT prophets and the Mesopotamian prophet Balaam, whom the king of Moab hired to curse Israel (Deut. 23:4). The Mari tablets frequently mention a tribe ruled by chieftains and elders, which largely had given up a nomadic way of life to settle in towns and villages, the names of whose individual members are West Semitic. The Akkadian name given to this tribe seems to indicate that it was related in some way to the Israelite tribe of Benjamin.

It was not long until the great Babylonian monarch Hammurabi (1728–1686 B.C. according to Albright,

1792–1750 B.C. according to Oppenheim); overran Mari and established a strong Babylonian rule over the territory. Copies of earlier Babylonian accounts of creation and the flood were made during his reign. The form and subject matter of his famous law code, which contains some 282 articles, indicate that the law of Moses was typical for its day (this is not to imply that the law of Moses is a wholesale borrowing from the code of Hammurabi).

During Hammurabi's reign, Hurrians began pushing into the Fertile Crescent from the north and establishing themselves throughout the region. Soon they founded the kingdom of Mitanni and gradually transmitted the culture of the Sumerians and Akkadians to the Hittites in Asia Minor. In excavations at the Hurrian city of Nuzi between 1925 and 1931, archeologists discovered thousands of cuneiform tablets dating from the fifteenth and fourteenth centuries B.C. Many of these tablets help explain customs reflected in the OT patriachal narratives but previously obscure for lack of information.

A few specific examples may be cited. At Nuzi, if a prominent man and wife had no children, their possessions became the inheritance of their chief servant. Thus it was natural for Abram to conclude that since he had no son, Eliezer of Damascus would be his heir (Gen. 15:2). According to Nuzi law, an upper-class wife who had borne her husband no sons was supposed to give him a slave girl as a concubine, and any child born to this girl was regarded as the wife's own child. Sarai's proposal to give Hagar to Abram (16:2) corresponds to this custom. In Nuzi, a slave girl was occasionally given to a new bride. This agrees with Laban giving Zilpah to Leah (19:24) and Bilhah to Rachel (29:29). (Note that Laban lived in Paddan-aram, Gen. 28:2, which was in the Mesopotamian region.)

At Nuzi, the birthright was not determined by the sequence of births of a man's sons, but by the father's decree, and the most binding decree was given in the form of a deathbed proclamation which contained the introductory formula "Now that I have grown old." This helps one understand the significance of Isaac's blessing Jacob above

Esau (Gen. 27:18-41), which is introduced in just this way (27:2). Nuzi law decreed that a man's property could be deeded over to his son-in-law only if he gave his son-in-law the household gods. This would explain why Rachel stole Laban's household gods or teraphim when she fled with Jacob from her father (31:19; see vss. 14-16) and why Laban pursued Jacob and his family in search of them (31:22-35).

When Abram and his family left Ur of the Chaldees, they settled in Haran in the north until Abram's father, Terah, died (Gen. 11:32–12:3). Later, when they moved to Canaan, they still considered Haran and its surrounding region as their home. (See 24:3-4, 10.) Haran was the main town in the region called Paddan-aram (see 28:2; 29:4; etc.), which was a strong Amorite center. There is good evidence, therefore, that Abram's movement into Canaan was connected with the Amorite migrations that were taking place in his day. Some of the names of Abram's ancestors and relatives, such as Peleg, Serug, Nahor, and Terah (11:16-31), were also names of towns in the vicinity of Haran. The names Abram and Jacob have been found among the personal names of the Amorites. The Hebrew expression for the name by which Abram knew God is *El Shaddai* (RSV, "God Almighty," see Gen. 17:1; Exod. 6:2-3), but "Shaddai" is a Mesopotamian word meaning "the mountain one."

Egypt. The patriarchs also had interesting connections with Egypt. Both Abram (Gen. 12:10) and Jacob's sons (41:53–42:5) went there for food when a severe famine drove them out of Canaan. The time of Abram overlapped with the Middle Kingdom in Egypt (twenty-first to eighteenth centuries B.C.), which was predominantly ruled by the Pharaohs of the Twelfth Dynasty (1991–1778 B.C.). The Egyptian story of Sinuhe (ca. 1900 B.C.) tells how a high Egyptian official named Sinuhe fled from Egypt for political reasons and settled in the country of the East, the same territory as "the land of the people of the east" where Jacob came (29:1). He learned to live a seminomadic life, tending flocks and herds and following occasional agricultural pursuits like the partriarchs (13:2-12; 30:14-43).

Asia Minor. The patriarchs had a number of contacts with Hittites living in Palestine. Abraham purchased the cave of Machpelah from Ephron the Hittite (Gen. 23:1-20; 25:9-10; 49:29-30; 50:13), Esau married Hittite women (26:34; 36:2), and Ezekiel says to the city of Jerusalem, "Your mother was a Hittite" (Ezek. 16:3, 45). The discovery of numerous Hittite documents at Boghazköy in Turkey, which began to be unearthed by B. Winckler in 1906 and deciphered by B. Hrozny in 1915, has revealed a veritable wealth of information for modern scholarship. There is good reason to believe that Hittites began moving into the Fertile Crescent and the Palestinian area ca. 2000 B.C. By the middle of the sixteenth century B.C. they were pressing into Syria in large numbers, and ca. 1530 B.C. they overran Babylon.

Palestine. Canaan or Palestine was a rather unsettled, disorganized region in the patriarchal age. Various tribes or groups from differing origins had settled there. (See Gen. 15:18-21.) City states began to spring up. Many of them were protected by strong walls to guard the inhabitants from possible invasion from other city states in the region or from foreign invaders. There were also large tracts of land, particularly in the central highlands, that were thinly populated or not populated at all.

The Israelites in Egyptian Bondage (1720–1290 B.C.)

The Hyksos invasion of Egypt. About 1720 B.C., invaders from Asia Minor called Hyksos (a word meaning "rulers of foreign lands") swept through the regions of Syria and Palestine and gained control over Egypt. They made their capital in the Delta region of Egypt at Avaris (or Tanis; OT Zoan, see Ps. 78:12, 43), near the land of Goshen, where the Israelites settled (Gen. 46:28-34), and controlled Egypt until ca. 1550 B.C.

This would have been an ideal time for foreigners like Jacob's family to be welcomed into Egypt and for an outsider like Joseph to rise to a significant position in the government. Exodus 12:40-41 states that the Israelites dwelt in Egypt 430 years (cf. Gen. 15:13, which rounds this off to 400 years). If the exodus took place ca. 1290 B.C., the date of the migration of Jacob's family to Egypt would fall ca. 1720 B.C.

Many details in the story of Joseph (Gen. 37–50) agree admirably with data gleaned from Egyptian sources. The title "overseer of the house" (39:4; 41:40) is a legitimate Egyptian official title. The gifts of the Pharaoh and the customs described in connection with Joseph's induction to the office of second in command in Egypt (41:42-43) correspond to Egyptian practices. Egyptian writings speak of palace officials with the titles "chief of the butlers" and "chief of the bakers" (40:2). The Pharaoh's birthday was an occasion of much joy, and on this day prisoners possibly were released each year (40:20). Magicians are often mentioned in Egyptian texts (cf. 41:8). Egyptians considered shepherds an abomination (43:32; 46:34). Famines are frequently mentioned on Egyptian inscriptions. An inscription from ca. 100 B.C. tells of a seven-year famine during the reign of Pharaoh Zoser (ca. 2700 B.C.), and of storehouses where grain had been kept to feed the people (cf. 41:46-49). Egyptian writings state that the length of a happy and prosperous life is 110 years, and Joseph lived to be 110 (50:22). The Egyptians embalmed or mummified important people, and both Jacob (50:2) and Joseph (50:26) were embalmed.

Egyptian control of Palestine. The Egyptians successfully drove out the Hyksos ca. 1550 B.C. and gained a rather loose control over Syria and Palestine. It was probably early in this period that "there arose a new king over Egypt, who did not know Joseph" (Exod. 1:8). The Israelites were put under heavy bondage and were forced to help in building the store cities of Pithom and Raamses (1:11). Scholars generally agree that the Bible here alludes to the building projects of Pharaoh Seti I (1308–1290 B.C.) and Pharaoh Ramses II (1290–1224 B.C.).

In 1887 some Egyptian peasants discovered approximately three hundred tablets, written primarily in Babylonian cuneiform, in the archives of Pharaoh Amen-hotep IV or Akh-en-Aton (1370–1353 B.C.) at the ancient city of Akhetaton, the modern Tell el-Amarna, about two hundred miles south of Cairo. Amen-hotep IV had moved the capital from Thebes to

Akhetaton in protest against the worship of Amon and other Egyptian gods and as a devout worshiper of the god Aton, the sun disk. The majority of the Amarna letters were sent to the Egyptian court by local Canaanite kings and princes. They are filled with claims of fidelity to their Egyptian overlords and with complaints that other Canaanite rulers in the area were unfaithful to Egypt and had tried to attack them. Amen-hotep IV was not concerned with politics nearly as much as he was with religion, and thus he was willing for the Canaanite princes to fight among themselves as long as they continued to send their annual tributes and taxes to Egypt. In Canaan, there was a constant struggle among the local rulers called "governors" internally and between these governors and Egyptian officials called "inspectors." As time went on, the situation became more and more chaotic, so that the country was in an ideal condition to be overrun by foreign invaders when the Israelites entered the land.

In 1929, archeologists began to unearth hundreds of cuneiform tablets at Ugarit (Ras Shamra) on the Phoenician coast in Syria, dating from the fifteenth and fourteenth centuries B.C. Ugarit was a Canaanite city, and these tablets therefore shed a great deal of light on the religion and culture of Canaan when the Israelites entered the land. El was the name of the chief god in the Ugaritic pantheon. He and his wife Asherah gave birth to approximately seventy gods and goddesses, one of whom was Hadad or Baal (a word meaning "lord" or "owner"). According to the Baal Epic in the Ras Shamra tablets, Baal defeats the god Yamm (Sea) and confines him to his proper habitation (the sea). But then the god Mot (Death) kills Baal and he is carried into the underworld. Since Baal is a god of rain and vegetation, the rains cease and all vegetation dies. Baal's consort, Anat, forces Mot to revive Baal during half of each year. When this happens, the rains come again and vegetation springs forth. In order to "help" Baal revive vegetation and breeding among animals, as a sort of ancient "sympathetic magic," the Canaanites practiced a number of religious rites which are repulsive to Christianity, such as drunken orgies, sacred prostitution, snake worship, and child sacrifice. (See Hos. 4:11-14.)

In the Ugaritic legend of King Keret, Keret's wife and children die in a severe calamity. Keret takes another wife by defeating her father in battle, and El blesses the new couple with many children. When Keret becomes very sick in his old age, El restores his health in reply to a prayer of one of Keret's daughters. Later one of Keret's sons rebels against him for judging unrighteously.

The Ras Shamra tablets also contain the story of a certain Danel, to whom the gods gave a son named Aqhat. When the gods give Aqhat a bow, the goddess Anat kills him to get it.

Many details in the Ugaritic literature give insight into the meaning of the OT text. There was a feast of the first sheaves of the grain harvest at Ugarit, very much like that described in Leviticus 23:10. The prohibition against Israelites boiling a kid in its mother's milk (Exod. 23:19; 34:26; Deut. 14:21) is a polemic against this Canaanite practice reflected in the Ugaritic materials. The Ras Shamra texts describe Lotan (Leviathan) in terms strikingly similar to Job 3:8; 26:12-13 (where Rahab is used instead of Leviathan); 41:1ff.; Pss. 74:13-14; 104:26; Isa. 27:1. Old Testament references to the mountain in the far north where the gods assemble (Pss. 48:2; 82:1; Isa. 14:12-14; Ezek. 28:14) find close parallels in Ugaritic language and thought.

The Hebrews. One of the most vexing questions in OT study today is the meaning of the term "Hebrew" or "Hebrews" when it is applied to the Israelites and their ancestors. Genesis 14:13 refers to Abram as "the Hebrew," and Potiphar's wife calls Joseph "a Hebrew" (Gen. 39:14, 17), apparently in a derogatory sense. The Egyptians refer to Shiphrah and Puah as "Hebrew midwives" to the "Hebrew women" (Exod. 1:15-16), and the Philistines used the term "Hebrews" in speaking of the Israelites at Aphek (1 Sam. 4:6), etc. During the last several decades of archeological discovery, scholars have found numerous references to Habiru or Hapiru people during the reign of Hammurabi of Babylon, in the Mari texts, in texts from

Alalakh, in the Nuzi materials, at Boghazköy in Turkey among the Hittite literature, and in the Tell el-Amarna tablets sent from Syria and Palestine to Egypt. When one views all the references to the Habiru from these various places, it appears that sometimes they are an ethnic group, but sometimes they are a certain social class including a variety of ethnic groups. As a social class, they seem to stand between the free citizens and the slaves and often appear as mercenary soldiers in some army. Whether the Habiru are connected with the OT Hebrews has not yet been determined with certainty. It seems most likely at the present time that the OT Hebrews were a smaller group of (or within) the much larger ancient Near Eastern social class or ethnic group called Habiru.

THE EXODUS AND THE WILDERNESS WANDERINGS (1290–1250 B.C.)

The Exodus

The date of the exodus. A great deal of effort has been expended by many scholars in an attempt to determine the date of the Israelite exodus from Egypt. Four theories have emerged, which can be outlined only briefly here.

(1) Some critics believe the exodus occurred ca. 1440 B.C. They interpret literally the 480 years from the exodus to the fourth year of Solomon's reign (ca. 958 B.C.), when the temple was begun (1 Kings 6:1). They appeal to Jephthah's statement (ca. 1100 B.C.) that the period of time that elapsed from the conquest of the territory east of Jordan under Moses to his day was 300 years (Judg. 11:26). And they espouse Garstang's view (1930–1936) that since imported Mycenaean pottery is found throughout Palestine after 1400 B.C. and since no Mycenaean pottery has been found at Jericho, that town must have fallen before 1400 B.C., thus corroborating the date 1440 B.C.

(2) Because of the allusions to Habiru troublemakers in Palestine in the Tell el-Amarna tablets dating from the reign of Amen-hotep IV (1370–1353 B.C.), others have concluded that the exodus took place ca. 1370 B.C.

(3) The most widely held view is that the exodus took place ca. 1290 B.C. Several arguments support this view. First, if Jacob's family moved into Egypt contemporaneously with the Hyksos invasion in 1720 B.C., and the period of Israel's sojourn in Egypt was 430 years (Exod. 12:40-41; Gal. 3:17; cf. Gen. 15:13; Acts 7:6), the date of the exodus would be 1290 B.C. Second, the number 480 in 1 Kings 6:1 may be interpreted as twelve generations (assuming that "forty years" can sometimes be a Hebrew idiom meaning "generation"). Computing a generation as approximately twenty-five years, the length of time from the exodus to the fourth year of Solomon's reign is satisfied. The 300 years in Judges 11:26 can be explained in a similar way. Third, the building of the store cities of Pithom and Raamses just before the exodus evidently is to be equated with the building programs in these cities by the Egyptian Pharaohs Seti I (1308–1290 B.C.) and Ramses II (1290–1224 B.C.). Fourth, the Merneptah (or Marniptah) stele (1220 B.C.), which contains the first extrabiblical mention of "Israel," speaks of Israelites as being in Palestine, but refers to them in a way indicating that they were a people in the land of Palestine, and not that they were the dominant power in the land. Fifth, Numbers 20–21 states that on their way to Canaan the Israelites went around Edom and Moab because these nations would not allow them to pass through their lands. But the kingdoms of Moab and Edom were not established east of the Jordan until the thirteenth century B.C. Sixth, over the past several years, archeologists have discovered that the towns of Lachish, Bethel, Eglon, Debir, and Succoth in central and southern Palestine, and Hazor in northern Palestine, were violently destroyed and burned during the last half of the thirteenth century B.C. Since the exodus occurred forty years before this, the evidence points to a date ca. 1290 B.C. Seventh, in excavations at Jericho beginning in 1952, Kathleen Kenyon discovered that Garstang's position on Jericho was far from conclusive. Archeological evidence shows that this location was inhabited off and on from 6800 B.C. It was destroyed ca. 1500 B.C. and not inhabited again in large numbers until

ca. 800 B.C. It is generally agreed, however, that Jericho had a small population ca. 1250 B.C. when Joshua and the Israelites probably began their invasion. In other words, there is no real evidence that Jericho was violently destroyed by invaders in the fifteenth century B.C.

(4) Some scholars feel that there were several Israelite migrations from Egypt to Canaan over a period of 300 years and that the Bible either records one of these or combines and compresses them into brief narratives. The first wave was driven out of Egypt with the Hyksos ca. 1550 B.C. The second is to be equated with part of the Habiru movement reflected in the Tell el-Amarna tablets ca. 1370 B.C. And the third consists of those who served under Moses and Joshua and overran Canaanite towns and cities by force.

It must be admitted that all these views have good arguments for and against them, and they all have been defended by liberal and conservative scholars alike. Viewed on the whole, the evidence seems to indicate that the exodus occurred ca. 1290 B.C., but the present writer offers this only as a tentative position.

The route of the exodus. It is most difficult to reconstruct the route that the Israelites followed when they fled from Egypt, because some of the places mentioned in the Bible have not been identified with certainty. The Israelites went from Rameses to Succoth to Etham on the edge of the wilderness, then turned back to Pi-hahiroth, encamped before Migdol, and crossed the Reed Sea (Exod. 12:37; 13:20; 14:2, 9, 21-22; Num. 33:5-8). In 1929, P. Montet excavated Rameses and discovered it was to be identified with Tanis (biblical Zoan). Succoth is the modern Tell el-Mashkutah near the Wadi Tumilat south of Rameses. So the Israelites at Rameses must have travelled south to the interior of the land of Goshen to gather their fellows to go with them if they wished, intending to leave Egypt along the course of the Wadi Tumilat in the region of Lake Timsah. Now the Karnak Inscription of Seti I (1304-1290 B.C.) states that the Egyptians had built fortresses all along their eastern frontier. Unfortunately, Pi-hahiroth and Migdol have not been identified. The Reed Sea (Hebrew *yam suph*; not "Red

Sea" as many Bibles have it) must be a region where "reeds" or "papyrus plants" grow (which in itself rules out the Red Sea).

Scholars have proposed three theories as to the place where the Israelites crossed the Reed Sea. One is that they journeyed from Rameses south to Succoth, then from Succoth on south to a point not far from the northern tip of the Gulf of Suez, so that the Reed Sea is the Bitter Lakes. A second hypothesis is that when they came to Succoth they turned east and crossed Lake Timsah, which is the Reed Sea. The third view (which seems most likely) is that after the Israelites left Succoth they moved on south a bit until they came to Etham (Exod. 13:20). Here they "turned back" (Exod. 14:2) north, perhaps because Etham was one of the Egyptian frontier fortresses that they felt unable to pass. As this would take them back in the direction of Rameses, the Reed Sea should probably be located in this region. Archeologists have discovered an Egyptian text that mentions two bodies of water near Rameses: "the water of Horus," which is the Shihor of Isaiah 23:3, and "the Papyrus Marsh." Thus the Reed Sea may be Lake Sirbonis, or more likely the southern extension of Lake Menzaleh (Manzala).

The Wilderness Wanderings

From the Reed Sea to Mount Sinai. The Bible names five places where the Israelites encamped between the Reed Sea and Mount Sinai: Marah, Elim, Dophkah, Alush, and Rephidim (Exod. 15:22-23, 27; 17:1; Num. 33:8-15). None of these places has been identified with certainty, and the location of Mount Sinai itself is not sure. Marah could be 'Ain Hawarah, 'Ain Musa, or some unknown spring near the Bitter Lakes. Since Elim has many springs and trees, it could be the Wadi Gharandel. Dophkah might be the Egyptian mining town of Serabit el-Khadim, and Rephaim the Wadi Rafayid. Mount Sinai is frequently identified with Jebel Musa near ancient copper and turquoise mines. The tradition that this is the location of Mount Sinai is about fifteen hundred years old. This identification would help explain why Midianites and

Kenites (metal smiths) were there, because they had interest in copper mining and smelting available in this region. Moses' father-in-law, Jethro (Reuel), lived in this area (Exod. 2:15-22; 18:1-27; Num. 10:29; Judg. 4:11).

Two other sites have been suggested as the location of Mount Sinai. Some think it is located in Arabia east of the Gulf of Aqabah, because the description of Mount Sinai in Exodus 19 would seem to fit volcanic action and some mountains in this territory are volcanic. Others want to place it near Kadesh-barnea, because Mount Sinai and Kadesh-barnea are closely associated in the OT. The problem with both of these views is that they are hard to square with possible locations of other sites mentioned in the biblical texts where the Israelites camped.

From Mount Sinai to Kadesh-barnea. Some forty campsites of the Israelites between Mount Sinai and Kadesh-barnea are mentioned in Numbers 33:16-36, only a very few of which can be identified. Evidently the Israelites passed through a number of interlocking valleys between Mount Sinai and Ezion-geber (Num. 33:35), located on the northern tip of the Gulf of Aqabah. Then they moved inland over high ridges until they reached Kadesh-barnea in the wilderness of Zin (Num. 20:1; 33:36). This wilderness must have been a portion of the wilderness of Paran, because Kadesh-barnea is also located in this wilderness (Num. 13:26). The distance between Mount Sinai and Kadesh-barnea could be covered on foot in eleven days (Deut. 1:2), but the Israelites took almost thirty-nine years in their wanderings to do it. (See Num. 10:11; 20:22-29; 33:38-39.)

THE BEGINNING OF THE CONQUEST AND SETTLEMENT OF CANAAN (1250–1200 B.C.)

Canaan at the Time of the Conquest

The Tell el-Amarna tablets, the Ras Shamra materials, and the Bible show that when the Israelites began the conquest and settlement of Canaan, the country was inhabited by a variety of peoples who were not united, who lived in isolation from each other, and who themselves were often hostile to each other. Deuteronomy 7:1 and Joshua 3:10 and 24:11 mention seven nations that lived there. The stories of the people of Gibeon (Josh. 9) and Laish (Judg. 18:27-28) show how poor communication was between the different peoples and cities. West of the Jordan it was common for each city state to have its own king (see Josh. 2:2; 6:2; 8:1-2; 10:1-4, 28-39; 11:1; 12:13-24; etc.) and its own god, usually some Baal, so that frequently the books of Joshua, Judges, and Samuel refer to the "Baals" and the "Asherim" or "Ashtaroth" (Asherah was the consort of Baal) or to a plurality of gods (Josh. 23:7-8, 16; 24:15-18, 20, 23; Judg. 2:3, 11-13; 3:7; 6:25; 8:33; 10:6; 1 Sam. 7:3-4; etc.). Large areas of Canaan were thinly populated or not populated at all.

The Course of the Conquest and Settlement of Canaan

The overthrow of the land east of Jordan. When the Israelites under Moses had gone around Edom and Moab to reach the region east of the Jordan just north of the Dead Sea at Shittim or Baal-peor (Num. 25:1-2; 33:49; Mic. 6:5), they entered into military conflict with two Amorite kings who governed small nations there. One was Sihon, the king of Heshbon in the south, and the other, Og, the king of Bashan in the north (Num. 21:21-35). When these kings had been defeated, Moses gave this region to the tribes of Reuben, Gad, and the half-tribe of Manasseh (Num. 32:33-42; Deut. 2:26–3:17; etc.) with the understanding that their men of war would help the other tribes seize the land west of Jordan.

Conquests and settlements in central Canaan. After Moses died, Joshua led the Israelites across the Jordan to the west and set up headquarters at Gilgal, an unoccupied region. They overran and/or made alliances with various central Palestinian peoples, including Jericho (Josh. 6), Ai (Josh. 7–8), Gibeon, Beeroth, Chephirah, Kiriath-jearim (Josh. 9, especially vss. 17-18), and Debir (Josh. 10:38-39).

Conquests and settlements in southern Canaan. After making inroads into central Palestine, the Israelites moved southward. Here they overran such strategic towns as Makkedah, Libnah, Lachish, Eglon, and Hebron (Josh. 10:28-37) and began to settle in this region.

Conquests in northern Canaan. After several successful campaigns in central and southern Palestine, the Israelites apparently engaged in a series of wars against Hazor and surrounding cities in the region around the Sea of Galilee in northern Canaan (Josh. 11, especially vss. 10-14, 18).

The Speed and Nature of Israel's Possession of Canaan

On the basis of Joshua 10:40-43; 11:15-17, 23; 18:1; 21:43-45; and 23:14-15, it might be concluded that the OT contains affirmations that the Israelites completely conquered Canaan during Joshua's lifetime. However, this is clearly not the picture painted in other texts, nor is it historically accurate. When Joshua was an old man, there was "very much land" yet to be possessed by the Israelites (Josh. 13:1-7; 18:3-7). Joshua had "allotted" or "apportioned" the land to the various tribes, but when he died by no means had they already "possessed" it (Josh. 13:6-7; 18:2-3, 10). Judges 1 describes many Israelite conquests of Canaanite cities and towns "after the death of Joshua" (Judg. 1:1) and tells how Israelites and Canaanites lived side by side in the land long after Joshua's death. The tribe of Dan did not seize its territory in the north until late in the period of the Judges (Judg. 18). And it was not until the time of David (ca. 1000 B.C. or later) that the Jebusites were dislodged from Jerusalem (2 Sam. 5:6-8) and the Israelite possession of Canaan completed.

Israel's possession of the land of Canaan was very irregular. They settled in regions that were not populated or thinly populated; they made leagues with peoples living in the land and coexisted with them (Josh. 9; 11:19; Judg. 1:27-36); they burned and overran certain city states. It seems that after the Israelites defeated some city states they did not inhabit them or, if they did, their enemies later drove them out because they had to conquer some towns more than once, such as Hebron (Josh. 10:36-37; 14:13-15; 15:13-14; Judg. 1:10), Debir (Josh. 10:38-39; 15:15-19; Judg. 1:11-15), Jerusalem

(Judg. 1:8-9; 2 Sam 5:6-8), and Hazor (Josh. 11:1-15; Judg. 4–5). This agrees with the repeated statement that they returned to Gilgal after defeating certain Canaanite cities.

In view of these facts, certain comments may be in order with regard to the above-mentioned passages that at first sight might be taken to mean that the Israelites under Joshua quickly and completely subdued the land of Canaan. (1) Joshua 10:40-43 has reference only to southern and central Palestine, as a simple reading of this text shows. (2) In the other passages, the word "all"is not to be taken in an absolute sense. Paul says: "from Jerusalem and as far round as Illyricum I have *fully* preached the gospel of Christ" (Rom. 15:19), and again: "the gospel . . . has been preached to *every creature* under heaven" (Col. 1:23). Yet it is quite clear that there were many people in the Roman Empire in Paul's day who had never seen or heard him and who had never heard about Christ. He means that the disciples had carried the gospel to the main cities of the world at that time. (3) Joshua 11:15-17, 23; 18:1; 21:43-45; 23:14-15 mean that Joshua had led Israel in enough military victories so that when he died the land that had been under the control of the Canaanites was now under Israelite control. Israel was now the dominant power in the land, and the individual tribes could begin trying to take possession of the territories allotted to them.

THE PERIOD OF THE JUDGES (1200–1020 B.C.)

Israel's Instability in Canaan

Although the Israelites had gained the upper hand in the land of Canaan by the time of Joshua's death, surrounding nations continued to give them trouble, and the tribes were not solidly united, but often fought with one another.

Israel was subdued by Mesopotamian peoples from the north (Judg. 3:8), Canaanites in the northern part of Palestine (Judg. 4:2), Midianites in the south (Judg. 6:1), Moabites (Judg. 3:14) and Ammonites (Judg. 10:8; 1 Sam 11:1-11; 12:12) from the east, Philistines from the west (Judg. 13:1; 1 Sam. 4–7; 13–14; 29–31; 2 Sam. 5:17-25), and probably other peoples not mentioned in the biblical text. The Philistines were a sea-going people who swept into Egypt in the eighth year of Ramses III (ca. 1188 B.C.). The Egyptians were able to drive them out ca. 1180 B.C., and thus they moved into Canaan. Archeological excavations by Danish specialists at Shiloh in 1926–1932 and in more recent days indicate that this town was violently destroyed by invading forces ca. 1050 B.C. It is generally agreed that this is to be correlated with the Philistine battles against Israel in the days of Samuel (1 Sam. 4:1-22; Jer. 7:14; 26:6, 9; Ps. 78:59-66). They were a constant threat to the Israelites until David finally defeated them soundly (2 Sam. 5:17-25) and even after this continued to be a menace. It is from them that the word "Palestine" came to be used of the land of Canaan.

The Israelite tribes were poorly organized until David solidified them. They had to be specially convened to take care of important matters, and even then many times only designated tribal officials attended. To cite only a few examples, they were called together at Mount Ebal so that the law could be read to them (Josh. 8:30-35), at Shiloh to set up the tent of meeting (Josh. 18:1), at Shechem to make or renew the covenant with Yahweh (Josh. 24:1, 25-28), and at Gilgal to renew the kingdom (1 Sam. 11:14-15). But more than this, when a common enemy attacked or threatened to attack, the fighting men of the pertinent tribes had to be convened, as when Deborah and Barak summoned certain tribes to help fight against Jabin (Judg. 4:10; 5:12-18) or when Israel determined to punish the Benjaminites for raping and killing the Levite's concubine (Judg. 10:1-2, 8-11; 21:5, 8; etc.) or when Saul called the tribes to help defend Jabesh-gilead against Nahash (1 Sam. 11:7-8).

Moreover, the Israelite tribes were constantly bickering and fighting with each other. Deborah chided the clans and tribes of Reuben, Gilead, Manasseh, Dan, Asher, and Meroz for not helping their brethren in war against the Canaanites (Judg. 5:15-17, 23). Ephraim was jealous when Gideon defeated the Midianites (8:1-3), and the men of Succoth and Penuel refused to help Gideon against Zebah and Zalmunna (8:4-9, 13-17). There was strife between Abimelech and Jotham (9:5-21), Abimelech and the men of Shechem (9:23, 26-49), and Abimelech and the men of Thebez (9:50-55). Jephthah's brothers bitterly opposed him and drove him away (11:1-3), and Ephraim was jealous of his victory over the Ammonites (12:1-6). The Israelites were divided over Saul's selection as king (1 Sam. 10:25-27; 11:12-13). Saul and David were enemies several years during Saul's reign (1 Sam. 17ff.). It is not surprising, therefore, that after the reigns of David and Solomon the kingdom was divided.

The Chronological Problem of the Period of the Judges

If one were to interpret the chronological data in the book of Judges sequentially, he would conclude that the period in which judges governed Israel covered 410 years, as Chart 1 shows.

Chart 1

Chronology of the Book of Judges

Text in Book of Judges	Event	Number of Years Involved
3:8	Israel subject to Mesopotamia	8
3:11	Peace under Othniel	40
3:14	Israel subject to Moab	18
3:30	Peace under Ehud	80
4:3	Israel oppressed by Jabin	20
5:31	Peace under Deborah and Barak	40
6:1	Israel subject to Midian	7
8:28	Peace under Gideon	40
9:22	Rule of Abimelech	3
10:2	Rule of Tola	23
10:3	Rule of Jair	22
10:8	Israel oppressed by Ammonites	18
12:7	Peace under Jephthah	6
12:9	Rule of Ibzan	7
12:11	Rule of Elon	10
12:14	Rule of Abdon	8
13:1	Israel dominated by Philistines	40
15:20 (16:31)	Peace under Samson	20
	Total	410

Now 1 Kings 6:1 states that there were 480 years from the exodus to the beginning of the building of the temple in the fourth year of Solomon's reign. However, if the biblical data pertaining to the time covered between these two events is taken sequentially, the number of years involved would be over six hundred years, as Chart 2 demonstrates.

Chart 2

Hypothetical Sequential Chronology from the Exodus to the Beginning of the Building of the Temple

Biblical Text	Event	Number of Years Years Involved
Num. 14:34 Deut. 1:3	Wilderness Wanderings	40
Josh. 24:31	Joshua's Leadership	x
Texts in Chart 1	Period of the Judges through Samson	410
1 Sam. 4:18	Eli's judgeship	40
1 Sam. 7:15	Samuel's judgeship	y
Acts 13:21 2 Sam. 5:4-5	Saul's kingship	40
1 Kings 2:11	David's kingship	40
1 Kings 6:1	Beginning of building of temple in 4th year of Solomon's reign	4
	Total	$574+x+y$

Even if Eli's judgeship is reduced to twenty years (following the LXX) and Saul's kingship is reduced to twenty years (because of the textual problem in 1 Sam. 13:1), the number still must be near six hundred years (including the unspecified time that Joshua led Israel and that Samuel judged—x and y on the chart).

Although the Bible does not give enough information to help one solve this problem in all its details, two general considerations point toward a solution. First, the number forty (with its multiples and fractions) may be a Hebrew idiom for a generation in a number of cases and need not be taken literally each time it occurs. The biblical breakdown of the wilderness wanderings (the second year, Num. 1:1; 10:11; the fortieth year, Num. 33:38; Deut. 1:3) and of David's reign (seven and one-half years over Judah at Hebron and thirty-three years over all Israel at Jerusalem,

2 Sam. 5:4-5) would suggest that the number forty should be taken literally in these two cases, but this would not necessarily be true in all instances. Second, there is no reason that different alien oppressions and Israelite judges could not have overlapped one another. In most cases, the OT takes care to specify the tribe from which a certain judge comes (Ehud from Benjamin, Judg. 3:15; Gideon from Manasseh, Judg. 6:15; Tola from Issachar, Judg. 10:1; Jair from Gilead east of the Jordan, Judg. 10:3; etc.). Possibly only his tribe was affected by the hostile attack described in the biblical text. (Deborah's summoning of several tribes, Judg. 4:6, 10; 5:12-18, 23, seems to have been the exception rather than the rule.) Then the word "Israel" in the book of Judges may be a case in which the more comprehensive term is used for a part of the whole.

The Work of Judges

It would be a grave mistake to think of the "judges" in the book of Judges in the modern sense of this word. The word "judge" is used of at least three functions in the OT. First and foremost, the judge was a military leader guided by God (his spirit or angel) to deliver the Israelites from foreign oppression (Judg. 2:16, 18; 3:9, 10, 15, 31; 6:36, 37; 7:2; 8:22; 10:1; 1 Sam. 8:20). Second, he was a man who heard court cases between tribes or individuals and decided how the problem was to be resolved on the basis of the law (Judg. 10:1-5; 12:8-15; 1 Sam. 7:15–8:3). Third, he was a teacher of the people, who encouraged them to be faithful to Yahweh and his law and warned them not to serve other gods (Judg. 2:17; 1 Sam. 12). Some of the judges may have discharged all of these functions, but most of them seem to have done only one of them.

THE REIGN OF SAUL (1020–1000 B.C.)

Change in Israel's Government

The transition from a disorganized tribal system under judges to an organized monarchical system under a king in Israel took place very slowly. On the one hand, there were several attempts to institute some sort of monarchical government in Israel before this was finally accomplished with Saul. After Gideon defeated the Midianites, the men of Israel said to him: "Rule over us, you and your son and your grandson also" (Judg. 8:22). This language suggests that they were asking him to establish a dynasty. Gideon's wicked son, Abimelech, became king over the citizens of Shechem (9:6-22). The elders of Gilead urged Jephthah to become their "leader" or "head" (11:5-11), probably suggesting some sort of kingship. Now it may very well be that what the people wanted was a king over a certain city state or district like the Canaanites had, but such requests indicate that they were unhappy with existing conditions and yearned for a more stable government. On the other hand, in the early years of Saul's rule, he functioned much more like a judge than a king. The spirit of God came mightily upon him (1 Sam. 10:6, 9-10; 11:6) as on the judges (Judg. 13:25; 14:6, 19). When Israel was attacked by an invading force (the Ammonites), Saul had to gather an army from the various tribes (1 Sam. 11:5-11) just like the judges (Judg. 4:6, 10). When the elders of Israel asked Samuel for a king, they used the verb "judge" (Hebrew *shaphat;* RSV, "govern") to describe the work that they wanted him to do (1 Sam. 8:5-6, 20). They wanted a leader, they said, to "go out before us and fight our battles" (1 Sam. 8:20), which was the primary function of a judge (Judg. 2:16, 18; etc.).

When Israel's monarchy began, at least three views of kingship existed. (1) The popular feeling apparently was that stability and security could be gained only by organizing the people under one earthly head, like the nations (1 Sam. 8:5, 19-20). The ultimate implication of such thinking is that Yahweh's leadership was not sufficient to deliver Israel from her enemies and that rule by charismatic judges was very unsatisfactory. (2) The view of Gideon (Judg. 8:23) and Samuel (1 Sam. 8:6-7) was that God alone should be recognized as king and that no earthly leader was necessary until God raised him up when the need required. (3) Yahweh's view seems to have been that it was best under the circumstances to give Israel a king, as long as he was the kind of man who would subject his will to God's will as his representative and let God rule through him (1 Sam. 8:7-9, 22). When Samuel anointed Saul, Saul possessed that type of humble spirit which would lend itself to such a philosophy (9:21; 15:17), although his attitude changed later. Possibly the statements that David was a man after God's own heart (13:14) and "better than" Saul (15:28) are to be understood in this context. (See 28:17-18.) Unlike Saul, he strove to allow God to be the real king in Israel's governmental system. It is this kind of king that the author of the book of Judges envisioned with his statement "In those days there was no king in Israel; every man did what was right in his own eyes" (Judg. 17:6; 18:1; 19:1; 21:25).

The Emergence of Prophetism

It seems to be no accident that the prophetic movement in Israel began about the same time as the monarchy. (Peter traces its origins back to Samuel, Acts 3:24, while recognizing that Moses also performed prophetic functions, Acts 3:22-23.) If God was to be the real king and the earthly king his representative, it was necessary for him to speak to the king and the people and to have a way to let it be known publicly that he was in charge. The prophets discharged these tasks.

The manner in which God designated a certain man as king was to have his prophet *anoint* him. Thus, Samuel anointed Saul (1 Sam. 9:16), but when he did so he said: "Has not *the Lord* anointed you to be prince over his people Israel?" (10:1). After this, Saul is called "the Lord's anointed" (24:6; 26:11; 2 Sam. 1:14). Samuel anointed David after the Lord had rejected Saul (1 Sam. 16:12-13), Nathan anointed Solomon (1 Kings 1:34), and one of the sons of the prophets anointed Jehu at the commission of Elisha (2 Kings 9:1-6). Hittite documents discovered at Boghazköy indicate that it was customary for a suzerain to have vassal kings subject to him anointed as a sign of their subjection and fidelity to him. The OT clearly indicates that at least one idea connected with anointing kings is that the king was thereby subject to God and set apart in a special way to be faithful to him. The Hebrew word for "anoint" is *mashach*, whence comes the noun *meshiach*, "anointed one" (the Greek word that translates this noun is *christos*, and from these two words come the English "messiah" and "christ"). All kings of Israel were the Lord's messiahs, or christs, or anointed ones. This language provided an excellent background for terminology already familiar to the people to be applied to Jesus. In a fuller sense than any OT personality, Jesus is the Lord's Messiah or Christ (Matt. 16:13-19; John 1:41).

The prophets also reproached and condemned kings when they acted in a way contrary to God's will. Samuel rebuked Saul for offering the burnt offering at Gilgal before he arrived (1 Sam. 10:8; 13:8-13a); Nathan reproached David for committing adultery with Bathsheba and having Uriah killed on the battlefield at Rabbah (2 Sam. 12:1-15); God offered David three alternate divine punishments when he numbered the people (2 Sam. 24:1-14); etc. The prophets also announced God's rejection of a king, as when Samuel declared that the Lord had rejected Saul (1 Sam. 13:13b-14; 15:26, 28; 28:16-18).

It was customary throughout the ancient Near East for a messenger of a king to introduce his message with the formula "Thus says . . . ." Accordingly, when the Rabshakeh conveys Sennacherib's message to Hezekiah, he introduces it with the words "Thus says the great king, the king of Assyria" (2 Kings 18:19; Isa. 36:4) or "Thus says Sennacherib king of Assyria" (2 Chron. 32:10). Again, the messengers of Ben-hadad introduced his words to Ahab by saying "Thus says Ben-hadad" (1 Kings 20:2, 5). In view of this, it seems clear that when the prophets used the formula "Thus says Yahweh (the Lord)," they assume that he is the real king over Israel.

Major Developments during Saul's Reign

Although Saul's kingdom never attained the power and glory that characterized the empire of David and Solomon, he was able to lift Israel somewhat above conditions that had prevailed previously. In 1922–1923 and 1933, excavators of the American School of Oriental Research unearthed a portion of a fortress or citadel at Gibeah (modern Tell el-Ful) dating from the end of the eleventh century B.C., which now is generally acknowledged to be Saul's stronghold in his capital city. The OT suggests that Saul made his home town (1 Sam. 10:5, 10, 26) his governmental center (14:2, 16; 15:34; 22:6; 23:19; 26:1). To be sure, this location and Saul's fortress were not nearly so imposing as those of David and Solomon later in Jerusalem, but Saul's work was a beginning in that direction.

Saul led Israel in a number of successful military campaigns against the Moabites, the Ammonites, the Edomites, the kings of Zobah, the Philistines, and the Amalekites (1 Sam. 11:1-11; 13–14; 15:1-9). This enabled the Israelites to secure greater control of the land of Canaan than they had ever enjoyed. However, the Philistines were determined to gain control of Canaan if they could. First Samuel 16–2 Samuel 1 alludes to numerous encounters between the Israelites and the Philistines. In time, Saul and Jonathan were killed while fighting against the Philistines on Mount Gilboa (1 Sam. 31).

In a rather crude way Saul began an organized military and political system among the Israelites. When he found any strong or brave man, he enlisted him in his army (1 Sam. 14:52). One of his most promising soldiers was David (16:21; 18:2). Evidently he hired foreign mercenaries who were especially skilled in warfare, such as Doeg the Edomite (22:9, 18), the chief of Saul's herdsmen (21:7). The commander of his army was Abner the Son of Ner, Saul's uncle (14:50). Under him were commanders of thousands and commanders of hundreds (22:7). Saul had personal armorbearers (16:21; 31:4-6), a bodyguard (22:14, 17), a three-man cabinet or council consisting of Abner, Jonathan, and David (20:25; cf. vss. 5, 18, 27), and a corps of eighty-five priests under Ahimelech (22:11-19, especially vs. 18).

Saul's failure in his personal life and as a national leader was due largely to great fear of his enemies and constant suspicion of his own men. His fear of the Philistines motivated him to offer the burnt offering before Samuel arrived at Gilgal (1 Sam. 13:11-12) and to consult the medium at Enzor (28:7-25, especially vs. 15). His suspicion of David led him to try to kill him in various ways on different occasions, as demanding that he kill 100 Philistines to qualify to marry Michal (18:25), trying to kill him with his spear several times (18:10-11; 19:9-10), etc. His suspicion of Ahimelech made him command that he and the eighty-five priests of Nob be killed (22:11-19). His suspicion of Jonathan moved him to try to kill him with his spear (20:30-33).

THE REIGN OF DAVID (1000–961 B.C.)

David's Rise to Israel's Throne

The OT emphasizes that David's successful rise to the throne (like that of Saul's) was due first and foremost to the intervention and continual working of the living God. Yahweh sought out, appointed, and provided David to be king (1 Sam. 13:14; 16:1) and gave the kingdom to him (15:28). He sent Samuel to anoint David for this work (16:1, 12-13). He was with David in all his undertakings (18:12, 14, 28; 2 Sam. 5:10), would not give him into Saul's hand (1 Sam. 23:14), and gave him victory over his enemies wherever he went (2 Sam. 8:6, 14). Under this large umbrella of divine intervention, many other factors worked together in bringing about David's elevation to Israel's throne.

First, David enjoyed the support of Israel's most influential religious leaders, namely, Samuel and the prophets under his charge (1 Sam. 16:1-13; 19:18-24), and Ahimelech and the priests of Nob (21:1-9; 22:7-19). Both of these groups had undoubtedly watched Saul's spiritual decline with deep regrets and looked for the day when Saul could be replaced by a man who would function more adequately as Yahweh's anointed one and representative (see 15:17-35; 22:14-15). When Saul killed the priests of Nob, it was only natural for Abiathar, one of Ahimelech's sons, to flee to David for refuge (22:20-23; 23:6).

Second, David frequently demonstrated his military skill

as a soldier in Saul's army. In keeping with the military custom of his day, he frequently engaged Philistines in single combats and defeated them (1 Sam. 17:48-51; 18:30 —"The Philistine officers used to come out to offer single combat; and whenever they did, David had more success against them than all the rest of Saul's men, and he won a name for himself," NEB). Saul made him one of his armor-bearers (16:21; 18:2), set him over the men of war (18:5), elevated him to the rank of commander of a thousand (18:13), made him one of his three personal confidants (along with Jonathan and Abner—20:25), and appointed him captain over his bodyguard (22:14). It is not clear whether this is the order in which David held these posts or whether he held some of them simultaneously. David steadily attracted mighty warriors to himself, men whom Saul repulsed by his general attitude and, particularly, by his negative attitude toward David. These included members of David's own family (22:1), fellow Judeans who were not happy with Saul's rule (22:2) and eventually joined David at the stronghold to help him take the throne from the house of Saul (1 Chron. 11:10), prominent North Israelite soldiers, Saul's own relatives, and foreign mercenaries. Of the thirty-seven heroes of David listed in 2 Samuel 23:8-37, twenty-one were Judeans, nine were North Israelites, and seven were foreigners. Other than Jonathan, perhaps the most impressive member of Saul's family that defected to David was Ishmaiah (1 Chron. 12:2-4).

Third, Saul's suspicion of those around him and especially of David caused many to become disenchanted with Saul and to turn to David. Samuel hesitated to go to Bethlehem because he knew Saul would suspect his intentions (1 Sam. 16:2). Saul sharply rebuked Jonathan for his friendship with David (20:30-31). He chastised the most trusted members of his army because they looked favorably on David (22:7-8). It is human nature to sympathize with the oppressed. The more Saul attacked David, the more popular David became, especially among those whom Saul harassed.

Fourth, David's relationship with Saul's family put him in a good position for the throne in the eyes of the people.

Jonathan could probably see his father's faults very clearly, realized that he was not cut out to be king of Israel, and really believed that David was the man for the job. Jonathan's dream seems to have been that David be the next king of Israel and that he be "next to him" (1 Sam. 23:17), (i.e., second in command). As the husband of Michal (Saul's daughter), David was son-in-law of the king (18:23); and, since Saul came from Gibeah in North Israel, this put David in a favorable light in the eyes of the people living in northern Palestine. It is politically significant that when David sought to bring the northern tribes under his rule after Saul and Jonathan were killed at Mount Gilboa, he demanded that Michal be returned to him as his wife (2 Sam. 3:13-16—while David was a fugitive in the latter part of Saul's reign, Saul had given Michal to Palti, 1 Sam. 25:44).

Fifth, David's unique ability to deal with the northern tribes played an important role in his accession to the throne. Although he had several opportunities to kill Saul, David refused to do so because Saul was the Lord's anointed (1 Sam. 24:6; 26:11, 23). Undoubtedly this put David in a favorable position with Saul's soldiers and followers. When David learned that Saul and Jonathan had been killed by the Philistines, he killed the Amalekite who claimed to have killed Saul (2 Sam. 1:14-16) and publicly mourned their loss (1:11-12, 17-27). His first public act when he was made king over Judah at Hebron was to send an official embassy to Jabesh-gilead in North Israel east of the Jordan, commending the men of that city for giving Saul and Jonathan a proper burial (2:4-7; cf. 1 Sam. 31:11-13). When David discovered that Joab had murdered Abner (who had been commander-in-chief of the armies of Saul and his son Ish-baal or Ish-bosheth), he publicly cursed the house of Joab (2 Sam. 3:28-29, 39), lamented Abner's loss to Israel, and gave him an honorable burial at Hebron (3:31-38). Similarly, when he learned that two of his own men had murdered Ish-bosheth, he had them killed and buried Ish-bosheth's head in Abner's tomb (4:9-12). Perhaps one of David's most spectacular political maneuvers was to select the neutral city of Jerusalem as his capital (5:6-8). It lay in

the borderland between Israel and Judah and since it had
been under Jebusite control could not be said to be either
uniquely Israelite or uniquely Judean. His transfer of the ark
of the covenant to Jerusalem (2 Sam. 6) must have made a
great positive impression on the North Israelites, because
the previous location where it had actually been used to any
extent at all was Shiloh in North Israel (1 Sam. 1–4).

Sixth, David had an uncanny ability to deal with foreign nations to Israel's advantage. His dealings with the
Philistines are a good example of this. Early in his career he
killed many Philistines in single combats and in battles.
When he first became a fugitive from Saul, he seems to have
been on unfriendly terms with Saul and the Philistines alike.
He was driven out of Gath by the men of Achish because
they thought he was "the king of the land" of Israel
(1 Sam. 21:11).

However, later David was able to convince the
Philistines that Saul had banished him, and thus he was
Saul's enemy. The Philistines gave David asylum in their
land, and he became their vassal with his own city for himself and his men at Ziklag (1 Sam. 27:5-6). Ultimately David
defeated the Philistines and made them special soldiers in
his army. Many scholars believe that the Cherethites and
Pelethites who fought in David's army (2 Sam. 8:18; 20:23;
1 Chron. 18:17) were Cretans and Philistines.

David's Achievements

David was a great, magnetic personality who welded
Israel into a unified state and provided her with sufficient
strength to continue as the controlling force in Palestine
for several succeeding decades (even after the tribes
split again). He captured Jerusalem from the Jebusites
(2 Sam. 5:6-8) and made it a strong, fortified city, able to
resist powerful military attacks by Israel's enemies (5:9).
Here he had an impressive royal palace built for himself and
his successors (5:11), and to the six wives he had married
earlier (3:2-5) he added several wives and concubines in
Jerusalem (5:13), some undoubtedly as a result of political
marriages. These gave birth to several sons, who became

princes under David, and ultimately contenders for the throne.

David defeated Israel's enemies and thus prepared the way for Solomon's peaceful rule. He defeated the Philistines on the west (2 Sam. 5:17-25; 8:1, 12), the Edomites on the south (8:12-14), the Moabites and Ammonites on the east (8:12; 10:1-19), and the Syrians or Arameans on the north (8:3-8; 10:1-19), and made peaceful alliances with Phoenicia on the west (5:11) and with Hamath on the north (8:9-10). During his reign, Israel actually came to possess and control the land of Canaan for the first time.

David made significant advances on Saul's governmental organization. His cabinet consisted of a commander of the army (Joab, the son of David's sister Zeruiah, 2 Sam. 8:16; 20:23; 1 Chron. 2:15-16; 27:34), a recorder (Jehoshaphat, 2 Sam. 8:16; 20:24), two high priests (Abiathar and Zadok, 8:17; 20:25), a secretary (Seraiah, 8:17; Sheva, 20:25), two counselors (Ahithophel and Hushai, 15:32-37; 16:15–17:23; 1 Chron. 27:33), court prophets (Nathan, 2 Sam. 7:1-17; 12:1-15, 24-25; 1 Kings 1:22-27, 32-40; Gad, 2 Sam. 24), a leader of the Cherethites and Pelethites (Benaiah, 2 Sam. 8:18; 20:23), and a leader of his forced labor gangs (Adoram, 20:24). He had a group of three mighty men (23:8-17) and thirty valiant men (23:18-39), who apparently were willing to give their very lives for him if necessary, even to satisfy his smallest desire (23:13-17). He also had overseers of the various works that were being done throughout the kingdom (1 Chron. 27:2-32).

David also made great contributions to Israel's religious activities. He brought the ark of the covenant to Jerusalem and temporarily housed it in a tent (2 Sam. 6). The ark was the throne-chariot of Yahweh and symbolized his presence with his people as king (1 Sam. 4:3-4; 2 Sam. 6:2). David longed to build a temple for the ark but could not do so because he was so involved in withstanding and overrunning Israel's enemies (2 Sam. 7; 1 Kings 5:3-4). Therefore, he drew up an architectural plan of the temple for Solomon to follow (1 Chron. 28:11-19) and had his servants gather many materials in preparation for the building of the temple

(22:2-5). Furthermore, he organized the priests and Levites in divisions (23–24), designated certain men and their descendants to be responsible for the instrumental and vocal music to be used in the temple (1 Chron. 25) according to the commandment from the Lord through his prophets (2 Chron. 29:25-26), and appointed gatekeepers, treasurers, officers, judges, and various other leaders (1 Chron. 26–27) so that the temple work and worship could begin smoothly and effectively. He appreciated and practiced animal sacrifice as a vital part of OT worship (2 Sam. 5:12-19; 24:18-25; 1 Chron. 23:13, 26-32).

David's Sins and Their Consequences

With all his good qualities, like all men David was a sinner. He committed adultery with Bathsheba, the wife of one of his hired foreign mercenaries, Uriah the Hittite (2 Sam. 11:1-5; cf. 23:39), had Uriah murdered on the battlefield at Rabbah (11:14-25), and (apparently from egotistical motives) took a count of his fighting men (2 Sam. 24:1-9; 1 Chron. 21:1-6).

As a consequence of his adultery with Bathsheba and murder of Uriah, the Lord brought four punishments on David. (1) He decreed that the sword should not depart from David's house (2 Sam. 12:10). Accordingly, Absalom killed Amnon, his half-brother, for committing fornication with Tamar (Absalom's sister—ch. 13), Joab killed Absalom in battle (ch. 18), and Solomon had Adonijah killed when he asked for Abishag to be given to him as a wife (1 Kings 2:13-25). (2) He announced that he would raise up evil against him out of his own house (2 Sam. 12:11). Thus Amnon committed adultery with Tamar (ch. 13); Absalom led a military rebellion against David and tried to usurp the throne (ch. 15), and Adonijah tried to seize the throne in David's old age (1 Kings 1:5-10, 41-53). (3) He stated that he would give David's wives to a neighbor of his, who would commit adultery with them publicly (2 Sam. 12:11). And when Absalom seized Jerusalem, on Ahithophel's advice he pitched a tent on the roof of the royal palace and went in to David's concubines in the sight of all Israel (16:21-22).

(4) He declared that the child born to David's adulterous relationship with Bathsheba would die (12:14), and it did at seven days of age (12:16-18).

As a result of numbering the warriors from Israel and Judah, God gave David the choice of a three-year famine (some ancient manuscripts read "seven years of famine" in 2 Samuel), three months of fleeing before his enemies, or three days of pestilence in the land (2 Sam. 24:13; 1 Chron. 21:12). David put himself into the Lord's hands by asking for the pestilence, because he knew God's mercy is great (2 Sam. 24:14; 1 Chron. 21:13).

THE REIGN OF SOLOMON (961–922 B.C.)

Solomon's Military and Political Achievements

Solomon came to the throne of Israel under tense circumstances. Adonijah, his half-brother, had succeeded in securing a rather strong following in Joab and Abiathar (1 Kings 1:7). But with the public support of David, Bathsheba, Benaiah, Zadok, and Nathan, Solomon was successful in attaining the throne (1:8, 11-40). Early in his reign Solomon got rid of his political rivals. He had Benaiah, the commander of his army, kill Joab (2:28-35), Adonijah (2:13-25), and Shimei, a member of Saul's house (2:36-46; cf. 2 Sam. 16:5-14); he banished Abiathar the priest to Anathoth (1 Kings 2:26-27, 35).

Solomon's governmental organization followed the pattern laid down by David to a large extent, except that it was expanded to care for growing needs in a more effective manner. His cabinet included a chief of district governors (Azariah), two secretaries or scribes (Elihoreph and Ahijah), a recorder (Jehoshaphat), a commander of the army (Benaiah), four priests (Zadok, Abiathar, Azariah, and Zabud), a steward of his royal palace (Ahishar), and a taskmaster over his forced labor gangs (Adoniram; cf. 1 Kings 4:2-6). Solomon divided his empire into twelve districts, each under an officer or prefect (4:7-19). Each district was responsible for providing food for the royal table, feed for the king's livestock, and manual labor for his building projects (4:22-28; 5:13-18;

2 Chron. 2:17-18). The forced labor inaugurated by David and continued by Solomon later proved to be a major cause for the renewed division between North and South Israel after Solomon's death (1 Kings 12:18). Solomon's building projects in Jerusalem included his own palace (7:1-8) with its great ivory throne (10:18-20), a house for Pharaoh's daughter (7:8; 9:24), and the Millo (apparently a stronghold or fortification of some sort—9:15, 24; 11:27).

Solomon also fortified strategic cities throughout his empire in order to protect Israel from possible invasions. In excavations between 1925 and 1939 at Megiddo, archeologists unearthed paved stables, complete with mangers and pillars for tying horses, some of which were undoubtedly built by Solomon (1 Kings 9:15, 19; 10:26), as well as impressive fortifications. Similar stalls and fortresses have been found at Gezer, Taanach, Tell el-Hesi, and perhaps Hazor. Excavators found a well-built governor's palace in Megiddo, which at one time may have been inhabited by Baana, Solomon's prefect in that district (4:12). In digs at the modern Tell el-Khaleifeh between 1938 and 1940, N. Glueck found what he claimed to be a great refinery at Ezion-geber built by Solomon, equipped with holes or flues ingeniously arranged so as to utilize the winds that generally blew from the north and northwest to fan the flames necessary for smelting large quantities of copper and iron. However, more recent work by B. Rothenberg suggests that Ezion-geber may have been located about three miles south of Tell el-Khaleifeh, that what Glueck had thought to be a refinery was actually a storehouse or granary, and that the holes were not flues but places where large, wooden beams were inserted to support the floor and ceiling. In 1965, Glueck himself admitted that he had been wrong on these identifications. Of course, Ezion-geber was an important industrial and trading center at the head of the Gulf of Aqabah during Solomon's reign (1 Kings 9:26-28; 2 Chron. 8:17-18).

Solomon had far-reaching international visions for Israel. Many of his marriages were political, designed to weld Israel into strong military and economic alliances with foreign nations. He married the daughter of the Pharaoh, who gave him the city of Gezer as a dowry for his daughter (1 Kings 3:1; 9:16). He had a treaty with Hiram the king of Tyre (in Phoenicia) to receive from him materials for his building programs and to trade with other nations (5:1-12; 9:10-14, 26-28; 10:11-12). Solomon's fleet of ships from Tarshish frequently made a round-trip cruise to Ophir, which is probably located on the east coast of Africa, and traded Israel's goods for gold, silver, ivory, apes, and peacocks (9:26-28; 10:11-12, 22; cf. 2 Chron. 9:21. [There is a technical textual problem in some of these passages as to whether Solomon's ships went to Tarshish in Spain or to Ophir in Africa on ships of Tarshish. Because of the products traded, the latter seems to be the case]). He was also engaged in extensive trading with Egypt for horses and chariots (1 Kings 10:28-29).

Solomon's Inconsistent Religion and Its Consequences

Solomon promoted numerous religious activities in Israel that were upbuilding to the people and were destined to have a strong impact on future generations. He erected the temple as the center of Israelite worship (1 Kings 6–7). Archeological discoveries in Ugarit, Qatna, Tainat, and Megiddo show that the pattern of the Solomonic temple is very similar to that of contemporary Syrian temples, although some of the temple decorations are closer to Assyrian and Egyptian parallels. Of course, Solomon knew that God did not dwell in temples made by men's hands (8:27-30), and he certainly did not build the temple to leave such an impression. His primary purposes in building it were to provide a dwelling place for the ark, which was the symbol of God's presence with his people (8:1-21), and to assure the people that when they sinned God would forgive them when they turned to him (8:28-61). Solomon offered animal sacrifices as a manifestation of his love for and loyalty to Yahweh (3:15; 8:62-66). His wisdom was known far and wide. At Gibeon he asked God for an understanding mind to govern the people (3:5-14). His wisdom surpassed the wisdom of all the people of the East and of Egypt, and he uttered many proverbs and songs

(4:29-34). Rulers and peoples from many lands came to Solomon to hear his wisdom, including the Queen of Sheba (10:1-10, 23-25).

But Solomon also adopted and promoted foreign elements in conjunction with Israelite worship. Such a merging is called syncretism. He sacrificed on the Canaanite high places in the land (1 Kings 3:2-4). He married many foreign women (many of his marriages were politically oriented) and built high places for their gods (11:1-4). Out of deference to his wives, he worshiped and sacrificed to such gods as Ashtoreth, the goddess of the Sidonians; Milcom or Molech, the god of the Ammonites; and Chemosh, the god of the Moabites (11:5-8, 33; cf. Neh. 13:23-27).

Because of Solomon's idolatry, God raised up three adversaries against him toward the end of his reign: Hadad the Edomite (1 Kings 11:14-22); Rezon of Zobah, who ruled Syria (11:23-25); and Jeroboam I, an Israelite from the tribe of Ephraim (11:26-28). The prophet Ahijah came to Jeroboam I and performed a symbolic act to indicate what was to happen after Solomon's death. Ahijah tore his own new garment into twelve pieces and gave ten pieces to Jeroboam I, symbolizing that he would rule the ten North Israelite tribes, leaving only one tribe to the Davidic dynasty, viz., the tribe of Judah (11:29-40). First Kings 12-14 tells the tragic story of the new division between North and South Israel after Solomon's death, with Jeroboam I ruling the ten northern tribes and Solomon's son Rehoboam ruling Judah in Jerusalem.

BIBLIOGRAPHY

For further details on specific points, the responsible student should consult a good Bible dictionary, such as:

The Interpreter's Dictionary of the Bible, G.A. Buttrick, ed., 4 vols. Nashville: Abingdon Press, 1962.

McKenzie, John L., S.J. *Dictionary of the Bible.* New York: The Bruce Publishing Company, 1965.

In addition, a few standard works dealing with OT history may be listed:

Albright, W.F. *From the Stone Age to Christianity.* 2nd edition. Garden City, N.Y.: Doubleday, 1957.

Bright, John. *A History of Israel.* 2nd edition. Philadelphia: The Westminster Press, 1972.

Huesman, J.E. *The World of Moses*. Englewood Cliffs, N.J.: Prentice-Hall, Inc., 1966.

Hunt, I. *The World of the Patriarchs*. Englewood Cliffs, N.J.: Prentice-Hall, Inc., 1966.

Maly, E.H. *The World of David and Solomon*. Englewood Cliffs, N.J.: Prentice-Hall, Inc., 1966.

McKenzie, J.L. *The World of the Judges*. Englewood Cliffs, N.J.: Prentice-Hall, Inc., 1966.

Mendenhall, G.E. *The Tenth Generation*. Baltimore: The Johns Hopkins University Press, 1973.

Noth, Martin. *The History of Israel*. 2nd edition. London: A.&C. Black, 1965.

Parrot, A. *Abraham and His Times*. Translated by J.H. Farley. Philadelphia: Fortress Press, 1968.

Wright, G.E., and F.V. Filson. *The Westminster Historical Atlas to the Bible*. Revision edition. Philadelphia: The Westminster Press, 1956.

V

History of
Old Testament Times, Part II

FROM JEROBOAM I AND REHOBOAM
THROUGH SIMON MACCABEUS

F. Furman Kearley

The history of Israel and of the OT times which is under consideration in this chapter is quite extensive and considerably involved. First, it covers a period of approximately eight hundred years, from 930 B.C. until about 135 B.C. This eight hundred years is filled with many leading persons, important events, and complex problems. Many transitions of power take place in the Middle East and among the Hebrews during this period. The sources which tell about this era are quite extensive and also varied in nature. There are the historical sources, which include 1 and 2 Kings, 1 and 2 Chronicles, Ezra, Nehemiah, and Esther. Further, the prophetic literature was all composed during this time and reflects much historical, social, and religious information concerning the people and the nations.

One of the most complex problems concerns the chronology of events, especially of the divided kingdom period. History and chronology are inseparably connected because there cannot be accurate history without an accurate placing of persons and events in the proper sequence. The chronological problems are too involved to be treated in this brief study. (For a more detailed study of these problems cf. Edwin R. Thiele, *The Mysterious Numbers of the Hebrew Kings* [Grand Rapids: Wm. B. Eerdmans Publishing Co.]. The author has adopted, with some modifications, the dates settled upon by Thiele.)

The OT times under consideration in this study may be logically divided into at least six distinct periods:

    I. The divided kingdom, 930–722 B.C.
    II. The monarchy of Judah, 722–586 B.C.
    III. The Babylonian captivity, 586–539 B.C.
    IV. Restoration and resettlement under the Persians, 539–333 B.C.
    V. The Hellenistic period, 333–165 B.C.
    VI. The Maccabean period, 165–135 B.C.

THE DIVIDED KINGDOM (930–722 B.C.)

Background of the Division

Throughout its history as a nation, Israel had been plagued by divisions. In the wilderness Moses had to contend with those of other tribes such as Korah, Dathan, and Abiram, who were jealous of his authority (Num. 16–17). During the time of Joshua the tribes of the sons of Joseph, Ephraim and Manasseh, complained about the division of the land and were ambitious for more territory (Josh. 17:14-18). The period of the judges reflects an increase in division among the tribes. The men of Ephraim "did chide sharply" with Gideon, who was of the tribe of Manasseh (Judg. 8:1, KJV). There was violent combat between Abimelech and the men of Shechem (Judg. 9:22-57). Civil war took place between Jephthah and the men of Ephraim, during which the famous password "Shibboleth" came into existence (Judg. 12:1-6). An extensive civil war took place between the tribe of Benjamin and the rest of the tribes, which almost resulted in the annihilation of the tribe of Benjamin (Judg. 19–21).

Unity, to some extent, was achieved under Saul during the early part of his reign. However, when he grew hostile to David and forced him to flee, a division arose between Judah and Israel. This division was quite apparent during the early years after Saul's death. David reigned for seven and one-half years over the house of Judah while Ishbosheth, a son of Saul, was king over Israel. Second Samuel 3:1 states, "There was a long war between the house of Saul and the house of David; and David grew stronger and stronger, while the house of Saul became weaker and weaker." During the middle part of David's reign he was considerably successful in uniting all the people of Israel into the united kingdom. However, his rebellious son, Absalom, stole the hearts of the men of Israel and led a rebellion which forced David out of Jerusalem and resulted in a great battle which culminated in the death of Absalom. When David returned to Jerusalem, a dispute arose between Israel and Judah, which clearly indicates that a basic division was present between them even at a time of comparative unity (2 Sam. 19:40-43).

In David's final years he united and solidified the kingdom and attempted to pass it on to Solomon in this fashion. However, the smooth transition of power into Solomon's hands was marred by the unsuccessful attempt of David's son, Adonijah, to usurp the throne. After Solomon gained the throne and punished those responsible for the usurpation, he proceeded with the blessings of God to unify and expand the kingdom. Under him the Hebrew nation reached its golden age, when it had its greatest unity, geographical extent, and political impact on the Near East. Solomon's hard driving and ambitious policies created enemies, and his sins in loving many foreign women and in building high places for his wives' pagan gods alienated God's blessings from him and his posterity.

God made use of one of Solomon's adversaries, Jeroboam, the son of Nebat. God sent the prophet Ahijah to inform Jeroboam that he would rend the kingdom out of the hand of Solomon and give Jeroboam ten tribes (1 Kings 11:26-40). God promised to leave the tribe of Judah to the descendants of Solomon for David's sake. Solomon sought to kill Jeroboam, but Jeroboam fled to Egypt.

After Solomon's death, Rehoboam, his son, reigned in his

stead. Jeroboam, who had been a labor force leader for the house of Joseph, returned from Egypt and came with all the assembly of Israel and requested Rehoboam to reduce the heavy taxes and labor service which had been required under Solomon. Rehoboam, rejecting the wise counsel of the old men and following the foolish counsel of the younger men, threatened to make their burdens heavier. First Kings 12:15 says that this was brought about by Jehovah that he might establish his word which he spoke by Ahijah. Upon hearing Rehoboam's threat, the men of Israel said, "What portion have we in David? We have no inheritance in the son of Jesse. To your tents, O Israel! Look now to your own house, David" (1 Kings 12:16). Rehoboam attempted to gather an army to prevent the secession of the northern kingdom, but God forbade him to do so by his prophet Shemaiah. Thus the kingdom was divided into two kingdoms never to be reunited as an earthly kingdom under a monarch of the house of David.

Jeroboam's Apostasy

God had promised Jeroboam, when he indicated that he would give him the kingdom:

> If you will hearken to all that I command you, and will walk in my ways, and do what is right in my eyes by keeping my statutes and my commandments, as David my servant did, I will be with you, and will build you a sure house, as I built for David, and I will give Israel to you.
>
> 1 Kings 11:38

However, Jeroboam refused to walk in God's commandments. He reasoned that if the people continued to sacrifice at Jerusalem they would turn again unto Rehoboam. Therefore, he led North Israel in committing four basic apostasies. First, he changed the object of worship from the Lord Jehovah, who had commanded that no graven images should be made, and commanded the people to look upon two calves of gold, which he made as their gods. Second, he changed the place of worship from Jerusalem, where the Lord had caused his name to dwell, and urged the people to worship in Bethel and Dan, where he placed the golden calves. Third, he expelled the Levites from priestly service and made priests from among all the people that were not of the sons of Levi. Fourth, he changed the time of worship from the three annual occasions when all men were to gather at the place where God caused his name to dwell and instead ordained a feast in the eighth month on the fifteenth day of the month.

Jeroboam continued in his sinful ways for the rest of the twenty-two years which he reigned. God indicated that he would give Israel up "because of the sins of Jeroboam, which he sinned and which he made Israel to sin" (1 Kings 14:16). This phrase became Jeroboam's epitaph and the epithet which was attached to nearly every king of Israel that followed him. It is said of nearly every one of the kings of Israel that he walked in the sins of Jeroboam which he sinned and which he made Israel to sin. It is no wonder that eventually it became necessary for God to destroy the northern kingdom and send them into Assyrian captivity.

Synchronistic History of the Two Kingdoms

The southern kingdom of Judah and the northern kingdom of Israel thus existed side by side for approximately 208 years (930–722 B.C.). Sometimes they warred against each other. On other occasions they were indifferent toward each other and concerned with internal matters or affairs with other nations. On a few occasions they were allied against a common foe. The main source of information about the northern kingdom and the interrelationship of the two kingdoms is the synchronistic history recorded in 1 Kings 12–22 and 2 Kings 1–25. Some information is reflected about the period from Joel, Jonah, Amos, Micah, Hosea, and Isaiah. The books of Kings are a synchronistic record which attempts to relate the history of Israel and Judah alternately, covering the same general period. The subject matter constantly shifts back and forth from Judah to Israel and from Israel to Judah. This synchronistic record attempts to tie the history of the two kingdoms together by indicating the year of the king of Judah when a king of Israel began to reign, and vice versa. Due to the nature of a synchronistic history, the books of Kings are somewhat complicated to follow and outline. A general outline which may be helpful follows:

1 Kings 12–14	The acts of Rehoboam of Judah and Jeroboam of Israel.
1 Kings 15–16	The acts of Abijah (Abijam) and Asa, kings of Judah; and Nadab, Baasha, Elah, Zimri, Tibni, Omri, kings of Israel.
1 Kings 17–22	The acts of Ahab, the king of Israel; the acts of Elijah, the prophet of God, and partially of Jehoshaphat, king of Judah.
2 Kings 1–8	The acts of Ahaziah and Jehoram, kings of Israel; Jehoshaphat, Jehoram, and Ahaziah, kings of Judah; and some of the acts of Elisha, the prophet.
2 Kings 9–14	The acts of the dynasty of Jehu including his sons Jehoahaz, Jehoash, Jeroboam II of Israel; and the acts of Athaliah, Joash, and Amaziah of Judah.
2 Kings 15–17	The acts of Uzziah (Azariah), Jotham and Ahaz of Judah; and Zechariah, Shallum, Menahem, Pekahiah, Pekah, Hoshea, of Israel, and the fall of Samaria (722 B.C.).
2 Kings 18–20	The acts of Hezekiah, king of Judah.
2 Kings 21	The acts of Manasseh and Amon, kings of Judah.
2 Kings 22–23	The acts of Josiah and Jehoahaz, kings of Judah.
2 Kings 24–25	The acts of Jehoiakim, Jehoiachin, and Zedekiah, kings of Judah; and the fall of Jerusalem (586 B.C.).

Second Chronicles 10–36 gives the history of Judah alone, both during the divided kingdom (930–722 B.C.) and the time of the monarchy of Judah (722–586 B.C.). The northern kingdom, Israel, is only mentioned occasionally when there is a direct contact between the two kingdoms. Consequently, the book of 2 Chronicles is easily outlined according to the reigns of the respective kings of Judah. These kings are the direct descendants of the house of David and of course are therefore in the direct ancestral line of Christ. A brief outline of 2 Chronicles and the kings of Judah follows:

2 Chronicles 10–12   Reign of Rehoboam (930–913 B.C.)

2 Chronicles 13   Reign of Abijah (913–910 B.C.)

2 Chronicles 14–16   Reign of Asa (910–869 B.C.)

2 Chronicles 17–20   Reign of Jehoshaphat (869–848 B.C.)

2 Chronicles 21   Reign of Jehoram (848–841 B.C.)

2 Chronicles 22   Reign of Ahaziah and the usurpation of his mother, Athaliah (841–835 B.C.)

2 Chronicles 23–24   Reign of Joash (835–796 B.C.)

2 Chronicles 25   Reign of Amaziah (796–767 B.C.)

2 Chronicles 26   Reign of Uzziah (Azariah) (767–739 B.C.)

2 Chronicles 27   Reign of Jotham (739–731 B.C.)

2 Chronicles 28   Reign of Ahaz (731–715 B.C.)

2 Chronicles 29–32   Reign of Hezekiah (727–699 or 715–686 B.C.)

2 Chronicles 33   Reign of Manasseh and Amon (698–642 or 686–642 B.C.)

2 Chronicles 34–35   Reign of Josiah (640–609 B.C.)

2 Chronicles 36   Reign of Jehoahaz (609 B.C.), Jehoiakim (609–598 B.C.), Jehoiachin (598–597 B.C.), and Zedekiah (597–586 B.C.)

Judah during the Divided Kingdom

The kingdom of Judah, for its entire existence, was under the leadership of only one dynasty, the house of David. Most of these descendants of David, however, did not follow the Lord with all their heart but sinned and led their people into sin. Since the inspired record centers the history of the kingdoms around their kings, the best way to summarize the highlights of the period is to summarize the reign of the king.

Rehoboam, 930–913 B.C. This son of Solomon reigned seventeen years. His foolish decision to increase the burdens of the people led to the division of the kingdom. After having been forbidden by God to fight against the northern tribes, Rehoboam proceeded to build the defenses of Judah. He fortified many strongholds and placed provisions, weapons, and soldiers in them. As a result of Jeroboam's changing the priesthood, many of the priests and Levites who were in the northern kingdom came to Judah and Jerusalem and became a part of the southern kingdom. However, Rehoboam also forsook the law of Jehovah and did that which was evil because he did not set his heart to seek the Lord. He allowed the people of Judah to build high places for pagan worship practices and he also allowed the Sodomites to continue in the land. Because of the sins of Rehoboam and of Judah, God sent against them Shishak, the king of Egypt, who took away the treasures of the house of the Lord and of the king's house. Shishak or Sheshonk I has left an inscription at Karnak which confirms his raid into Judah and the extracting of tribute from the land (See James B. Pritchard, *Ancient Near Eastern Texts,* pp. 263-64). Rehoboam humbled himself, and the Lord turned his wrath and did not completely destroy him. However, there was continual war between Rehoboam and Jeroboam throughout his reign (1 Kings 12–14; 2 Chron. 10–14).

Abijam or Abijah, 913–910 B.C. Abijam or Abijah succeeded Rehoboam. He reigned only three years. War continued between Jeroboam and him, with Abijah prevailing because Judah relied upon the Lord. However, on the whole, he walked in the sins of his father and his heart was not perfect with Jehovah (1 Kings 14:31–15:8; 2 Chron. 13:1-22).

Asa, 910–869 B.C. Abijah's son Asa became the third king of Judah. He came to the throne in the twentieth year of Jeroboam and reigned forty-one years over Judah. Asa is the first of four righteous, reformer kings who reigned over Judah. He "did what was right in the eyes of the Lord" (1 Kings 15:11). He removed the altars and the high places and ordered Judah to seek the Lord and to keep the law. He attempted to eradicate pagan worship in Judah. He also built fortified cities and strengthened the army. The Lord blessed him with peace and prosperity at the beginning of his reign. Later he engaged in war with the Ethiopian army and was victorious due to a prayer of reliance on God. After a further warning from the prophet of God, Asa put into effect even greater reforms. He put the Sodomites out of the land and removed all the idols and abominations. The Scripture says, ". . . the heart of Asa was perfect all his days" (2 Chron. 15:17). His reform included not only Judah and Benjamin but those that sojourned with them from Ephraim, Manasseh, and Simeon and all who desired to seek the Lord. Toward the end of Asa's reign there was war between Judah and the northern kingdom with Baasha as their king. Asa obtained the assistance of Benhadad, the king of Syria, against Baasha. For this he was rebuked by Hanani, the seer. The end of Asa's reign was marred by his reliance upon Syria and physicians, instead of upon the Lord, and by his putting Hanani in the prison house (1 Kings 15:8-24; 2 Chronicles 14–16).

Jehoshaphat, 869–848 B.C. After Asa's death Jehoshaphat ascended the throne as the fourth king of Judah. He was contemporary with the wicked king of Israel Ahab, beginning his reign in the fourth year of Ahab. Thiele proposes that he was coregent with Asa for about four years. Jehoshaphat was also a righteous and good king. He removed the remnant of the Sodomites. He sent circuit teachers with the book of the law throughout all the cities of Judah to teach the people. The Lord caused the nations to respect him and gave him peace. The Philistines and Arabians brought him tribute.

Jehoshaphat's great mistake was to make peace with the king of Israel and to confirm this by taking Ahab and Jezebel's daughter, Athaliah, as a wife for his son, Jehoram. The sins of Ahab, Jezebel, and their daughter Athaliah brought much grief to the kingdoms of Israel and Judah in later years. Due to this alliance with Ahab, Jehoshaphat later joined him in battle against Syria. The Lord was against this battle, as indicated by the prophet Micaiah, and it resulted in death for Ahab and in defeat for Jehoshaphat. The prophet Jehu rebuked Jehoshaphat for helping the wicked Ahab and loving those that hate the Lord. Following this, Jehoshaphat returned to his reforms, going to the people from Beersheba to the hill country of Ephraim and bringing them back to the Lord. He set judges in the land and warned them to judge according to the standard of the Lord. At the end of his reign, because of his reliance upon the Lord and his prayer for the Lord's help against the Moabites and the Ammonites, the Lord gave him victory over these enemies. Jehoshaphat continued his alliance with the house of Ahab by assisting Jehoram, king of Israel, in an expedition against the Moabites and their king, Mesha. They were successful in subduing the Moabites this time, but later Mesha successfully rebelled against Israel and erected the Moabite Stone to tell of his success. (See Pritchard, *Ancient Near Eastern Texts,* pp. 320-21.) Evidently, in his last years his own son, Jehoram, joined him as coregent (1 Kings 22:41-50; 2 Kings 3; 2 Chron. 17–20).

Jehoram, 848–841 B.C. Judah's fifth king, Jehoram, the son of Jehoshaphat, married Athaliah, the daughter of Ahab and Jezebel of the northern kingdom. Unfortunately, he walked in the ways of the kings of Israel, as did the house of Ahab because he had the daughter of Ahab as his wife. He made high places in the mountains of Judah and caused the people of his kingdom to commit spiritual adultery. The subject kingdoms of Edom and Libnah successfully revolted against him. During his reign, and because of his sins, the Philistines, the Arabians, and the Ethiopians raided Judah and carried away the substance of the king's house, along with his sons and his wives. A written message came to Jehoram from Elijah rebuking him for his sins and pronouncing his death by means of a disease of the bowels (2 Kings 8:16-24; 2 Chron. 21).

Ahaziah, 841 B.C. The son of the wicked Athaliah, Ahaziah, reigned only one year as the sixth king of Judah. He also was an unrighteous king who walked in the way of the house of Ahab, his grandfather. Second Chronicles 22:3

affirms, "his mother was his counselor in doing wickedly." He continued in alliance with his uncle Jehoram, king of Israel, and went to war with him against Hazael, king of Syria. His death came through the providential working of God to fulfill the prophecies he had made through Elijah against the house of Ahab. Ahaziah went to visit Jehoram, king of Israel and son of Ahab, because he was sick. It was at this time that God raised up Jehu to annihilate the dynasty of Omri and Ahab and to become king of Israel. Conveniently, Jehoram and Ahaziah were together at Jezreel when Jehu came. Jehu smote both kings at the same time and proceeded to destroy all of the house of Ahab (2 Kings 8:24–9:29; 2 Chron. 22:1-9).

Athaliah, 841–835 B.C. When Athaliah, the wicked daughter of Ahab and Jezebel, saw that her son Ahaziah had been killed, she destroyed all the seed royal and usurped the throne of Judah. It may be recalled that Athaliah's husband had been Jehoram, king of Judah. Again through God's providence Jehosheba, daughter of King Jehoram and wife of Jehoiada the priest, hid Joash, the son of Ahaziah, so he would not be slain (2 Kings 11:1-3; 2 Chron. 22:10-12).

Joash, 835–796 B.C. Jehoiada and his wife hid Joash (or Jehoash) securely for six years. When the lad was seven years old, Jehoiada, with the assistance of captains, nobles, and the people in general, broke down the house of Baal, slew Athaliah, and made Joash king. During his minority and while Jehoiada was priest and his instructor, he did what was right. A reform was instituted and the breaches of the house of the Lord were repaired. However, after the death of Jehoiada, Joash forsook the house of the Lord and served idols. He would not listen to the prophets of God. He forgot the kindness of Jehoiada and consented to the stoning of his son Zechariah. Because of his sins, the Lord allowed the army of the Syrians to sack Judah. They left Joash severely wounded, whereupon his servants conspired against him and slew him on his bed (2 Kings 11:4–12:21; 2 Chron. 23–24).

Amaziah, 796–767 B.C. Amaziah, who succeeded his father Joash, is described as doing right, but not with a perfect heart. He slew those who had assassinated his father. Amaziah organized an expedition against Edom and hired mercenaries from Israel to assist him. However, a man of God rebuked him for aligning himself with Israel, and he forfeited a hundred talents of silver to the mercenaries rather than go against the prophet and the Lord. He recognized, as the prophet said, that "the Lord is able to give you much more than this" (2 Chron. 25:9). He had a successful campaign against the Edomites. He sinned, however, in bringing back the gods of Seir, setting them up to be his gods, and rejecting the counsel of God's prophet. He challenged Jehoash, king of Israel, to battle but was defeated, and Jehoash broke down the wall of Jerusalem and carried away treasures and hostages. Amaziah's end came when a conspiracy was made against him and he was slain at Lachish (2 Kings 14:1-20; 2 Chron. 25).

Azariah or Uzziah, 767-739 B.C. In the twenty-seventh year of the reign of Jeroboam II, king of Israel, the people of Judah made Azariah king in the place of his father, Amaziah. Thiele postulates that Azariah had a coregency with his father from 791 to 767 B.C. His character description credits him with doing what was right and setting himself to seek God. Because of this, God made him prosper. He engaged in war with the Philistines and the Arabians and received tribute from the Ammonites. He fortified Jerusalem and made engines to shoot arrows and stones. He built a great army and expanded the southern kingdom to the greatest extent that it had been since the time of Solomon. However, he sinned by burning incense upon the altar of incense and became a leper (2 Kings 14:21-15:7; 2 Chron. 26).

Jotham, 739-731 B.C. It is possible that Jotham was co-regent with his father Azariah during his leprous years, 750-739 B.C. Generally, Jotham did good. However, the high places were not removed. He engaged in building and fortifying activities and defeated the children of Ammon, exacting tribute from them. The Syro-Ephraimitic War seems to have begun while Jotham was still reigning, for the Lord sent Rezin, king of Syria, and Pekah, king of Israel, against Judah in Jotham's days (2 Kings 15:37-38; 2 Chron. 27:1-9).

Ahaz, 731–715 B.C. Ahaz, the twelfth king of Judah, reigned alone sixteen years, after a coregency with his father, Jotham, 735–731 B.C. Ahaz displeased God and walked in the ways of the kings of Israel, engaging in child sacrifice and idol worship. Rezin, king of Syria, and Pekah, king of Israel, warred against him with the intent of placing the son of Tabeel on the throne in his stead (Isa. 7:1-9). They killed many in Judah and carried a great multitude captive. In order to retain his throne, Ahaz became tributary to Tiglath-pileser III, king of Assyria. In response, Tiglath-pileser III came against Syria and Israel, captured Damascus and a number of cities of Galilee, and carried many captive to Assyria. Ahaz had a pagan altar built in Jerusalem and offered sacrifices upon it. Isaiah had an encounter with Ahaz concerning the outcome of the Syro-Ephraimitic War and prophesied the destruction of these two kingdoms (2 Kings 15:38–16:20; 2 Chron. 28).

Hezekiah, 727–698 or 715–686 B.C. Hezekiah was the last king of Judah during the divided kingdom. In the fourth year of his reign, Shalmaneser V, king of Assyria, besieged Samaria. In his sixth year, or 722 B.C., Samaria fell, and the northern kingdom was carried into captivity and ceased to exist as a kingdom. More will be said of Hezekiah, but the fall of Samaria brings to an end the period of the divided kingdom.

Israel during the Divided Kingdom

Unlike the southern kingdom of Judah, which was ruled by only one dynasty, the dynasty of David, the northern kingdom, Israel, had frequent changes in dynasties. Also, whereas Judah did have some good kings who served as righteous reformers, the northern kingdom was without any kings who did right in the eyes of the Lord. It is said of nearly every king of the northern kingdom that he followed in the sins of Jeroboam and the ways in which he caused Israel to sin.

The dynasty of Jeroboam I. This dynasty consisted of the reign of Jeroboam I, 930–909 B.C., and his son Nadab, 909–908 B.C. As noted above, Jeroboam I led the rebellion against Rehoboam. God established him as king, but Jeroboam I turned and sinned grievously against God, leading his kingdom into apostasy. Because of his sins God indicated he would sweep away the house of Jeroboam I. Nadab, his son, came to the throne but reigned only two years and "walked in the way of his father, and in his sin which he made Israel to sin" (1 Kings 15:26). Baasha conspired against him and assassinated him. He then fulfilled God's promise against the house of Jeroboam I by killing all of the house of Jeroboam.

The dynasty of Baasha. God exalted Baasha to punish the house of Jeroboam and allowed him to reign twenty-four years (908–885 B.C.). However, Baasha also proved wicked and walked in the way of Jeroboam I to provoke the Lord to anger. He engaged in war against King Asa of Judah but was unsuccessful. Because of his sins God decreed that he would make his house like the house of Jeroboam I. He was succeeded by his son, Elah, for two years (885–884 B.C.). Zimri, the captain of half his chariots, conspired against him and killed him.

Period of civil strife. Zimri was able to assume power for only seven days. He completely destroyed the house of Baasha, fulfilling God's plan. When the people heard of the assassination of Elah, they made Omri, who was serving as the captain of the hosts, king over Israel. He besieged Zimri in Tirzah and took the city, whereupon Zimri burned down the king's house. About the same time another segment of the people exalted Tibni and followed him as king. For a period of four years (884–880 B.C.) the northern kingdom was divided between these two. However the people who followed Omri prevailed over Tibni and his followers, and Omri became the sole ruler for eight years (880–873 B.C.).

The dynasty of Omri. Omri bought the hill Samaria and built the city here. Scripture does not give much information about his reign. However, he did establish a dynasty that consisted of the reigns of himself, his son, Ahab (twenty-two years), his grandson, Ahaziah (two years), and his grandson, Jehoram (twelve years). He made an impression upon the Assyrians, for a number of times in the annals of the Assyrian kings they call the land of Israel *Bit Huumria* (Omri-land) well over a century after the death of Omri. Omri acted more wickedly than the kings before him and walked in the sins of Jeroboam I.

Omri's son, Ahab, succeeded him and reigned approximately 873–853 B.C. He was more sinful than any of the kings before him and probably after him. He married Jezebel, the daughter of Ethbaal, king of the Sidonians. Together they engaged in and promoted Baal worship extensively. The prophet Elijah was contemporary with them and opposed their sinful practices. Jezebel sought to kill Elijah, but God protected him. He confronted the prophets of Baal and slew 450 of them. When Jezebel treacherously killed Naboth so Ahab could take his vineyard, Elijah met Ahab at the vineyard and indicated that, as the dogs had licked the blood of Naboth, so they would lick Ahab's blood, and they would eat Jezebel. Ahab warred with Benhadad, king of Syria, on several occasions. However, about 854 B.C. when both kingdoms were threatened by Shalmaneser III, king of Assyria, they joined forces with ten other kings of the region to fight him at the battle of Qarqar (see Pritchard, *Ancient Near Eastern Texts,* pp. 278-79, and W. W. Hallo, "From Qarqar to Carchemish," *The Biblical Archaeologist* 23:2 [1960], 33-61). Though this battle is not mentioned in the Bible, it is most significant for biblical history. The Assyrian records indicate that it was in the sixth year of Shalmaneser III. The Black Obelisk of Shalmaneser III and other Assyrian records indicate that Jehu had become king of Israel and paid tribute to Shalmaneser III in the eighteenth year of Shalmaneser's reign, which evidently was the first year of Jehu's reign. Thus, since only the two-year reign of Ahaziah and the twelve-year reign of Jehoram (which together probably covered approximately twelve calendar years) came between Jehu and Ahab, the battle of Qarqar must have been about the last year of Ahab's reign. Thus, with the last year of Ahab's reign reckoned at about 853 B.C. and the first year of Jehu's reign at about 841 B.C., it is possible to arrive at the approximate dates of all the kings of Israel. Ahab continued his sinful ways in his last year by warring against Syria, rejecting the counsel of Micaiah, God's prophet, and putting him in prison. Ahab was slain in this battle, and the dogs licked his blood (1 Kings 16:29–22:40).

Ahab's son Ahaziah (853–852 B.C.) succeeded his father as king of Israel. He continued the sinful ways of his father, his mother, and Jeroboam I. He sent messengers to inquire of Beelzebub, the god of Ekron, concerning his sickness. After consuming two companies by calling down fire from heaven, the prophet Elijah accompanied the third company to Ahaziah, rebuked him for his sins, and prophesied his death.

Ahaziah's brother Jehoram succeeded him and reigned 852–841 B.C. The Scripture indicates that, while he was not as wicked as his father and mother, he continued in the sins of Jeroboam I. Many of the activities of the prophet Elisha seem to have occurred during his reign. Jehoram was contemporary with Jehoshaphat and Jehoram of Judah and continued the alliance that Ahab had made with Judah. His sister Athaliah was married to Jehoram of Judah. Therefore, he was joined by Jehoshaphat in a successful expedition against Mesha, king of the Moabites. At the close of his reign Ahaziah, Jehoram's nephew and the son of Jehoram and Athaliah, became king of Judah. They joined in battle against Hazael, king of Syria, at Ramoth-Gilead. In this battle Jehoram of Israel was wounded. While he was recuperating, Ahaziah came to visit him. At this time God (through the work of Elisha) raised up Jehu to fulfill his prophecies against the house of Ahab. Jehu was proclaimed king by the other officers of the army. He came to Jezreel, met Jehoram and Ahaziah, and slew them both. He proceeded to destroy the entire house of Ahab, thus bringing to an end the dynasty of Omri and Ahab in the northern kingdom and removing the king from the throne in Judah at the same time.

The dynasty of Jehu. Having annihilated the house of Ahab, Jehu reigned over Israel for twenty-eight years (841–813 B.C.). He had Jezebel thrown out a window, and she was trampled by the horses. He proceeded to entrap and destroy a multitude of Baal worshipers and to destroy Baal worship out of Israel. While he removed many of the sins of Ahab and Jezebel, he did not depart from the sins of Jeroboam I, but maintained the golden calves in Bethel and Dan. He did not walk in the law of the Lord, but because of his faithfulness in executing God's will against the house of Ahab, God promised to allow his sons to the fourth generation to sit on the throne of Israel. Jehu is the only king of the Hebrew people represented pictorially in extant material. He is pictured on the Black Obelisk of Shalmaneser III, bowing before Shalmaneser to present tribute, apparently during the first year of his reign (841 B.C.).

The reigning descendants of Jehu were Jehoahaz (813–798 B.C.), Jehoash (798–781 B.C.), Jeroboam II, perhaps a co-regent (792–781 B.C. and sole king 781–753 B.C.), and Zechariah, who ruled for less than a year about 752 B.C. It is said of each of these that he did evil and followed in the sins of Jeroboam I, the son of Nebat. The only one of these kings who was really significant is Jeroboam II. According to a prophecy made by Jonah, he extended the border of Israel from the entrance of Hamath unto the Sea of the Arabah (2 Kings 14:25). The book of Amos reflects that Israel was experiencing tremendous prosperity under the reign of Jeroboam II. The dynasty of Jehu came to an end when Shallum conspired against Zechariah, killed him, and reigned in his place, thus fulfilling the word of the Lord that the sons of Jehu to the fourth generation would sit upon the throne of Israel.

The final period of anarchy. Shallum could maintain the throne for only the space of a month during 752 B.C. Menahem killed him and assumed the throne. Menahem reigned from 752–742 B.C. Pekahiah, his son, replaced him and reigned for two years (741–739 B.C.). There is a chronological difficulty in the dating of Pekah's reign. Thiele postulates that there was a division in the northern kingdom at this time and that Pekah exercised a rival reign in Gilead east of the Jordan, beginning the same year that Menahem assumed the throne in Samaria. Other theories have been proposed (see Thiele, *The Mysterious Numbers of the*

Hebrew Kings, pp. 122ff.). If this is the case, he would have been in contention for kingship 752–739 B.C. and would have exercised complete kingship 739–731 B.C. Pekah, in league with Rezin of Syria, attempted to fight against Ahaz of Judah. However, Ahaz secured the aid of Tiglath-pileser III, king of Assyria, who took many Syrians and Israelites of the region of Galilee into captivity. The last king of Israel, Hoshea (731–722 B.C.), was placed on the throne of Israel by Tiglath-pileser III according to his annals. (See Pritchard, *Ancient Near Eastern Texts,* pp. 283-84.) Shalmaneser V found Hoshea conspiring with So (Siwa), king of Egypt. He besieged Samaria for three years. Samaria fell in 722 B.C. to the Assyrians, who were now led by Sargon II. Many of Israel were carried captive and transported into cities of Assyria. Thus the sinful ways of Jeroboam I, the son of Nebat, which were imitated by every king of Israel, finally resulted in the destruction of the northern kingdom.

The Prophets and the Divided Kingdom

The prophetic movement had been developing among the Hebrew people at least since the time of the judges. During the divided kingdom the prophets came to be more and more significant in the history and literature of the Hebrews. A number of prophets are mentioned who have left no written messages, except the part they may have played in recording the historical books. Ahijah the Shilonite guided Jeroboam I in rebelling against Rehoboam and condemned him when he sinned. Shemaiah commanded the authority to restrain Rehoboam from battle with Israel and to rebuke him for his sins. Iddo, Hanani, Jehu ben Hanani, and Azariah ben Obed all moved freely about the courts of the kings and performed their functions in an authoritative manner.

The two most prominent prophets were Elijah, who was contemporary with Ahab, and Elisha, his successor, who was contemporary with Jehoram and Jehu. Many stories are related of the outstanding exploits of these two prophets. They were held in high respect and exercised tremendous authority.

The prophets of the most enduring influence left written

accounts of their messages. The earliest one certainly known is Jonah, who preceded or was contemporary with Jeroboam II (2 Kings 14:25). (Some scholars date Joel earlier, but the book of Joel contains no specific date, and the evidence is indefinite.) The book of Jonah is not really prophetic in nature but is historical and biographical in that it tells of Jonah's mission to warn Nineveh of her forthcoming destruction and of Jonah's own reactions.

Next, the book of Amos specifically dates this prophet in the days of Uzziah, king of Judah, and in the days of Jeroboam, king of Israel (Amos 1:1). Amos was from Judah, but the Lord sent him to the northern kingdom to rebuke Israel for their sins. The prophet Hosea enjoyed a lengthy ministry, which began in the days of Jeroboam II, king of Israel, and Uzziah, king of Judah, and continued through the reigns of Jotham, Ahaz, and Hezekiah of Judah (Hos. 1:1). The message of Hosea is also directed to the northern kingdom. It compares their heinous sins with the repeated adultery of Hosea's wife, Gomer. The time of Isaiah's ministry was almost identical to Hosea's, beginning in the year that Uzziah died and continuing well into Hezekiah's reign, if not beyond (Isa. 1:1; 6:1). Isaiah served as a prophet in the court of the kings of Judah, rebuking sins on the one hand and prophesying hope and bright prospects on the other. The prophet Micah seems to have been a younger contemporary, since he dates his ministry in the days of Jotham, Ahaz, and Hezekiah. Micah uttered messages concerning things he saw about both Samaria and Jerusalem.

THE MONARCHY OF JUDAH (722-586 B.C.)

During the time of Tiglath-pileser III (745-727 B.C.), both Israel and Judah became tributary kingdoms to the Assyrians. Judah voluntarily became tributary when Ahaz paid tribute to Tiglath-pileser III so he would war against Pekah, king of Israel, and Rezin, king of Syria, who were making war in league against Judah. Israel became subject as a result of Tiglath-pileser III's victorious conquest of the land, which resulted in his placing Hoshea on the throne of Israel. When Hoshea and Israel conspired with Egypt against Assyria, Shalmaneser V began war against Israel. His successor, Sargon II, destroyed Samaria and carried many of the northern kingdom into captivity. (See Pritchard, *Ancient Near Eastern Texts,* pp. 284ff.) Thus the kingdom of Judah was left as the only Hebrew kingdom. Hezekiah was only in the fourth year of his reign when the siege of Samaria began, and the northern kingdom fell in the sixth year of his reign. The alliance between Judah and Assyria seems to have been in force, though the change in kingship, both in Assyria and in Judah, may have left many matters unclear.

Hezekiah and the Assyrians

Scholars differ widely on exactly when Hezekiah began his reign in Jerusalem. They are generally agreed that he reigned 727–698 B.C., 715–686 B.C., or somewhere in between. (See Thiele, *The Mysterious Numbers of the Hebrew Kings,* pp. 132ff.) At any rate, Hezekiah came to the throne about the time of the collapse of the northern kingdom. He departed drastically from the policies of Ahaz, his father, and started a major religious reform in Judah. He even extended this reform to the remnant of the northern kingdom and involved many of them in the renewed and refreshed worship of Jehovah. Naturally, this meant disposing of the idols and altars, which included the one his father, Ahaz, had erected after his alliance with Tiglath-pileser III of Assyria. This also signified that Hezekiah was rebelling against Assyria. The Assyrian King, Sargon II (722–705 B.C.), was busily engaged in quelling a rebellion in the Babylonian area, which was being led by Merodach-baladan II. Some of the facts seem to indicate that there was an agreement between Merodach-baladan II and Hezekiah to rebel simultaneously on opposite fronts of the Assyrian Empire. At any rate, Hezekiah was free to carry out his reforms in Judah for the early part of his reign because the Assyrians were busy fighting on their eastern front. However, Hezekiah anticipated eventual reprisals by the Assyrians and prepared for siege by building a tunnel to bring water into the city. In 701 B.C., Sennacherib, king of Assyria (704–681 B.C.), came against Judah. He claims in his annals that he laid siege to forty-six of the cities of Judah and to many small villages in their vicinity. He says that he shut up Hezekiah in Jerusalem like a bird in a cage. However, his annals do not claim ultimate victory, and the biblical record indicates that the Lord intervened through his angel and caused Sennacherib to flee from Judah. Hezekiah seems to have been able to reign fifteen more years after his sickness with peace, prosperity, and continued religious reforms.

The Wicked Manasseh

Wicked Manasseh reigned fifty-five years in Jerusalem 697–642 B.C. He completely reversed the reforms of his father, Hezekiah, and was more wicked than any of the other kings of Judah. He encouraged Baal worship and worshiped all the hosts of heaven. He practiced sorcery and enchantments and passed his children through the fire, as well as other sinful things. He is charged with shedding much innocent blood in the city, and the ultimate fall of Judah must be laid at his feet because of his sins and the innocent blood that he shed.

Manasseh also returned to a tributary relationship with Assyria under Sennacherib, Esarhaddon (680–669 B.C.), and Ashurbanipal (668–630 B.C.). Both Esarhaddon and Ashurbanipal recorded in their annals that Manasseh was forced to provide assistance in their Egyptian campaigns and to furnish building materials and labor for construction activities at Nineveh. Second Chronicles 33:11 mentions that Manasseh was placed in chains and carried to Babylon by the Assyrians. However, he was allowed to return to Jerusalem later and manifested some penitent attitude afterwards. But the wickedness he had encouraged was so prevalent among the people that no change was made in the sinful direction of the land.

Amon, his son, succeeded him for only two years (742–740 B.C.). He continued the evil ways of his father. His servants conspired against him and assassinated him.

The Reforms of Josiah

At this point God raised up king Josiah, of whom he had prophesied to Jeroboam I. Josiah was only eight years old when he began to reign, and he reigned thirty-one years in Jerusalem (640–609 B.C.). When he was sixteen years old, he began to seek after God. In the twelfth year of his reign he began to purge Judah and Jerusalem of the idolatrous images and worship places. He even carried his reform into the areas of Manasseh, Ephraim, Simeon, and Napthali in North Israel. In the eighteenth year of his reign he started repairing the house of the Lord. In the process of cleaning and repairing it, Hilkiah the high priest found the book of the law. He gave it to Shaphan the secretary, who read it and then brought it to King Josiah. After hearing it and checking with the prophetess Huldah, Josiah launched an extensive effort to keep the law contained in the book. He gathered the elders and the inhabitants of Judah and Jerusalem and read the contents of the book to them. They made a covenant to keep the commandments of the Lord. He intensified his efforts to purge the land of Baal worship and the worship of the hosts of heaven. He broke down the houses of the Sodomites. He fulfilled God's prophecy found in 1 Kings 13:1-3 by breaking down the altar that Jeroboam I had erected in Bethel. He caused the people to keep the Passover in a manner that had not been observed since the days of Samuel.

Josiah was, no doubt, aided and encouraged in his reform by the prophet Jeremiah. God raised up Jeremiah to be a prophet in the thirteenth year of the reign of Josiah. Thus for eighteen or nineteen years Jeremiah was busy preaching against the sins of the people and urging them to repent while Josiah was administering his kingdom and reform.

However, in spite of all the efforts of Josiah, Jeremiah, and other righteous men of the period, it seems that the reforms were only surface in nature. It was impossible for Josiah to legislate righteousness. For the most part, the hearts of the people of Judah and Jerusalem had not been changed from the ways they had learned under sinful Manasseh.

Therefore, when Josiah was killed at Megiddo in an attempt to keep Pharaoh-necho, king of Egypt, from assisting the Assyrians against the Babylonians, and was succeeded by his sons, they almost immediately forgot their father's reforms and returned to the wicked ways of the nation before him. Jeremiah, under the successors of Josiah, became a persecuted and hounded prophet who saw his nation die before his eyes in spite of his pleading and preaching with tears and many sacrifices for them to repent.

The Fall of Assyria and the Rise of Babylon

One of the reasons Josiah was able to carry out his reforms is that Assyria was in the process of being overthrown by Babylon during the same years that Josiah and Jeremiah were pushing reform in Judah. According to the Neo-Babylonian chronicles (see D. J. Wiseman, *Chronicles of the Chaldean Kings*), Nabopolasser ascended the throne of Babylon in 626 B.C., one or two years after Josiah began his reforms and Jeremiah was called to be a prophet. The Babylonians had forced the Assyrians to withdraw from there. For several years there were insignificant encounters between the Babylonians and the Assyrians, as Babylon was gaining in strength. In 615 B.C., the Babylonians were confident enough to besiege Asshur, a chief city of Assyria. In 614 the Babylonians were assisted independently by the Medes, who captured Asshur. In 612 the Babylonians besieged Nineveh and brought about its fall. The Assyrian king, Assur-uballit, assumed the rule of Assyria and set up his headquarters at Harran. In the meanwhile, the Babylonians, under Nabopolassar, continued to subdue various areas that had formerly been a part of the Assyrian Empire. In 610 B.C. the Babylonians with the Medes captured Harran. In 609 Assur-uballit was joined by Pharaoh-necho of Egypt in an attempt to retake Harran, but they were unsuccessful. Finally, Babylon gained undisputed control of the Fertile Crescent through a decisive victory over the Egyptians at the Battle of Carchemish in 605. This victory was led by the crown prince, Nebuchadnezzar II. While he was following up on this victory and conquering all of the Syrian-Palestinian area he received word that Nabopolassar had died, and he returned to Babylon to ascend the throne as the new king.

The Decline and Fall of Judah and Jerusalem

While Babylon was struggling to gain control of the Fertile Crescent against dying Assyria and the aspiring Egyptians, there developed in Judah two opposing parties in terms of their foreign policy with regard to these nations. In 609 B.C. Pharaoh-necho had killed Josiah, and the Jewish people placed his son Jehoahaz on the throne in Jerusalem for three months. Pharaoh-necho made Judah tributary to him, deposed Jehoahaz, and put Jehoiakim (608–598 B.C.) on the throne. Then, according to Daniel 1:1, in the third year of the reign of Jehoiakim, Nebuchadnezzar besieged Jerusalem, took part of the vessels of the house of God and certain fine young men of the seed royal and of the nobles, including Daniel, Hananiah, Mishael, and Azariah to Babylon for training and as hostages. The one party in Judah wanted to make alliance with Egypt, and the other wanted to submit to Babylon. Jeremiah was caught in the middle of this dilemma. He knew by revelation from God that the only way for Judah to survive was to submit to Babylon. However, the other party considered him a traitor when he urged such action.

The Egyptian party prevailed, and after serving Babylon three years Jehoiakim rebelled. Nebuchadnezzar II came again against Jerusalem and accomplished the second exile about 597 B.C., deporting Jehoiakim to Babylon. Jehoiakim's son Jehoiachin had been on the throne only three months and ten days when Nebuchadnezzar besieged Jerusalem. He took Jehoiachin, his mother, and others, including Ezekiel, into captivity.

Nebuchadnezzar II made Zedekiah, another son of Josiah, king in Jerusalem. He reigned for eleven years (597–586 BC.). He was extremely weak, and though he seemed to want to listen to Jeremiah, the Egyptian party prevailed over him and he rebelled against the king of Babylon. Therefore, Nebuchadnezzar II laid siege against Jerusalem in the ninth year of the reign of Zedekiah and continued until the eleventh year. Finally, the city was taken and destroyed, including the great temple. Many of the people were killed. Zedekiah's sons were slain before his eyes and then his eyes were put out. Jeremiah was given a choice of going to Babylon or staying in the land, and he chose to stay. Thus Judah was carried away captive because of her transgressions.

THE BABYLONIAN CAPTIVITY (586–539 B.C.)

The Length of the Captivity

One of the problems concerning the captivity or exile is its exact length. According to Jeremiah 25:10-14, the captivity would last seventy years. The writer of Chronicles indicates that Jeremiah's prophecy was fulfilled and that the land enjoyed seventy years of sabbath keeping (2 Chron. 36:20-23). However, the biblical sources do not indicate exactly when this period started and when it ended. At any rate, there are two seventy-year periods that quite adequately fulfill what may be called a seventy-year captivity. The first time that Nebuchadnezzar subjugated Judah and carried away some of the nobles was approximately 605 B.C., the fourth year of Jehoiakim when the prediction in Jeremiah 25 was given. It is not known exactly when Zerubbabel and Jeshua arrived in Palestine with the first Jews who returned under the edict of Cyrus, but it must have been about 536 or 535 B.C. This would give one possible seventy-year period for the captivity. Another way of calculating the captivity would be from the destruction of the temple until it was rebuilt. The temple was destroyed in 586 B.C., but due to various delays, even after many returned from captivity, it was not completed until the sixth year of the reign of Darius I, king of Persia, in 516 B.C. Either way, Jeremiah's prophecy of seventy years of captivity would be fulfilled.

The Captives of the Mesopotamian Area

Daniel and his friends. The book of Daniel provides the only direct source of information about these captives. Critics have attempted to undermine the historicity of the book of Daniel. However, much archeological evidence of recent years gives reason to have confidence in the history of Daniel. In the third year of Jehoiakim, Nebuchadnezzar II besieged Jerusalem. He carried back to Babylon part of the vessels of the house of God and certain of the finest young men from the seed royal and the nobles. This account from Daniel 1:1-7 agrees with other information from 2 Kings 24:1-7, Jeremiah 35:11, as well as the information obtained from the Babylonian chronicles and the Aramaic papyrus from Saqqarah. (See Charles F. Pfeiffer, *The Biblical World,* pp. 133-37.)

Among those carried away were Daniel, Hananiah or Shadrach, Mishael or Meshach, and Azariah or Abednego. According to Daniel 1, these purposed not to defile themselves with the king's dainties and his wine. They fared better on their diet of water and vegetables than those on the royal diet and were found to be superior to all the others. In the second year of Nebuchadnezzar II's reign, he had his dream concerning the golden image, which Daniel interpreted. As a result, Daniel and his friends received high appointments in the land. Chapter 3, however, tells of the severe trial by fire that Shadrach, Meshach, and Abednego had to face. Through God's blessings and their faith they overcame the fiery furnace and were promoted by Nebuchadnezzar II. Chapter 4 tells how Daniel interpreted another dream of Nebuchadnezzar II, which was fulfilled when the haughty king went temporarily mad, in order that God might humble him. After mentioning these four events under the reign of Nebuchadnezzar II, the history skips over all the intervening period of the captivity until the last year, 539 B.C. Chapter 5 tells of the feast of Belshazzar and the handwriting on the wall, which was interpreted by Daniel and came to pass that night. The rest of the book of Daniel concerns events and prophecies of Daniel under Persian rule.

Jehoiachin and the deportation. According to the Babylonian chronicles, in 601 B.C. Nebuchadnezzar fought against the Egyptian army of Pharaoh-necho II. This battle resulted in great losses to both armies and in virtual defeat for Babylon. Evidently this encouraged the Egyptian party of Judah to rebel against Babylon. For some time the Babylonians were busy elsewhere, but in 598/97 they came to hold Judah in account for the rebellion. About this time Jehoiakim died and Jehoiachin reigned for three months. Then Nebuchadnezzar captured Jerusalem and carried Jehoiachin, his mother, his servants, his princes, his officers, and others captive to Babylon. Second Kings 24:10-16 reports that this captivity included the chief men of the land, including the smiths and craftsmen. Only the poorest of the people were left in Judah. Nothing definite is known about these captives. After Jehoiachin had been in captivity thirty-seven years, Evil-merodach, king of Babylon, brought him out of prison and gave him a more exalted position. He provided him with finer garments and with a regular allowance for the rest of his life. This is confirmed by a clay tablet found near the Ishtar Gate of Babylon. The tablet, which dates from the reign of Nebuchadnezzar II, lists Jehoiachin as king of Judah and indicates that he, along with five other royal princes, received rations of barley and oil. The Babylonians thus continued to regard him as the legitimate king of Judah.

Ezekiel and his fellow captives. Judging from the fact that Ezekiel dates his activities from the beginning of the reign of Jehoiachin, it seems probable that he and the other captives were brought to the river Chebar about the same time that Jehoiachin was carried to Babylon. These, then, must have been some of the chief men of the land and the leaders of the people. According to various references in Ezekiel and to information recorded in Jeremiah 29, some false prophets tried to deceive the people into thinking that they would return from captivity very soon. The task of Ezekiel and Jeremiah was to convince these people that they should settle down, build houses, engage in agriculture, and continue family life in that place, because the captivity was going to be long and Jerusalem was going to be completely destroyed in a few years. Thus Ezekiel portrayed the siege and destruction of Jerusalem and in other ways encouraged the people to recognize their sins and to repent. From

Ezekiel 8:1 and 20:1, it is evident that the Jewish community in exile recognized elders or leaders and that these had gatherings and gave counsel and leadership to the people. From the fact that they sought guidance from Ezekiel it may be assumed that they continued to hear the word of the Lord, both from his prophets and from the reading of the law. As some have inferred, the synagogue may well have had its beginning in the very type meetings mentioned in Ezekiel.

Jeremiah and the People Left in Judah

The great prophet Jeremiah saw his nation reject the reform which he preached and which King Josiah instituted. He saw Nebuchadnezzar II invade the land of Judah and carry away some of its people on at least five different occasions. In spite of his inspired counsel, he saw the Egyptian party persuade Jehoiakim and later Zedekiah to rely on Egypt and rebel against Babylon, which brought further repression from Babylon. Finally, in 588 B.C., he saw Nebuchadnezzar II march into the land and begin a three-year siege of Jerusalem, which ended with the total destruction of the city and the temple in 586 B.C. Zedekiah was taken to Nebuchadnezzar II at Riblah. There his sons were killed before his eyes, his eyes were put out, and he was carried captive to Babylon. Many of Zedekiah's officers were killed. According to Jeremiah 52:29, an additional 832 persons were carried into captivity. Only the poorest of the land were left to be vinedressers and husbandmen.

Nebuchadnezzar II gave charge concerning Jeremiah that his soldiers should look well to him and do him no harm. He was freed after being carried to Ramah with the other captives and was given free choice to go on to Babylon or to return to Judah. Jeremiah chose to go back with Gedaliah, whom the Babylonians had appointed governor, to be among the people that were left in the land. Gedaliah set up his headquarters at Mizpah and attempted to reorganize the community under Babylonian rule. However, Baalis, king of Ammon, sent Ishmael to assassinate Gedaliah, which eventually he did. The people, now led by Johanan, were fearful of what the Babylonians might do and wanted to flee to Egypt. Jeremiah urged them to remain in the land, but Johanan and the people took the prophet and Baruch into the land of Egypt.

The Exiles in Egypt

No specific source gives systematic information about the exiled Jews in Egypt. However, many allusions and prophecies concerning the Jews going to Egypt and being in Egypt are made in the Scriptures. The most specific information concerns the Jews who brought Jeremiah to Egypt and settled in Tahpanhes, Migdol, Memphis, and the country of Pathros.

Jeremiah 44 indicates that they burned incense to the queen of heaven and committed abominations against the Lord in these places. Later history testifies clearly to the fact that many Jewish exiles did live and develop communities in Egypt.

The Elephantine Papyri give positive evidence of a Jewish settlement on this island at the first cataract of the Nile at the close of the fifth century B.C. Josephus refers to Jewish communities in Egypt, and it is certainly known that during the Hellenistic period the Jews constituted a large part of the population of Alexandria.

The evidence is conclusive that the Babylonian and Assyrian captivities caused the Jewish people to be scattered in all directions, so that by NT times there were Jewish communities in every major city and country of the Roman Empire. The captivity served a definite purpose in bringing what Scripture calls "the fullness of time." Through the Jewish exiles, people throughout North Africa, Western Asia, and Europe became acquainted with monotheism and the OT. In every major city there were synagogues, which served as a good medium for the preaching of the gospel and the establishment of the church.

Further, the captivity served as had no other act of God to help turn the Jewish people, especially those who returned from captivity, from idolatry and to the worship of Jehovah alone.

THE RETURN AND RESTORATION (539–333 B.C.)

The Decline and Fall of Babylon

During Nebuchadnezzar II's long reign of forty-four years, the Babylonian empire was strong and firmly in control. However, his son, Evil-merodach (562–560 B.C.), reigned only two years. In all likelihood he was assassinated by his successor, Nergal-shar-usur (Neriglissar, 560–556 B.C.), who died within four years and left a minor son, Labashi-Marduk, on the throne. This son was quickly removed by Nabonidus, who reigned 556–539 B.C. Nabonidus seemed to have forgotten the affairs of the kingdom in his fanatical devotion to the moon god, Sin. Because of his neglect of the traditional Babylonian religion, the priests of Marduk became hostile to him. Around 549 B.C. he transferred his residence from Babylon to the Oasis of Teima in the Arabian Desert southeast of Edom. The affairs in Babylon were left in the hands of the crown prince, Belshazzar.

In the meantime, Cyrus the Persian had rebelled against the Median king, Astyages, and by 550 B.C. had seized the vast Median Empire. He continued the expansion of this empire until finally he confronted Babylonia and overthrew it with the conquest of the city of Babylon in 539 B.C.

Cyrus' Policy and Edict of Restoration

In 538 B.C. Cyrus issued a decree which provided for the restoration of the Jews in exile to their homeland, the rebuilding of the temple, and the revival of Jewish worship. (See Ezra 1:1-4; 6:1-5.) This decree is in harmony with the general policy of Cyrus, which has been confirmed by archeology. (See Pritchard, *Ancient Near Eastern Texts,* pp. 312ff.) Cyrus reversed the deportation policy of the Assyrians and Babylonians. He allowed and assisted the people to resettle in their own homeland if they desired.

The restoration of the Jewish captives and the life of the Jews under the Persian Empire may be briefly outlined as follows:

    I. The biblical period, 539–423 B.C.

        A. The first return to the rebuilding of the temple, 539–515.

The First Return to Rebuild the Temple

Cyrus placed Sheshbazzar in charge of the first party of Jews to return to the land and allowed him to take back many of the spoils that Nebuchadnezzar II had removed from Jerusalem. Very little is said of the activities of this first group of returnees. Ezra 5:16 credits Sheshbazzar with laying the foundations of the house of God in Jerusalem. However, the book of Haggai makes it clear that the first returning Jews became involved in their own activities and did not complete the temple. In part, this was caused by opposition from adversaries, but the details of this are shrouded in the problem of understanding Ezra 4.

At any rate, the temple lay incomplete until 520 B.C. when the prophets Haggai and Zechariah urged Zerubbabel, the governor, and Jeshua, the priest, and the rest of the people to resume work on the house of God. They obtained authorization from the Persian authorities and proceeded with the work. They finished the temple in the sixth year of the reign of Darius I, king of Persia, about 516 B.C. They dedicated the house of God with great sacrifices and the observance of the Passover.

The period from 515 to 458 B.C., when Ezra led a group of the Jews back to Palestine, is a blank in the history of the Jews in Palestine. Almost nothing is known of events that transpired in Palestine between the time of Zerubbabel and Ezra. Scholars have made many conjectures and speculations based on vague references and theories concerning the books of Joel, Malachi, Zechariah, and others. However, there are no certain facts about this period. Perhaps some day archeology will bring forth evidence that will help to clarify this period in history.

Esther and the Jews in Persia

The events of the book of Esther take place in the

days of Ahasuerus. He is usually equated with Xerxes I (486–465 B.C.). If this identification is correct, then the book of Esther provides the only concrete information concerning the Jews during the silent or blank period of history mentioned above. The central message of the book of Esther is concerned with how this young Jewish heroine came to be queen, in order that she might save the Jewish people from annihilation at the hands of Xerxes I's cruel minister, Haman. Through Esther's intervention and influence Haman was overthrown, Mordecai, her elder cousin, was exalted, and the Jews were allowed to defend themselves against those who would destroy them; thus they were preserved from annihilation.

The Restoration under Ezra and Nehemiah

Considerable debate exists among scholars as to the exact dates when Ezra and Nehemiah lived and worked and as to whether they were contemporaries. The present author believes that both of them led movements of returned captives to Palestine during the reign of Artaxerxes I (465–424 B.C.; see John Bright, *A History of Israel*, pp. 392ff.). Accordingly, Ezra came to Jerusalem in the seventh year of Artaxerxes I, or about 458 B.C. Ezra's primary goal was to restore the understanding and practice of the law among the Jews. Very few details of his work are given. Emphasis is placed on his letter of authority from Artaxerxes, the journey from Babylon to Jerusalem, Ezra's penitent prayer for the Jewish nation, and the people's repentance expressed mainly in abandoning their mixed marriages.

In the twentieth year of Artaxerxes I or about 445 B.C., Nehemiah heard of the desolate state in Jerusalem and began seeking permission to come to the aid of the beloved city. He obtained permission from Artaxerxes I, gathered a group to accompany him back to the city, and made that perilous journey. The story of Nehemiah and his work is one of great faith and perseverance. In the face of great hardship and much opposition he manifested the qualities of an outstanding leader and successfully completed the task of rebuilding the walls of Jerusalem and making it a protected and defensible city once again. Then he and Ezra joined in reading the law of Moses to the people, observing the Feast of Tabernacles, and in making a public confession of sin, with the people making a covenant to keep the law. This resulted in the resumption of the temple service, the separation of Israel from the mixed multitude, the forbidding of Sabbath violation, and the condemnation of mixed marriages.

The Last Century of Persian Rule

The inspired biblical history of Israel ends with the work of Ezra and Nehemiah, at approximately the end of the reign of Artaxerxes I about 424 B.C. The next ninety years, 423–333 B.C., during which the Jews continued to live under the Persian Empire, is a period of almost total obscurity. The Elephantine texts shed some light on the Jewish settlement at the first cataract of the Nile. However, of the Jews in Palestine and in the rest of the Persian Empire very little is known.

ISRAEL UNDER HELLENISTIC RULE (333–165 B.C.)

The Conquest by Alexander the Great

Beginning with Darius I, the Persians had attempted to expand their empire to include Greece and had engaged in wars against Greece. However, these actions by the Persians only resulted in the eventual unification of the Greeks and in creating a strong desire to defeat Persia. Finally, about 336 B.C., Alexander succeeded his father, Philip, when he was but twenty years of age, unified the Greek city states, and planned the conquest of Persia. In 334 he crossed the Hellespont and marched to meet the Persians. He defeated Darius III at the Granicus River in Asia Minor and at Issus in Syria in 333. From there he proceeded to take Tyre and Gaza after extended sieges. According to Josephus, he marched to Jerusalem and was welcomed by the priests and people (Antiquities XI, 8, 4). Thus Palestine and the Jews in it came to be under the control of Alexander the

Great. Of course, Alexander proceeded to Egypt, then turned to the Persian front and defeated Darius III at Arbela in 331 B.C., thereby gaining control of the Persian Empire. He continued expeditions into Media and into India. After gaining military control of all this territory, he inaugurated policies which led to the Hellenization of the Near East and Egypt. He encouraged the merging of society, socially and commercially. He married a Persian princess and urged his men to take Persian wives. Through the providence of God, the Greek language and culture became widely adopted throughout his empire.

Alexander became ill with malaria, and due to a generally weakened condition he died in 323 B.C. His kingdom was divided among four of his generals. Cassander obtained Macedonia, Lysimachus became ruler over Asia Minor, Ptolemy I gained control of Egypt, and Seleucus I ruled over Syria and Mesopotamia.

The Jews under the Ptolemies

For some years there was contention between Ptolemy I and Seleucus I for the control of Palestine. After various maneuvers, Ptolemy I was successful and Palestine came to be under the control of this dynasty until about 198 B.C. Ptolemy I placed his capital in the new city of Alexandria and it soon became one of the great cities of the world. Under him many Jews were settled at Alexandria, and this city became the center for the Hellenistic, Jewish influence. Some time during the middle of the third century B.C. the Hebrew Bible began to be translated into Greek under the influence, most likely, of Ptolemy II Philadelphus. Various other evidences indicate that Jewish communities flourished in Egypt. However, concerning the fortunes of the Jews in Palestine during this period of time, we know very little.

From 204 to 198 B.C. there was war between Ptolemy V and Antiochus III of the Seleucid Empire. Finally, Antiochus III gained control of Palestine and the Jews' fate fell into the hands of the Seleucid rulers.

The Jews under the Seleucids

From 198 to 165 B.C. Palestine was under the control of

the Seleucid rulers. In 175 Antiochus IV Epiphanes began to rule. He instituted policies aimed toward the Hellenization of the Jews. He attempted to force them to sacrifice to idols, to profane the Sabbath, to cease circumcision, and to do many other things contrary to Jewish practice. In 169 he plundered Jerusalem. Then in 167 he returned, burned it, tore down some of its houses and walls, and finally erected a desolating sacrilege on the altar of burnt offering. Some Jews happily associated themselves with this new Hellenization, but most resisted. Many chose to die rather than to yield to the oppressive policies of Antiochus IV. The desperate Jews were urgently in need of brave leaders, which they found in Mattathias and his sons.

THE MACCABEAN PERIOD (165–135 B.C.)

In the process of the oppression by Antiochus IV, the king's officers, who were enforcing the Hellenization policy, came to the city of Modein to make the people there offer sacrifice. However, they were opposed by a priest named Mattathias. When a Jew came forward in response to the order by the king's officer, Mattathias ran and killed him upon the altar. He also killed the king's officer, who was forcing them to sacrifice, and tore down the pagan altar. He and his sons fled to the hills and many Jews began to follow them.

Mattathias had five sons whose names were John, Simon, Judas, Eleazar, and Jonathan. These were all able men and they were joined by many other Jews dedicated to their religion and to freedom.

Mattathias, his sons, and other dedicated Jews carried on a guerrilla warfare against the Syrian army for a good while. At first they did not fight on the Sabbath and were attacked on that day with about a thousand being killed. Afterward the policy was changed, so the Jews could defend themselves on the Sabbath. Then Mattathias and his army went about and tore down the altars, slew apostate Jews, and circumcised many in the land. Mattathias became ill and died in 166 B.C. Before he died, he appointed Judas, who is also called Maccabeus, as the general to lead the army.

Judas Maccabeus, 166–161 B.C.

With Judas as the leader, the Jews proceeded to defeat the Syrians in one battle after another until finally they were able to reenter Jerusalem. Here they cleansed the sanctuary and rededicated it. This rededication took place in an elaborate festival which lasted eight days in the month Chislev, equivalent to our December, in the year 164 B.C. This is the feast referred to in the New Testament in John 10:22 as the Feast of Dedication. Today it is commonly called the Hanukkah Festival. Judas continued to strengthen the Maccabean kingdom until his death in 161 B.C. However, his death came in a fierce battle and defeat for himself and his troops against the Syrian army led by Bacchides. Such a tragic defeat threatened to bring an end to the Maccabean revolt.

Jonathan, a brother of Judas, was selected as his successor, although the Syrians had essentially regained control of the land. The period from 160 to 153 B.C. is quite obscure. However, it must have been a very important period for the reinvigorating of the Maccabean party, for at its end Jonathan and the Maccabean party were in control of Judea. The Graeco-Jewish party had no real root among the people. The Seleucid government itself had become weak and could no longer force upon the Jewish people a Hellenistic government, but were obliged to do all in their power to conciliate and win the favor of the Maccabean party. By 153 B.C. Jonathan was again able to gain control of Jerusalem. Because of a division in the Syrian rulers, Jonathan was able to play one against the other and gain further strength for himself and the Maccabean kingdom. By various political maneuvers and some successful military tactics, Jonathan gained a great extent of independence from the Seleucid kingdom. Finally, however, Jonathan was outmaneuvered by a Seleucid leader named Trypho and was made a prisoner. Later Trypho had Jonathan murdered and proceeded in his attempts to overthrow the Maccabean kingdom. Concerning Jonathan's accomplishments, Schurer observes:

> By the heroic deeds and successes of Jonathan, the Maccabean party had passed out far beyond its original aims. It had not at

first intended to strive for anything more than the restoration of the Jewish worship, and the securing of the free exercise of the Jewish religion. But even Judas, when he had attained this end, did not rest satisfied therewith. He and his party then wished also to gain the supremacy in the control of home affairs. In the time of Jonathan this end was completely won. By Jonathan's appointment as high priest the ruling power was placed in the hands of the Maccabean party, and the Hellenistic party was driven out. But even this no longer seemed sufficient. Favorable circumstances—the weakness of the Syrian Empire—tempted them to strive after thorough emancipation from the Syrian suzerainty. The last acts of Jonathan were important steps in this direction.
Emil Schurer, *A History of the Jewish People in the Time of Jesus,* (New York: Schocken Books, 1961), p. 57.

Jonathan was succeeded by his brother Simon, who reigned 142–135 B.C. The significance of the reign of Simon is that he completed the work of Jonathan and made the Jewish people completely independent of the Syrian or Seleucid Empire. After Trypho's deceptive and hostile acts resulting in the murder of Jonathan, Simon turned his support to the Syrian ruler Demetrius, having exacted the promise from him that he would recognize the freedom of the Jews and exempt them from tribute. Simon then proceeded to take the Syrian fortresses at the city of Gazara and the citadel of Jerusalem. Since the Syrian kings were divided and not in a position to give real attention to events in Judea, Simon's rule proceeded in undisturbed prosperity and peace for the Jews. In September 141 B.C., a great assembly of the priests, the people, and the princes of the people, and the elders of the land decreed that Simon should be high priest, military commander, and civil governor of the Jews until there should arise a faithful prophet (1 Maccabees 14:41-43). However, toward the end of Simon's reign the Syrians again turned their attention toward Judea and attempted to overthrow Simon. But by this time he was strong enough to maintain his position and the position of Jewish independence. Unfortunately, intrigue from within by his own son-in-law, Ptolemy, led to his assassination in February 135 B.C.

Thus the last of the sons of Mattathias was killed.

A new phase of the Maccabean kingdom began with John Hyrcanus, the third son of Simon, who assumed the position of his father, which had been declared hereditary. Through negotiations, military feats, and the weakness of the Syrians, he and his successors were able to maintain the shaky Maccabean kingdom until Palestine was conquered by the Romans in 63 B.C.

The Maccabean period contributed tremendously to the fullness of time and to the development of Jewish practices, concepts, and attitudes. Principally, a new nationalistic spirit was developed during this period and a sharpened, though diversified, messianic hope. Also the Jewish sects of the Pharisees and Sadducees seemed to have gained clear, distinct existences during this period.

Conclusion

The preceding survey of the history of the Jewish people is highly selective and very abbreviated. However, it does serve to show that God acted in the history of this nation as in the history of none other. The principal purpose for his actions was for the redemption, not of Israel alone, but for all the world through Jesus the Christ, whom he brought into the world through the Jewish people. God overruled the actions of the Jews, as well as the actions of the neighboring nations, to lead to the development of the fullness of time for the sending of the Redeemer.

BIBLIOGRAPHY

Ackroyd, Peter R. *Exile and Restoration.* Philadelphia: The Westminster Press, 1968.

_____. *Israel under Babylon and Persia.* London: The Oxford University Press, 1970.

Bright, John. *A History of Israel.* 2d ed. Philadelphia: The Westminster Press, 1972.

Crockett, William Day. *A Harmony of the Books of Samuel, Kings, and Chronicles.* Grand Rapids: Baker Book House, 1954.

Gottwald, Norman K. *A Light to the Nations.* New York, Evanston, and London: Harper and Row, Publishers, 1959.

Heaton, E. W. *The Hebrew Kingdoms.* London: Oxford University Press, 1968.

Pfeiffer, Charles F. *Old Testament History*. Grand Rapids: Baker Book House, 1973.

Pritchard, James B., ed. *Ancient Near Eastern Texts*. 2d ed. Princeton: Princeton University Press, 1955.

Thiele, Edwin R. *The Mysterious Numbers of the Hebrew Kings*. Grand Rapids: Wm. B. Eerdmans Publishing Company, 1965.

Young, Edward J. *My Servants the Prophets*. Grand Rapids: Wm. B. Eerdmans Publishing Company, 1961.

VI

Types of Old Testament Literature

Clyde M. Miller

NARRATIVES

Narrative is the major form of literature in the OT, although several other forms are also used. Since much of the OT involves persons and events within the context of history, it is to be expected that narrative would be used to communicate this information. Old Testament narrative can be divided into three major types: genealogies, epic poetry, and historical prose narrative.

Genealogies

Biblical genealogies are something more than mere listings of names and family groups. Genealogies are so placed in the OT as to become a framework for the historical narrative surrounding them. The four major genealogies in Genesis give clear indication of their purpose to link together family groups to emphasize the unfolding of God's scheme of redemption to be realized through the Hebrew people. Ten generations from Adam to Noah are given (ch. 5), thus giving coherence to the course of human history from creation to the flood. Ten generations are given from Shem, the son of Noah, to Abram (ch. 11), thus bringing the reader at once to the beginning of God's

communication with and direction of his special covenant
people. To further this purpose, the genealogies of Isaac,
the son of Abraham (25:19-26), and of Jacob, son of
Isaac (35:22b-29), are given. Even the minor genealogies in
Genesis fit into the historical framework of the book.
The genealogies of Shem, Ham, and Japheth, sons of Noah
(ch. 10), are given for the express purpose of indicating how
men were dispersed over the face of the earth after the
flood. The genealogies of Ishmael (25:12-18) and Esau
(ch. 36) serve a double function. They show God's loyalty to
Abraham, even in regard to the noncovenant people, and
they give the necessary background of two tribes of people
who figure prominently in their contacts with the Hebrew
people.

The book of Chronicles also shows the historical purpose
behind the genealogies. Chapters 1–3 move quickly through
the families from Adam to David. Chapter 4 gives the tribe
of Judah, followed by the rest of the sons of Jacob
(chs. 5–8). From chapter 9 forward, the Davidic covenant is
kept in the forefront. Hence, the genealogies in Chronicles
emphasize the unfolding of the messianic covenant through
the family of David.

Epic Poetry

The book of Genesis is sprinkled with brief epic poems
which fix the mind of the reader on certain important events
or persons. These epic poems, like the genealogies, do not
interrupt the historical narrative, but rather enhance it.
These poems in Genesis take one of the earliest covenant
forms, emphasizing the blessing of obedience or the curse of
disobedience. Curses are pronounced upon the serpent, the
woman, and the ground as a result of sin entering the human
family (3:14-19). A curse is placed upon Lamech for the sin
of murder (4:23-24) and upon Canaan for the sin of his
father (9:25-27). Blessings are pronounced upon Abraham
(14:19-20), Jacob (25:23; 27:27b-29), and Esau (27:39-40). A
mixture of blessings and curses is pronounced upon the
Patriarchs, the sons of Jacob (49:2-27).

Other parts of the Pentateuch employ epic psalms to

enhance the historical record. The deliverance from Egypt and the Egyptian armies is celebrated in Exodus 15:1-18. The Book of the Wars of the Lord is quoted in Numbers 21:14b-15 to enhance the Israelites' journey through the territory of the Amorites. The Israelites sang a brief praise hymn to celebrate God's giving them water in the desert (Num. 21:17b-18), and a ballad concerning Heshbon is also recorded (Num. 21:27b-30). The Balaam oracles (Num. 23:7b-10, 18b-24; 24:3b-9, 15b-24) are familiar to every Bible reader. The book of Deuteronomy records the song (32:143) and the blessing of Moses (33:2-29) to the people of Israel. A number of psalms within the book of Psalms also follow the form of epic narrative (e.g., 68, 78, 105, 106). These generally begin a historical retrospect with God's promise made to Abraham, or they begin with the exodus.

The Former Prophets (Joshua, Judges, Samuel, and Kings), according to the Hebrew classification, also contain epic poems. The celebration of the sun's standing still (Josh. 10:12-13), the Song of Deborah (Judg. 5:2-31), Hannah's prayer of thanksgiving for a child (1 Sam. 2:1-10), and David's laments over Jonathan and Saul (2 Sam. 1:19-27) and over Abner (2 Sam. 3:33b-34a) all celebrate momentous occasions. So it is with David's thanksgiving psalm (2 Sam. 22 = Ps. 18) after God had given him rest from all his enemies, and David's "last words" (2 Sam. 23:1b-7). Isaiah's oracle of doom against Assyria (2 Kings 19:21b-28) and the liturgy made up of parts of Psalms 96, 105, and 106 to celebrate David's bringing the ark to Jerusalem (1 Chron. 16:8-36) complete the epic poetry.

Historical Prose Narrative

The history recorded in the OT does not claim to be complete, but it is selective in nature. Only that which is necessary to show God's dealings with man in the working out of the scheme of redemption is included. For this reason, a disproportionate amount of space is given to various events and periods of history. Genesis, even by the most conservative estimate, covers more history than all the rest of the Bible combined. Yet, even within this book, a disproportionate amount of space is given to the events recorded. Twenty generations are covered in chapters 1–11, but only four generations are covered in chapters 12–50. It is obvious that the intent of the book is primarily to tell us of the Abrahamic covenant and its working in the lives of Abraham, Isaac, Jacob, and the Patriarchs.

By contrast, Exodus covers only one year of history, centered mainly around the giving of the law and the instructions for and erection of the tabernacle. Numbers takes us through the forty-year period of the wilderness wandering. Joshua and Judges carry the reader from the conquest of Canaan to the beginning of the monarchy, comprising a period of several hundred years. First and Second Samuel take us through the careers of Samuel, Saul, and David (ca. 1050–970 B.C.), and 1 and 2 Kings continue the history through the career of Solomon, the period of the divided kingdom, and the period of Judah alone after the exile of North Israel (ca. 970–587 B.C.). Esther and parts of Daniel and Ezekiel give the history of the exile. Ezra and Nehemiah recount the work of restoration after the return from exile (ca. 457–433 B.C.). First and Second Chronicles give the history from David's career to the return from exile, repeating much of what is in Samuel and Kings, but giving special emphasis to the southern kingdom.

Almost every book in the OT includes some historical notations, but those given above are basically the ones which contain the bulk of OT history. Some brief historical narratives are found in prophetic books not mentioned above, but this material is comparatively negligible.

LEGAL FORMS

Covenant Forms

The discovery of Hittite legal codes which come from the same general period as Israel's national beginnings has added to our understanding of covenant forms in the OT. While the OT does not follow the Hittite forms precisely, traces of these forms can be found. There are six close comparisons which can be made between the Hittite suzerainty treaty and God's covenant with Israel. God employs familiar forms to communicate his will to man.

In these covenants there is (1) a *preamble,* in which the author of the covenant is identified (cf. Exod. 19:3; Josh. 24:2). This is followed by (2) a *historical prologue,* which recounts the past favors of the sovereign to his subjects (cf. Exod. 19:4; Josh. 24:2b-13). Next comes (3) the *stipulations,* with detailed obligations imposed upon and accepted by the subjects (cf. Exod. 20–23; Josh. 24:14-15). Provision is then made for (4) *deposit* in the temple and *periodic reading* of the covenant terms (cf. Exod. 25:21; 31:18; Deut. 10:1-5; 31:9-13). In the Hittite covenants (5) a list of the gods is given as *witnesses* to the covenant. This is not to be expected in a monotheistic society. Israel witnesses against herself (cf. Exod. 19:8; 24:3, 7; Josh. 24:16-28). Finally, there is (6) a list of *curses and blessings* to be suffered or enjoyed as a result of disobedience or obedience (cf. Deut. 27–28). Prophets, priests, sages, and singers keep calling Israel back to a covenant which has so frequently been forgotten.

Casuistic (Case) Laws

Casuistic laws are introduced by a conditional clause beginning with the word "if," "when," or "whoever." Frequently there is a statement of a general principle followed by subsidiary circumstances which pertain to it. In such cases, it is best to begin the general principle with the word "when," "whoever," etc. (Heb. *kî*), and the subsidiary clauses with the word, "if" (Heb. *'im*), as is done in the RSV (cf. Exod. 21:1-6, 7-11, 18-19, 20-21, 22-25, 26-27, 28-32).

The subsidiary clauses give the case law the specific limitations intended by the lawgiver. Frequently the Hebrew word *mishpatim* (judgments, ordinances) is used to refer to these laws. Many interpreters believe that casuistic laws were customary laws which were found in varied forms throughout the ancient world, as many parallels would seem to indicate. Additional examples of casuistic law can be found in Exodus 22 and 23.

Apodictic Laws

These laws may take one of three forms. (1) They may be given in direct command, as in the decalogue (Exod. 20:1-17); (2) they may take the curse form (Deut. 27:15-26); or (3) they may take the participial form (Exod. 21:12-17). In the participial form, the subject is stated in the form of a Hebrew participle (translated as a relative clause) placed at the beginning for emphasis. The participle is followed by its object which is in turn followed by the penalty. In some cases the principal clause may be followed by subordinate clauses which further clarify or limit the law (cf. Exod. 21:1-14).

These varied law forms are not divided into neat categories in the OT. Rather they are interspersed throughout the law of Moses and the forms interchange freely. There is no reason to think that one form of law is any more binding than another.

PROPHETIC ORACLES

Hope Oracles

Almost all the prophetic books (preexilic, exilic, and postexilic) contain oracles of hope for the future. These are so numerous as to preclude the possibility of enumerating all of them in this chapter. A few of the more forceful ones must suffice. The prophets found it necessary to condemn the sins of the people and to warn of coming calamity, but they also held out hope for the righteous and the penitent. Amos holds out little hope for the nation, but he does show that God makes a distinction between the righteous and the sinner (9:8) and that there is always hope for the righteous (9:9-10). Hosea expresses more hope than does Amos. In beautiful poetry, he pictures God as the husband who arranges a new betrothal with his bride, Israel, who has become unfaithful to him (2:14-23). God himself provides a fivefold bride price because Israel is helpless to restore herself. The book ends on this same happy note, indicating the exercise of God's free grace in taking the penitent people back to himself (ch. 14). Throughout the preexilic prophets this attitude is manifested, except in Jonah, who unfortunately did not share God's lovingkindness and, therefore, could not rejoice over the repentance of the Ninevites (Jonah 4:1-4).

Sometimes this hope for the future extends beyond the future involved in the restoration of the righteous remnant from exile. This restoration often becomes a type of a greater worldwide restoration which includes people of all nations. God's Spirit will be poured out upon all flesh (Joel 2:28-32), God's word will go forth from Jerusalem to all people (Micah 4:1-3 = Isa. 2:1-4), there will be a perfect ruler who judges with righteousness and equity (Isa. 11:1-5), all of which will result in salvation and a harmonious society (Isa. 11:6-9). The booth of David will be restored (Amos 9:11-15), and a Davidic descendant will rule over all God's people (Hos. 3:5; Jer. 30:9; 50:4-5; Ezek. 34:24). A careful check of the NT references to these and other OT passages will reveal that the ultimate fulfillment of these ideas was in and through Jesus Christ and his kingdom on earth, the church.

Doom Oracles

Sometimes the prophets refer to calamities of the past as prefiguring the greater coming calamity of the exile of the nation (cf. Amos 4:6-11). This historical retrospect may go back to the distant past. For instance, the destruction of Sodom and Gomorrah is alluded to by Isaiah (3:9), Jeremiah (23:14), and Ezekiel (16:44-50). Since the sins of God's people in the present era are similar to those of the people of Sodom and Gomorrah, Israel and Judah must also suffer destruction (Isa. 1:9; Amos 4:11). Frequently, the prophets predict the doom of the nation (whether Israel or Judah) (e.g., Amos 2:4-5; 3:11-15; 4:1-3; 5:5, 27; 7:17; Hos. 1:4-5; 8:10; 9:3; 11:5, 7). The frequency of such predictions indicated in the above references is characteristic of the pre-exilic prophets. Amos goes so far as to say that there will be no restoration of North Israel as a nation (5:2; 8:14).

Occasionally these predictions of exile are extended to include a still greater eschatological day of the Lord when

198 / TYPES OF OLD TESTAMENT LITERATURE

he will take vengeance upon the whole world. It is clear from Joel's use of the expression "the day of the Lord" that there is a development of the meaning of this expresion in his book. The locust plague which he so vividly describes is used as a warning of a coming day of vengeance against the covenant people (1:15; 2:1-2, 11). A fourth passage (2:28-32; cf. 3:1-2) is transitional in that it contains a mixture of hope and doom. Devastation is coming upon Jerusalem, but there shall be those that escape. And when God restores the fortunes of his people, Jerusalem will be exalted. This prepares the way for the final use of the expression "the day of the Lord" (3:14), in which the nations are judged and condemned for their sins, and Jerusalem is delivered and glorified. The whole context of this final scene in Joel and its interpretation in the NT (Acts 2:17-21) indicate that the symbolism is ultimately fulfilled in the rejection of the Jewish nation by the Lord and the coming in of the worldwide spiritual kingdom, the church.

It is not uncommon for the prophets to pronounce doom upon Gentile nations (cf. Amos 1:3-2:3; Isa. 13-23; Jer. 46-51). It is not always easy to determine whether these predictions are meant to be fulfilled historically or eschatologically, or both.

Frequently the prophets lament the evil which they have predicted. Amos, who is sometimes erroneously described as the stern prophet of God's judgments, laments the fall of the nation of Israel (5:1-2). Micah laments the coming destruction of Judah (7:1-7) and then indicates the confession which the nation ought to make (7:8-10), with the promise of deliverance if they will repent (7:11-17). Jeremiah seems to have been the most sensitive of the prophets (cf. 8:18-19, 21-22; 9:1). The fact that the prophets predicted what they themselves did not wish to happen indicates that they were speaking the will of God.

The Covenant Lawsuit

A popular method of communication used by the preexilic prophets is based on the law courts of their day. Since court was often held in the gates of the cities, the people had opportunity to see the judicial system in action. They would, therefore, readily understand the meaning implied in the use of this device by the prophets. In the covenant lawsuit, God serves the double function of judge and plaintiff (accuser), and the nation is the defendant. A clear example of this figure is found in Micah 6:1-8. God charges the people with ingratitude for the saving acts of the Lord (vss. 3-5). The people respond by declaring that their sacrifices and offerings have been made in abundance and asking what more they could do to please God (vss. 6-7). God answers that the requirements are simple: to do justice, love kindness, and walk humbly with God (vs. 8). Verses 9-16 may be the enumeration of Israel's sins and the pronouncement of the sentence, although some interpreters do not believe that the figure of the covenant lawsuit extends to these verses. Other clear examples of the covenant lawsuit are found in Isaiah 1:2-9; 3:13-15; Micah 1:2-7; and Hosea 4:1-3.

Prophetic Intercession

The prophets sometimes successfully interceded on behalf of their people (cf. Amos 7:1-6). However, though Jeremiah prayed earnestly for his people (13:17; 17:16; 18:20), God eventually told him to quit praying for them because they were hopelessly doomed (7:16; 11:14; 14:11-12). Amos also was told that the doom of Israel was certainly coming (7:7-9; 8:2). The important thing is that the prophets cared enough to intercede on behalf of the people whom God had chosen for his own.

Biography and Autobiography

Several portions of the prophetic books contain information about the prophets and events in their lives. Some are in poetry and some in prose. Some are written in the first person (autobiography) and some in the third (biography). Of course it is possible that a prophet wrote about himself in the third person, but usually when the third person is used it was probably written by the prophet's secretary or disciple, as when Baruch wrote of Jeremiah.

The varied types of material found in the prophetic books need not be taken as evidence of diverse authorship of the books. Variety of form indicates skill on the part of the prophets in communicating the messages received from God, and in some cases it indicates changing circumstances within the nation or suggests that the prophet is addressing different elements within his audience.

PSALMODY IN ISRAEL

In addition to those psalms included in the section above on narratives, there are also some psalms to be found in the Prophets which will not be enumerated here. The vast majority of the psalms in the OT are to be found in the book of Psalms, comprising in our English Bible 150 separate psalms written and collected over a period extending possibly from 1000 to 300 B.C. Though scholars are not in agreement as to how the psalms should be classified, there are four major types which are generally recognized by all interpreters.

Praise and Thanksgiving Psalms

The lines of demarcation between psalms of praise and those of thanksgiving are not easily drawn, but it can be generally established that the latter usually reflect a recent deliverance. Because of the great similarity between these two types, they will be discussed together. While the following literary characteristics of these two types of psalms are not always clearly manifested, frequently several of these characteristics can be noted.

There will usually be an *announcement* of the praise or thanks. This may take the form of an *invitation* to Israel, the world, or the heavenly host to praise God; or the psalm may simply begin with an *ascription* of praise to God. In other cases, the psalm may begin with a *prayer* for God to protect Israel or with an *exhortation* to Israel to trust in God.

In the body of these psalms God is praised for his general works of *creation* and *providence* and sometimes specifically for certain *historical evidences* of his goodness to Israel.

Sometimes a *motive* for praising God is indicated by the word "for," although at other times the motive is more subtly expressed.

If the psalm has a *formal conclusion*, it may take one of three forms: (1) resume the opening line, (2) repeat the thought of the opening verse, or (3) add a brief prayer as a plea for God's continual blessings to be upon Israel. In a psalm of thanksgiving the psalmist may bid bystanders join him in praise, announce his intention to pay his vows, or exhort his fellow worshipers to trust in God's deliverance. The following are good examples of praise and thanksgiving psalms: 8, 33, 104–106, and 136.

There are also some specialized psalms which belong in the category of praise and thanksgiving psalms. There is a group of enthronement psalms which emphasize the fact that God is king of the universe (93, 95–99). Another special category involves psalms which emphasize that God has put his name in Zion (e.g., 24, 46–48, 84, 87, 122). Some psalm interpreters put these two groups in separate categories and designate them *enthronement psalms* and *psalms of Zion,* respectively.

Psalms of Lament and Petition

These psalms comprise the largest single category of psalms in the Psalter, with psalms of praise and thanksgiving forming the second largest category. There are two, possibly three, major types of these psalms. *Psalms of innocence* are those in which no guilt is 'confessed or felt by the author. *Psalms of penitence* are those in which sin is acknowledged as a cause of the calamity. There is a large group of *psalms of confidence* which seem to have come from the same kind of distressing circumstances as the other two categories. In this last category the psalmist's faith and trust are so strong as to preclude the element of lament.

A psalm of lament contains a description of the distress or danger which the psalmist and/or the nation is suffering. This lament is often stated in hyperbolic and/or emblematic language. Some of these psalms do not contain a lament, but they all contain a petition to God, except that *psalms of confidence* may only imply the petition. There may be a statement of the *motivation* which should prompt God to answer the petition. Three statements of motivation recur frequently in these psalms. The psalmist may appeal to God to uphold God's own reputation, suggesting that if Israel is not delivered from her enemies the nations will mock the name of God (cf. 42:3b, 10b). Or the psalmist may say, "If I die, there will be one less worshiper," for ancient Israel did not understand that God can be praised in the afterlife (cf. 6:5; 88:10-12). Or, in the third place, the psalmist may say, "I have repented, so God should forgive" (cf. 39:7-9; 51:3, 16-17). Sometimes the psalmist *promises* to do certain things if God will grant deliverance. He may promise to praise God (51:15; 69:30; 35:28), to offer a sacrifice (54:6-7), or to pay a vow (22:25).

Occasionally the psalmist prays for the destruction of his enemies. So frequent is this element that some interpreters designate a special category of *imprecatory psalms*. Often it can be determined that the psalmist is not praying for personal vengeance but is only asking God to vindicate his own name or the nation Israel as his covenant people. Perhaps the strongest imprecation is found in Psalm 109:6-19. The Christian should follow the example of Christ, who prayed for his enemies (Luke 23:34) and taught his disciples to do the same (Matt. 5:43-48).

In most psalms of lament and petition there is a great expression of trust in God. These psalms, therefore, were not uttered out of a lack of faith, but they are appeals to God to manifest his covenant loyalty anew on behalf of his people in their present crisis. These psalms vividly contrast human weakness and divine strength.

A good example of a public declaration of innocence is Psalm 44, and Psalm 26 is a good example of a personal declaration of innocence. The frustration of the psalmist is greater in a psalm of innocence because it is more difficult to account for the calamity than it would be if his sin or the sin of the nation were the clear cause of the trouble. The frustration may be greater in a personal psalm of innocence than in a community psalm of innocence because in the former case there is no one else to share the sense of alienation from God or the worshiping community. Examples of psalms of penitence are Psalms 38 and 51. Examples of psalms of confidence are Psalms 23 and 139.

Didactic Psalms

These are psalms which, in the main, are not directed to God as praise or prayer, but to men for the purpose of edification. Some of the topics included in these psalms are the following : (1) the knowledge (cf. 19, 119) and fear (cf. 112, 128) of the Lord, coupled with obedience; (2) a contrast between the righteous and the wicked (1, 14); (3) trust in God (49, 91); (4) justice in society (52,82), and (5) brotherhood among men (127, 133).

Royal Psalms

These psalms are grouped together, not because they form a separate literary group, but because they have to do with the subject of the king. They may be written in the form of a praise hymn, a psalm of thanksgiving, a didactic psalm, or a psalm of lament and petition. These psalms may involve God's unconditional promise to David of a continuing dynasty (cf. 2 Sam. 7:14-16; Pss. 132, 89). The king is God's anointed son whom God himself inducts into office (Ps. 2). The king functions as a priest before God (Ps. 110) in that he offers sacrifices of thanksgiving and praise to God on behalf of the nation (cf. 2 Sam. 6:14; 1 Kings 8:62-64; 9:25). The king's personal prayers and sacrifices are important as evidence of his loyalty to God (Ps. 20), and he is expected to rejoice in the Lord and not in himself (Ps. 21). The throne of the king is be characterized by equity and righteousness (Ps. 45), for he is to be endowed with and to execute God's righteousness and justice (Ps.72). The king promises to faithfully execute righteousness and justice (Ps. 101). David is the example *par excellence* of one who was loyal to God and who thus achieved amazing success (Ps. 18).

There are six important ways in which the Davidic king serves as a type of Christ, just as the nation Israel serves as a type of the church. (1) The king and Christ are God's anointed (Ps. 2:1-2; Acts 4:25-26); (2), God's Son (Ps. 2:7; Heb. 1:5; 5:5-6; Acts 13:33); (3) they both perform priestly functions (Ps. 110:4; Heb. 5:5-6); (4) they are expected to rule with righteousness and justice (Ps. 45:6-7; Heb. 1:8-9); (5) they are promised success (Ps. 110:5-7; Luke 1:46-55); and (6) they are promised an eternal kingdom (Ps. 89:28-37; Luke 1:32-33). The movement from the type to the antitype is always from the imperfect to the perfect. No Davidic king ever perfectly accomplished his mission, but Christ is the perfect mediator between God and man. Much of the messianic material found in the Psalms is understandably in connection with the Davidic king.

WISDOM LITERATURE

Proverbs

While it is true that there are proverbs in the OT outside the book of Proverbs, the discussion here will be confined to that book. The principles discussed here, however, would apply to other proverbs as well. The Hebrew word *māshāl*, translated "proverb," can carry any one of three basic meanings: (1) a likeness or comparison, (2) a rule or standard of behavior, or (3) a riddle or, more particularly, the setting forth of God's mysterious unseen world order to which man must conform. The English word "proverbs" can be defined as short, pithy sayings in common use. They may include epigrams (short, cryptic, witty sayings, frequently involving antithesis), aphorisms (short, concise statements of principles), or maxims (precepts or rules of conduct). It can readily be seen that the English word "proverb"does not in all respects correspond to the Hebrew word *māshāl*, although this is the best English equivalent available.

The serious student who expects to be an effective teacher of the word will find a knowledge of the Hebrew language very helpful here. The non-Hebrew student should make use of commentaries that treat the Hebrew text. A close study of the introduction to the book of Proverbs (1:2-6) will yield a good understanding of what the book proposes to do. The writer or collector intends that his readers shall know wisdom (Heb. *chokhmâh* = Grk. *sophia* = intellectual instruction) and instruction (Heb. *mûsar* = Grk. *paideian* = a balanced education, self-discipline) (vs. 2a). The student is expected to discern (*hābîn*) the sayings of understanding (Heb. *bînāh* = Grk. *phronēsis* = practical application of wisdom) (vs. 2b). He is to receive instruction in wise behavior (Heb. *haskēl* = Grk. *noēsai* = to intellectually discern), namely, righteousness, justice, and equity (hence, this = Grk. *sunesis* = moral judgment) (vs. 3). Verse four employs synonymous parallelism, so that "simple" = "youth," and "knowledge" and "discretion" = "prudence." The simple person is one whose mind is not set so that it cannot be changed through instruction. The book, therefore, is for anyone who is still willing to learn. Verse five also employs synonymous parallelism, so that "wise man" = "man of understanding," and "increase in learning" = "acquire skill." Verse six is also synonymous parallelism, so that "proverb" = "words of the wise," and "figure" = "riddles." Hence, the book contains material which will enable the immature to so understand the words of the wise as to be able to apply these truths to daily living. "Proverb" in this book can be defined as "the word of the wise."

The book of Proverbs contains heterogeneous materials. Included are short, sentence proverbs without any context (comprising most of the book), brief poems (30:1-9; 31:1-9), a numerical poem (30:11-31), and an alphabetic poem on the worthy woman (31:10-31). The sentence proverbs are the most difficult to interpret since they have no context. There are three main classes of these short proberbs: (1) those which contrast the wise man with the fool, (2) those which contrast the righteous man with the wicked, and (3) those which emphasize man's relationship to God. These proverbs deal in generalizations and should not be interpreted as containing all truth in and of themselves. They may deal with only one item which contributes to financial success, social well-being, or fellowship with God. To make them mean more than they say is detrimental to their intent.

The authors of proverbs are fond of personification, so that Folly is personified (cf. 1:10-19; 4:14-17; ch. 5; ch. 7; 9:13-18) and contrasted with a personified Wisdom (cf. 1:20-33; 8:1-21; 9:1-6). The characteristics and fruits of the good life (chs. 2-3) are contrasted with the characteristics and fruits of folly (ch. 6). The relationship of this personified wisdom to creation is set forth (3:19-20; 8:22-31). Blessings are pronounced upon the one who learns good speech (10:11-14), beneficence (11:24-26), discipline (12:1, 15), and contentment (14:30). Warnings are issued to the sluggard (12:11), the arrogant (16:18), one who trusts his own conscience (14:12), and one who refuses discipline (15:5). These are just a few illustrations of the variety of wise sayings in the book of Proverbs.

Proverbs frequently employ emblematic parallelism by which everyday matters are compared with spiritual truths (cf. 25:3, 11-14, 18-20, 25-26, 28). They also make use of progressive parallelism whereby relative values are compared (cf. 25:24; 27:5; 28:6, 23). These proverbs follow a common pattern used by other Eastern peoples as well as by the Egyptians. They attempt to make the abstract spiritual truths relevant by communicating them in everyday language. Poetry aids the memory, and the memorization of many of these proverbs could be a worthwhile adventure.

Ecclesiastes

The book of Ecclesiastes is written in the form of a soliloquy. The author often muses with himself in his effort to work out the problem of human happiness. Some of his statements, if isolated from their context, could lend themselves to pessimism or even skepticism. But the entire book needs to be interpreted in light of the conclusion which is stated in 12:9-14. After the author had weighed, studied, and arranged his material, he concluded that the only wise thing for man to do is to fear God and keep his commandments, for God will judge man on the basis of his deeds.

The primary difference between Ecclesiastes and an ordinary soliloquy is that "The Preacher" declares that he has actually experienced the things about which he writes. However, it is quite obvious that his reflections on these experiences did not always yield the same conclusions. For instance, at one time he may declare that work and labor are a vanity and striving after wind (or vexation of spirit) (2:9-23), but again he may conclude that there is something good and rewarding in labor (2:24-26). These different conclusions do not indicate a contradiction in the book; rather it can be determined that the author came to realize that labor and toil are only valuable when a man lives to please God. This is the method by which a soliloquy must be interpreted. One must not analyze the parts so as to lose sight of the whole. This is true of all biblical interpretation, but especially of this kind of literature.

Job

The book of Job provides us with still a third type of wisdom literature. This book contains a prose prologue and epilogue and a poetic dialogue which constitutes the bulk of the book. Other ancient books of wisdom have been found which follow the same pattern. While it seems quite evident that Job was a historical character (cf. Ezek. 14:14, 20; James 5:11), it seems just as evident that the debate which he had with his fellow philosophers was not originally delivered in the beautiful poetry contained in the book. Apparently some skilled poet has taken the material which may have been handed down orally or in written form and has skillfully written the controversy in poetic style. This is the same thing that our song writers are constantly doing. We frequently sing hymns based on some narrative of the Bible, but the poet has restructured the material to compose a poem which says the same thing. Poetry captures and holds the attention so that the mind of the reader can be focused on the issue until its final conclusion.

One must not suppose that in such a dialogue everything that is said is true. Not everything that Job says is true (cf. 9:13-24 and 40:3-5; 42:1-6), nor is everything which the "friends" say false (cf. 4:17 with Rom. 3:1-26). The reader must pay close attention to three elements within the book if the dialogue is to be properly understood. He must notice what God says about Job in the prologue (1–2) and epilogue (42:7-9), while at the same time not failing to consider what God says about Job in the Jehovah speeches which end the dialogue (chs. 38–41). These philosophers acknowledge that their conclusions were reached through human thought processes; therefore, their words must be weighed against divine truth (cf. 4:7-8; 5:27; 8:8-10; 12:1-2; 13:1-4; 15:7-10; 20:1-5; 26:14; 32:6, 10). Always, when one studies the Bible, he must ask: Who is speaking? An inspired person or an uninspired person? The necessity of so analyzing the material is much greater in a book like Job.

THE FORM OF HEBREW POETRY

Since two-fifths of the OT is poetry, it is essential that the serious student study from a translation which writes the poetry as such. Unfortunately, the KJV does not do this. The ASV (1901) writes most of the poetry as poetry, but fails to do so with Ecclesiastes and the Prophets. The New American Standard Bible and the RSV, as well as most modern translations, write all of the poetry as poetry.

It is also essential that the student know something of the form of Hebrew poetry, which differs considerably from English poetry. Rhyme and rhythm are not major features of Hebrew poetry. The primary feature of Hebrew poetry is *parallelism*, which means a balanced thought pattern by which the thought of one line of poetry is compared with the thought of a succeeding line or lines. The most basic forms of Hebrew parallelism are given here.

Internal Parallelism

Internal parallelism involves the shortest possible unit, usually the comparison of only two lines of poetry. The three basic forms, with their subdivisions, are as follows. The examples are from the Psalms.

Synonymous parallelism. In this form the thought of the first line is repeated in other words in the second line. This form may be subdivided into two subforms. In *identical parallelism* the second line uses exact synonyms of key words in the first line:

The earth is the Lord's, and the fullness thereof;
the world, and they that dwell therein.

24:1

In *similar parallelism* the key terms in the two lines are not precisely synonymous, but the thoughts are similar:

Day unto day pours forth speech,
and night unto night declares knowledge.

19:2

Antithetic parallelism. In this form the second line provides a contrast to the thought of the first line:

They will collapse and fall;
but we shall rise and stand upright.

20:8

Synthetic parallelism. The second line adds something to the thought of the first line in synthetic parallelism. There are five basic subdivisions of synthetic parallelism:

(1) *Completion type*, which is laregly a parallelism of rhythm rather than of sense:

Yet have I set my king
upon Zion, my holy hill.

2:6

(2) *Comparison* (or *progressive*) *type*:

I would rather be a doorkeeper in the house of my God
than dwell in the tents of wickedness.

84:10

(3) *Reason type*, in which the second line provides a reason for the thought of the first line:

But there is forgiveness with thee,
that thou mayest be feared.

130:4

(4) *Stairlike* (or *climactic*), in which part of the preceding line is repeated in the succeeding line and is made the starting point for an additional idea:

Ascribe to the Lord, O heavenly beings,
ascribe to the Lord glory and strength.

29:1

(5) *Emblematic*, in which one part of the verse becomes a figure to enhance the thought of the other line:

For as the heavens are high above the earth,
so great is his steadfast love toward those
who fear him.

103:11

Any of the above forms may be written in *complete* or *incomplete* form. The example given above under *similar parallelism* involves complete parallelism because there is a corresponding key word or phrase in the second line to match every key word or phrase in the first line. "Day unto day" corresponds to "night unto night," and "pours forth speech" corresponds to "declares knowledge.'The example given under *identical parallelism* involves incomplete parallelism. The phrase, "is the Lord's," is not repeated in the writing of the second line, but must be understood as applying to both lines. External parallelism may also involve either complete or incomplete parallelism.

A second variation of any of the above forms is that the lines may be written in *inverted* or *chiastic* form. The syntactical arrangement of the first line is reversed in the writing of the second line. Psalm 91:14 ia a good example:

Because he cleaves to me in love (a), I will deliver him (b);
I will protect him (b), because he knows my name (a).

"Because he cleaves to me in love" is equivalent to "because he knows my name," and "I will deliver him" is equivalent to "I will protect him." Thus, we have an a-b-b-a arrangement. This chiastic arrangement may apply to either internal or external parallelism.

External Parallelism

External parallelism is an extension of internal parallelism in that pairs of parallel lines are combined to form a larger unit. There are three major subdivisions of external parallelism.

Synonymous. In this case, all four (or more) lines of poetry say the same thing in other words. This follows the a-b-c-d pattern:

> The cords of death encompassed me,
> The torrents of perdition assailed me;
> The cords of Sheol entangled me,
> The snares of death confronted me.

Psalm 18:45

Antithetic. This may take one of two forms. (1) It may follow the a-b, a-b pattern in which the first two lines are synonymous and the third and fourth lines are synonymous, but the two sets of lines form a contrast:

> Yet a little while, and the wicked will be no more;
> Though you look well at his place, he will not be there.
> But the meek shall possess the land,
> And delight themselves in abundant prosperity.

37:10,11

(2) It may follow the a-c, b-d pattern in which the first and third lines correspond and the second and fourth lines correspond, but the a-c, b-d pattern forms a double contrast:

> Though with thine own hand didst drive out the nations,
>   but them thou didst plant;
> thou didst afflict the peoples,
>   but them thou didst set free.

44:2

Synthetic. This may take more than one form. (1) It may follow the a-b-c-d pattern in which each succeeding line adds something to the thought of what precedes:

> If we had forgotten the name of our God,
>   or spread forth our hands to a strange god,
> would not God discover this?
>   For he knows the secrets of the heart.

44:20,21

(2) It may follow the a-b-b-a pattern in which lines one and four are parallel and lines two and three are parallel.

> If I forget you, O Jerusalem,
> Let my right hand wither!

Let my tongue cleave to the roof of my mouth,
If I do not remember you.

137:5,6

There is no definite method of *stanza arrangement* discernible in Hebrew poetry, although most of the more recent English translations leave a blank line where the translators felt that a stanza division was desirable. Recurring refrains often indicate the movement of thought in a poem, but these divisions do not always correspond to English or American stanza arrangement. Good examples of recurring refrains are Psalms 42:5, 11; 43:5; 46:7, 11; 49:12, 20; 59:6, 14: Amos 1:3, 6, 9, 11, 13; 2:1, 4, 6; Isa. 9:12b, 17b, 21b; 10:4b.

There are several Hebrew *acrostics* or alphabetic poems in which each succeeding line, verse, or series of verses begins with the next succeeding letter of the Hebrew alphabet. The book of Lamentations is written in a series of acrostics. The familiar poem about the worthy woman in Proverbs 31:10-31 is also an acrostic, as are Psalms 9–10, 25, 34, 37, 111, 112, 119, and 145. The alphabetic arrangement is not discernible in translation, so the Hebrew student should consult the Hebrew text, and the non-Hebrew student should consult a good commentary based on the Hebrew text. In Psalms 9–10, 25, 35, and 37, every two verses begin with the next succeeding letter of the Hebrew alphabet. The intervening lines are neutral and may begin with any letter. In Psalms 111 and 112, each line of poetry (each half verse in English) begins with the next succeeding letter. In Psalm 119, each of the first eight verses begins with the first letter of the Hebrew alphabet, each of the second eight verses with the second letter, etc. Each English verse contains two lines of poetry, the first of which begins with the designated letter and the second of which is neutral.

There are two great values to be received by the student who understands Hebrew poetry. In the first place, he will learn not to be over technical in his interpretation of words used in poetic repetition for the sake of effect. In the second place, he will grasp the flow of thought much better through an understanding of the poetic form in use.

APOCALYPTIC LITERATURE

Characteristics

A possible definition of apocalyptic literature is that it is a highly symbolic portrayal of coming destruction on the wicked world, which also promises triumph for the righteous. Within this general definition there are several specific characteristics.

Mysterious. Apocalyptic literature has a tendency to deal with the esoteric and mysterious. The secrets of God's intervention into human history are revealed, but usually only in a general way. Daniel saw some things in visions which he found extremely difficult to understand (cf. 7:15-22; 8:27; 12:6,8). The apostle John indicates that some things in the book of Revelation are hard to interpret (cf. 13:18; 17:9).

A significant difference between canonical and non-canonical apocalypses needs to be noted. Daniel is told to shut up the vision (8:26; 12:9) because the fulfillment is for the distant future, but the word *satham* (preserve), not *sathar* (hide, conceal) is used. In noncanonical apocalypses of the intertestamental period, the writer may claim that the angel commanded the original writer to conceal the material until a later time (2 Esdras 12:37), or the claim is made that the writings are concealed until the last age (2 Enoch 33:10-11). Perhaps it is because of this attempted imitation of the book of Daniel, involving a misunderstanding of Daniel, that John is told not to seal up his book (Rev. 22:10).

Eschatological. Apocalyptic literature involves eschatology, the doctrine of the last things and days. Old Testament eschatology may refer to the first coming of Christ (cf. Joel 2:28-32; Acts 2:16-21) or the end of all things at his second coming (cf. Daniel 12). New Testament eschatology may refer to the inauguration of the "last days," at Christ's first coming (cf. Heb. 1:1-2; 2:1-4) or to the consummation of all things at his second coming (cf. 1 Pet. 1:3-5).

In time of crisis. Apocalyptic literature is written in a time of crisis. When men are disillusioned with the present world situation, they long for some assurance that God's justice will eventually right the wrongs. The parts of the OT which can safely be designated as apocalyptic give evidence of the element of crisis. Daniel and Ezekiel were exiles in Babylon along with their fellow-Israelites, and it must have seemed to many that God's promises to David of an everlasting kingdom could not be realized. Zechariah lived in a time of great opposition to the reconstruction era following the Babylonian exile. It may have appeared to many faithful Jews that the temple would never be rebuilt. Joel pictures some great calamity which is coming on the Lord's people, possibly the Babylonian exile. Several noncanonical apocalypses were written during the time of Syrian corruption and persecution in the second pre-Christian century. The book of Revelation was written at the beginning of the outbreak of Roman persecution against the church.

Epochal. There is a tendency in apocalyptic literature to divide time into periods or epochs marked by divine intervention into human affairs. The rise and decline of empires is a major feature of the book of Daniel (chs. 2, 7). There is the 1,260-day period of Satanic persecution against the church, during which time the church witnesses for God while clothed in sackcloth (Rev. 11–12). This symbolizes the breaking of the persecuting power of Rome. It is evident that OT apocalyptic, especially the book of Daniel, greatly influenced the language of the book of Revelation.

Symbolic. There is a great deal of symbolism in apocalyptic literature. There is fondness for the symbolic use of numbers, especially three, four, six, seven, ten, twelve, and multiples of these. The great struggle is between God and Satan or between Christ and the antichrist. The strength and swiftness of animals and birds symbolize the great forces of evil or good which often meet in conflict. Wars between God's servants and the world power may be pictured in highly symbolic language (cf. Dan. 10; Rev. 12). Daniel's nondescript beast (ch. 7), representing his fourth world power, and Ezekiel's vision of wheels within wheels (ch. 1), along with the four living creatures, almost defy description. One needs to understand that proper interpretation of these symbols often requires that the details be understood as serving no other purpose than to heighten the dramatic setting in which they are cast. The central truth is usually evident, but sometimes the particulars are extremely difficult to comprehend. It is obvious in all this symbolism that the primary lesson is that God's sovereignty will eventually triumph over the evil forces of Satan.

Predictive. The predictive element is paramount in apocalyptic literature. Daniel 2, 7, and 8 predict the successive rise and fall of the Medo-Persian, Macedonian (Grecian), and Roman empires.

Survey of Old Testament Apocalypses

While there is a great deal of difference among interpreters as to whether certain passages are apocalyptic in style and nature, it is generally agreed that the following are to be classed as apocalyptic literature.

Joel portrays invading armies as a great locust plague devastating Judah, and the impending judgment awaiting the covenant people is designated as the day of the Lord (chs. 1–2). Then he pictures a worldwide judgment which destroys the ungodly nations and vindicates God's loyal people (ch. 3).

Daniel emphasizes the establishment of the kingdom of God during the time of the fourth world empire (chs. 2, 7). He describes a "little horn" from the Grecian Empire, which turns out to be the "abomination of desolation" which attempts to completely wipe out Judaism; but God intervenes on behalf of his people and overthrows the tyrant (8:8-14, 21-26). He also decribes a "little horn" from the fourth world power which exalted himself against the saints until the Ancient of Days came and put an end to his power and gave the kingdom to the saints forever (7:7-22).

Ezekiel sees the glory of the Lord portrayed before his eyes in vivid symbolism (ch. 1). At a later time he sees the glory of the Lord removed from Jerusalem (chs. 10–11) as a symbol of the exile resulting from Judah's sins. The famous vision of the valley of dry bones signifies the restoration of Israel and Judah from captivity (ch. 37). In some distant future time Gog, prince of Meshech and Tubal, is to be destroyed (chs. 38–39). The many interpretations of these symbols are treated in the respective commentaries. There are other apocalyptic pictures in Ezekiel, but these will suffice here.

Zechariah describes the conflict between God's two anointed ones, the prince and the priest, and Satan and pictures the cleansing of the priest, which in turn symbolizes the cleansing of the nation (chs. 3–4). Later he sees God's four horsemen go out to patrol the earth to "set my Spirit at rest in the north country" so that the temple could be completed (ch. 6). Finally, after many conflicts, victory comes to the saints in the final judgment (ch. 14). Other apocalyptic pictures are also given in Zechariah.

Perhaps it would be well to include a brief resume of a noncanonical apocalypse in order to indicate how these works imitated and yet departed from the recognized authoritative scriptures. First Enoch was apparently written in the second or first pre-Christian century. In this book the fall of the angels brings on the judgment (ch. 1–5) because of the corruption brought about through the cohabitation of angels and human beings (chs. 6–8), which results in the flood (chs. 9–11). According to this work, it is not the fall of man (cf. Gen. 6) which brings on the flood, but it is the fall of angels. The idea of the cohabitation of angels with men involves a strange but popular interpretation of the Genesis declaration that the "sons of God" married the "daughters of men." According to 1 Enoch, Azazel, the chief watcher, is destroyed by the flood, but his offspring become demons in the air all about us (chs. 12–16). Enoch is allowed to view the deep valleys of the dead (chs. 17–36) and to see visions of a pre-existent Messiah, the Son of Man (chs. 37–71) who will judge the mighty rulers and deliver the oppressed. The degrees of punishment in the valleys of the dead, depending on how much meritorious atonement for their sins had taken place in this life, is out of keeping with biblical teaching, but the idea of a pre-existent Son of Man is in keeping with NT teaching.

FIGURATIVE LANGUAGE

While it is true that most of the Bible is written in direct, literal language, it also contains much figurative language. This is sometimes couched in very simple similes or metaphors, but at other times the figure is more extended. Sometimes symbolic language, which has a tendency to be mystical and esoteric, is also used. Great care needs to be exercised in the interpretation of figurative language in the Bible.

Extended Figures of Speech
In addition to the simple figures of speech discussed in Chapter 1, the Bible sometimes employs more extended figures which frequently require greater care in interpretation.
Similitudes and allegories. A similitude (parable) is an extended simile, and an allegory is an extended metaphor. There are few similitudes in the OT. Those which do exist frequently contain a mixture of other types, which suggests that they could be better classified as fables or allegories. The classic OT parable or similitude is Nathan's parable of the little ewe lamb in 2 Samuel 12:1-6. This story vividly illustrates the fact that a parable can withhold the application of the essential truth until the crucial moment when the application will be most effective.

Allegories are more frequently found in the OT than are similitudes. In an allegory, several points of comparison are made instead of only one point of comparison which is made in a metaphor. Psalm 80:8-16 (cf. Isa. 5:1-7) describes Israel under the allegory of a vine. Proverbs 5:15-18 describes sexual purity under the allegory of a pure body of water in a cistern, well, or spring (cf. vss. 19-23). Ecclesiastes 12:3-7 describes old age as a gathering storm. Ezekiel 13:8-16 describes the activities of false prophets as being like one who builds a house and covers it with whitewash.
Riddles and fables. The word "riddle" in our English versions can be misleading. Sometimes this word is used in a general rather than a technical sense. For instance, the

"riddle" and "allegory" of Ezekiel 17:1-24 are better described technically as a fable. The "dark sayings" occasionally mentioned in the OT (Ps. 78:2; Prov. 1:6) are not necessarily, or usually, riddles in the technical sense, but are only figures that reflect the wisdom sayings of the day. A riddle, in the strictest sense, seems to have been told for the very purpose of taxing the ingenuity of the reader. The example of a riddle in the OT in Judges 14:14. The context of the entire chapter explains the riddle.

A fable is a fictitious story which teaches a moral lesson. Aesop's Fables are probably the best examples. There are several fables in the OT, all of which are explained by the context (cf. Judg. 9:1-20; 2 Kings 14:9-10; Ezek. 17). Note that all of these involve times of stress when vividness of communication was highly desirable.

Numerology in the Old Testament

Graded numerical sequence. This involves a sequential use of numbers in which any number may be used with the next highest number to form a climax. This has frequently been designated as the $x/x + 1$ formula. Any series may be used. Those which in fact are used in the OT are the 1/2, 2/3, 3/4, 5/6, 7/8, and 1,000/10,000 sequences. The two significant things in this sequential use of numbers are the title line and the list which follows. By comparing these two items, the $x/x + 1$ sequence can be seen to fall into one of three patterns: (1) the second number is the only one to be considered in the listing, (2) the first number is the only one to be considered in the listing, or (3) neither numeral is to be taken literally.

Several examples of the first group are found in the OT. The list of items following the title line shows that the first numeral is included only for poetic effect to fill out the parallel structure. A good example of this first type is Proverbs 30:15b-16:

> Three things are never satisfied;
>   four never say, "Enough":
> Sheol, the barren womb,

the earth, ever thirsty for water,
and the fire which never says, "Enough."

Since four things (Sheol, the barren womb, the earth, and fire) are listed, the number three has no numerical significance but is only used to provide a climax by means of poetic parallelism. Other examples of this use of sequential numbers are Proverbs 30:18-19, 21-23, 29-31; 6:16-19; and possibly Job 5:19-22.

While it is true that the second numeral is the one usually emphasized in the graded numerical sequence, it is possible for the first numeral to be taken literally and for the second to be used figuratively. Deuteronomy 17:6 says, "On the evidence of two witnesses or three witnesses he that is to die shall be put to death; a person shall not be put to death on the evidence of one witness." It is obvious from the last clause that the statement means to say that two or more witnesses are required before the death penalty can be executed. The number three is not to be taken literally in this case.

Sometimes sequential numbers are used in a way that indicates that neither numeral is to be taken literally. In this case, the numerals provide merely a poetic device to indicate an indefinite number, usually a small number. This is the sense in which Amos refers to the "three transgressions of . . . , for four" of the nations which he has under consideration (Amos 1:3, 6, 9, 11, 13; 2:1, 4, 6). He mentions neither three nor four transgressions of any of the nations, but he is using this device to indicate their sin is continual. It is interesting that Amos accuses none of these nations of being idolaters, though he certainly could have. He intends only to refer to the kind of sin which man's conscience should condemn. Other examples which could be included in this category which indicate indefinite numbers are Judges 5:30; Ezra 10:13; 2 Kings 9:32; Jeremiah 36:23; 2 Kings 13:19; Ecclesiastes 11:2.

It seems likely that word-pairs which do not involve numerals may occasionally be used in a sense similar to the graded sequence numerical equation. This means that only one of the words in the word-pair is essential to the discussion at hand and that the other word simply fills in the poetic parallelism. In these cases, words which were already established as word-pairs were used. Either of the words in the word-pair may be the one which is emphasized. Only the context can determine which.

An example of a broken word-pair in which the meaning is restricted to the second word can be illustrated by Proverbs 24:30-32. Verse 30 mentions both "field" and "vineyard," but verses 31-32 describe only a vineyard enclosed by a stone wall. Fields were marked by boundary stones (Deut. 19:14; 27:17; Prov. 22:28; 23:10), rather than being enclosed by stone walls; therefore, our passage is not describing a field. Since "field" and "vineyard" had already become word-pairs in the minds of the people (cf. Exod. 22:5; Num. 16:14; 20:17; 21:22; 1 Sam. 8:14), the word "field" can be used by the wise man to fill in the parallel structure, even though he had only a vineyard in mind.

In these broken-up word-pairs, the meaning may be restricted to the first word in the pair. Since "father" and "mother" were frequently used as word-pairs (cf. Prov. 19:26; 20:20; 23:22; 30:11, 17), these two words may be used in parallel structure when only one of the parents is meant. Both "father" and "mother" may be used in synonymous parallelism, in which case equal treatment is given to both parents (cf. Prov. 10:1; 15:20; 30:11, 17). But in some passages only the responsibility of the father in Israelite society is under consideration. Proverbs 4:3-4a says,

> When I was a son with my father
>   tender, the only one
>   in the sight of my mother,
> he taught me, and said to me,

The singular pronouns used in 4a indicate that only the father is under consideration. The word "mother" is used only as a poetic device.

Symbolic use of numbers. While numerals are usually used in their literal sense in the OT, there is also evidence that they may be used with a symbolic meaning which goes beyond their literal import. There is wide divergence of opinion on the part of OT interpreters in regard to symbolic language in general and symbolic numerology in particular. These views range all the way from those who deny that any symbolic material is found in the OT to those who tend to take almost everything symbolically. Systems of theology should not be based on some strange, symbolic interpretation of Scripture which ignores the literal import of most of its language. On the other hand, those passages which do lend themselves readily to a symbolic interpretation, especially where the literal meaning renders the passage unintelligible or contradictory, should not be neglected.

Symbolic use of numbers in the OT seems to be somewhat rare. Yet it does seem that the numbers three, four, seven, and ten stood as symbols of completeness or perfection. This, or course, does not mean that these numerals were not often used literally. The three annual festivals of Israel (Exod. 23:17), Balaam's blessing Israel three times (Num. 24:10), Elijah's pouring out water three times (1 Kings 18:34), the threefold betrothal in Hosea 2:19-20, the thrice-given "Holy, holy, holy" (Isa. 6:3), and the priestly benediction which repeated the name of God three times (Num. 6:24-26) all seem to follow the Babylonian and Egyptian patterns of the triad which stood for the superlative degree, completion, or perfection.

The number four frequently is used in connection with the four cardinal points of the compass to indicate the whole earth (cf. Ezek. 37:9; Dan. 7:2; Zech. 6:5).

The number seven gives the clearest evidence of having symbolic significance. The seventh day (Exod. 20:8-11), month (Lev. 23:24), and year (Exod. 23:10-11) were sacred to Israel. Ceremonial cleansing from touching a dead body (Num. 19:11; 12:14) or from leprosy (Lev. 13:4) lasted for seven days. A young animal could not be sacrificed until it was seven days old (Lev. 22:27). Balaam offered seven bullocks and seven rams upon seven altars (Num. 23:29). Israel was commanded to march around Jericho once each day for six days and seven times on the seventh day, at which time the walls would fall down (Josh. 6). Zechariah 3:9 pictures a stone with seven eyes, which are interpreted as the eyes of the Lord which range through the whole earth (Zech. 4:10). On the Day of Atonement blood was sprinkled by the high priest seven times (Lev. 16:14), and the Feast of Weeks (Lev. 23:15) came seven weeks after the seven-day Feast of Unleavened Bread (Lev. 23:6). These and other considerations indicate that the number seven had a symbolic meaning beyond its literal import.

Since a decimal system of numeration prevailed generally in the ancient world of Israel's national era, it is most likely that the number ten also stood for completion since all other numbers are composed of the first ten. The fact that many numbers in the OT were rounded off to the nearest ten is too common knowledge to need elaboration here. The number ten also seems to be used in a symbolic sense on occasion. Jacob's wages were changed ten times (Gen. 31:7), there are ten plagues in Egypt (Exod. 7–11). The Law is summarized in the Ten Commandments (Exod. 20:1-17), the Israelites tempted God ten times (Num. 14:22), Job said he was reproached ten times (Job 19:3). The dimensions of the ark in Noah's day (300 x 50 x 30 cubits, Gen. 6:15) and of the tabernacle (10 x 10 x 20 cubits) are given in multiples of ten. It seems, therefore, that God intended for the numbers three, four, seven, and ten to stand as symbols of completeness or perfection.

There is also some evidence that the number twelve, based on the twelve-month year, indicated completeness. When the tribe of Levi was chosen as the priestly tribe and thus given no specific inheritance in Canaan, the sons of Joseph, Ephraim and Manasseh, had tribes assigned to them (Num. 34:13-29). Apparently this was done to keep the number at twelve.

While there is considerable controversy in regard to the matter, it may be that the number forty is also sometimes used symbolically. The number recurs many times in the OT. The rains of the flood lasted forty days (Gen. 7:4, 12, 17) and Egyptian embalming required forty days (Gen. 50:3). Moses and Elijah fasted forty days

(Exod. 24:18; 1 Kings 19:8). The spies spent forty days in Canaan (Num. 13:25) and Goliath challenged the armies of Israel for forty days (1 Sam. 17:16). Forty stripes are exacted of certain criminals (Deut. 25:3). A forty-day period of purification was required of a woman after giving birth to a male child, and eighty days were required after giving birth to a female (Lev. 12:2-5). Judges mentions several periods of forty years or multiples of forty (cf. 3:11; 5:31; 8:28; 13:1). These and other possible examples indicate the fondness for the number forty.

Many scholars believe, with good reason, that the number forty stood as a symbol of a generation. It is believed by some that 1 Kings 6:1, which designates 480 years as the time between the Exodus and the building of the temple in the fourth year of Solomon, is not meant to be taken literally, but as representing twelve generations. Actually, twelve generations are given between these two events. First Kings 4:1-4 indicates that Zadok lived in the time of Solomon. First Chronicles 6:3-8 (Heb. 5:29-34) gives twelve generations from Amram, the father of Moses, to Zadok, who was serving as high priest at the time Solomon's temple was built. There were also twelve generations from Ahimaaz, son of Zadok, to Jehozadak, who was priest when Nebuchadnezzar destroyed the temple and took Judah captive (1 Chron. 6:8-15; [Heb. 5:34-41]). There may have been a studied effort to work out the chronological pattern in poetically balanced form, just as Genesis 5 gives ten generations from Adam to Noah, and Genesis 11 gives ten generations from Shem to Abram. Matthew poetically balances his genealogical list to have fourteen generations from Abraham to David, fourteen from David to the Babylonian captivity, and fourteen from the captivity to Christ (Matt. 1:17). A comparison of Matthew's genealogy with Luke's indicates that several generations were omitted from Matthew's list (cf. Luke 3:23-34). While this method of reckoning may seem very strange to us, it must have been common and acceptable in ancient days.

It is not necessary to assume that every number had a symbolic meaning in the OT or that the numbers three, four, seven, ten, and twelve had a symbolic meaning every time they were used.

BIBLIOGRAPHY

Berkhof, L. *Principles of Biblical Interpretation.* Grand Rapids: Baker Book House, 1950.

Farbridge, Maurice H. *Studies in Biblical and Semitic Symbolism: The Library of Biblical Studies.* Harry M. Orlinsky, ed. New York: KTAV Pub. House, Inc., 1970.

David, John J. *Bibical Numerology.* Grand Rapids: Baker Book House, 1968.

Haran, Menahem. "The Graded Numerical Sequence and the Phenomenon of 'Automatism' in Biblical Poetry," *Supplements to Vetus Testamentum.* Vol. 22. G. W. Anderson et al, eds. Leiden: E. J. Brill, 1972, pp. 238-67.

Mickelsen, A. Berkeley. *Interpreting the Bible.* Grand Rapids: William B. Eerdmans Publishing Company, 1963.

Noth, M., and Thomas, D. Winton, eds. *Wisdom in Israel and the Ancient Near East: Supplements to Vetus Testamentum.* Vol. 3. Leiden: E. J. Brill, 1960.

Roth, W. M. W. *Numerical Sayings in the Old Testament: Supplements to Vetus Testamentum.* Vol. 13. G. W. Anderson et al., eds. Leiden: E. J. Brill, 1965.

Willis, John T. *Insights from the Psalms: The Way of Life Series,* nos. 131–133. 3 vols. Abilene, Texas: Biblical Research Press, 1974.

——. *My Servants the Prophets: The Way of Life Series,* nos. 116–118. 3 vols. Abilene, Texas: Biblical Research Press, 1972.

VII

The Making of Old Testament Books

Thomas H. Olbricht

A contemporary person embarking upon the reading of the OT enters a different world. It is as if one in a few short hours flew from New York, landed in Teheran, traveled by Land Rover for two hours, and took up a stay with a nomadic group who rode camels, herded goats, ate figs, dates, and goat milk cheese, and kept a harem. In fact, this is exactly the life of certain people one comes to know from reading the OT.

The OT is different, not just because of the people one comes upon there, but also because of the very books from which one reads about them. Written documents differ considerably in terms of the manner in which they are put together. The reading of a letter from my wife's sister is a work of art. I am more accustomed to reading a letter from my mother. She sits down, picks up a pen, and in about thirty minutes turns out a two-page letter written on one side of the paper. She always writes her letters at one sitting and on pages consecutively. Not so with my wife's sister. She commences a letter which she may not finish for a couple of weeks. In different sections she puts Monday, Wednesday, Thursday. She makes later comments on remarks she has written earlier. She writes on five pages on one side then starts writing on the other side. By the time she is through it takes someone with a Master's degree to decide what is supposed to follow what and how all the various ideas and comments fit together.

There are similar problems reading other documents. Take the Constitution of the United States, for example. We are not certain how it was produced. It is supposed that Thomas Jefferson had much to do with the final form. But it was not just Jefferson's work. It represented the thinking of the Constitutional Convention, made up of a number of men from the various states. Then, too, it was not all produced at one time. At the back are the amendments which have been added intermittently over almost a 200-year period. In order to make heads or tails out of this or any other document, it is necessary to have some understanding as to how it was put together. To assume that my sister-in-law's letters are just like my mother's would cause me to reach false conclusions about what she wrote. To assume that the Constitution of the United States was compiled by one man at one sitting is to fail to understand that document.

In order to understand the books of the OT it is necessary to have some vision of how they came to be. They were not each put together in the same way, obviously. The book of Psalms was not composed like the book of Isaiah. The books of 1 and 2 Chronicles were not put together like the book of Amos. One cannot presuppose how a book of the OT was put together. He must examine the book as closely as possible to determine what clues are found in it as to the manner of its composition.

Some assume, on the basis of a preconceived doctrine of inspiration, that all books of the Bible are produced just like a letter in the NT. Take an epistle such as 1 Thessalonians, for example. It is commonly assumed that Paul, guided by the Holy Spirit, sat down and wrote his first letter to the Thessalonians at one sitting. The assumption is made that all books of the Bible were produced in a like manner. In fact, it is claimed that if they were given by God, that is, inspired, this would have to be the method by which they were produced. Luke does not seem to share this assumption. At the beginning of his gospel, Luke states that he has collected materials which others have written, as well as utilized stories about Jesus which he has heard orally. From these materials he has put together the Jesus story according to his own preference in content and order.

> Inasmuch as many have undertaken to compile a narrative of the things which have been accomplished among us, just as they were delivered to us by those who from the beginning were eyewitnesses and ministers of the word, it seemed good to me also, having followed all things closely for some time past, to write an orderly account for you, most excellent Theophilus.
>
> Luke 1:1-3

There is no biblical a priori as such as to how a document may be produced. One cannot argue that if Luke collected materials in order to produce his gospel, it is not a God-inspired document. In fact, if he claims he collected materials and if his work shows evidences of collected materials, then that must be considered as the means through which God worked. There is no a priori reason that God could not have been at work in Luke's process of collection. There is apparently no one way in which all books of the Bible were produced. At the same time there was no one way in which they were inspired. According to the writer of Hebrews, inspiration was multifold. "In many and various ways God spoke of old to our fathers by the prophets; but in these last days he has spoken to us by a Son" (Heb. 1:1-2).

From claims in the Bible itself, biblical documents are inspired in various ways. Therefore, one who seeks the method through which a biblical document is put together is by no means denying the inspiration of the Bible. He, of course, could be, if in fact he does not believe the Bible inspired. But if he believes in inspiration, he can in good conscience seek to discover the various means through which OT materials were worked into a book. In fact, he claims that the very manner in which they were inspired has to be determined by looking at the book itself and examining the evidence. One cannot determine before looking at a specific book how it was inspired. If one can determine with some plausibility the manner in which a book was put together, then he understands something of the way in which God worked to make the words his own. In so doing the biblical student enhances his understanding of the work. In having a glimpse of how it was put together, he understands how to read it. The difference between various OT books may be as much as the letters of my mother and my sister-in-law. Without understanding how differently they were written one really would not understand the letters. The same holds true for books of the OT.

THE MAKING OF THE BOOK OF THE PSALMS

Most Christians have received considerable enjoyment and comfort from reading the Psalms. All have favorites such as Psalms 23, 19, and 119. Many persons have searched out these Psalms individually without being much concerned to find out about overall structure. It is of some help in understanding the Psalms to see the larger pattern, to raise the question of how the larger book of the Psalms was composed.

In the NT one reads such statements as "For David himself says in the Book of Psalms . . ." (Luke 20:42). From this statement the conclusion could be drawn that the book of Psalms is a product of David's authorship. Should one form this conclusion he might conceive David near the end of his career, say about 965 B.C., getting the word from God one day that he was going to dictate the book of Psalms to him. Therefore, on that day he was to be prepared with ink, quills, and animal skins. On that day, then, God delivered to David, word for word, Psalms 1–150. An alternate version could be that rather than on one day, God gave to David the Psalms one by one over a period of years. As David received the Psalms, he put them into a box face down. At the end of his career he turned them over and there neat and nice were the 150 Psalms. Neither of these versions is possible, however, if one follows the evidence found within the book of the Psalms.

In the first place, only 73 of the 150 Psalms are ascribed to David. Of the rest, some are ascribed to Solomon, Moses, Asaph, the Sons of Korah, Heman, and Ethan. Fifty-three of the total are ascribed to no person. Others have superscriptions commenting on the psalm, but thirty-four are without superscription altogether. It seems unlikely that these superscriptions go back to the original authors of these Psalms. If they do, certainly God did not reveal the Psalms to David as a unit. Those of the other authors would have been revealed individually. If this is the case, then the question remains as to who collected them and when.

But it seems unlikely that at least all the superscriptions originally belonged to the Psalms. Should this be the case, then two conclusions follow. First, it is clear that whoever added these superscriptions considered the book of Psalms a collection of psalms, much like a twentieth-century hymnal, rather than the production of one author. Second, it would seem that someone later than the age of Solomon (about 961–922 B.C.) put the Psalter into its present form. How much later depends on the date of the latest Psalms. It is apparent to this author that Psalm 74 was written after the Babylonians destroyed Jerusalem in 587 B.C. Psalm 137 was obviously written a few months or years later by those who were taken as exiles to Babylon. Psalm 126 apparently was written after the captives returned and rebuilt houses, the city wall, and the temple, or sometime around 500 B.C. This means that the book of the Psalms as we now have it is probably no earlier than 500 B.C. and may have been put into its present form as late as 300 B.C., as numerous scholars think. Third, since the superscriptions are later, it is not necessary that all the psalms ascribed to David be written by him. In fact, the Hebrew *ledhawidh* may mean "to David," that is, a psalm dedicated to David, rather than by him, in which case the Psalm could have been written after his death. Despite the scepticism of certain scholars, however, there is no reason that David may not have written some of the Psalms himself. Clearly, he is identified as a psalmist (1 Sam. 16:18, 2 Sam 23:1; 2 Chron. 29:30). But he is even better known as one who commissioned the writing of Psalms (1 Chron. 16:4-7).

With these facts in mind we can now turn to the book of the Psalms to see what we can learn about it, then propose conclusions as to how it came to be that way. As we examine the Psalms, we discover first that it is divided into five books—Book I, Psalms 1–41; II, 42–72; III, 73–89, IV, 90–106; and V, 107–150. At the end of each of these books is a doxology or expression of praise, so 41:13; 72:18-19; 89:52; 106:48, and 150:6 (or the whole of 150 may be considered as a doxology to the whole Psalter). Second, at the beginning of the book are to be found a number of laments, while toward the end hymns of praise prevail. Despite this general trend, however, the pattern is not rigorous. Third, the Psalter can be divided into three sections based on the preference of the name ascribed to God. In Psalms 1–41 the name Yahweh appears 273 times while Elohim occurs only 15. In Psalms 42–89 Yahweh is used 74 times while Elohim appears 207 times. In Psalms 90–150 Yahweh is found 339 times, while Elohim occurs only 7. Fourth, there are evidences of smaller collections within the larger five-book framework. At the end of Book II are found these remarks, "The prayers of David, the son of Jesse, are ended" (Ps. 72:20). Since psalms attributed to David are found after this in the Psalter, for example 86 and 101, apparently a collection ended with Psalm 72, possibly 1–72. In addition, in 2 Chronicles 29:30, the statement is made that words of David and Asaph the seer were available in the time of Hezekiah (715–686 B.C.). All the Psalms attributed to Asaph are found in Book III, 73–89 with the exception of Psalm 50. The statement by the chronicler may imply that a collection was known starting with Psalm 1 and ending with 89, or it could have been 73–89. Other groupings of the Psalms may also be found. In Psalms 95–100 are a group of similar Psalms which, due to the influence of Sigmund Mowinckel, a Scandinavian, have been called enthronement Psalms. Psalms 120–134 include the super-scription "A Song of Ascents." These psalms may have been used by the people as they left their homes and traveled to Jerusalem for the religious festivals. Psalms 113–118 commence or end with "Hallelujah" or "Praise the Lord" and thus are called Hallel Psalms. They were prob-ably sung at the three great feasts. Psalms 146–150 both begin and end with "Hallelujah."

With this information we can now piece together some suggestions as to why the book of Psalms in our Bible turned out as it did. It seems likely that about the time of David's death the priests assigned to the music in the temple (1 Chron. 16:4-7) collected certain Psalms of David as well as those of Asaph and others. It is doubtful that all those available were added to the collection, since there are various Psalms in the Bible which did not make their way into the Psalter, for example Exodus 15:1-18 and Judges 5. As time went along, the priests added other Psalms to this collection. By the time of Hezekiah the collection may have totaled as many as eighty-nine Psalms. Not all the Psalms were written or collected in Jerusalem. Some of them apparently were written in the north because of the tribe and place names cited, for example Psalms 77, 80, and 81. There may have been a collection formed there which was brought to Jerusalem at the fall of Samaria in 722 B.C. These would not have immediately been added to the Jerusalem Psalms, though they may have been added by the time of Josiah (621-609 B.C.) or more likely at the time of the exile (587 B.C.) or later. During and after the exile, the leaders and people felt constrained to reconstitute the faith of old. They thus became especially interested in the Scriptures (Neh. 8–9). They were also interested in cultic worship at the temple, including the temple music (Neh. 12:27-30). In the process they no doubt spent some time rummaging around and collecting Psalms. There is tradition to the effect that Ezra the scribe finished the collection of the Psalms and put the book into the form in which we now have it. While this is doubtful, the importance of the period for collecting Psalms should not be underestimated.

Finally, in the fifth and fourth centuries B.C. the collections of the important Psalms had pretty well congealed. Some of the priests assigned to the temple music, or perhaps just one, started arranging these various collections into final form. He had one set of Psalms which used, for the most part, Elohim for God. These he kept essentially intact. He added other collections. The whole he divided into five books, perhaps in some measure preserving the groupings in which they came to him. Why they were originally grouped into five books will likely never be known. The best surmise is that the fivefold division was laid out analogously to the five books of the law of Moses. So now there were five books of the law and five books of the Psalms. To these books the collector added certain beginnings and endings. We have already noted the doxologies. It may be that the collector himself "inserted," perhaps from certain traditional materials, Psalms 1 and 150 to serve as an introduction and conclusion to the whole book. Of course, a certain amount of guesswork has gone into this reconstruction, but the evidence of the case provides fairly certain data for these conclusions.

The question remains as to the manner in which the book of the Psalms is the inspired word of God. If one believes in the inspiration of the Scriptures he believes that God somehow was at work in each of these authors as the Psalms were produced. Just how God was at work is not always clear. It could be as with the prophets (e. g., Isa. 6:1-13), but we cannot be sure. But aside from individual authors, the question remains as to how the whole turns out as the word of God. The only suggestion forthcoming is that God was at work in the collectors as well as in the authors. There is no a priori reason which could rule out his presence. Therefore, the search for the way in which a book was put together is in part the search to uncover the presence of the Spirit of God in those who collected and put together the materials of the OT. Of course, one could claim that collecting and organizing is purely human activity, as radical biblical critics have done. But one can claim, as this author does, that such activity is not the mere effort of man, but each collector and editor received assistance from the Spirit of God.

With the process of the making of the book of the Psalms before us, we now are better prepared to understand its contents. We can perceive the larger framework in which individual Psalms are situated. We are sensitive to the need to examine each Psalm individually, to ascertain its origin, date, and setting, even apart from the superscription if necessary. We are prevented from making hasty judgments trying to tie all the Psalms in some way or another into the details of the life of David. By these efforts the Psalms become alive, for they are the word of God to concrete men and women who lived before God with all the cares of man. In their human situation they suffered, complained, and approached death. But at other times they rejoiced and praised God for his good gifts.

We have employed the Psalms as something of a test case. Now that we have made observations on matters that may trouble our readers, these need not be repeated. We hopefully are now prepared to take up other OT books and draw conclusions from these documents themselves as to the manner in which they have come down to us in the form in which we have them.

THE MAKING OF THE BOOK OF PROVERBS

The book of Proverbs is much like the book of Psalms in that it consists of materials collected from more than one author. The main difference is that the units, for the most part, are much smaller, being often a proverb of two lines.

Headings in the book provide us with the following information. The first heading (1:1) reads "The proverbs of Solomon, son of David, King of Israel." A second heading is found at the beginning of 10:1, "The proverbs of Solomon." The reason for the second heading is apparent from the form, if not in some measure the content, of the material. The material in the first nine chapters contains ideas that are worked out at considerable length. The literary structure has continuity for a number of verses. Much more interest in God is manifested as well as citations of his name. The Proverbs after chapter 10 running at least through 22:17 are almost all two-line proverbs. The subject matter from one proverb to another may or may not relate to the same topic. The form most often is antithetical parallelism:

A wise son hears his father's instruction,
But a scoffer does not listen to rebuke.

Proverbs 13:1

Though some reference is made to God in this section, the theological underpinning of these proverbs is slight.

The third heading is found at the beginning of chapter 25, "These also are proverbs of Solomon which the men of Hezekiah king of Judah copied." This heading indicates that the proverbs attributed to Solomon were not all collected during his lifetime (961–922 B.C.); some were collected two centuries later in the days of Hezekiah (715–686 B.C.). The proverbs in this section have characteristics both like those of 1–9, and 10 following. The fourth heading is found at the beginning of chapter 30, "The words of Agur son of Jakeh of Massa." The final heading commences Proverbs 31, "The words of Lemuel, king of Massa, which his mother taught him." These two headings openly attribute these proverbs to someone other than Solomon. We thus learn that Proverbs is not a book produced at one sitting, but is at least five collections of materials from a minimum of three authors. These different parts have different characteristics, so it is important to recognize these sections in reading and attempting to understand these materials.

In additon to these professed divisions in the book itself, scholars find certain other sections which seem to be self-contained units. Proverbs 22:17–24:22 are different in that they consist, for the most part, of two or three verses for each period. They also stand apart because of their similarity to a collection of Egyptian proverbs titled *The Wisdom Amen-em-opet*. Another short collection is found in 24:23-34. This collection may be seen as having a heading "These also are sayings of the wise" (24:23). If so, then the phrase may be a reference to the first statement of 22:17, "Incline your ear, and hear the words of the wise."

These headings are helpful in that they call our attention to differences in form and content in the Proverbs. But just as with the Psalms, we need to be careful about insisting that these are endemic in the text. In other words, not all the Proverbs attributed to Solomon need be claimed as authored by him. Obviously Solomon was heralded to be a wise man (2 Chron. 9) and a framer of proverbs (1 Kings 4:32; 10:23-24). There is no reason for denying that a number of the Proverbs may be attributed to him.

The question is left as to the manner in which the book of Proverbs was compiled. Solomon in his time gave special attention to wise sayings, not only of Palestinian origin, but also from the other courts of Near Eastern nations, one of which was apparently Egypt. He had contact with these nations through his various wives (1 Kings 11:1-8). He no doubt added to these collections certain wise sayings of his own. So in the days of Hezekiah there was available a collection of Proverbs which probably was initiated in the time of Solomon and included some of Solomon's sayings as well as other materials, to which others were added in the intervening two hundred years, though perhaps not in any large number. To these proverbs were joined those collected by the men of Hezekiah. Some of these additional sayings may have been from the pen of Solomon. Others may have been assigned to him by way of recognizing his interest in the Proverbs and encouragement of their collection. As with certain Psalms, they may have been more associated with Solomon by way of paying tribute than because of actual authorship. Then after Hezekiah's time, to the former materials were added those attributed to the two kings of Massa. These may have been conjoined during the period of the exile and the final form given the book at that time.

Having this insight into the making of Proverbs sensitizes us to looking at the various sections of the book for the differences in structure and thought. By so doing we better understand what is going on. The Proverbs thus become more than a collection of wise insights to help young people. They become the word of God to specific persons with specific problems in specific times. But at the same time they speak to our problems, which are analogous.

But if this was the manner in which the book of Proverbs was formed, then how can it be the word of God? It seems to come more from the insights of man than from God. The writer of Proverbs himself provides an answer.

If you cry out for insight
and raise your voice for understanding,

if you seek it like silver
and search for it as for hidden treasures;
  then you will understand the fear of the Lord
and find the knowledge of God.
  For the Lord gives wisdom;
from his mouth come knowledge and understanding.

Proverbs 2:3-6

The man who struggles, observing life and the world, finds answers, but they are not alone from his knowing powers. They likewise come from God. This is the case whether or not one belongs to Israel, as with Agur and Lemuel. Numerous Proverbs existed from ancient times, but these the Spirit of God especially identified to be preserved age after age as a word for his people. God was at work in those who collected and preserved these words of wisdom.

THE MAKING OF THE BOOKS OF THE CHRONICLER

Four books of the OT are attributed to one author, commonly referred to as the Chronicler because his name is unknown. Various persons have assigned these works to Ezra the scribe, but, while this is possible, it seems unlikely. The four books are 1 and 2 Chronicles, Ezra, and Nehemiah. These works differ from the Psalms and the Proverbs by the fact that they are produced by one author or a few authors working together. They come from the same period of time and are consciously written to produce a continuous, integrated, and consistent account. At an initial glance they appear to be a history of the people of God from the beginning until the days of the author(s). Some scholars raise the question as to whether these documents should actually be called history, for they are not history in the modern, so-called objective sense. In this author's view they qualify as history, but a special sort of history, constructed not so much to set forth the facts as to bring the past to bear, as the Chronicler understood it, upon the present.

We are interested in this essay in the manner in which the Chronicler put together these four works. In order to see this we need to look over his shoulder and observe him at work. We need to ascertain his purpose and what he hoped to accomplish in these writings. We need some understanding of the people for whom he was writing and what he was trying to say to them. We need an inventory of the sorts of material available to him and a determination of the ones he employed and how he employed them. With this information we can then advance conclusions as to the reasons for the form in which these books turned out. The other historical materials in the OT are not exactly the same as that of the Chronicler, but some similarities exist. With these insights into the manner of OT history writing, we will be better prepared to appreciate and understand these historical documents in the OT.

There are a number of question marks in trying to establish an exact date for the work of the Chronicler. Most scholars place the writing at about 400 B.C. In 587 B.C. Jerusalem fell to the Babylonians. The leaders and craftmen of the land were transported to Babylonia to assure that no effective uprising would be forthcoming against Babylonia or Palestine. About forty years later, Cyrus the Persian overthrew the Babylonians. He adopted a different policy for controlling far-flung peoples and permitted the Jews to return to their native land. After some years of struggle, the city, the city wall, and the temple were rebuilt. Then an effort was undertaken to reestablish the people in the faith of old. This was not an easy task, as we learn from various incidents in Ezra and Nehemiah. In his reforming efforts, Ezra made special use of the priests and Levites (Neh. 13:30). The problems as seen in Nehemiah centered upon paying the tithes, keeping the Sabbath, and marrying foreign women (Neh. 13:4-29).

It was out of being plunged into the middle of these events that the Chronicler produced his magnum opus. He was aware that the catastrophe of fall and destruction weighed heavily upon the people, but not necessarily so as to change the manner in which they lived. The Chronicler wished to provide a rationale for the retribution of the past and to offer a program for the present, which entailed the reestablishment of the cult with its functionaries and a rigorous adherence to the law of God. A piece of poetry identified as a prayer in 2 Chronicles does an excellent job of summing up the central message of the Chronicler.

"And now arise, O Lord God, and go to thy resting
   place,
thou and the ark of thy might.
Let thy priests, O Lord God, be clothed with salvation, and let they saints rejoice in thy goodness.
O Lord God, do not turn away the face of thy anointed
   one!
Remember thy steadfast love for David thy servant."

                                              6:41-42

The Chronicler has a deep conviction that victory comes
through God acting on behalf of his people (2 Chron. 14:7;
18:31; 20:17; 32:21); therefore, in this poem Yahweh is
called on to rise and act. In contrast, failure to depend on
God, to be prideful of one's own ability, brings downfall and
defeat (2 Chron. 13:15; 16:7; 26:16). The ark is cited as the
center from which the power of Yahweh radiates. This
emphasizes the temple and its role in the salvation and
sustenance of God's people. In the view of the Chronicler,
life in Palestine should revolve about the temple. Since the
temple is the place from which the power of God radiates,
the cult functionaries, the priests and the Levites become
the most crucial figures in the land (1 Chron. 15:11-15). The
northern kingdom fell upon hard times because the priests
were driven out (2 Chron. 11:14ff.). The Levites served as
teachers, instructing the people in the ways of God, securing the gifts he promised (2 Chron. 17:9; Neh. 8:1-13). The
Chronicler says almost nothing about the priests. The
people should support the priests with tithes and keep the
law of God. When they do so, they will be immersed in
God's love (2 Chron. 33:7-8). But most of all, as this poem
indicates, the Chronicler saw the hope of God's people
resting with David and his dynasty (2 Chron. 21:7; 33:7-8).
For him God's presence was with the south, the kingdom of
Judah. Hence he spent very little time discussing the north.
He selected material which presented Judah in a favorable
light and deprecated Israel.

   Now that we have in mind the situation of the people to
whom the Chronicler wrote and the message he wished to
put across, we need to characterize the manner in which he

carried out his program in these four books. The indications are that at one time these books were one. They were divided at a later time for convenience and sequence in the canon. First Chronicles commences with the broadest possible genealogical survey from Adam to Saul (1 Chron. 1-9). Special attention is given to the two favorite lines, those of Judah (4:1-23) and of Levi (5:27-6:66). Saul is given one short chapter (10), then almost immediately the Chronicler turns to David, with chapters 11-29 devoted to him. The point is made that David was first of all recognized as king in the south (1 Chron. 12:38). David was given victory by Yahweh because he inquired of God in whatever task he undertook (1 Chron. 14:13-17), and God was with him (1 Chron. 17:2).

Second Chronicles commences with a long statement on Solomon (chs. 1-9). Solomon is depicted as taking up the work of David, especially in connection with the temple. He comes in for little criticism concerning his wives and waywardness, as in 1 Kings 11. In connection with the temple, David is seen as a second Moses, which is an important point for the Chronicler. Just as Moses gave the regulations concerning sacrifice, so David gave the regulations concerning temple worship (2 Chron. 8:12-15; cf. 29:25-30, Neh. 12:44-47). The last section of 2 Chronicles (chs. 10-36) contains the division of the Kingdom and the rise and fall of the various kings until the Babylonian exile. The kingdom is depicted as dividing because of God's promise to Jeroboam I (2 Chron. 10:15-16), but also because he "did evil, for he did not set his heart to seek the Lord" (2 Chron. 12:14). The history of the various kings was evaluated according to a set, if not single-minded, formula: "If you seek him, he will be found by you, but if you forsake him, he will forsake you" (2 Chron. 15:2).

Ezra 1-6 tells the story of the return to Jerusalem and the restoration of the temple. The importance of the temple to the welfare of Judah is highlighted. The Chronicler makes a point of the significance of Zerubbabel (Ezra 3:8-9) because of his Davidic origins (1 Chron. 3:10-24). Ezra 7-10 tells of Ezra's efforts to bring the people to a rigorous keeping of the Law and highlights the importance of the Levites. Nehemiah 1-7 tells the story of rebuilding the wall of Jerusalem. The last half of the work

(8-13) depicts the period of dedication and the efforts of Ezra to see that the people are faithful to the ways of God.

> Thus I cleansed them from everything foreign, and I established the duties of the priests and Levites, each in his work; and I provided for the wood offering, at appointed times, and for the first fruits.
>
> Nehemiah 13:30-31

The expectation is that by keeping the law of God, God in turn will be their keeper and prosper every activity.

We have now arrived at the situation to which the Chronicler spoke, the message conveyed, and an outline of the story through which he conveyed it. The final question is crucial. It is obvious that the Chronicler wrote of matters of which he was without firsthand acquaintance. He took his story back to the beginning, commencing with Adam. His observations were more genealogical than historical until the time of David; then he took up historical detail. David reigned from 1000–961 B.C., and the Chronicler did his writing about 400 B.C. In fact, much of the story about which he wrote preceded his days, with the exception of certain events found in Ezra and Nehemiah. The question then occurs, how did he generate the information to put together books of history? There are various options. (1) He could have received it all from God by direct revelation. (2) He could have received the details from some wise old religious man. (3) He could have searched in a number of available manuscripts and pieced together the story from them. It could also be that all three of these avenues were involved. At minimum, we know from his work that he claimed dependency on written sources at various points for his information. We now turn to noticing the sources which he himself cites.

In his Anchor Bible commentary on 1 Chronicles, Jacob M. Myers (1965) has collected the following references to sources in 1 and 2 Chronicles. [The citations here are Myers' translation; the RSV reads slightly different.] (1) Official records: "The book of the chronicles of King David" (1 Chron. 27:24), "The chronicles of the kings of Israel and Judah (2 Chron. 27:7; 35:27; 36:8), "The chronicles of the kings of Judah and Israel" (2 Chron. 16:11; 25:26; 28:26; 32:32), "The chronicles of the kings of Israel" (1 Chron. 9:1; 2 Chron. 20:34), "The records of the kings of Israel" (2 Chron. 33:18), "The treatise (midrash) of the chronicle of the kings" (2 Chron. 24:27), and "The decree of David the king of Israel and the decree of Solomon his son" (2 Chron. 35:4). This is the language of the Chronicler. In some cases one suspects these titles may be different language for the same document. It is not clear how many of these sources were available and examined by the Chronicler, but likely some were. (2) Official genealogical lists: "They had an official genealogy" (1 Chron. 4:33), "All of them were included in the official genealogy" (1 Chron. 5:17), "Their official genealogy" (1 Chron. 7:9; cf. 1 Chron. 7:40; 9:1, 22; 2 Chron. 12:15). From what he says, it seems likely that he was in possession of the lists. (3) Prophetic records: "The records of Samuel the seer" (1 Chron. 29:29), "The records of Nathan the prophet" (1 Chron. 29:29; 2 Chron. 9:29), "The records of Gad the seer" (1 Chron. 29:29), "The prophecy of Ahijah the Shilonite" (2 Chron. 9:29), "The visions of Iddo the seer concerning Jeroboam the son of Nebat" (2 Chron. 9:29), "The records of Shemaiah the prophet" (2 Chron. 12:15), "The visions of Iddo the seer" (2 Chron. 12:15), "The treatise (midrash) of the prophet Iddo (2 Chron. 13:22), "The records of Jehu ben Hanani" (2 Chron. 20:34), "The history of Uzziah which Isaiah the prophet, the son of Amoz, has written down" (2 Chron. 26:22), "The vision of Isaiah, the son of Amoz, the prophet in the chronicle of the kings of Judah and Israel" (2 Chron. 32:32), and "The records of his seers (referring to Manasseh)" (2 Chron. 33:19). It may seem surprising that prophets kept official court records, but from these notices their role as official chroniclers and historians cannot be denied. (4) Other documents: "Message of Sennacherib to Hezekiah" (2 Chron. 32:10-15), "Other letters of Sennacherib (2 Chron. 32:17), "The words of David and Asaph" (2 Chron. 29:30), "The document with plans for the temple" (1 Chron. 28:19), and "The Lamentations" (2 Chron. 35:25).

All these sources are extrabiblical (extracanonical). In addition to the extrabiblical materials the Chronicler had canonical OT books to draw upon, including the books of the law,

242 / THE MAKING OF OLD TESTAMENT BOOKS

the histories, and the prophets. It is obvious that he drew upon these materials and had before him 1 Samuel—2 Kings as he wrote. He may have drawn upon these works for about half of his information and on the extracanonical materials for the other half.

In his commentary on Ezra and Nehemiah, Myers noted the sources cited there (1965): (1) Ezra: "The edict of Cyrus" (1:2-4), "List of temple vessels returned to Sheshbazzar" (1:9-11), "List of returnees with Zerubbabel" (2:1-70), "Letter of Rehum and Shimshai to Artaxerxes" (4:11-16), "Reply of Artaxerxes to Rehum, Shimshai, and their partners" (4:17d-22), "Letter of Tattenai and Shethar-bozenai to Darius" (5:7b-17), "Memorandum of Cyrus located from the archives at Ecbatana" (6:2c-5, "The reply of Darius to Tattenai, Shethar-bonzenai and their partners" (6:6-12), "Rescript of Artaxerxes to Ezra" (7:12-26), "List of family heads of those returning with Ezra" (8:1-14), "Inventory of vessels and bowls" (8:26, 27), "Ezra's prayer" (9:6-15), "List of those who had married foreign wives" (10:18-44). (2) Nehemiah: "The prayer of Nehemiah" (1:5-11), "List of builders" (3:1-32), "Complaint of Sanballat against Nehemiah" (6:6-7), "Note of Nehemiah to Sanballat" (6:8), "Census list" (7:6-72a), "Ceremony of dedication of walls" (12:27-43), "Law reading ceremony" (7:72-8:18), "Ezra's prayer" (9:6-37), "Signatories to agreement" (10:1-28), "The code of 'Nehemiah'" (10:31-40), "List of residents of Jerusalem" (11:3-24), "List of towns occupied in Judah and Benjamin" (11:25-36), and "List of priests and Levites" (12:1-26). These materials probably came from the temple archives. Some may even have come from the Persian archives, supplied to the Chronicler by someone who had access to them.

From the willingness of the Chronicler to identify his sources, we can be certain that he himself spent considerable time looking through biblical and official documents to tell the story and make the point he had in mind. It is also possible that he talked with older persons and those interested in history and received some information in oral form.

From reading the works of the Chronicler, we therefore receive the above glimpses into the making of his work. Some time about 400 B.C. a religious man in Jerusalem, quite likely a Levite, decided to write a lengthy story of his people, told from a particular perspective. He was especially interested in the southern kingdom and the reasons for its ups and downs. He was convinced that it had managed to survive because of God's love for David and his promise to him. But at the same time the nation had been on the brink of disaster because it had not been faithful to God. He therefore wished to tell the story in such a way that God's care for David and his descendants would be obvious, as well as the need for life to revolve about the temple and the Levites and for the people to be faithful to the law. How was he to tell the story? Apparently he was a person who had access to the archival materials available in Jerusalem as well as elsewhere. He therefore read numerous documents and poured over the canonical books. As he gleaned pertinent information, he wrote his story, utilizing some of it and putting aside considerable as not directly related to his purpose. When he finished, his product was what we now refer to in the OT as 1 Chronicles, 2 Chronicles, Ezra, and Nehemiah.

We have already affirmed that a person working in this manner might well be under the influence of the Spirit of God. Does this mean that such a person, by incorporating statements from secular documents, elevated them to the status of inspiration? That is a difficult question to answer. But at minimum, if God was at work with the Chronicler in turning out his history, then not only was this the account which the Chronicler wished to give to his time to be available to posterity, but God himself desired special preservation of the story as told in this manner. For this reason, the work of the Chronicler and all that is contained therein has come down to us as the word of God.

THE MAKING OF THE BOOK OF AMOS

Various suppositions might be advanced concerning the making of a prophetic book. One could suppose, for example, that the book of Amos was produced in one day when God told Amos to take a pen in hand and write down these words in nine chapters. This supposition, however, runs counter to what can be discovered in the book of Amos itself. From an examination of a prophetic book, it becomes apparent that the word of the Lord which came to the prophets normally was in short oracles and not in extended utterances. A rather typical utterance may be found in Amos 3:1-2:

> Hear this word that the Lord has spoken against you,
> people of Israel, against the whole family which I
> brought up out of the land of Egypt:
> "You only have I known of all the families of the
> earth;
> therefore I will punish you for all your iniquities."

One reason for thinking that these were all the words the Lord said to the prophet at that time is the fact that the material in 3:3-8 does not take up the same point. In fact, 3:3-8 seems to be one utterance of the prophet, then 3:9-11 another. Two kinds of material are found in 3:1-2. First, the prophet makes an observation about the words which the Lord told him to speak. Second, he quotes the word which the Lord himself has spoken or given. Verses 3-8 contain only the first of these elements. Ostensibly, these verses are Amos' comments on the prophetic word and the basis upon which God gives it. But the book of Amos contains even a third type of material. Amos 1:1 is words neither from God nor from Amos, but rather comments on Amos made by a third party. There is another such section in the book, Amos 7:10-17.

From looking at the contents in Amos, therefore, we arrive at these conclusions. First, Amos does not contain a long, extended argument such as one finds, for example, in the book of Romans, or an extended narrative as in Esther. Rather, the comments are short and often appear without any bridge or continuity from one passage to another. Unlike the proverbs in Proverbs 10–22, there is no predictable length of utterance. Each section must be taken up and, on the ground of content and form, a decision made as to the length of the oracle. Second, there are at least three sorts of comments in the prophets, and we have identified these three in Amos: (1) the word of the Lord, (2) observations of the prophet upon the word of the Lord, and (3) observations on the prophet by a third party. How then did these materials come to be molded into a prophetic book?

A second supposition might be that each time a prophet received a word from the Lord he either memorized it and wrote it down on papyrus when he got home or else wrote it down at the time it was given him so it could be read to those intended. A case of the latter is obvious in the famous situation in which Jeremiah was prevented from speaking at the temple, so he dictated a statement to Baruch, who in turn was to take the document and read it at the temple (Jer. 36:1-6). When the prophet was finished with the oracle, he placed it in a box for safekeeping. At some date late in his life he took out the materials and had some scribe transcribe them on a long scroll in the order in which they were preserved in the box. There are two problems with positing this as the manner in which a prophetic book was made. The first is that it fails to account either for the prophet's own comments on the word he received or comments contained in the book by someone else about the prophet. Second, it assumes that the material in a prophetic book is always in chronological order. Whether the oracles in the book of Amos are in chronological order is difficult to determine since few indications of place or date are obvious. But in certain prophetic books where such details are apparent, for example in Jeremiah, as we shall see, we find clear indications that chronology was not altogether the basis upon which the material in the book was organized.

With these facts we are in a somewhat better position to describe the making of a prophetic book. The first ingredient of a prophetic book is a word which has come from the Lord, an oracle. These oracles are usually short and are either written before being given or after. On the other hand, perhaps they were often memorized and only written at a considerably later date. Or it is also possible that the prophet had some of his disciples present when he uttered the saying and they memorized it, or he gave it to them orally at a later time so they could memorize it. (That prophets had disciples may be ascertained from the "sons of the prophets"of an earlier day. See 2 Kings 4:38-41.) Then after preserving the word from the Lord, the prophet added his own comments and observations. These he might do either orally or in writing. At some time in his career a prophet probably organized some of his sayings according to a scheme, but not necessarily chronologically. Or it is possible that he did very little organizing or any other work on his sayings. At his death, when his disciples wished to preserve the sayings and writings of their master, they organized the materials, made certain chronological and biographical comments, and put it all in manuscript form. The final result may, of course, be basically the sayings of the prophet, but other elements are found.

With these observations before us, we are now ready to turn to the book of Amos to see what we can ascertain about the manner in which it was produced. There are three clear elements: (1) oracles from the Lord, (2) comments by the prophet upon the oracles, and (3) comments on the life and activities of Amos. Because of the last (Amos 1:1; 7:10-17), the supposition seems justified that Amos did not give the book its final form, but that someone else, possibly a disciple, at least an admirer of his, did so after his death. But the next question is difficult to answer. In what form was the material preserved when this disciple started to work on it? Had Amos already collected his materials and arranged them, or was this the work of the one who produced the book as we have it? Of course it is also possible that someone else had been working with the material even before the final editor. Before we attempt any answer to these questions we need to look at the arrangement of Amos.

Since there is an absence of historical references in Amos, it is almost impossible to determine whether the material is in chronological order. From the book itself there is nothing to prevent all of it, except the editorial comments, from being uttered on one occasion, though in this writer's view such a prospect is unlikely. If the order is not chronological, what sense can we make of it? The book commences with oracles of Amos against the nations (1:3–2:3), then follows with oracles against Judah (2:4-5) and Israel (2:6-8). The oracles against the nations are all collected in this one place. It could well be that these oracles were given at disparate times and places, but were placed together in the book for topical and literary continuity. In one sense, not just 2:6-8, but the rest of the book also is an oracle against Israel.

The remainder of the book is divided into two parts: the oracles against Israel (2:6–6:14) and the visions against Israel (7:1-9; 8:1–9:15). A pattern in the oracles is not immediately apparent. They could well be a series of unrelated sayings. There is some flow, however, perhaps suggesting an effort on someone's part to provide order. The oracles move from Amos' declaration of the basis upon which Israel stands guilty before God (3:1-9) to her concrete guilt (3:9–5:15) to the coming of God (5:16-25) and inevitable invasion and exile (5:26–6:14). The visions are more clearly organized, though the biographical note serves as an interlude. There are visions of locusts (7:1-3), devouring fire (7:4-6), the plumb line (7:7-9), and a basket of summer fruit (8:1-3). These belong together both in terms of content and form. After the visions follows a section identifying Israel's shortcoming and affirming that punishment is on the way. A final or fifth vision shows the destruction of the altar at Bethel (9:1-10). The end of the book is an oracle of hope professing that God will raise up what he has destroyed (9:9-15). Certain materials in Amos seem to have no context, for example the three famous doxologies (4:13; 5:8; 9:5-6). Some propose that the doxologies are from someone other than Amos, but this is not necessary; in fact, they make a point in each case in the text as the doxologies now stand. What is clear is that someone has given thought to organizing the book, whether Amos or another. To this writer, this organization, especially in the section 2:9–6:14, does not represent the order of the material as originally given by Amos but is a later arrangement.

We cannot be too adamant, then, about the manner in which the book of Amos received its final form. A number of hypotheses have been presented. The best this writer can do is to conclude that Amos received a series of oracles and visions over a period of time. Some of these may have been recorded and arranged according to his instructions. The rest were preserved without any particular arrangement. Then toward the end of Amos' career, or perhaps after his death, an admirer or disciple collected Amos' utterances, arranged them in a manner which appealed to him, added a historical and biographical note, and copied the book onto a manuscript. Not only then is the word from God to Amos God's message for man in all ages, but likewise the comments of Amos on the oracles, as well as the remarks of the editor and arranger who gave the book its final form.

Now we are in a much better position to set about understanding it. In the first place, we do not assume that it was given at one sitting. At the same time, we look for overall arrangement, understanding that this may be provided by someone other than Amos. Second, we are aware that prophetic oracles come in short utterances. As we look at the book, we must therefore try to determine what the boundaries of each saying are. We do not presume to find a continuity from one oracle to another. Furthermore, we do not suppose that the materials are in chronological order, though in some cases they may be. In other words, we check through the materials to determine what the facts of the case are rather than assuming ahead of time any particular characteristics of a prophetic book.

THE MAKING OF THE BOOK OF JEREMIAH

The book of Jeremiah has the essential characteristics of the book of Amos so that we can build upon observations already made. In addition to oracles, visions, comments of Jeremiah, and comments about Jeremiah, one also discovers historical material (Jer. 52) taken almost verbatim from 2 Kings 24–25. Apparently Jeremiah has received more editing than Amos, since many sections are basically prose, for example 32–45. The assumption is, perhaps not altogether justified, that prophetic oracles were always in poetic form. But Jeremiah gives us an opportunity to do what we were unable to do with Amos, namely, to reflect on the historical and chronological settings of the material.

Jeremiah contains numerous references to kings, battles, and incidents. From these references we can date much of the material in Jeremiah and ascertain to what extent the whole is chronological in sequence.

In presenting observations on the book of Jeremiah as we have it in our OT, we need first to lay a historical base so that comments made on the chronological flow in the work will be obvious. Second, we need to see what we can make out by way of overall pattern in the book. Third, we want to examine the historical allusions in the book, to reconstruct it chronologically. Finally, we want to bring together what insight these facts reveal as to the manner in which the book was put together.

Certain dates and facts are important in grasping the historical background of Jeremiah. Jeremiah commenced prophesying in the thirteenth year of the reign of Josiah. Josiah reigned from 640–609 B.C., which means that Jeremiah began his prophetic career in 627. The dates of the reigns of the kings of Judah during Jeremiah's work are as follows:

Josiah, 640–609
Jehoahaz, 609 (three months)
Jehoiakim, 609–598
Jehoiachin, 597 (three months)
Zedekiah, 597–587
Gedaliah, 587 (served as governor)

As well as knowing the kings in Judah, we need to know events in the large empires of Assyria an Babylonia.

Nineveh, the capital of Assyria, fell to the
   Babylonians, 612 B.C.
Neco II was the king of Egypt, 609–597.
Nebuchadnezzar defeated Egypt at Carchemish, 605.
Nebuchadnezzar became king in Babylonia, 604.
Rebellion arose in Babylon, 595–94.
Nebuchadnezzar took Jerusalem, August 587.

The one other fact of considerable importance is that in 621 B.C. a book of the law was found in the temple in Jerusalem, which provided great impetus for the reform of Josiah.

We are not altogether in the dark as to major aggregations of materials in the book of Jeremiah. We are told about the writing down of the earlier oracles of the Lord to Jeremiah.

> In the fourth year of Jehoiakim the son of Josiah, king of Judah, this word came to Jeremiah from the Lord: "Take a scroll and write on it all the words that I have spoken to you against Israel and Judah and all the nations, from the day I spoke to you, from the days of Josiah until today."
>
> Jeremiah 36:1-2

This scroll was destroyed by Jehoiakim with his penknife and the fire in the brazier (Jer. 36:22-23), but Jeremiah was told to rewrite the scroll (vss. 27-29). Jeremiah did not write down the words himself. "Then Jeremiah called Baruch the son of Neriah, and Baruch wrote upon a scroll at the dictation of Jeremiah all the words of the Lord which he had spoken to him" (Jer. 36:4). This command came from God in the fourth year of Jehoiakim's reign, or 605 B.C. By that time Jeremiah had prophesied for twenty-two years. If we take the command seriously, Jeremiah has gone for twenty-two years without writing down the words of the Lord given him. Now he is asked to recall them all. With us such a feat would likely be impossible. But in societies where writing is scant, oral memory abounds. This indicates that prophets may or may not have written down their own materials. It further tells us that we have no way of predicting when or how such writing occurred.

The question now occurs as to whether we have the Baruch scroll in the book of Jeremiah. Obviously the scroll is not the book of Jeremiah as we now have it, for Jeremiah continued to prophesy until at least 587 B.C., or another eighteen years. But is it possible that somewhere within the book of Jeremiah this scroll may be located? The reply will no doubt always be under dispute, but a statement in Jeremiah 25:13 is of interest: "I will bring upon that land all the words which I have uttered against it, everything written in this book, which Jeremiah prophesied against all the nations." This seems to be a reference to a book which is not the entirety of Jeremiah. These words likewise come from the fourth year of Jehoiakim (Jer. 25:1). In addition, Jeremiah 25:8-13 contains language sounding like Jeremiah 1:15-16. For these reasons, some have supposed that we have in Jeremiah 1–25 the contents of the scroll dictated to Baruch. If so (and this writer considers it a good possibility), Jeremiah 1–25 is not just the scroll, for we can identify some material which has been added, for example, comments about Zedekiah, who reigned 597–587 B.C. (Jer. 21), and on Jehoiachin, who reigned briefly in 597 B.C. (Jer. 13:15-27; 22:24; 20:7-18). So we do not know exactly how much of 1–25 is the Baruch scroll, but it may be all there with other materials added by Baruch if he was the one who put together the final manuscript.

Another section referred to as a book in the Hebrew text (Jer. 46:1) is a collection of prophecies against the nations (Jer. 46–51). It is obvious from what dates can be determined that these sayings were not given to Jeremiah at the same time. Neither are they arranged in chronological order. The first section is against Egypt and because of the citation in 46:2 is to be dated 605 B.C. The heading in verse 13 may indicate oracles against Egypt delivered at another time, but internal citations do not enable us to date them should there be any. Chapter 47 is against the Philistines. It is probably to be dated when Neco was in the land, which could be anywhere from 609 to 605 B.C. Chapter 48 contains a series of oracles against Moab. No datable material is immediately obvious, but it would seem that the comments fall after Jehoiakim rebelled in 600–598 B.C., but Moab remained loyal to Babylonia, assisting in restoring Judah to Babylonian hegemony. Chapter 49 contains comments on the Ammonites, Edom, Damascus, and Elam. The comments against Ammon probably are to be dated at the same time as those against Moab. The comments against Edom best fit the situation after the fall of Jerusalem in 587 B.C., since the Edomites took advantage of Judah's defeat. The date of the comments against Damascus is uncertain, but they possibly fall before Nebuchadnezzar consolidated his occupation of the region, or before 600 B.C. The prophecy against Elam (Jer. 49:34-39) is dated at the beginning of the reign of Zedekiah or 597 B.C.. Chapters 50 and 51 are against

Babylon and may be from the time of the final destruction of Jerusalem in 587 B.C., but there is little way of knowing for sure. The last section in 51:59-64 comes from the time when Zedekiah went to Babylon, 594. Jeremiah 51:60 speaks of a book, but, unless this has in mind chapters 50 and 51, we do not have these materials. The section ends with the statement "Thus far are the words of Jeremiah" (51:64), indicating an awareness that what follows in chapter 52 is not from Jeremiah.

We have located two books in Jeremiah. We now turn to a third. The first verse of Jeremiah 30 contains this statement: "The word that came to Jeremiah from the Lord: 'Thus says the Lord, the God of Israel: Write in a book all the words that I have spoken to you.'" This book apparently ends with chapter 31, inasmuch as in these two chapters the content and style are similar. The section is designated "the Book of Consolation," since it contains oracles of hope depicting the action of God in restoring his people beyond destruction. Apparently these materials have been collected by Jeremiah or someone else and put in this form. As to setting, they likely come from after the fall of Jerusalem in 587 B.C., since the destruction seems presupposed (Jer. 30:18-21; 31:23-28).

By discovering these three books in Jeremiah we can see that a pattern is beginning to unfold. The books comprise (1) chapters 1–25, (2) chapters 30–31, and (3) chapters 46–51. The remaining material consists of chapters 26–29, 32–45, and 52. What is interesting about the materials in 26–29 and 32–45 is that they are prose and narratives written in the third person about Jeremiah. They contain almost no oracular material. These historical narratives could well have been composed by the one who gave the book its final form, perhaps Jeremiah's friend and scribe Baruch. Chapter 52, as we have already noted, is taken almost verbatim from historical materials in 2 Kings. It was apparently added to relate the narrative of the final days of Jerusalem in historical form.

Standing back from the book of Jeremiah, we thus obtain this picture: We have three books, transitional material, and a historical appendix. There is something of a historical sequence involved, but anyone interested in following the book through from a chronological perspective has to provide his own outline. The earliest materials of Jeremiah are probably all in the first ten chapters. The materials relating to events from the death of Josiah (609 B.C.) to the fall of Jerusalem (587 B.C.) flow somewhat chronologically from chapters 7–45, with 30 and 31 as an interlude. But a sizeable amount is out of phase. Certain sections are, of course, not datable. Chapters 30 and 31, as we have dated them, should properly come toward the end of the book. Chapters 46–51, as we noted, are not in chronological sequence. They fall in the years 609–587 B.C. We thus conclude that whoever put together the book may have had some interest in chronology, but it was not a controlling factor. Rather, he utilized blocks of material that were already together, put certain oracles and narratives together according to subject matter, inserted oracles and transitions at places, and added a historical ending.

Much of the material in Jeremiah can be dated, but some cannot. We could spend considerable time giving detailed information about the dating of various materials. With the chronological details provided earlier, however, most persons can do this on their own by noticing section headings. For example, at the beginning of chapter 21 the remark is made, "This is the word which came to Jeremiah from the Lord, when King Zedekiah sent to him Pashhur the son of Malchiah and Zephaniah the priest" (Jer. 21:1). We know, therefore, that this falls in the reign of Zedekiah (597–587 B.C.) and probably at the last part of the reign. To show how a chronological reconstruction of Jeremiah would look, the following outline is presented. The prophecies against the foreign nations are left together at the end rather than being redistributed. In their form in Jeremiah they may have been written after the fall of Jerusalem.

CHRONOLOGICAL OUTLINE OF THE BOOK OF JEREMIAH

I. Jeremiah's Earliest Prophecies (616[?]–609 B.C.)

A. His call, chapter 1 (ca. 627 B.C.)

B. The northern peril, 1:13-19; 4:5-31; 5:15-17; 6 (also 8:13-17 and 10:22)

C. Indictment of the people of the nation, 2:1–4:4, 5–6

D. Jeremiah and the great reform under Josiah, 6:16; 4:10 (622 B.C.)

II. Prophecies mostly from the Reign of Jehoiakim, (609–598 B.C.)

A. The temple sermon, 26–27

B. Further indictment and lamentation, 8–10

C. Writing of the scroll, 36, 45

D. Prophecy of the Babylonian captivity, 25

E. About Jehoiakim, 22:1-9, 13–19

F. Parables on the edge of doom, 13, 18–19

G. Trouble with the authorities, 20:1-6

III. The Personal Life and Problems of the Prophet

A. Spiritual struggles, 12, 14–17, 20:7-18

B. Enemies, 23:9-40, 28

IV. The First Captivity (598 B.C.)

A. About Jehoiachin, 13:15-17; 22:24–23:4; 24

B. Lesson from the Rechabites, 35

V. Rebuke of False Hopes about a Speedy Return of the Exiles, 27–29 (ca. 594–593 B.C.) Cf. 28:1

VI. The Last Days of Judah, (ca. 589–587 B.C.)

A. Commissions from Zedekiah, 21; 34:1-7

B. Fortunes of Jeremiah during the siege, 37

C. Redemption of family land at Anathoth, 32–33

D. Last days of the siege, 38

E. Cancelled liberation of slaves, 34:8-22

F. Fall of Jerusalem and the new order, 39–40, 52

G. Subsequent events in 587–586 B.C., 40:1–43:7

H. The Book of Consolation, 30–31

VII. Prophecies against Foreign Nations

A. Egypt, 43:8-13, 44, 46

B. Syro-Palestinian countries, 47:1–49:33

C. Elam and Babylon, 49:34-51

VIII. Historical Appendix, 52

From the preceding information we can now offer conclusions about the making of the book of Jeremiah. Apparently the first remarks of Jeremiah were put on papyrus by Baruch in 605 B.C. after Jeremiah had been prophesying some twenty-two years. Very little of this material, with the exception of that relating to the call of Jeremiah in chapter 1, preceded the discovery of the book of the law in the temple in 621 B.C. and the waves which went out from Josiah's attempt to take the book seriously. Most of the oracles in the book dictated to Baruch are from 616 to 605 B.C. Baruch preserved his book and with that as the beginning probably commenced recording certain of Jeremiah's other utterances. Some of these he kept together in chronological order; others he stored topically. At the death of Jeremiah he probably gave the book the form in which we now have it.

First of all, as with the other prophetic books, he wrote a historical introduction to the whole (Jer. 1:1-3). Next he placed the materials he had written down in the dictated scroll. At certain points, where he thought pertinent, he added items he had preserved, which occurred later. After this first book, he placed a narrative account of the actions of Jeremiah, which he may have been working on for some time or which he may have composed as the form of Jeremiah took shape in his mind. He broke up this narrative with the Book of Consolation, which he apparently felt was needed in order to show the future of Israel and Judah as anticipated by the prophet. Last of all, he included the oracles against the nations which he had been collecting for some time. Then at the end he provided a historical appendix, which he pieced together from materials in 2 Kings.

The end product of the work of Baruch, or perhaps someone else, is preserved for the people of God as the book of Jeremiah. It is a book of many elements. Among these are oracles from God, comments on the oracles by Jeremiah, comments on Jeremiah and his oracles by Baruch and perhaps others, and historical materials borrowed elsewhere. Because of the manner in which the book of Jeremiah was created, it is not easy to discern the particular context for certain sections. But obviously if one is to have more than a cursory insight into what he reads, it is extremely important that he have an idea of how the book was put together, how one goes about determining the beginning and end of the various sections, and the contexts to which they are spoken.

The book of Jeremiah as we have it is the inspired word of God providing nourishment for those who are his from then to now. Much of the material in the book was, first of all, a word from God to those who lived in a particular time and under a particular set of circumstances. It can only be the word of God for those who live in later times and later circumstances when they are sensitive to the first set of circumstances. For that reason an insight into the manner in which the book was put together is of utmost importance. It is only when insights such as these are obtained that the word of God then can be transferred to the present. This is possible when the present set of circumstances is parallel. When the then and the now can be lined up and are analogous, God's word reaches into our lives just as it did into theirs. In this manner God's word becomes the living word. It comes to us as prophetic oracle, comment, or third-party reflection. All this is human word, but, upon reaching us, it is deeply and profoundly the inspired word of God.

CONCLUSIONS

The making of the books of the OT is a very complex matter. One can almost offer the suggestion that the rule is that there are no rules. Apparently certain documents were essentially the work of one author in a short span of time, for example, the book of Ruth. What we have provided in this chapter at best serves only as an introduction to the whole subject. If it has created a sensitivity to the means by which the composition and structure of an OT book may be discovered, then it has been successful. As the student takes up each book, he should read introductory remarks to the book calling attention to its composition. Then as he reads the work itself, he should pick up clues along the way.

Through these means he will secure the necessary insight for a more profound understanding of the word of God. The most significant conclusion of this chapter is that each OT book must be approached on its own grounds. The inspiration of God produced the Bible as it is, not as some scholar, however conservative or liberal, professes it to be apart from a hard-nosed look at the books. In the words of the hymn, "God moves in a mysterious way, His wonders to perform." This is true, not only of his work in nature and history, but also of the manner in which he produced and preserved his word. The action of God is wondrous and multiplex. We should be very careful about declaring limits on the manner of God's inspiration. After all, he is God, and we have no franchise for providing arbitrary rules as to how he may or may not breathe his very way into his word. Just as it is exciting to discover the astounding and multifold ways in which God works in history, so also it is an exciting adventure to discover the manner in which the books of the Bible were made through which he spoke then and through which he speaks even now.

BIBLIOGRAPHY

The best means of finding information on the making of specific OT books is to read in introductions and commentaries. These are some of the important introductions:

Anderson, G. W. *A Critical Introduction to the Old Testament,* 1959.

Bentzen, A. *Introduction to the Old Testament,* 1959.

Driver, S. R. *Introduction to the Literature of the Old Testament.* Reprint, 1961.

Eissfeldt, O. *The Old Testament: an Introduction,* 1965.

Fohrer, G. *Introduction to the Old Testament,* 1965.

Harrison, R. K. *Introduction to the Old Testament,* 1969.

Pfeiffer, R. H. *Introduction to the Old Testament,* 1957.

Sandmel, S. *The Hebrew Scriptures: An Introduction to Their Literature and Religious Ideas,* 1963.

Weiser, A. *The Old Testament: Its Formation and Development,* 1961.

Young, E. J. *An Introduction to the Old Testament,* 1954.

VIII

A Brief History of Modern Criticism In Old Testament Study

Wendell Willis

METHODOLOGY IN OLD TESTAMENT STUDY

The Literary-Historical Approach

Modern study of the OT, as the modern study of other documents and histories, is an outgrowth of the eighteenth-century renaissance in learning. Prior to this, the study of the OT was largely carried out as a subdiscipline in dogmatic theology (as were NT studies and church history). **J. G. Eichhorn** (1780–1783) is generally regarded as the "father of OT Criticism" for his attempt to locate sources used in the writing of the Pentateuch on the basis of literary study. **Jean Astruc** had done a similar work in 1753, but Eichhorn refined and established the methodology.

Eichhorn and his students, such as **K. H. Graf** and **H. Hupfeld**, located four major documents in the Pentateuch and explained their relation to each other. This resulted in the famous "four-document hypothesis" widely referred to as the Graf-Wellhausen hypothesis. The four documents were described as "J" (for the Yahwist source, which referred to God as Yahweh [the *J* comes from the German spelling, *Jahweh*]); "E" (a source calling God Elohim);

"D" (a revision of the law by a "Deuteronomist" author with a prophetic theology); and "P" (the final document by a writer with "priestly" concerns). This solution, while no longer used as originally formulated, has had an abiding influence for over a century of OT study.

The synthesis of earlier ideas by **J. Wellhausen** gave a classic formulation in OT criticism, especially in his work *Prolegomena to the History of Israel* (1878). It was he who first clearly formulated a reconstruction of the history of Israel based on the four-document solution. His reconstruction was so complete and widely accepted that subsequent study, even beyond literary criticism, has characteristically used it as a starting place, whether endorsing or refuting it. His work is a good example of the liberal approach which consciously rejected all theological interpretation for a naturalistic history (based on an evolutionary view of history).

For Wellhausen, the history of Israel began with the exodus from Egypt, that is, with Moses. At this initial stage Israel had a primitive nomadic religion replete with rituals (Wellhausen was deeply sympathetic to primitive, uncorrupted society). This primitive religion was complicated by adoption of Canaanite practices. The second stage of Israel's religion was the prophetic creation of an ethical monotheism in protest to these primitive practices. The prophets in turn called forth the legal teachings of the OT and a centralized worship at Jerusalem. This third stage was the development of a church-state union which deprived Israel of a free and spirited religion and resulted in cold formalism.

With this reconstruction, Wellhausen felt he had given a "life situation" for the development of the literature of the OT. Subsequent OT scholarship tended to reverse his conclusions and see the prophets as the later stage in the development of Israel's religious thought and as the opponents of the cultic worship.

Wellhausen's solution became almost canonical for OT study in subsequent generations. *The International Critical Commentary on the Holy Scriptures* is a good example of the literary-historical concern in English. It contains neither homiletical nor theological emphasis.

Others in this tradition of OT study pressed the search for literary documents contained in present books of the OT. Using the criteria of linguistic style and historical setting, increasingly they found more documents. Especially the Pentateuch was subdivided by scholars such as **R. Smend, J. Hempel** and **O. Eissfeldt**. But this proliferation of sources produced an increasing dissatisfaction at what seemed a sterile approach.

Even in Europe, the literary-historical school was not without conservative critics. They pointed to this embarrassment of riches in the numerous sources as a refutation of the method. And the explicit disinterest in theology (and an accompanying bootlegging of a naturalistic theology) was found especially offensive. **J. Dahse, B. D. Eerdmans** and **W. Moeller** attacked the use of divine names as a criterion for locating sources. Eerdmans also claimed the literary school failed to account for much older traditions which were formalized at a later date (thus prefiguring the tradition-history approach). Moreover, he said Wellhausen's reconstruction was too unappreciative of the patriarchal age.

The literary-historical method has never been generally rejected by OT scholars, but issues have changed. This resulted in new methodologies, such as *form criticism,* developed around World War I. Form criticism sought to move behind the literary documents to the earlier oral period, before the life and religious teachings of Israel were put into written form. Then the *comparative religions* approach sought to understand Israel's religious life and thought in its historical context. A third approach emphasized the use of archeology to illuminate the OT.

Each of these will be discussed individually, but it is crucial to realize that they are not separable from each other. Each method interrelates with the others (including the textual and literary-historical methods) in varying ways. Whether a particular scholar's approach is placed in this category or that is largely a question of emphasis. Nor can any approach be wholly aligned with a particular theological persuasion (although some conservative scholars have rejected all but archeology as denying the integrity and inspiration of the Bible).

The Form-Critical Method

This approach is similar to the literary-historical in that it concentrates on traditions as contained in the OT. It arose when there appeared a need to supplement literary criticism by asking new questions. Both form and literary approaches seek to locate an earlier stage of traditions now found in the canonical books. While literary study seeks earlier *written* sources, form criticism seeks earlier *oral* sources. Thus the latter concentrates on oral forms, rather than on documents.

Most prominently recognized as the initiator of the form-critical school is **H. Gunkel.** Gunkel observed that creativity was not as prized in the thought expressions and faith of the ancient world as it is in the modern. Rather the ancient world, including Israel, had a customary form which was expected to be followed in composing a victory song, a lament, a prayer of thanksgiving or a request. From this insight Gunkel drew several implications. First, these forms, being stylized, could be recovered from our written OT. Second, doing this would move one to the preliterary stage, and thus to the ideas and beliefs of the common people (rather than to an exceptionally creative writer). Finally, one could discover the *situation* in which these forms were used and thereby recover the worship of ancient Israel.

Gunkel investigated both Genesis and the Psalms with his new method. Rather than seeking various documents now incorporated into the OT historical books, he sought to find individual stories which he felt were told and retold orally over a long period before being written down (e.g., the story of Abraham's migration from Ur). Gunkel found this method of study less formal and cold than the literary school's use of documents.

H. Gressmann applied Gunkel's form study to the Pentateuch, especially the various stories about Moses. He stressed that OT narratives were not creations of artistic

writers, but were old stories transmitted orally by generations of Israelites. They were a community heritage.

Gunkel's most famous work was on the Psalms, where he
isolated various styles of songs used virtually unchanged in
generations of Israelites. Gunkel's view was supplemented
by historians who investigated other ancient Near Eastern
cultures and found similar poetical forms. **S. Mowinckel,**
one of Gunkel's pupils, contributed the most in continuing
the study of the Psalms. Mowinckel stressed the community, rather than individuals, as composing religious songs
(see his *The Psalms in Israel's Worship*). Mowinckel also
went beyond Gunkel in postulating a situation for which
these Psalms were created. He thought they were designed
to be used in an annual New Year Festival in which God
was praised as the King. (Mowinckel has often been criticized for this. Others have noted there is not explicit
evidence for such a festival in Israel. Mowinckel assumed
there was such from analogy with other contemporary
cultures, especially Babylon.) But even if many scholars
remain unconvinced by the New Year Festival, most accept
the thesis that the OT traditions are closely related to
worship in Israel.

Following the same method, others have sought to locate
forms used in Israel in addition to stories and songs. In
particular the prophetic literature has been studied for such
forms. Three basic forms are widely used: *accounts* of the
prophet's call and other biographical material; *prayers*, the
most famous being Jeremiah's "complaints;" and *oracles*,
which have been subdivided into more specific forms.
The oracle of judgment is the most easily described (see
Amos 1:6-8). It begins with a formula like "Thus says the
Lord . . ." which is followed by a reason for the coming
disaster, then a "therefore" (or "so," "thus") and a description of the coming judgment, and is concluded by a formula
like "says the Lord God." (A convenient summary both of
these forms and of the history of their investigation appears
in **C. Westermann,** *Basic Forms of Prophetic Speech*.)

The last of the OT to receive serious attention with the
form-critical method was the legal portion of the Pentateuch.

A. Jirku and **A. Jepsen** both gave pioneering form research into this material in 1927. But the most famous form study of the legal traditions is that of **A. Alt.** Using the form-critical method, Alt located two distinct forms of legal materials. The first was "decisions," or "case law," which followed the common practice in the ancient world of describing a situation ("If any man . . .") and its legal result ("He shall . . ."), often called "casuistic law." Alt felt that the second form, more unique to Israel, came from the covenant at Sinai. This is the "apodictic" law, which is formulated as an injunction ("Thou shall not . . ." or "Cursed be the man who . . ."), the most famous of which are the Ten Commandments in Exodus 20. (A succinct introduction to Alt's work can be found in his essay "The Origins of Israelite Law" in his *Essays on OT History and Religion*.)

The form-critical method has been a dominant methodology in OT study up to the present time. It made two important contributions beyond the method itself. First, it showed that the OT traditions were the common property of Israel and what gave them a peculiar sense of identity and unity. Second, it suggested that the old liberal view of the prophet as the antagonist of the priest was wrong. Form criticism showed that prophet, priest, and lawgiver were all closely related in the religion of Israel. Even when the prophets denounced the cult worship, they did so on the basis of old and well-known teachings and laws.

Finally, mention must be made of the most recent trend in methodology which builds upon both literary and form-critical methods. This is variously called *redaction criticism* and *editorial criticism*. This method is a direct heir of the preceding methods of OT study. It begins with locating the older oral forms but then seeks the intent of the present arrangement of those forms in the books as they now stand. In this way, redaction criticism is concerned to move beyond the analytical work of locating old traditions. For example, given the fact that the final compiler of Jeremiah possessed oracles, biographical stories, and prayers (according to form-critical study) of the prophet, why did he arrange them as he did in the final book of Jeremiah?

Redaction criticism's interest in *written* work reflects its closeness to the older literary method, but it is drastically different because of form study.

This method is still in its formative stage in the study of the OT. For that reason it is less clear which scholars may be taken as pivotal. The important point in relation to the two previous methods of study is that redaction study is a step forward in that it deals with the books *as they now exist.*

The History of Religions School

Unlike redaction criticism, the history of religions method does not directly build on literary and form methods and thus is not a specialized type of those methods. But neither should the history of religions approach be considered a competitor; it is more a compatriot. This method, now over a century old, emphasizes the comparison of OT ideas with those in the cultures contemporary with, and prior to, the national life of Israel. Thus there is a built-in tendency to attend to the similarities, but the differences are also noted. The key point is that it is necessary to place OT religion in a broad context and to understand it in relation to other ideas in the ancient world.

There has been a tendency to think that, when two cultures (for example, Israel and Canaan) have similar religious practices or theological concepts, one must have borrowed from the other, or both from yet a third. Thus when similarities were found between Israelite law and the code of Hammurabi, history of religions scholars tended to see Israelite dependence on the Babylonian traditions. Even if this were so, what could one conclude? Some have used it to show Israelite law as a poor stepchild; others see in the similarities proof of the antiquity of OT law codes. But both positions are using the history of religions approach.

Wellhausen, and the early literary study, had tended to consider Israelite religion and its developments as a rather self-contained entity. But Gunkel and the form-critical school turned outward, because they sought to learn about oral forms in other cultures as an aid in understanding forms among the Israelites. It was really the great strides of archeology beginning in the last quarter of the nineteenth century that furnished the raw materials for the history of religions approach by making possible the comparative study of many ancient cultures.

One of the most famous names in the development of the history of religions approach is **F. Delitzsch,** remembered for his view that everywhere the OT showed a deep dependence on Babylonian thought and life (the old "Bible" vs. "Babel" debate early in this century). But Gunkel and others made a more careful use of the approach by focusing on the OT materials as the place of investigation and proceeding from it to other cultures. H. Gressmann, examining Israelite eschatology, demonstrated that apocalyptic thinking was not a late development after the exile, but a way of thinking with century-old precedents in Babylon and Egypt (thus undercutting many literary scholars who denied that eschatological portions of the prophetic books could have been authentic).

Conservative response to this new method of OT study was divided. Some rejected it, thinking that the concern for old non-Israelite parallels was a move to deny the genius and originality of the OT faith itself. Conversely, some appropriated it as a means of securing confidence in the accuracy of the biblical record. For example, **P. Volz** examined Egyptian texts to show that the ethical principles of the decalogue could be established in Egyptian records before Moses. He then claimed to prove the Mosaic authorship of the decalogue and its significance in Israel's early history. In a similar way **B. D. Eerdmans,** by studying Babylonian and Assyrian religion, sought to show the Mosaic character of the Levitical worship. (To properly appreciate this point, one must recall that Wellhausen's followers tended to see Levitical laws and worship as added to Israel's life *after* the prophetic period.)

Between the "Babylonists," who sought to explain the OT as a mere shadow of older non-Israelite ideas, and the orthodox response which sought to prove the total originality and truthfulness of Israelite faith, there developed a mediating position. **R. Kittel** was a founding member of this group. For example, while not accepting the view that from Moses onward Israel had been wholly monotheistic, Kittel also rejected the view that monotheism was a postprophetic belief in Israel. He said Moses had taught an ethical monolatry, one high God worthy of worship, who was the ruler and judge of Israel (although in the Mosaic period other gods may have been recognized as belonging to the other nations). **E. Sellin** also sought to work out this thesis and to give equal attention to development and antiquity in the religion of Israel.

Another facet of the mediating position of Kittel and Sellin was their insistence that Israelite faith was never uniform but had always consisted of different levels of theology and practice. Thus even in the prophetic period when monotheism was normative for Israel, many Hebrews could be found flocking to the Baals. Loyalties to God had always persisted but were widely varied and distributed among the different groups in the nation.

In the middle half of this century, a wealth of new and exciting archeological discoveries became very important for the history of religions approach. The Ras Shamra tablets found in 1929 revealed a great deal about Canaanite civilization. **S. H. Hooke** examined the similarities between the Canaanite and Levitical priesthoods using these tablets. Other history of religions scholars pointed out also the differences in Israelite and Canaanite religion, including the latter's essential polytheism and fertility focus.

The similarities between the Canaanite culture and that of the OT gave rise to a movement within the history of religions school known as the "myth and ritual" school. These men, led by Hooke, emphasized that OT worship had close relations with the patterns of religion in Canaanite cultus and that the prophetic protest could best be understood as a criticism of Israelite adoption of Canaanite ideas. Others said the basic flaw in the "myth and ritual" approach is its tendency to assume that similar practices and language proved a similar meaning and understanding.

The Archeological Approach

In the last century there has been a rapid increase in the knowledge of the ancient Near East from archeology. Most of the significant discoveries have taken place in the last fifty years. It is difficult to exaggerate the way such knowledge has multiplied. Cities, temples, and palaces have been unearthed, along with countless documents. Archeology has provided physical and written remains to allow for a good reconstruction of the background of OT history.

The lead in archeological study has been held by American scholars. **W. F. Albright** was probably the most knowledgable mind on ancient Near Eastern archeology in this century. In copious writings he brought the available information into relation to the OT. Between the two world wars, great archeological projects were done in the area of Palestine; and, when World War II temporarily interrupted the physical research, time was found for synthesis and the interpretation of such findings.

As far back as the world of the Patriarchs, archeology provided insights. Some earlier scholars had doubted there ever were such OT heroes as the pre-Mosaic figures and had viewed the accounts of the patriarchs as totally fanciful. But Albright and others have demonstrated by archeological findings a high accuracy of the world described in these early stories. The nomadic life-styles of the patriarchs, their legal customs, and even an occasional name of Abraham's descendants have been documented in the world of the time in which they are presented in the OT (that is, between 2000 and 1700 B.C.). (A useful summary is available in W. F. Albright's *From the Stone Age to Christianity.*)

Others using archeology, such as **H. H. Rowley** and **J. Garstang**, have examined the exodus with the aid of findings in Canaan and Egypt. The evidence is, of course, given varying interpretations, especially in regard to dates. Albright and **G. E. Wright** concluded that the remains of the cities referred to in the conquest narratives of Joshua and Judges confirm a quick and destructive invasion of southern Palestine in the period the OT describes. Of course, beyond

locating places and dates for the study of the OT, archeology
has also done a great deal to advance knowledge of culture
in early Canaan.

One of the pioneering attempts to use this archeological
method to rewrite Israelite history was by **W. C. Graham
and H. G. May** in *Culture and Conscience.* It has been
superceded by other worthwhile contributions, such as
Albright's *From the Stone Age to Christianity* and **R. K.
Harrison's,** *Archaeology of the Old Testament.* Because of
the wide availability of popularly written reports on the
work of archeologists, little more needs to be said here.

In conclusion it should be noted, first, that the archeological school had a real impact in securing serious attention
to OT history, especially those early chapters once so
shrouded in mystery. Second, there has been a lack of
clarity about what can and cannot be done with archeology,
especially by nonarcheologists writing on "Archeology and
the Bible." Archeology cannot prove the accuracy of the
biblical narratives, much less the inspiration of Scripture,
partly because archeology is less than a precise science, but
also because archeology cannot investigate certain questions. For example, even if all scholars were convinced by
archeological evidence that a group of slave laborers left
Egypt in a certain year, that would not confirm that it was
God who provided the means for the exodus and gave it his
stamp of approval. What archeology has done, and rightly
can do, is to help interpret OT events and thoughts by
throwing light on their background. Finally, archeology has
been able to raise certain issues in a way that requires that
they be investigated. In this way some of the "assured
results" of other approaches have been called in question.
Archeology will continue to exercise great influence in OT
study insofar as it avoids the tendency either to dominate
interpretation or to neglect it completely.

The Theological Approach

To many it will seem strange that a "theological approach" to OT study has only come to the fore in the last
generation. In a way, this new method and the previous

refusal to use a theological approach are both results of a desire to be serious in recent OT study. The originators of the literary school wished to be *nontheological* in reaction to orthodoxy's use of church traditions to determine what the OT must mean. They sought to study Israel's religious history, not its theology. But scholars who were first trained in this method also first raised the objection that to analyze documents and forms, and to relate archeology's findings, was too shortsighted. They also wanted to understand the *theology* of the OT.

Of course there had always been some who felt such "objective" study was both impossible and inadequate. But this objection, even when raised by men of H. Gunkel's stature, was not heeded. Among such scholars, the first modern study of the OT which was avowedly interested in theology was **W. Eichrodt**'s two-volume *Theology of the Old Testament*. Eichrodt's work went behind the study of individual details and events in Israel's history to locate the basic unity of Israelite faith (which he saw as the covenant). He did not neglect differences and development in Israel's religion but sought its core, its center, also. Thus Eichrodt combined historical and literary investigation with interpretation of theological interests.

The crises in the Western world evoked by two world wars and the world depression of the 1930s raised theological questions to the foreground. In this way the view of Eichrodt and a few others was vindicated. Many books were written during and immediately after World War II which sought once again "the relevance of the Bible" (from the title of such a book by H. H. Rowley. A similar book was produced in America by **B. W. Anderson,** *Rediscovering the Bible*). The most recent major example of the theological approach is **G. von Rad**'s *Theology of the Old Testament*. Many similar studies have been done with more limited scope, such as **D. Hillars'** *Covenant: The History of a Biblical Idea*.

Since the theological approach is not definable in respect to methodology, it is difficult to point to common assumptions of scholars using it. Perhaps the real common factor is the insistence that, while other approaches (literary, form, historical, and archeological) are necessary, they are not sufficient for an adequate understanding of the OT. It has a significance and a message beyond the simple historical meaning.

Summary

This survey indicates that OT study has changed from a subdiscipline under church doctrine to a field of great interest and variety of its own. It has also been noted that new methods of study develop to answer questions for which the older methods were not adequate, but these new methods in turn also evoke new questions. How these questions have been treated with regard to specific portions of the OT will be the concern of the remainder of this chapter.

THE NARRATIVE BOOKS

There are basically two subdivisions in the narrative books: the Pentateuch (Genesis through Deuteronomy) and the historical books (Joshua through Esther). These divisions have been widely assumed in Christian scholarship on the OT. The Jewish tradition, based on the Hebrew OT, has a slightly different arrangement. In it the first five books constitute the *Torah* (law), and the rest are included in the *Former Prophets* (Joshua to Kings) or the *Writings* (Chronicles, Esther, Ruth, Ezra, and Nehemiah).

Because of necessary limitations this section will focus on the Pentateuch (where modern scholars have been most active) and give some attention to Joshua, Judges, Samuel, Kings, and Chronicles. Only slight space will be devoted to Ezra and Nehemiah, and Esther and Ruth will not come under discussion.

The Pentateuch

A good deal of attention to Pentateuchal study was given in the introductory section. This is appropriate both because that was the locus for modern study's beginnings and because it continues to receive such a large share of OT study. One recalls the rise and dominance of the so-called "documentary solution," also known as the Graf-Wellhausen hypothesis. This emphasized that earlier documents (J, E, P, D) had been united into the present Pentateuch. Through World War I this theory dominated OT study, although most conservative scholars rejected this approach altogether. Roman Catholics denounced it as disloyal to the church. Some "mediating" scholars disagreed with the Wellhausen consensus, although they used similar methods of study. Of course the majority of critical scholars were unconcerned about the opinions of Protestant orthodoxy or Roman ecclesiology. And the minor dissident voices within their own circles were few enough not to evoke serious attention.

The Jewish tradition, continued in the NT, generally held that the first five books were written by Moses. The JEPD solution replaced the idea of a single author, Moses in particular. The reasons given included: (1) The common references to Moses in the third person, rather than the first person; (2) some apparent anachronisms such as Genesis 36:31, "before ˙ any king reigned over the Israelites"; (3) differences in the names referring to God—in the Hebrew language Yahweh, Elohim, El Shaddai (this was the phenomenon that began the source theory); (4) differences in language and style, a point which must be seen with a Hebrew OT.

These observations and others the documentary hypothesis explained by positing different *sources* for the Pentateuch. The crucial source was D or the Deuteronomist (a source including the present Deuteronomy, but also found in the other historical books). This document was equated with the law code discovered in the temple and used as a basis of Josiah's reform. (See 2 Kings 22:8ff.) Since Josiah's reform began in 621 B.C., the law code, D, was dated shortly before this. From this "fixed document" the documentary theory located the other three documents (J, E, P) and dated them. J (so named because of a preference to call God "Yahweh," [German *Jahweh*]) was dated between 950 and 850. It was believed to have been written in Judah and found largely in Genesis and Exodus 1–16. The third document, E (from the preference for the name "Elohim" for God), was thought to have come from North Israel between 850 and 750. The fourth document, P (for its "priestly" interests), was held to have been written during or after the exile. These four documents were thought to have been combined after the return from exile.

Conservative replies to this reconstruction may be divided into two basic types, with much overlapping. The first is that Moses must have authored these five books because the Christian (and/or Jewish) community had said he did for so long. A special form of this judgment is that NT references, particularly words of Jesus (e.g., Matt. 19:8; John 5:46–47; and 7:19), assume Mosaic authorship and thus the matter is settled by inspiration. A good presentation of this is by E. J. Young, *Introduction to the Old Testament.*

Another conservative approach defending Mosaic authorship is investigative, that is, joining issue on the accuracy of the various traditions and on the defects of the four-document hypothesis. Here the various individual issues remain open for investigation. For example, the argument depending on the different names used for God in the books was assessed and demonstrated to be far from evident as was being claimed by W. H. Green and others.

A more surprising critique of Wellhausen developed among critical scholars and those without confessional concerns. G. Hoelscher and R. H. Kennett argued that D was to be dated a century after Josiah. A. C. Welch, on the other hand, sought to push D back to Solomon's time, and E. Robertson, to the entrance into Canaan. These investigations had an unsettling effect upon the one assured date, and thus the viability, of the Wellhausen solution.

More distressing for the theory was the tendency to find more documents than four. O. Eissfeldt and G. von Rad with one more, and P. Baentsch, with seven sub-P sources, are typical and atypical representatives of this tendency. Other literary critics proposed reducing the sources to two (P. Volz) or even one, with supplements.

This does not mean that OT scholars have rejected the

Wellhausen solution. They have modified it and become less dogmatic about dates and contents of the documents, yet the solution is still widely accepted. It was not that it was deemed inaccurate by its users, but rather inadequate. This led to the form-critical work of the "Uppsala school."

The Uppsala school of OT study replaced the Wellhausen interest in documents with an emphasis upon oral tradition. In 1931 J. Pedersen, an eminent Scandinavian OT scholar, announced his break with the documentary theory. He suggested that various stories and narratives had been retold in overlapping traditions. While their sequence cannot be established on the basis of documents, *each* individual story, law, or song can be studied and dated on its own merits.

One of Pedersen's students, I. Engnell, proposed "traditio-historical" OT study, which he envisioned as superseding literary and form criticism. He rejected documents in favor of two "circles of tradition" which shaped and preserved Genesis through Numbers, and Deuteronomy through 2 Kings, respectively. But even these two circles (loosely termed P and D) interwove written and oral traditions. Thus any search for a "foundational document(s)" is misdirected. Engnell thought these traditions were first written down in the time of Ezra or Nehemiah but had received their shape centuries before.

A similar shift in German OT study was worked out by G. von Rad, who still allows for JEPD but is less strict about defining their limits or dates. He allows for a long, formative oral period of the various stories and theology. He speaks of a Hexateuch (the first six OT books) with sources drawn from particular cultic traditions, rather than creative authors. One basic tradition, nurtured at Shechem's annual autumn festival, centered around the events of Sinai and the law. The second major tradition was the conquest of the land, celebrated at Gilgal.

Von Rad's reconstruction has been challenged for a lack of hard evidence of the festivals so important to his view. The "creeds" of Joshua 24 and Deuteronomy 26 that he elaborates may have repeated Israelite confessions, but there is little evidence for the festivals he assumes they represent. (For more criticism of von Rad, see **A. Weiser,** *The Old Testament; Its Formation and Development.*)

The more recent trends in Pentateuch study have not emphasized sources, written or oral, but have either looked at possible parallels to certain points in other cultures (**E. A. Speiser** on Genesis in *The Anchor Bible*) or have sought to account in other ways for the present form of the Pentateuch.

Two important issues in Pentateuch studies have been (1) the historical value of the descriptions from Genesis 1 to the death of Moses and (2) the use of the Pentateuch in reconstructing Israelite history from the exodus to the return from exile. Recently, the more common practice has been to avoid searching for "bare history" and to concentrate on the traditions telling of God's dealings with men as now recorded in the OT. Regarding the second question, one view, following the Uppsala school, eschews documents and attempts to write a developmental history of Israel's religion (I. Engnell is representative). The second view, still working with documents, is more confident of demonstrating to some degree the development of Israelite religion (von Rad is representative).

The American Albright school, foremost in the archeological approach, has tended to emphasize the basic trustworthiness of these traditions as well as their confessional role in Israel. They consider the OT traditions to contain both event and interpretation. For example, the conquest of the land includes both the history (in a degree demonstrated by archeology) and the interpretation as being God's work, not simply Israel's. This seems to be something of a mediating position between some who use archeology to prove the truth of biblical claims and Uppsala scholars who have contented themselves with traditions alone.

The Former Prophets

Joshua, Judges, 1 and 2 Samuel, 1 and 2 Kings, 1 and 2 Chronicles, Ezra, and Nehemiah are the "Former Prophets" in the Hebrew Bible (the prophetic books are called the "Latter Prophets"). All these are anonymous books, both in their present form and in tradition. In modern study two focal questions have been discussed: (1) whether for Joshua through 2 Kings the JEDP sources are continued and, if so, to what extent, and (2) whether the Deuteronomic element is decisive or only one of a number of layers in the editorial production of these books.

The book of Joshua has received perhaps the most attention among these books. Those who argue for the continuation of JEDP beyond the Pentateuch believe the strongest case can be made for Joshua. As early as Wellhausen it was common among some who felt Joshua shared more with the first five books than with those following it to speak of the Hexateuch (rather than Pentateuch). **C. R. North** and **J. Bright** believe J and E are thoroughly interwoven in Joshua. Others (e.g., **W. Rudolph**) find only J. Generally those who have emphasized the sources in the Pentateuch have been more open to their presence in Joshua.

M. Noth has been a leader among those who deny JEDP in Joshua. Noth suggests that stories about cities and places preserved at Gilgal (chs. 1–9) and two collections of hero stories all come from the time of the division of the kingdom. A similar emphasis upon stories about places (aetiologies) is made by A. Alt and Engnell. Aetiologies are explanations of the origins of some observable phenomenon (a stone heap, a destroyed city, etc.). These have been particularly located in Joshua 5–11. The aetiological approach has found both acceptance and criticism. W. F. Albright criticized the extreme use of this method and argued that these places and persons were more substantial than many have suggested.

E. J. Young has sought to show that Joshua does not have such close ties to the Pentateuch (which he holds to be Mosaic) and therefore does not make a "Hexateuch." He does not think Joshua himself wrote the book, however.

Much research has been given to the date and character of the conquest of Canaan. The "traditio-historical" approach emphasized the theological focus: *God gave* the land. Others, agreeing with this, still think the historicity of the conquest is important. Albright and Bright have emphasized the archeological evidence of a major onslaught in southern Palestine about the thirteenth century, in which several leading cities were thoroughly and quickly destroyed. They argue that this confirms the accuracy of the Joshua account.

The book of Judges presents similar questions, and scholarship is similarly divided over whether aetiologies or JE are at the base of the writing. Most agree the Deuteronomist has been involved, but few like **R. Pfeiffer** still find J and E. The aetiological approach of Alt, von Rad, and Pedersen has been prominent. Also Albright, Bright, and Wright have emphasized the historical reliability of Judges and renounced the aetiologists' excesses.

There are many similarities between Joshua and Judges which suggest they are more like contemporary books than successors (for example, note the references to parallels given in the RSV footnotes in Judges 1–2). In the modern study of Judges there have been two tendencies: first, to study the individual stories (of the judges) and, second, to explain the present framework (the work of the Deuteronomist editor).

Our 1 and 2 Samuel are all one book in the Hebrew Bible. In the Greek Bible of the early Christians they were 1 and 2 Kingdoms with our books of Kings being 3 and 4 Kingdoms. In this way the divisions followed by most English translations agree with neither the Hebrew nor the Greek version. The books of Samuel form a unit in that they cover the rise of the Israelite kingship to David (under Samuel's guidance). While Samuel is a key figure, especially in the first fifteen chapters, he was never considered the author of these books, nor were the other chief figures, Saul and David.

Two traditions have been located in these books by many scholars: The older critics (K. Budde) identified these with J and E, and recently O. Eissfeldt defended this view. (The origin of this speculation notes two accounts of how Saul became king in 1 Sam. 8 and 9 and two accounts of how David came to Saul's notice in 1 Sam. 16 and 17.) Others, doubting two documents, have suggested two different traditions in Israel, one recognizing kingship, the other antagonistic to it (see A. Bentzen).

Apart from these two traditions, another document has been widely accepted. This is the section of 2 Samuel 9–20 and 1 Kings 1 and 2, where David's rule and succession by Solomon is given. This is often called the Davidic Court History, or the Succession Narrative. It is recognized as one of the best pieces of historiography in the ancient world because, although probably written under the patronage of the Davidic kingship, it is very honest about the good and bad aspects of David's rule. Young rejects this "succession narrative" as a source, but thinks 1 Chronicles 29:29 suggests that possible documents were used. The date of the finished books is difficult to estimate, but it is usually thought to have been after the division of the nation under Rehoboam. (See 1 Sam. 27:6.)

There is widespread agreement that the purpose of 1 and 2 Samuel is to describe and evaluate the kingship in Israel. This was a religious issue, because the Sinai covenant had assumed God was Israel's king, so how could there be a human king? The books of Samuel see it as a mixed blessing and perhaps a necessary evil. David, Israel's great king, was a paradigm of how kingship is both a blessing and a curse.

Like the books of Samuel, 1 and 2 Kings were originally one book. Their contents divide into four sections: 1 Kings 1:1–2:10 deals with the transfer of the throne from David to Solomon (thus uniting these books with Samuel); 1 Kings 2:12–11:43 describes the united kingdom after David; 1 Kings 12–2 Kings 17 pictures the divided kingdoms of Israel and Judah; and 2 Kings 18–25 deals with Judah and the beginning of the exile. Because of the similarities between Kings and Samuel many have argued that the same editor was responsible for the final edition of both works.

The same trends noted in regard to sources in the books of Samuel are continued in the case of 1 and 2 Kings. Some (Eissfeldt and Hoelscher) find J and/or E, but most do not. One type of source that is located is the court annal (such as the Acts of Solomon in 1 Kings 11:41), the Book of the Chronicles of the Kings of Israel (see 1 Kings 14:19), and the

Book of the Chronicles of the Kings of Judah. (See 1 Kings 14:29.) Perhaps other official records were also used. A second source type proposed by many is the story collection about key persons such as Elijah, Elisha, and Isaiah. Understandably, those scholars who have de-emphasized literary sources find some embarrassment at this wealth of documents acknowledged by the biblical writers.

It has been observed that the various kings are presented in a stylized way (date of accession, age upon taking the throne, mother's name, a judgment of each king's rule, and an obituary notice). These forms constitute a framework used by the writer to present material from official annals.

Modern study has found little interest in the Kings. There has been some interest in a chronology of the kings (see H. G. May, *Oxford Bible Atlas,* p. 16) or in nonbiblical information from archeologists. The other main interest has been in the persons of Elijah, Elisha, and Isaiah, but these have been mostly studied as a prelude to the later prophetic writings, rather than focusing on the Kings' account.

Another interest has been whether the Kings are a part of a "Deuteronomic" history, running from Deuteronomy through 2 Kings. M. Noth is widely known for this thesis, which sees the Deuteronomist as interpreting the history of Israel using the criterion of loyalty to God (understood as support of the Jerusalem temple and opposition to the "high places"). Thus all the northern kings are unfavorably viewed, and only a few Judean kings are favored. This thesis emphasizes the theological viewpoint of the writer(s) of Kings. Conservative scholars such as Young and Harrison criticize unnecessary skepticism about the historicity of these accounts. They think the possibility of a single, final author for the entire collection is possible.

First and Second Chronicles, Ezra and Nehemiah in recent study have been widely regarded as originally parts of a single work. This view is accepted by such divergent people as R. H. Pfeiffer, G. E. Wright, H. H. Rowley, and A. Bentzen. Others (A. C. Welch and Young) have found more than one author.

The reasons for holding one author for these four books

include: (1) a similar religious standpoint emphasizing the temple and the priesthood, (2) the same interest in statistical records and genealogies, (3) language and style, and (4) the seeming overlap between the conclusion of Chronicles and the beginning of Ezra.

The books are usually dated between about 400 and 250 B.C. W. F. Albright, who thought that Ezra was the author, dated them ca. 427. Those favoring a late date point to the Aramaic (a late-developing language from biblical Hebrew) sections of Ezra. But recent discoveries have shown the use of Aramaic in Egypt ca. 400 B.C. and has muted that objection.

The question of sources in Chronicles is somewhat confused. Accepting a date after about 300 B.C., it is conceivable that the author had the use of Genesis to 2 Kings. This would explain the frequent overlapping with these works. Those scholars who have not thought that the author had access to these books have tended to stress his affinities with the D and P documents, especially the "Deuteronomist's" style of evaluating the kings of Israel.

Ezra and Nehemiah, as separate works, have received little attention. There has been some discussion on the dating of Ezra (ca. 457 or 397, that is, before or after Nehemiah). Many have accepted "memoirs" of Ezra and Nehemiah as sources for the books bearing their names, whether or not they wrote the books. The theological focus of both is the solidifying of Israel as the elect people by reforming worship in Jerusalem and severing relations with non-Jewish (i.e., Samaritan) neighbors. One matter of considerable interest has been the "edict of Cyrus" in Ezra 1:2-4, and 6:3-5, recently discovered in Cyrus' own records (see J. Pritchard, *Ancient Near Eastern Texts*). A great value of all four books is the information they provide about a dark period in Israel's history, during which the Judaism of Jesus' and Paul's day was being formed.

THE PROPHETS

In the Hebrew OT the "Latter Prophets" is the designation given those books most English readers consider the prophets. The Hebrew Bible includes them in four scrolls: Isaiah, Jeremiah, Ezekiel, and the Book of the Twelve (Hosea to Malachi). Of course stories about prophets of God are found in the books of Samuel and Kings, but these are usually distinguished from the "writing prophets."

The number of the prophetic books and the amount of scholarly attention given them make it impossible to study them separately here. We will examine six major areas of modern study of the prophets.

What Is a Prophet?

There are a variety of words used in the OT to designate prophets. The most common Hebrew word, *navi'*, has received a good deal of attention in seeking to know who the prophets were. An early view (T. H. Robinson, T. J. Meek), taking the designation to stem from a word meaning to "bubble forth," argued that a *navi'* was one who was seized in ecstasy, lost control of his words, and became a mouthpiece for God. But the more recent interpretation derives *navi'* from an Akkadian word meaning "to call." Thus the prophet is one who "calls out" to Israel (E. Koenig) or, conversely, who was "called out" by God (R. B. Y. Scott, and especially W. F. Albright).

Two other common terms for a prophet are *ro'eh* and *hozeh*, both basically meaning "to see." The relation of these terms has been studied, because 1 Samuel 9:9 reads "he who is now called a *navi'* was previously called a *ro'eh*." Some (e.g., G. Hoelscher) have concluded from this that a seer was one who received special knowledge in dreams, and this was true of the later *navi'* (the development being in terminology for the same calling). Others have suggested a development in function: In the time of the kings, prophecy was moving out of a work of clairvoyance and becoming an institution of moral and religious instruction (thus a *navi'* was different from a *ro'eh* both in name and function). In the last half-century the discussion about the nature of a prophet has shifted away from the focus on philology.

The Call of the Prophet

Beyond the term *navi'*, many scholars have sought the significance of prophecy in the "call" of the prophet by God to become his messenger (this is one of the "prophetic" aspects of Abraham and Moses, Gen. 20:7 and Deut. 18:15f.). Some of the prophetic calls are explicit (Isa. 6) and are more than simply a report of how a man came to be a prophet. They also include his message given by God (see H. H. Rowley).

The idea of the call as a constitutive part of prophecy was developed by S. Mowinckel; G. von Rad makes a good deal of the call of the prophet in his study of the prophetic books. A general consensus (with some differences) suggests the call includes: (1) an autobiographical report, (2) an audience with God (described in the report), (3) the call of the individual as a prophet, (4) the prophet's response (often expressing reluctance to accept, (5) the prophet's authority and his message from God, (6) God's promises to support the prophet, and (7) the prophet's dismissal by God.

Prophet and Priest

In recent study no greater question has been raised than the relation of the prophets to the priestly cultus. In Wellhausen's view, the prophets proposed a new monotheistic faith developed after the settlement in Palestine. Because of their work the worship was centralized at Jerusalem, which prepared the way for later ritual worship conducted by the priests. Thus, in a sense, the prophets contributed to the growth of the sacrificial cult. Later students, early in this century, tended to reverse the roles (priests were prior to prophets) and picture a radical disjuncture or even hostility between prophets and priests.

The prophet vs priest view won widespread acceptance, especially in liberal American Protestantism. In this view the prophets were very sensitive individuals who saw that true faith was a proper respect for God as the loving Father and all men as his children. Thereby the prophets became spokesmen for ethical monotheism and antagonists of sacrificial worship, which they deemed the perversion of true religion (see R. H. Pfeiffer, and especially J. P. Hyatt's *Prophetic Religion*).

A third stage in interpretation placed the "classical" (or "writing") prophets in antagonism with the "false prophets" who were associated with the kings and made their work to insure stable politics in Israel by proclaiming "Peace be with you." (See Jer. 28.) These "cultic" prophets, attached to Israel's sanctuaries, were a common feature in OT study after the World War I. G. Hoelscher said they were derived from the Baal worship of the native Canaanites. But they were seen as completely different from the writing prophets.

The next stage proposed a close connection between the "cultic prophets" and the "classical prophets." This stemmed from the work of Gunkel and Mowinckel, who allowed a place in Israel's worship for a prophet to pronounce a word in God's name. But Mowinckel assumed the "cultic prophets" were ecstatics, who had little in common with the writing prophets except stylized forms of speech. He still considered the writing prophets a high-water mark in moral and religious development. A. Haldar strengthened Mowinckel's form studies by showing a similar prophetic aspect in the worship of other cultures.

Others, building on Mowinckel, argued for closer connections in function, words, and roles between the "cultic" and "writing" prophets. A very close association was defended by England's S. H. Hooke, who emphasized the centrality of the ritual for *all* life and institutions in Israel.

A. R. Johnson proposed that there was an established place for the prophets in the Jerusalem temple worship and that the prophets were part of the temple staff (thus they disappeared with the fall of the temple). I. Engnell championed a similar view in his work on the role of the king in the ancient Near East, especially in connection with cultic festivals.

In the 1940s the idea of a cultic base for the OT prophets came to dominate OT study, with dissident voices by B. D. Eerdmans (a conservative scholar who denied the existence of all cult prophets, true or false!), H. H. Rowley (who warned of making a theory a dogmatic assumption) and, of course, by "unreconstructed" liberal theologians like **J. P. Hyatt** (who continued to maintain prophets were anti-cultic).

A more mediating position held that the prophets were not against the cultic worship, including sacrifices, but did oppose some excesses, the appropriation of some Canaanite worship features, and/or lack of daily life character in the worshipers. Thus Amos, Isaiah, and Hosea attacked a debased and misused cult, but not sacrifice itself (H. H. Rowley, R. K. Harrison).

In summary, the view that the prophet was the antagonist of the priesthood finds few supporters today. Most scholars assume some connection between the prophets and the cult (perhaps only that the prophets delivered their oracles in the cult). Even so, this consensus has been recently challenged for neglecting the originality of the individual prophets, and their attacks on the cult are taken more seriously by **J. Ward** and **G. Fohrer**, who argue the eighth-century prophets foretold the total overthrow of Israel's institutions, both cult and king.

Prophetic Inspiration

When scholars saw the prophets as individuals with a loose relation to the cult, their "inspiration" was viewed as something like being a religious genius (perhaps an eccentric one). This rationalistic understanding is the antithesis of the ecstatic theory of Hoelscher and **T. H. Robinson**. The ecstatic view was congenial with prominent theories in sociological anthropology which stressed the significance of a "holy man" in primitive societies (assuming Israelite society of the eighth century was primitive). They declared that the "holy man" had an experience and was seized by the divine Spirit.

J. Lindblom distinguished between an ecstasy of "absorption" (where the individual is fused with God) and the ecstasy of "concentration" in the prophets. Mowinckel, still accepting some extraordinary experience (ecstasy) in the prophets, came to emphasize more the *message* of the prophets. He thought the ecstatic experience was more basic to the false prophets. H. H. Rowley summarized that "ecstasy" was not proved by etymology with *navi'*, that such "ecstasies" must have been shared by "true" and "false" prophets, and that what was constitutive of the true prophets was their message (recently G. Widengren has reintroduced the parapsychic experiences as foundational to prophecy).

The Prophetic Message

The message of the prophet has been the focus in prophetic studies for the last quarter-century, in both *form* and *content*.

For most of Christian history, the essence of the prophetic message was held to be predictions of future events, especially the details of Jesus' coming. Often this view minimized the work of the prophets in their own time and neglected their religious and moral teachings. Some modern scholars revolted against both the idea of prediction and the neglect of prophetic teachings.

Old Testament study for the first quarter of this century tended to diminish or deny prediction in the prophetic message. **J. P. Hyatt** and **W. R. Harper** stressed the ethical teaching of the prophets as social reformers in Israel. Predictions found in prophetic books were often deleted as later additions. A classical formulation of this view was the slogan that prophets were "forthtellers" rather than "foretellers." Many scholars, especially the more orthodox, objected that this was a criterion grounded in modern prejudices rather than in study of the OT books themselves.

The more rigid application of this principle quickly fell into disrespect among most scholars. For one thing, there were too many predictions in the prophets (especially of an impending political disaster for Israel) which were really constitutive of the book. Moreover, history of religions study revealed that prediction was a common work of "divine men" in ancient Greece, Egypt, Babylonia, and Phoenicia. Thus the Hebrew prophets would have been abnormal in *their time* if they refused to offer predictions. But scholars have retained the emphasis on the role of the prophet in his own times. The classical prophets gave a word from God to kings and peoples, rebuking sins, threatening divine judgment, and warning of the nation's fall. This prophetic work has been enrichingly studied in the last half-century.

Possible predictions have become more acceptable, and the differences among scholars have been on whether certain prophecies have either a primary or secondary reference to Jesus as the Christ. Here there is a relative division between conservative and liberal scholars according to assumptions about the nature of inspiration.

An aspect of the question of prediction is whether the classical prophets (especially Amos, Hosea, and Micah) spoke only a message of coming doom or if they included a word of hope. The dominant view since the turn of the century has been to limit or eliminate "hopeful" words in these prophets. Scholars have argued that a message of utter disaster facing Israel (found in these prophets) would have been rendered innocuous by any words of hope (J. M. Ward, *Amos and Isaiah*). Others have replied that the prophets may not have been too exercised about such an apparent lack of consistency.

This "despair" view of the prophetic message is related to recent studies on the form of prophetic oracles. Gunkel had proposed that the prophets were not basically writers, but orators who spoke in short oracles—only a few lines. This view holds that the prophets were sent with a message for a specific occasion. Gunkel analyzed the prophetic oracle as consisting of a *reproach* (Because you have . . .) and a *threat* (thus will I do to you . . .). This basic analysis has been widely accepted and developed by others and given a classical presentation in C. Westermann's *Basic Forms of Prophetic Speech*.

H. G. Reventlow, building upon the work by E. Würthwein, has argued there was an oracle of salvation form as well as of condemnation. T. Raitt suggests Jeremiah's message also included a call to repentance and that Israel's decision would determine either a hope-filled future, or destruction. A similar view has been defended recently by G. **Fohrer,** who argues that prophetic messages took account of both the action of God and the decision of men. These last two scholars have written recently, and it is still too soon to see what acceptance their proposals may find.

Conservative scholars have had little interest in the study of forms but have concentrated on the completed prophetic book. Young, in fact, is very critical of the form-study approach as a "foe of true exegesis." But such hostility is not expressed by other conservative scholars such as R. K. Harrison.

The Origin and Transmission of Prophetic Books

The work of Gunkel and Mowinckel gave impetus to the view that the oral stage of prophetic messages could be recovered out of the written books. With this theory, scholarly study turned increasingly towards the study of the *forms* of the oral prophetic speech.

Around World War I three stages in the production of prophetic books were widely recognized: (1) the oral stage, when the prophet gave short oracles to his contemporaries, (2) a later collection of these oracles which had been transmitted by his disciples, and (3) the production of prophetic books from such collections, with frequent additions not from the prophet himself.

H. S. Nyberg modified this view by insisting that the oral transmission was the longest period and that as a result it is highly doubtful that any *exact word* of the prophet survived. **H. Birkeland** argued for a highly faithful remembrance of the prophetic message but also doubted that any specific wording of that message was recoverable.

From the theory that the prophets had office at the cultic shrines, Haldar and Engnell argued that the prophetic words were passed on by cultic prophetic guilds. Placing even greater emphasis upon the oral transmission, Engnell once thought the bulk of the OT was not written down until the exile (he later accepted some books, such as Nahum and Habakkuk, as being written from the beginning).

Comparing the transmission of traditions in other ancient cultures, **G. Widengren** argued that written transmission played a greater role than scholars had allowed. Reversing the emphases, he places a greater significance on the written tradition, noting suggestions in Isaiah 8:1-4; 30:8; and Ezekiel 43:11-12. In the case of Jeremiah, there is an explicit description of one prophet committing his words to writing (Jer. 36).

In reply, **J. Muilenburg** and others have pointed to the style (poetic) and the content ("hear," not *read*, "this word!") as demanding an oral transmission. Muilenburg says, "The prophets were not primarily literary men, but speakers." This leads him to analyze the prophetic book by identifying the smaller individual parts (i.e., oracles) and defining them by form critical study. (See the article "Old Testament Prophecy" in *Peake's New Commentary on the Bible*, p. 478.)

Apart from the criticism of Widengren, conservative scholars have refuted the oral transmission approach on other grounds: (1) the Jewish tradition considered the prophetic books to have been authored by the prophets themselves, as they evidenced by adding the later superscriptions to them; (2) R. K. Harrison and others have said that the many interpolations which have been located in the prophetic books assume a process of editing and re-editing the prophets' words with little respect for the divine source of their message; (3) it has been noted that in Egypt and Babylonia important messages were characteristically committed to writing, to avoid any chance additions.

In summary, the nature of the origin and development of prophetic books is still far from having a consensus among OT scholars. While most agree the prophetic message was first presented orally, there is no real agreement on when it was subsequently put in written form and whether this was the work of the prophet himself or of his "disciples" (a phenomenon vital to the Uppsala School's view of oral transmission but questioned by many scholars).

THE WRITINGS

The Psalms

Probably the best-loved of the OT books is the Psalter. Like the Pentateuch, it has also been a major focus in modern OT study, especially since the work of H. Gunkel. Prior to Gunkel, the common view (whether orthodox or liberal) considered the Psalms as basically individual creations arising from personal faith. Gunkel overturned this view so that today the consensus is reversed, with most OT scholars emphasizing the *community* character of the Psalms.

Nineteenth-century critics tended to date the Psalms very late, after the return from exile and most even from the Maccabean Age. In the view of C. H. Cornill and W. Robertson Smith, the individual Psalms were collected as a "hymnbook of the second temple." Gunkel reversed this, arguing that the Psalms arose in Israel's public worship and were later "democratized" by individuals in Israel and appropriated for expression of individual piety. His pioneering work sprang both from his interest in form-critical study (see below for his classification of the Psalms) and from a study of Israel's neighbors and their cultic practices. Gunkel explained the possible significance of Babylonian and Egyptian worship for understanding the Psalms.

Gunkel's student S. Mowinckel represents the next major shift in Psalms study. He, too, saw the origins of the Psalms in cultic worship, but, unlike his teacher, Mowinckel was favorably disposed toward the cultus. Thus he came to explain the Psalms as almost entirely cultic, both in their origin and in their use in Israel. Mowinckel's most original contribution was to suggest a life setting for many of the Psalms in connection with an annual New Year Festival at the temple, where God was enthroned as the king of the world. Specifically, Mowinckel proposed a type of "enthronement psalms" (e.g., Pss. 93, 95, 100) used in this festival.

Mowinckel's theory has been widely accepted to explain the purpose and use of the Psalms. But many have criticized his idea of an enthronement festival because it is totally dependent on assumed analogies with Babylonian worship (see criticisms by O. Eissfeldt, L. I. Pap). Some have accepted a basic, annual, cultic use of Psalms without an "enthronement festival." **H.-J. Kraus** suggests that they were used in conjunction with a covenant-renewal ceremony where Israel rededicated herself to God. G. Widengren and I. Engnell, following their overall reconstruction of the life of Israel, proposed an ancient ritual of a dying and rising deity.

One of the most important aspects of Gunkel's work was to classify the "forms" of various Psalms. Of course the Psalms had long been classified by their subject matter (hymns of joy, meditation, penitence, royal songs, etc.) by conservative scholars like B. D. Eerdmans and **J. Cales**, an approach still favored by R. K. Harrison. But Gunkel's classifications were by *function* rather than *subject matter*.

Gunkel suggested five basic forms for the Psalms, with several additional less important types: (1) *hymns* praising God, such as individuals and/or choirs might have sung— Pss. 8, 19, 33; (2) *community laments*, evoked by a national crisis such as war or famine and begging God's intervention —Pss. 44, 79, 80; (3) *individual laments,* similar to type 2, except basically an individual's petition in personal crisis— Pss. 7, 13, 51; (4) *individual thanksgivings,* used in public worship, but chanted or sung by individuals; and (5) *royal psalms,* celebrating significant events in the life of an Israelite king—Pss. 2, 20, 101, 110. (Gunkel also allowed for "mixed" forms, which used parts of two or more of these.)

Basically Mowinckel worked with Gunkel's categories but greatly reduced the role of individual Psalms, partly by interpreting their "I" in a communal way (as today many songs used in public worship are first person singular). Mowinckel gave greatest attention to the category of "royal psalms" because of his view of an annual royal festival. His work refined Gunkel's theory and is in no way a refutation of it. H.-J. Kraus' suggestion of a cultic origin and development of the Psalter is similar, but without Mowinckel's king theory. Finally, the most recent major treatment of the

Psalms, by M. **Dahood** (*Anchor Bible*), still utilizes Gunkel's thesis, although it also makes extreme revisions of the actual text readings in the Psalms (for which his work has been widely and severely criticized).

The significance of the superscriptions ascribing authorship of the various Psalms has been variously assessed. Older critical scholars thought the Psalms claiming David as author (seventy-three in the Hebrew text) were a device to help give them importance in postexilic worship. R. H. Pfeiffer, perhaps an extreme example of this view, doubted there were any pre-exilic hymns in the collection.

Since then two major changes have occurred. First, scholars were increasingly agreeable to assign pre-exilic dates for many Psalms (most, I. Engnell) and also to accept David as the author of some. Second, linguistic study suggested the Hebrew phrase translated "psalm of David" could equally be rendered "a psalm for David" or "a psalm in the Davidic style." This view has been acceptable to conservative scholars like Young and Archer.

Other superscriptions in the Psalms were similarly discussed. Many conjectures were given, because in many instances the meaning of the Hebrew terms is difficult. Some were apparently for musical accompaniment; others gave directions to singers or choirmasters. Even the frequent word "selah" is of uncertain meaning.

Gunkel's proposals are still the watershed for modern Psalms study, because his insistence on the *communal* locus for the Psalms is foundational in almost all modern studies. It has undergone real refinement, but, unlike other important theories in OT study, it has not been rejected by any sizeable number of scholars.

Proverbs

The earliest representative of Hebrew wisdom literature, Proverbs, was a focal point in the recent increase of interest in the wisdom movement of the ancient world. Wisdom was the last major segment of OT literature to receive study by modern scholars, and that really began about fifty years ago with the discovery of other wisdom writings from the ancient Near East. In 1922 **E. A. W. Budge** began publishing extracts from an ancient Egyptian writing *The Wisdom of Amen-em-opet,* which appears to have parallel sections with Proverbs 22:17—23:11. **A. Erman** and later O Eissfeldt argued that this Egyptian text was used by the writer of Proverbs. Egyptologist **E. Drioton** argued that Proverbs was the source for *The Wisdom of Amen-em-opet.*

The discussion of who copied from whom was mitigated by the discovery that there was a widespread, international wisdom movement in the ancient world, including Egypt, Babylonia, Phoenicia, and Israel (W. O. E. Oesterly and H. Gressmann). This internationalism gives the Proverbs and other OT wisdom writings their uniqueness because they have a more universalist orientation (in content, form, and origin), make little or no use of distinctive Israelite ideas (the Sinai covenant, the exodus, the Davidic rule), and are more empirical in outlook.

Such internationalism provided frequent cross-exchange of ideas affecting the questions of authorship and date of the Proverbs. In few areas of OT study is there such disagreement among scholars employing the same methods of study. Very few would hold that Solomon was the author of the entire book (the book does not claim so; see 24:23; 30:1; 31:1). But some (including Albright) suggest Solomon was responsible for many of these proverbs (Young thinks for most). Others have thought Solomon the author of very few, if any (J. Skinner). Most recent scholars hold that Solomon was directly responsible for some, and indirectly for many, in that he was the patron who encouraged wise man/scribal schools in Israel (J. C. Rylaarsdam and W. Baumgartner). Thus Solomon was to the development of Proverbs what David was to the development of Psalms.

Of course the dating of the Proverbs is closely tied to the question of authorship, if one holds Solomon as their writer. Otherwise the date of the collection ranges from the time of Hezekiah (Albright, see Prov. 25:1) to after the exile (S. R. Driver, C. H. Toy). Of course the "oral transmission" theorists suggest a long oral history in the cult prior to a rather late date for writing (I. Engnell, A. Bentzen).

One of the questions arising in Proverbs studies is the "hypostatization," or personification, of Wisdom in Proverbs 8. Some have suggested that wisdom is pictured here as a divinity separate from God (similar to Christ). This has been seen to reflect Greek speculation about the Logos (E. Sellin, R. Kittel) or Canaanite thought (H. Ringgren). Others have suggested that wisdom is personified but not a distinct person (R. K. Harrison). H. Wheeler Robinson explained the idea as use of a poetic style. Apart from studies of ancient parallels to other particular proverbs, little modern study has been done on Proverbs. J. C. Rylaarsdam made the suggestion it was a "copybook" used by wisdom teachers to instruct their students.

Job

Of all the "Writings," Job has received the most attention in modern OT study. For centuries it has excited the minds and hearts of a great variety of readers. In the last century it was considered by some to be modeled on Greek drama (a parallel may be seen in A. MacLeish's modern play *J. B.*). Five basic sections within the book can be identified: (1) the prose prologue, chapters 1–2; (2) the dialogues of Job and his friends, 3–31; (3) Elihu's speeches, 32–37; (4) the speeches of God, 38:1–42:6; and (5) the prose epilogue, 42:7-17.

These five divisions have been variously interpreted. Some have regarded the entire book as a unit (E. Sellin, H. Hertzberg), while others have thought that the prose prologue and epilogue were earlier than the poetic materials (Wellhausen, C. Cornill, and K. Budde). Other scholars (e.g., Eerdmans) have reversed this. Several have suggested that the Elihu speeches are not originally part of the work (Dhorme, Koenig). The variety of possible combinations is examined in Young's *Introduction to the Old Testament*, although this is now rather dated.

Although one Jewish tradition ascribed the book to Moses, most scholars (ancient and modern) agree that the author of the book of Job is anonymous. With regard to dating, distinction must be made between the date of the story of Job and the present written form. Albright, by examining the customs presumed in the book, proposed that the hero himself belonged to the patriarchal age. The completed work has variously been dated in Solomon's time (Young, M. Unger, F. Delitzsch), in the time of Hezekiah (Gunkel, Koenig, and Albright), and after the exile (A. Weiser, S. R. Driver). If the book is divided into parts, these are often dated differently. Such great variety in dating among scholars from all theological positions suggests that any consensus is unlikely, pending new facts.

Despite the popular view that Job is focused on the question of God's justice (theodicy, accepted by W. Harrelson and W. A. Irwin), there are other suggestions. **E. Kraeling** thought the purpose was entertainment. **J. Pedersen** thought Job posed the problem of theodicy but did not seek to solve it (similarly, H. H. Rowley says it does not solve this problem). J. Hempel saw it as one man's complaint against the stereotyped answers of the wisdom school.

Perhaps part of Job's power to evoke interest, thought, and meditation about basic religious questions and at varying levels of study is the enigmatic quality which also makes it open to diversity in interpretations.

Ecclesiastes

This third example of OT "wisdom" books shows the variety within that category. If Proverbs is basically optimistic about human life and reasoning, Ecclesiastes is the reverse. It has been viewed as very pious (F. Delitzsch) and skeptical (Heine). As with Proverbs, Solomon has been considered its author (H. Moeller, R. K. Harrison) or its patron (Young), while others have denied any connection with Solomon (C. C. Torrey).

With regard to date, suggestions range from Solomon to the time of Herod the Great (H. Graetz; this is no longer possible since a copy was found in the Dead Sea Scrolls, insuring a date before 170 B.C.). Earlier in this century a late date was suggested on the basis of alleged dependence on Greek philosophies (G. Siegfried, H. Ranston).

Ecclesiastes has been regarded as a collection of earlier writings (Ranston) or as one writing with various interpolations to make an originally skeptical work more pious (P. Volz). Among critical scholars, the unity of the book has found a competent defense from C. **Cornill** and **R. Gordis**.

The older critical view located Greek influence in the book (O. Eissfeldt, R. Pfeiffer), but Babylonian (G. Barton, W. F. Albright), Egyptian (P. Humbert, W. Baumgartner), and even Phoenician (M. Dahood) origins have been proposed. As with Job, the purpose of Ecclesiastes has been variously explained. J. Pedersen saw it as a statement of Hebrew skepticism; **W. Zimmerli** thought that it was a critical assessment of wisdom theology. R. Gordis, a Jewish scholar, thinks it is a spiritual testament given to reject attempts to explain God's favor on the basis of success or failure in this world.

Only in recent years, since G. von Rad's *Theology of the Old Testament*, has there been real interest in assessing the significance of "wisdom" within the overall thought of the OT. W. Zimmerli tried to show that the idea of God as the Creator is behind Hebrew wisdom theology. One of the most recent attempts to explore this question, in relation to the prophetic writings, is **J. Crenshaw**'s *Prophetic Conflict*.

This brief survey of the history of modern criticism in OT thought is necessarily very incomplete. The author's desire has been to fairly represent major positions, although often it has been necessary to oversimplify. Refutation of erroneous views would require a massive, book-length undertaking, along with a much more detailed study of the history of the discipline.

BIBLIOGRAPHY

Albright, W. F. *From the Stone Age to Christianity*. 2d ed. Garden City, N.Y.: Doubleday, 1957.

Archer, G. L. *A Survey of Old Testament Introduction*. Chicago: Moody Press, 1974 rev. ed.

Clements, R. E. *One Hundred Years of Old Testament Interpretation*. Philadelphia: Westminster, 1976.

Eissfeldt, Otto. *The Old Testament: An Introduction*. New York: Harper and Row, 1965.

Flanders, H. J.; Crapps, R. W.; and Smith, D. A. *People of the Covenant*. New York: Roland Press, 1973.

Hahn, F. H. *The Old Testament and Modern Research.* Philadelphia: Muhlenberg Press, 1954.

Harrison, R. K. *Introduction to the Old Testament.* Grand Rapids: Wm. B. Eerdmans Co., 1969.

Rowley, H. H., ed. *The Old Testament and Modern Study.* Oxford: Clarendon Press, 1951.

Unger, Merrill. *Introductory Guide to the Old Testament.* Grand Rapids: Zondervan, 1952.

Von Rad, Gerhard. *Old Testament Theology.* 2 vols. New York: Harper & Row, 1962, 1965.

Young, E. J. *Introduction to the Old Testament.* Grand Rapids: Wm. B. Eerdmans, 1949.

IX

The Theology of the Old Testament

Thomas H. Olbricht

THE THEOLOGICAL STUDY OF THE BIBLE

What is involved in a theological study of the Bible? The Bible may be studied from a number of perspectives, one of which is theological. There are specialized studies, such as the animals of the Bible, the men and women of the Bible, the social customs of biblical times, and biblical archeology. There are also the biblical tools which include commentaries, lexicons, concordances, Bible dictionaries, and handbooks. Just as each of these approaches to the Bible is different, so is a theological study.

Scholars divide biblical studies into six major divisions. First is introduction, which is concerned with background information about each book as to its author, date, literary form, and audience. Second are textual studies, which take up the manner in which the Bible has come down to us in its various manuscript forms. Third is a study of developmental aspects of biblical times in the form of OT or NT history. Fourth are exegetical studies of the sort found in commentaries. The exegete explains biblical sections in their own setting, then puts them in words which make sense now. Fifth are studies in the history of religion, which trace the development of religion chronologically either in the OT or the NT. Sixth is the theology of the Bible.

A theological study of the Bible differs from other studies in that it is concerned with that which gives unity to the Bible, the nearness or distance of other matters to that center, and a manner of organizing the materials of the Bible around that center.

THE THEOLOGICAL STUDY OF THE OLD TESTAMENT

Old Testament theology is concerned with finding the center of the OT, then unifying the thought of the OT from that standpoint. Various proposals have been made as to how OT theology should be done; and, since the time when it began as a discipline in the seventeenth century, the major approaches have been four. (1) Some have suggested that no center to the OT is obvious, so they have put to the OT those questions typical of systematic theology. A case in point is the *Old Testament Theology* of Ludwig Köhler (1935, E.T., 1957) organized in three parts: I. God, II. Man, III. Judgment and salvation. Otto J. Baab (1949) makes a similar assumption. (2) Others have proposed that Christ is the center of the OT. These include Wilhelm Vischer (E.T., 1949) and George A. F. Knight, who titles his book *A Christian Theology of the Old Testament* (1964). (3) Still others have seen the covenant as the center of the OT, principally Walther Eichrodt in his monumental two-volume work (E.T., 1961, 1967) and J. Barton Payne (1962). (4) A fourth group have seen the OT centering around God, who is characterized by certain mighty acts which reappear thematically throughout the OT. These include Gerhard von Rad in his two-volume *Old Testament Theology* (E.T. 1962, 1965) and G. Ernest Wright, *The Old Testament and Theology* (1969).

The position taken in this essay is that the scholar should not decide this matter on his own but should search the pertinent OT passages which declare that which is central or most important. These are passages which envision Israel at worship proclaiming who she is before God (as in Deut. 26:1-11; Pss. 136, 105, 106), in covenant renewal ceremonies (as in Josh. 24:1-28; Neh. 9:6-37), and in prayer (as in Jer. 32:16-25; Dan. 9:3-19). An amazing similarity of affirmation appears in each of these places. At the center of OT thought is Yahweh, who is defined by certain great events in which he revealed himself to Israel. The most complete statement is that found in Nehemiah 9, which will essentially serve as the outline of OT theology in this essay.

From looking at the above Scriptures, one concludes that God is at the center of OT theology. But God is not so undefined that each scholar may fill in the blanks as he pleases. He is specifically the God who revealed himself to Israel through certain mighty events. He is known, not in his essence, but in his action. Therefore, the important affirmations about God in the OT are those mighty acts which receive recurring emphasis in the OT. These mighty events can serve as the manner of organizing the thought of the OT. They involve a God who creates and sustains, who made promises to the fathers, who acted in Egypt and at the sea, who trained his son in the wilderness, who put it in writing with his people, who cares by giving law, who commands the heavenly armies, who gives his son an inheritance, and who makes a promise to David.

THE THEOLOGY OF THE OLD TESTAMENT

God Who Creates and Sustains

In Psalm 136 the first mighty work of God is creation. God is praised for his goodness and steadfast love. That goodness or love is not some glow which hangs over the universe, stirring up human emotions. It is concretely realized in creation itself. The psalmist indicates why he declares these characteristics of God:

To him who alone does great wonders,
   for his steadfast love endures for ever;
to him who by understanding made the heavens,
   for his steadfast love endures for ever;
to him who spread out the earth upon the waters,
   for his steadfast love endures for ever;
to him who made the great lights,
   for his steadfast love endures for ever;

the sun to rule over the day,
> for his steadfast love endures for ever;
the moon and stars to rule over the night,
> for his steadfast love endures for ever.

Psalm 136:4-9

Unique in the view of the created order declared in the OT is that the physical universe reflects the warmth and love which come from God. There is no suggestion that the universe is impersonal, unfeeling, cold, and material. The God who saved Israel at the sea is the same God who called forth the material universe. They both alike function in behalf of man and reflect the goodness of God.

One of the basic affirmations about creation in Genesis 1 is that God "saw everything that he had made, and behold, it was very good" (1:31). Even after man's sin caused nature to slip toward the abyss, its goodness remained.

Thou dost cause the grass to grow for the cattle,
> and plants for man to cultivate,
that he may bring forth good from the earth,
> and wine to gladden the heart of man,
oil to make his face shine,
> and bread to strengthen man's heart.

Psalm 104:14-15

What does "good" mean in Genesis 1? The created order is good because it fulfills the purpose intended by God. Plants and grass are food for man and animals. They are good since they serve a function in the created order (Gen. 1:29-30). The goodness of creation is neither its orderly beauty, as with the Greeks, nor a moral quality, as with the Persians. The universe is good because each part contributes to and has function in the whole. (See Ps. 104:10-23.)

But because the function of these parts contributes to the welfare of man, the goodness of creation also has a moral dimension. One moral characteristic of the universe is its regularity or loyalty. The universe is faithful (regular) because God is faithful. Jeremiah indicates this quality as most obvious in the recurrence of day and night.

If you can break my covenant with the day and my covenant with the night, so that day and night will not come at their appointed time, then also my covenant with David my servant may be broken.

Jeremiah 33:20-21

Other qualities are helpfulness and love. The material universe has these qualities because God continues to bring his blessings through physical channels (Deut. 28:11-12). The universe is lawful, not because it contains within itself natural law, but because God, who is faithful in promise, sustains it (cf. Col. 1:16-17).

Evil is present in the universe, but it is not ultimate. Satan, the adversary of man, is nevertheless answerable to God (Job 2:2-6). But because of Satan, who has a degree of freedom, the universe is no longer solely good since there are powers which oppose God. When man violates the command of God, he too adds to the spread of evil. The snakes turn against man (Gen. 3:15), the woman suffers pain in childbirth (3:16), and thorns and thistles infect the earth (3:18).

Because of its view of the created order, the OT steers clear of various extremes. Physical existence is a blessing because it is from God. Even the extreme cries of Job (Job 3) and Ecclesiastes (8:17) do not denounce the material order. Even if the physical order is polluted by sin, it is still God's; and he is completing his work in it (Ps. 50:10-12). At the same time the physical universe is not to be worshiped since it is not God (Ps. 90:1-2). Furthermore, it is less than God because it has been infected by human sin. The OT view is thus not pantheistic, that is, that God is all and all is God. The universe does not emanate from God, nor is it his outer physical nature (1 Kings 8:27). At the same time, however, God is not radically separated from his universe. His power and presence extend throughout its vast reaches (Ps. 139:7-8). He is transcendent, but not radically so. He is loving, caring, and involved.

God created the universe by his word; and, inasmuch as it fulfills his purpose, it is good. The universe is meaningful and loving, but in its present state it is not final. Man lives in the world. It is his home. But he does not worship the world. His love and worship are directed to God, the Maker of heaven and earth (Deut. 6:4-5; Gen. 14:19-20).

In the OT, God not only brought the universe into existence, but he supports it through his sustaining word. The physical order continues moment by moment because of God's abiding presence. When his hand is opened, when his face shines upon the created order, all goes well.

> These all look to thee,
>> to give them their food in due season.
> When thou givest to them, they gather it up;
>> when thou openest thy hand, they are filled with good things.
> When thou hidest thy face, they are dismayed;
>> when thou takest away their breath, they die and return to their dust.
> When thou sendest forth thy Spirit, they are created;
>> and thou renewest the face of the ground.
>
> Psalm 104:27-30

The orderliness of the universe is not due to natural law, but to the promise of God.

> Neither will I ever again destroy every living creature as I have done. While the earth remains, seedtime and harvest, cold and heat, summer and winter, day and night, shall not cease.
>
> Genesis 8:21-22

He sustains it not only in its physical expression, but also in the life residing within it. He assists those who are his, even through the material order. When his people cry to him, he reaches out to assist. His appearance with his people in battle is often accompanied by natural phenomena, especially the thunderstorm (Judg. 5:4-5; 2 Sam. 22:8-16; Ps. 18:7-19). God is Creator and Sustainer. He also appears in the universe as Savior, rescuing those who cry out of their affliction. Even nature is affected by his action (Ps. 114). In fact, the OT does not distinguish among these three roles. He is one God. There is no dichotomy of spiritual and material, if by material one has in mind the physical universe. The only way in which the physical universe is less than spiritual (good) is through the forces in it which are at enmity with God. It is only where sin is present that the material stands against the spiritual.

Where sin is rampant, God withdraws his sustaining word and the created order sinks back into chaos (Job 34:13-15). Micah declares that, when God arrives to put down rebellion, creation itself is affected:

> For behold, the Lord is coming forth out of his place,
>   and will come down and tread upon the high places of
>   the earth.
> And the mountains will melt under him
>   and the valleys will be cleft,
> like wax before the fire,
>   like waters poured down a steep place.
> All this is for the transgression of Jacob
>   and for the sins of the house of Israel.

Micah 1:3-5

Jeremiah goes so far as to envision God reversing the order of original creation because of the transgressions of his people (Jer. 4:23-26). After the action of God, the countryside lies devastated. Everything has disappeared, leaving the earth as it was before God brought order out of chaos, light out of darkness, life out of death. The physical universe is not God himself, but neither is it impersonal material. The universe reflects the very person of God, for he is continually involved. He is Creator, Sustainer, and Activator.

But even after the universe sinks back into chaos, God does not abandon it. He is ever creating anew. This is especially the affirmation of the prophets as they envision events beyond the destruction of Israel. Jeremiah declares that the God who brought forth man and animals in the beginning can do it again:

> Behold, the days are coming, says the Lord, when I will sow the house of Israel and the house of Judah with the seed of man and the seed of beast. And it shall come to pass that as I have watched over them to pluck up and break down, to overthrow, destroy, and bring evil, so I will watch over them to build and to plant, says the Lord.

Jeremiah 31:27-28

Isaiah sees the postcaptivity events as resulting in new

action of God which he calls new creation:

> Remember not the former things,
>   nor consider the things of old.
> Behold, I am doing a new thing;
>   now it springs forth, do you not perceive it?
> I will make a way in the wilderness
>   and rivers in the desert.
> The wild beasts will honor me,
>   the jackals and ostriches;
> for I give water in the wilderness,
>   rivers in the desert,
> to give drink to my chosen people.
>
> Isaiah 43:18-20

In the thought of the OT, God is at the center of the universe and of human life because he brought it into existence. It reflects his steadfast love and goodness. Despite evil which has interrupted God's plans, he continues to work in his world as Sustainer and Savior. In OT theology God is defined through his loving concern for the universe he has brought forth and for man created in his image.

God Who Made Promises to the Fathers

God is defined in the OT not only in his relationship to the physical universe, but especially through his relationship with man. Man was created in the image of God (Gen. 1:26). He stands at the apex of God's creation. This is obvious in Genesis 1 in that he stands last in an ascending order, and in Genesis 2 in that the one who is of most importance is there mentioned first. From these accounts it is clear that man is the center around which the created order radiates (Gen. 1:29). He is the creature most like and nearest to God, since he is made in his image. Even though the world was made for man, he is not to utilize it to his own ends, but responsibly. Man has dominion over his sphere (Gen. 1:26) just as God has dominion over the whole. Man has responsibility for his world (Deut. 20:19-20) just as God has for the whole. This is man's uniqueness. In this manner he is like God. Man is different in that he has abilities that are

Godlike, not that he contains an everlasting principle within himself. Man was not created to live forever. He had that prospect only through eating from the tree of life (Gen. 3:22). Because of sin he was evicted from the garden and cut off from the tree. God is the source of life for man. He does not have life as a substance or principle within himself.

> If he should take back his spirit to himself,
> and gather to himself his breath,
> all flesh would perish together,
> and man would return to dust.
>
> Job 34:14-15

But man is also Godlike in his freedom. Just as God freely determines his universe, so man orders his own world. In his freedom man can live life on God's terms or on his own (Gen. 2:15-17). The rest of creation follows the course of nature.

> Even the stork in the heavens
> knows her times;
> and the turtledove, swallow, and crane
> keep the time of their coming;
> but my people know not
> the ordinance of the Lord.
>
> Jeremiah 8:7

But man can go his own way, and most frequently he does.

> The ox knows its owner,
> and the ass its master's crib;
> but Israel does not know,
> my people does not understand.
>
> Isaiah 1:3

So God creates the world, bestowing upon it his loving care and concern. But the one creature whom God addresses and who in turn addresses God (Gen. 3:8-13)—man made in his image—absconds from his responsibility under God, upsetting the created order, plunging it back toward the abyss. Man turns his back on God, and communication is broken off (Gen. 3:22-24). The result is that communication is likewise disrupted with his fellow (Gen. 11:1-9). Man is then concerned only for himself. In so doing he breaks off from the basic character of God, which is loving action, and from the created order which reflects the love of God. Man in his self-centeredness is man the sinner.

Man is created in the image of God to realize his love and goodness in the created order. Instead, man pursues his own interests and becomes a sinner.

> The Lord saw that the wickedness of man was great in the earth, and that every imagination of the thoughts of his heart was only evil continually.

> Genesis 6:5

So what is God to do? His first impulse is to wipe man out. He decided to destroy him through a flood (Gen. 6:11-13). But God saved Noah, and through him the problem started all over again. Then God promised he would never again set out to destroy man (Gen. 8:21). As a loving God, however, he could not sit idly by and watch an endless succession of evil. What God did was to make a promise to the fathers; first of all to Abraham, then to Isaac and Jacob. The intent of the promise was that through them the original goodness of creation might in some measure be restored. It is significant that God made this promise. Even more significant, however, is the reason he made it. Through the reason, the theology of the promise is disclosed.

The basic theology of the promise to the fathers is found in the statement to Abraham:

> Now the Lord said to Abram, "Go from your country and your kindred and your father's house to the land that I will show you. And I will make of you a great nation, and I will bless you, and make your name great, so that you will be a blessing. I will bless those who bless you, and him who curses you I will curse; and by you all the families of the earth shall bless themselves."

> Genesis 12:1-3

God is taking up anew the task of sharing his love and goodness with the universe he has made and man within it. He plans to do it through a chosen people. To that end he plans to bless those chosen and in turn bless those with whom they rub shoulders. The same promise was made to Isaac (Gen. 26:4) and to Jacob (28:13-14). The promise also looked ahead to a multitude of descendants who would form a great nation. It was an open-ended promise.

In Genesis particularly, the manner in which God fulfilled this promise is indicated. In these accounts the patriarchs are those through whom God sought to bestow his goodness on the families of the earth. Because of the blessing of God Abram was a very rich man (Gen. 13:2). This blessing in turn rubbed off on Lot so that they were unable to live in the same region (13:5-7). Even Sodom and Gomorrah were rescued from their enemies by the elect of God. Abram wanted to make sure he blessed them rather than they him (14:19-24). Isaac was richly blessed even in the midst of a drought when he was living in the land of the Philistines (26:12). He did so well the Philistines grew jealous. They were not aware that by Isaac's presence they themselves were being blessed. Upon his departure they sought out Isaac to make a covenant so their blessings would continue (26:27-29).

Jacob and his son Joseph brought the goodness of God upon those with whom they lived. After Jacob had been in the household of Laban for several years, Laban became aware that he prospered throughout his estate. He sought out the cause and said to Jacob, "If you will allow me to say so, I have learned by divination that the Lord has blessed me because of you" (Gen. 30:27). Not only was Laban blessed; but, when he turned parts of his holdings over to Jacob, Jacob was likewise blessed. Joseph in his early years was a person with a tragic streak. But those with whom he associated prospered. "From the time that he made him overseer in his house and over all that he had the Lord blessed the Egyptian's house for Joseph's sake" (39:5). Joseph eventually advanced until he was over all the granaries of Egypt. From that point on, Egypt was blessed. Pharaoh recognized this blessing and, when Joseph's family came to Egypt, requested that they be put in charge of his cattle (47:6).

Why did God bless these particular people? It was not

because of who they were or because of their great faith in God. Abraham's relatives served other gods when God called him (Josh. 24:2). There is no evidence in the OT to suggest that Abraham did otherwise before the call. Neither was it because the people of Israel were mighty among the nations (Deut. 7:7). Nor was it because they were holy people, though they were not as wicked as the other nations (9:4). The reason the Lord blessed them was "because the Lord loves you, and is keeping the oath which he swore to your fathers, that the Lord brought you out with a mighty hand" (7:8).

God chose Israel not just to shower gifts on them. He chose them as an avenue through whom to bless the nations. They were elected to service. As the prophets envisioned Israel's role in the world of the future, they saw her as a servant bringing blessings to the nations:

> It is too light a thing that you should be my servant
>   to raise up the tribes of Jacob
>   and to restore the preserved of Israel;
> I will give you as a light to the nations,
>   that my salvation may reach to the end of the earth.
>   Isaiah 49:6

Israel remembered the promise, at least part of the time, and her role in it. She identified God, not according to some quality or essence, but as the one who appeared to Abraham, Isaac, and Jacob and promised his presence (Ps. 105:1-11). She remembered him as Creator, who in those events made glad the life of man (Ps. 104:15). The Creator was the same God who promised to continue distributing his gifts through Abraham, Isaac, and Jacob, and their descendants (2 Kings 13:23).

God Who Acted in Egypt and at the Sea

It was particularly at the time of the exodus that God revealed himself as the one who held history in his hand. He did this through disclosing himself as Yahweh and through his action in Egypt and at the sea. But at the same time, he remained the Creator God who commanded the sea and it obeyed. He was also the one who promised the fathers that they would be a great nation, sharing the gifts of God with others. It was because of his action in creation and with the fathers that he turned out to be the sort of God who lifted Israel from bondage in her moment of despair.

God appeared to Moses in a burning bush on the mountain and told him he would lead Israel out of bondage. Moses asked God what he should say to the people if they asked, "What is his name?" God replied, "I am who I am" (Exod. 3:14). This phrase is a translation of the Hebrew verb *hayah*. In the context it is presupposed that from this root the Hebrew word Yahweh, translated "Lord," is derived. This is obvious from the next statement. "Say this to the people of Israel, 'The Lord, the God of Abraham, the God of Isaac, and the God of Jacob, has sent me to you': this is my name for ever" (Exod. 3:15). It is assumed that it was not until the period of the Exodus that God revealed this name to Israel.

And God said to Moses, "I am the Lord. I appeared to Abraham, to Isaac, and to Jacob, as God Almighty, but by my name the Lord I did not make myself known to them" (Exod. 6:3). The common name for God in the Semitic language is *'elohim*. The Hebrew phrase translated God Almighty is *El Shaddai*. The name Yahweh is of interest to us, for once again through it we are not given the essence or the inner nature of God. The RSV gives an alternate translation of *hayah* in the footnote "I will be what I will be." This is to say that Yahweh is the one who is known by his action. Man cannot hold God in a closed system and say this is the nature of God. God is the being whose future is open. He will define himself by what he does and it is not yet clear just what he will do in the future. By this action in Egypt and at the sea God disclosed the way in which during this time he fulfilled the promise to the fathers. It was not clear from the promise itself that these events would take place. On the other hand, God's helping hand in Egypt was consistent with the promise. But God is free to fulfill his promises in his own way. He will be what he will be. From the theology of the exodus period emerges additional knowledge about

God disclosed through his unique name Yahweh.

The clear affirmation from the OT is that God was at work in the series of events which occurred at the time of the exodus. The important question thus becomes what God hoped to accomplish through these actions. In Exodus 1–18 it is clear that God attempted (1) to create faith in his own people, and (2) convince Egypt and the nations of his might. These actions were, therefore, a continuation of the effort of God to pour forth his gifts upon all mankind. God could dole out all sorts of surprises for man, but they could turn out to be man's downfall rather than for his well-being. It is only when man recognizes that the gifts come from Yahweh and seeks his way that gifts can be utilized in a helpful manner (Deut. 8:11-20).

Before Israel left Egypt, Yahweh, through Moses and Aaron, undertook a series of signs and actions. The result was to bring the people to an intensity of faith. First, Moses and Aaron showed Israel the signs revealed by God in the wilderness. When the people saw, they "believed; and when they heard that the Lord had visited the people of Israel and that he had seen their affliction, they bowed their heads and worshiped" (Exod. 4:31). But that faith was not long lasting. When Pharaoh forced them to collect straw for their bricks, they began to doubt and lay the blame at the feet of Moses and Aaron (5:21). Then followed hard upon those signs the famous plagues. These too had the purpose of convincing the people of the power of Yahweh. This reason is given in Exodus 10:1-2:

> . . . that I may show these signs of mine among them, and that you may tell in the hearing of your son and of your son's son how I have made sport of the Egyptians and what signs I have done among them; that you may know that I am the Lord.

God is known by Israel, not as a heavenly spiritual substance or as an impersonal source of energy, but as one who shows himself to man in his might and power. His power is over the whole of nature and man. He is able to redeem his people, utilizing all the forces of creation—frogs, gnats, flies, bad water, darkness—because he is the one who created all things. All these events—this display of power—created a community of faith.

Through all these events the Pharaoh was finally persuaded to send the Israelites out of the land. But even as they left, he had regrets and sent his armies in pursuit. As the people neared the sea in the distance they saw the armies approaching. The enemy bore hard upon them, and they stood with their backs to the sea. They were once again plunged into doubt and great fear (Exod. 14:10-12). But the unexpected happened. The sea opened up. They crossed over on dry land. The pursuing Egyptians were destroyed as the sea came back together. Through these events they became believers. "And Israel saw the great work which the Lord did against the Egyptians, and the people feared the Lord; and they believed in the Lord and in his servant Moses" (14:31).

The events at the exodus became crucial in the theology of Israel. She came to remember herself chiefly as a group of defeated people whose situation changed when "the Lord brought us out of Egypt with a mighty hand and an outstretched arm, with great terror, with signs and wonders" (Deut. 26:8). It was these events which formed the nation. Forever after, she remembered in times of crisis that God was a God who heard his people when they cried to him. He once again acted as he did at the sea. The recital of these events was central in the worship of Israel, especially in the yearly celebration of the Passover. So at the time of that observance these explanations are to be offered. "And when in time to come your son asks you, 'What does this mean?' you shall say to him, 'By strength of hand the Lord brought us out of Egypt, from the house of bondage'" (Exod. 13:14).

But the mighty deeds of that crucial time were not simply for Israel. They were also for Egypt and the nations. In fact, it is this explanation which is more frequently offered in Exodus. Yahweh tells Moses:

I know that the king of Egypt will not let you go unless compelled by a mighty hand. So I will stretch out my hand and smite Egypt with all the wonders which I will do in it; after that he will let you go.

Exodus 3:19-20

This was not just to destroy the Egyptians because God was against them, but to teach them of the power of Yahweh. "And the Egyptians shall know that I am the Lord, when I stretch forth my hand upon Egypt and bring out the people of Israel from among them" (7:5). These events had results. The magicians became convinced that these were extraordinary acts. "This is the finger of God" (8:19). Several of those who owned cattle put them under shelters because of the hail (9:20). Even the Pharaoh himself was convinced (9:27), but he often relented (10:1). The hardening of the Pharaoh's heart served a purpose. The Pharaoh, because of his natural inclination to doubt the power of the God of these despised people, frequently relented (his heart was hardened) in permitting them to depart. But all this served God's purpose:

> For by now I could have put forth my hand and struck you and your people with pestilence, and you would have been cut off from the earth; but for this purpose have I let you live, to show you my power, so that my name may be declared throughout all the earth.

Exodus 9:15-16

Through these events the power of Yahweh became known among the nations. They had a means through which to identify him—his name. Now they, too, should they be inclined, could respond and share in his gifts.

The great works of God in Egypt and at the sea had the desired results.

> The peoples have heard, they tremble;
>   pangs have seized on the inhabitants
>   of Philistia.
> Terror and dread fall upon them;
>   because of the greatness of thy arm,
>   they are as still as a stone,

till thy people, O Lord, pass by,
    till the people pass by whom thou
        hast purchased.

                                Exodus 15:14, 16

Even Jethro, the priest of Midian and father-in-law of
Moses, heard and was convinced (Exod. 18:1). "Now
I know that the Lord is greater than all gods, because
he delivered the people from under the hand of the
Egyptians . . ." (Exod. 18:11). Jethro then proceeded to
offer a sacrifice to God.

Through the exodus events God made known his might,
power, and goodness, not just to Israel, but to the nations. Israel remembered these actions throughout her
existence. In a real sense, the faith of theology of Israel
centered around the exodus. It was the crucial manner in
which God disclosed his identity in her experience. In the
future as she contemplated her plight, she remembered that
once before when she was enslaved God brought her out
with a mighty hand. He could do it again, for he was that
sort of God. In the days of Gideon God's people were
oppressed. They cried to God as in the time of the exodus.
He reminded them of what he had done in Egypt, then
stated that they had come into this sad state of affairs
because they had not given heed to his voice (Judg. 6:7-10).
But he was still the God of the exodus. Through Gideon he
delivered them from the hands of their enemies. The God of
the exodus was also remembered in the days of destruction
at the hand of the great world powers Assyria and then
Babylon. Even when Israel was exiled in a distant land, her
homeland denuded and the temple lying in rubble, the
prophets remembered the God of the exodus and believed
that he would again do what he had done in the former days.

Thus says the Lord,
    who makes a way in the sea,
    a path in the mighty waters,
who brings forth chariot and horse,
    army and warrior;
they lie down, they cannot rise,
    they are extinguished, quenched like a wick:

> Remember not the former things,
> nor consider the things of old.
>
> Isaiah 43:16-18

Israel may have reversals. She may be sent back to Egypt (Hos. 8:11-14; 11:5-7). But there is always a new day. The God who engineered the first exodus is always capable of another. That is the hope in which Israel lives.

> Therefore, behold, the days are coming, says the Lord, when men shall no longer say, "As the Lord lives who brought up the people of Israel out of the land of Egypt," but "As the Lord lives who brought up and led the descendants of the house of Israel out of the north country and out of all the countries where he had driven them."
>
> Jeremiah 23:7, 8

Yahweh is the God who will be what he will be. The first exodus does not limit God. It gives assurance that the future is in his hands. He is defined by the mighty, loving deeds he performs on behalf of his people when they cry to him in the depths of despair. Yahweh is the one who again and again takes up the cause of his people, redeeming them from bondage.

God Who Trains His Son in the Wilderness

After God brought his son through the sea with a mighty hand, he introduced him to the wilderness. God promised the fathers he would give them a land "from the river of Egypt to the great river, the river Euphrates" (Gen. 15:18). Now the time seems ripe. So why the forty-year delay? What does God hope to accomplish in the wilderness? The modern church school answer is that Israel wandered forty years in the wilderness as a punishment for their failure to go up and take the land. This is one of the reasons provided in the OT (Num. 14:32). But it is not the only one. There is a great theological depth to the wilderness experience that often goes unexplored. In the wilderness God is not only (1) punishing his son, he also is (2) preparing him for war and life, (3) creating trust, (4) loving him, and (5) acting for the sake of his own name.

God punished his son with forty years of wilderness wandering, not because he violated the law of God, but because of his inexplicable doubt. Yahweh had exhibited his might and power in Egypt. His people knew the amazing event at the sea. Now he told them to go up and take the land he had given them (Deut. 1:21). They sent up spies who reported that the land was as great as God had said, but the inhabitants were giants "and we seemed to ourselves like grasshoppers" (Num. 13:33). The report of the spies set up a great murmur in the camp. God had done wonders for these people. He had fed them with manna. But now they found reason to doubt the power of God. With that God's patience ran out. So he said to Moses, "How long will this people despise me? And how long will they not believe in me, in spite of all the signs which I have wrought among them? I will strike them with the pestilence and disinherit them" (Num. 14:11-12). Moses, however, persuaded God against that action and encouraged him to forgive them. God forgave, but he did not let them off scot-free. None of the present faithless generation was to inhabit the land. They suffered for their faithlessness because there was every reason to expect that they should be persons of great faith (Deut. 1:29-33).

The wilderness experience, however, is not seen singularly as punishment. Just as a man may achieve more than one objective with his son in a single event, so may God. A son who leaves home without saying where he is going may be told that he cannot go anywhere for a week except for routine matters.

But during that week the father continues to sustain his son. He may also teach him how to play pool or chess. According to the OT, God was not just punishing his son in the wilderness. He was also training him for war and for life. The reason given in Exodus as to why God did not immediately take his people to the land promised was to prepare them for the struggles ahead:

When Pharaoh let the people go, God did not lead them by way of the land of the Philistines, although that was near; for God said, "Lest the people repent when they see war, and return to Egypt." But God led the people round by the way of the wilderness toward the Red Sea.

Exodus 13:17-18

In the wilderness, too, God disciplined his son, getting him ready for the tasks ahead. "Know then in your heart that, as a man disciplines his son, the Lord your God disciplines you" (Deut. 8:5). Through that action they learned that "man does not live by bread alone, but that man lives by everything that proceeds out of the mouth of the Lord" (8:3). The point is that if man looks to God for food and then sees that God provides it, he should be willing to trust him in all realms of life. If God says this is the way to live and spells it out in statutes and ordinances, the person who has experienced God's sustaining love should trust him in these ways, too. When things are working out right, man often becomes heady and thinks he has made it on his own (Deut. 8:11-13). But God's way is the only one which works out in the end. God's son must learn to trust in God. The reason for the wilderness experience was "that he might humble you and test you, to do you good in the end" (8:16). So God punished his son for forty years in the wilderness. But he did not simply mark time until the forty years were completed. He utilized the wilderness as a training camp to prepare his people for life in the land.

God shows himself to be a God of love in the wilderness even at the same time that he punishes his son. "God bore you, as a man bears his son, in all the way that you went until you came to this place" (Deut. 1:31). "Your clothing did not wear out upon you, and your foot did not swell, these forty years" (8:4). In fact, some of the prophets, working from the imagery of God and his bride, characterized the wilderness as Israel's honeymoon period. So Jeremiah, quoting God:

> I remember the devotion of your youth,
> your love as a bride,
> how you followed me in the wilderness,
> in a land not sown.

Jeremiah 2:2

Ezekiel likewise talks about it as a period of betrothal and marriage (Ezek. 16:8-14). But how can it be a time when God's love flowed freely to his bride if it was also a time in which the anger of God was obvious?

How can one reconcile the love and wrath of God? As the OT reports it God is both at once. What is the basis of God's anger? Is it vindictiveness? No, God becomes angry when he reaches out in love toward his bride, but his love is rejected. In Numbers 14 God had lovingly prepared his people to take the land. He planned to go along and assist them in all their needs. But when they heard of the problems, they turned their back on the eager love and helpfulness of God (Num. 14:4). At that point God became extremely upset. He burned. His love had been thwarted. In fact, there is no embarrassment in the OT over characterizing God as a lover who is jealous over his love. "For you shall worship no other god, for the Lord, whose name is Jealous, is a jealous God" (Exod. 34:14).

Can love and wrath go hand in hand? The fact is that the opposite of love is not, as might be thought, wrath, but indifference. A husband who laughs off his wife's infidelity is not thought to love her, but to be indifferent. If he loved her, he would be upset at her attention to other males. In the tradition of Western philosophy we have been led to believe that such personal characteristics cannot really be attributed to God. But the God of the philosophers is not the God of the Bible. The God of the Bible is personal as man is personal, for in fact man is made in his image. As personal, God has the traits of a person, though the height and depth of them far exceed these same traits in man. God is a loving God, but this at the same time entails wrath. The two go hand in hand. Wrath is not an independent characteristic of God. It is not the primary characteristic of God. Love is the primary characteristic of God. Wrath is secondary because it always follows upon the rejection of love by God's people. Love involves freedom—freedom to love or not to love. Freedom involves risk, for love may be rejected. Rejected love results in hurting, burning, suffering, and wrath. Therefore, despite the traditional Christian theology, which rejects the suffering of God and affirms his impassibility, the God of the OT suffers. He does not deteriorate; he does not dissipate. But he suffers because he loves. God burns over the manner in which he reaches out to bless his children, but they are always turning their backs and seeking other lovers:

> When I fed them to the full,
>   they committed adultery
>   and trooped to the houses of harlots.
> They were well-fed lusty stallions,
>   each neighing for his neighbor's wife.
> Shall I not punish them for these things? says the Lord;
>   and shall I not avenge myself
>   on a nation such as this?
>
> Jeremiah 5:7b-9

God loved his children in the wilderness but they continually rejected that love.

If God did not get anywhere in his efforts to obtain love from his people, why did he persist in seeking them out? From Numbers 11–36 it is particularly obvious that Israel was a stubborn and rebellious people. In the words of Ezekiel, in the wilderness "the children rebelled against me; they did not walk in my statutes, and were not careful to observe my ordinances" (Ezek. 20:21). Because of their infidelity God decided to pour out his wrath on them, to wipe them out right there in the wilderness (vs. 21b). But he did not. Why? "I withheld my hand, and acted for the sake of my name, that it should not be profaned in the sight of the nations, in whose sight I had brought them out" (Ezek. 20:22). God did not destroy them because he acted for the sake of his name. What can this mean?

The account in Numbers 14 helps us understand what is at stake in God acting for the sake of his name (see also Exodus 32). God is about to destroy his people in the wilderness (Num. 14:12). But Moses hears of it and reminds God what he is doing. God had brought his people up out of Egypt not only to give them a land and create faith in them, but also to make his name known among the peoples of the world so they too might be blessed (Exod. 9:16). His purposes were larger than simply the welfare of Israel. If these purposes were to be accomplished, God's name needed to be known among the nations. He needed to act in view of this larger goal. Moses spoke to God in the midst of his anger, and reminded him:

> Now if thou dost kill this people as one man, then the nations who have heard thy fame will say, "Because the Lord was not able to bring this people into the land which he swore to give to them, therefore he has slain them in the wilderness."
>
> Numbers 14:15-16

God therefore preserved his people, but they were not home free. He did not destroy them, but that was no reason for ignoring their faithlessness. He kept them and led them in the wilderness for forty years. In that manner he maintained his purposes with the nations while at the same time disciplining his children. God's people on more than one occasion received more than they deserved because it fit God's larger purposes—his name's sake.

It is of interest that not only did Moses argue with God, he won the argument. There are various reasons. First, Moses did not tell God anything new. He simply reminded him of the purposes for which God was already at work. It would pose problems if an observation of a man resulted in new divine purposes. Second, it is the duty of a mediating party to step in when a loved one is so upset he cannot see straight. Abigail did this for her husband Nabal (1 Sam. 25:23-31). God's friends, such as Moses (on more than one occasion) and Phinehas, did this for him (Num. 25:10-13). Third, such action seems out of place for a deity. So it is, with the deity of philosophers! But the God of the OT is a person, and persons have exactly these characteristics. If God did not have these characteristics, he would no longer be a person. Fourth, God seems unusually concerned with man to listen to Moses. But in the OT this is exactly who God is. He is the one who has created man in his image. He is the one who continually reaches out to man in his *hesedh* (steadfast love) and he does so whether man responds or not. He is the one who ever listens as to know how it is from the human side. The Christian should be the one least surprised that the Father of our Lord Jesus Christ has always had an ear open to man.

So important did certain prophets see the wilderness experience that they expected God to recreate his people after defeat and loss of their land, by bringing them once again into the wilderness. Hosea pictures God bringing his bride once again into the wilderness.

> Therefore, behold, I will allure her,
>   and bring her into the wilderness,
>   and speak tenderly to her.
> And there I will give her her vineyards,
>   and make the Valley of Achor a door of hope.
> And there she shall answer as in the days of her youth,
>   as at the time when she came out of the land of Egypt.
>
> Hosea 2:14-15

The wilderness is laden with a number of pregnant theological themes. It is especially instructive when God's people are in an in-between time. Those in Christ Jesus are so situated. They are between Christ's resurrection and their own.

God Who Put It in Writing with His People

Yahweh desires a continual, permanent relationship with his people. He is the God "showing steadfast love to thousands of those who love me and keep my commandments" (Exod. 20:6). Because he reveals himself as a God of this sort, his servants who preserved his word for later generations depicted him as one who entered into covenant affirmations with his people. These relationships were to continue into perpetuity (Exod. 31:16-17). Yahweh was not content to hang in there loose when it came to relationships. He desired something permanent. He put it into writing with his people.

Those who conveyed this characteristic of God's love utilized the ancient types of formal relationships or covenants. They used the forms of the time so that God in a genuine way would be disclosed in the experience of the men and women who were accustomed to formal relationships expressed in these ways. There were basically three types of transactions which put relationships on a permanent basis. (1) There were personal agreements, for example the covenant which Jonathan made with David (1 Sam. 18:3). (2) There were political agreements, as when Gibeon made a covenant with Israel (Josh. 9:15). (3) There was the marriage covenant (Mal. 2:14). In the OT all these types of covenants are employed analogically to depict the relationship of God with his people. We are here concerned not so much with the covenant types, but with the grounds or theology underlying the covenants.

Various permanent affirmations of God preceded the great Mosaic covenant. Especially memorable are the promises of God to Noah and Abraham. Both of these covenants have ramifications for all men, but in enactment and form they are like the personal covenant of Jonathan with David. With Noah and David God made a commitment which bound him in permanent fashion. What is permanent about God is not so much a philosophical trait, such as spiritual essence, unlimited intelligence, Being Itself, or boundless energy. The permanence of Yahweh is defined through the commitments he makes, the covenants into which he enters. He is the one who is faithful in covenant.

There are two sorts of personal covenants, those of equals, as Jonathan with David, and those in which a greater person makes a personal promise to a lesser. Obviously no man stands on a level equal with God. Man is in no position to force a covenant from God. He may make a covenant with God as did Jehoiada (2 Kings 11:17), but he does not lay the terms of the covenant on God. Rather, he makes a commitment upon the terms which God has already laid upon him. Such is the covenant made by Josiah:

> And the king stood in his place and made a covenant before the Lord, to walk after the Lord and to keep his commandments and his testimonies and his statutes, with all his heart and all his soul, to perform the words of the covenant that were written in this book.
>
> 2 Chronicles 34:31

It is important to see that the covenant which God made with Noah and Abraham is not a covenant between equals. It is not a covenant in which two persons get together and spell out the responsibilities of the party of the first part, then of the party of the second part. It is a one-sided covenant made by God, the terms of which are determined by him. In fact, in both these cases, it is not man who is bound by contractual obligations, but God. He takes the obligation willingly upon himself for he is the one who reaches out for relationship. To Noah God promised "that never again shall there be a flood to destroy the earth" (Gen. 9:11). This promise of God prevails regardless of what man does. God binds himself to man and creation. Though, of course, man is expected to be faithful to his Creator (Gen. 9:1-7), God remains bound in promise regardless of what man does. Man did nothing to secure this promise. It came as the loving concern of the Creator for creation. No work on man's part is requested or expected. God is the covenant keeper, not man. Man is a creature of the dust (Ps. 103:14). He has no hold over God.

God likewise entered freely into a permanent relationship with Abraham and his descendants (Gen. 12:1-3; 15:1-21; 17:1-27). God did this, not because of Abraham's righteous works prior to the covenant (Josh. 24:2) or because Abraham was equal with God. This is in contrast with Jacob and Laban, who were equals in covenant. God entered into covenant because of his desire to continue spreading his good gifts to his people. In Genesis 15 it is only God who binds himself in the covenant. He walked between the divided halves of the animals (Gen. 15:17-18) as was customary in covenant ratifications. (See Jer. 34:18-19.) As the description is given, Abraham did not take the customary walk. This is apparently to indicate that the covenant was God's idea, not Abraham's. Through it God bound himself to man, and not the other way around.

The sign of the covenant, just as the bow was the sign of the Noachian covenant (Gen. 9:12), was circumcision (Gen. 17:11). Circumcision was neither the manner through which the covenant was secured nor maintained. It was not a work of the one receiving it. But the covenant prevailed only where the sign was present (Gen. 17:14). Abraham and his descendants were expected to respond faithfully to the commandments, statutes, and laws of God (Gen. 26:4-5). But God would keep his promise even in face of gross violations of his will. He would keep it, not through all his people, but through the faithful remnant (Gen. 45:7; cf. Isa. 10:20-23).

In these covenant relationships God made his own personal promise to distribute his good gifts to men. He did this, not being forced to in any way, whether through human works or gentle persuasion through prayer. Nothing man could do made him worthy either to attain the covenant or remain in it once obtained. Through this relationship the nature of God is revealed. He is the one who pours himself out freely for man created in his image. He expects man's reciprocal love shown by his action in commandment keeping. But God's love is steadfast even in the face of flagrant human violation of that love.

The relationship of God with his people was also depicted in the manner of political agreements. The Mosaic covenant in form, if not in some measure in concept, is much like the ancient suzerainty treaty which was in widespread use in the Near East during the days of Moses. (For elaboration as well as reservations, see D. J. McCarthy, *Old Testament Covenant*, 1972.) The suzerainty treaty was one in which a powerful ancient emperor (suzerain) extended a covenant to a small vassal state on his borders. Preceding the extending of covenant was almost always some act in which the suzerain befriended the smaller country, usually through going to battle in its behalf when it was threatened by a large power. The suzerain then framed a covenant for the smaller country. He did not invite the vassal state's participation in the construction as if it had claims to advance. Rather, he set forth the terms of the covenant.

In the covenant the suzerain promised to continue to protect the small power. In return he expected faithful allegiance spelled out through specific stipulations. He himself gave his oath before the gods to uphold the covenant. He expected a similar oath from the small state. He concluded the covenant by advancing blessings which would accrue from faithful execution and curses which would be forthcoming for violations. The covenant was extended through the good graces of the suzerain. It was assumed that he would be faithful in promise. In turn, from the vassal nation he expected faithful support. The form of the covenant usually (1) identified the suzerain, (2) spelled out what he had done for the small nation, (3) advanced the stipulations the suzerain expected the smaller nation to fulfill, (4) indicated arrangements for storing and periodic reading, (5) cited a long list of deities as witnesses, and (6) declared curses and blessings.

In concept, the Mosaic covenant is much like the suzerainty treaty. It provided an excellent vehicle in which God revealed his relationship with his people in a manner which they had experienced and which they understood. God himself was a sovereign Lord who had befriended a small band of people when they were enslaved in Egypt. He acted powerfully on their behalf and rid them of their oppressors. He then proceeded to make them a nation in their own right. On the way to their land he offered a covenant. He did it, not because of anything they had done (Deut. 9:6-12), but out of his love (7:8). In the covenant he affirmed that he would be their God, guiding, loving, protecting them (4:37-39), just as he had already done in Egypt. He expected them in turn to behave as his people, fulfilling his ways, identified in statutes and laws (4:39-40; 5:1-21). Unlike the Noachian and Abrahamic covenants, God expected his people to accept (ratify) the covenant (5:27). He also laid out specific stipulations (laws) for them to keep.

In this covenant there were works for the people to fulfill —works of the law. But law keeping needs to be understood in its proper perspective. Israel did not secure the covenant from God because of what she had done. He offered it out of his own freedom and love. Neither did Israel keep the covenant in force by keeping the law. God desires with his whole being that his people share in his goodness (Deut. 5:29; 6:24), and it is out of his love that the covenant promises accrue. But man can cut himself off or out of the covenant with its blessing by a failure to keep its regulations (Deut. 8:19-20). Israel is therefore not in the covenant because of her lawkeeping. But when she fails to keep the law of God, he withholds the blessings which he so gladly wishes to extend (Judg. 6:7-10).

The form of the covenant reflects the ancient suzerainty treaty, and out of it this theology shines through. First, God identifies himself: "I am the Lord (Yahweh) your God" (Deut. 5:6). Second, he tells what he has done for these people before extending covenant, "who brought you out of the land of Egypt. . . ." Third, the terms of the covenant are set forth in the form of the Ten Commandments and the laws (5:7-21; 12–25). Fourth, the tables of the covenant are to be stored in the ark (10:5), and the covenant is to be read every seven years (31:10-11). Fifth, a list of deities would be cited as witnesses to the covenant. But Yahweh is one God (6:4), and he alone can serve as witness and prosecutor of the covenant. Sixth, the curses and blessings are listed:

> "Behold, I set before you this day a blessing and a curse: the blessing, if you obey the commandments of the Lord your God, which I command you this day, and the curse, if you do not obey the commandments of the Lord your God."
>
> Deuteronomy 11:26-28 (cf. chs. 27–28)

In various places in the OT, God's relationship with his people is conceived as a marriage covenant, especially by the prophets. In this analogy Yahweh is the husband and Israel the wife. Yahweh desires that his wife be faithful and loyal. But if his bride seeks out the gods of the other nations to worship, then she (Israel) is being unfaithful or playing the harlot (Exod. 34:13-16). The marriage relationship is the most compelling, intense relationship known by man. The prophets intentionally employed this means of depicting the God-man relationship, because in their view the most profound relationship which a human may experience is with God. The person who is in covenant relationship with Yahweh, yet thwarts that relationship by seeking out other gods, can only expect to be subjected to the same wrath and fury to which a wife is subjected who spends her time in the bed of other lovers.

Hosea, Ezekiel, and Jeremiah especially depict faithless Israel as a faithless wife. The use of this analogy presupposes that God's relationship with his people is not simply a legal one, but a relationship of love in which promises are made to reserve oneself for the lover. Of course this takes a legal exterior form, namely, the marriage contract or covenant, but the motivation results from intense love.

Hosea does his theology out of the crisis of his own marriage. He married Gomer, who after a time sought out other lovers. He continued to care for her, however, despite her faithlessness. He did what he could to restore her to himself. Yahweh did the same with Israel his bride (Hos. 2:6-15). In fact, just as Hosea was told to take back his harlot wife, so Yahweh was willing and eager to take back his. He was willing to take her back, no questions asked, but not without strings attached. "You must dwell as mine for many days; you shall not play the harlot, or belong to another man; so will I also be to you" (Hos. 3:3). God's love was so strong for his people that he continually struggled to return them to that relationship. To do so he tried various ways to bring them to their senses, including causing them to suffer. He caused them to suffer not because he is sadistic, liking to hear cries of anguish, but because this was the only way to bring them again to his love. "Come let us return to the Lord; for he has torn, that he may heal us . . ." (6:1). In some cases the only way a husband can secure faithful love from his wife is to deprive her of the checking account and threaten divorce. He does this not because he wants to see his wife squirm, but because he loves her and hopes that through this means she will return to his love.

Ezekiel employs the marriage analogy in a number of places but especially in chapters 16 and 23. The most vivid presentation is in chapter 16. There Ezekiel depicts Israel as a young girl who, unwanted by her parents, is left exposed in an open field (16:5). But God took her, cleaned her up, and entered into a pledge of marriage with her (16:8). God was giving and caring throughout the marriage (16:10-14). But Israel was not content with the love of God. "But you trusted in your beauty, and played the harlot because of your renown, and lavished your harlotries on any passer-by" (16:15). So strong was Israel's lust that she used no discrimination whatsoever in seeking out lovers (cf. 16:31-34). It is clear that this harlotry consisted in worshiping the gods of other peoples and building altars to them (16:23-29). Because of such unfaithfulness Yahweh threatened to expose Israel's lewdness to her neighbors by letting her enemies overrun the country (16:39). But the separation is not to be permanent. God still loves his bride and he will take her back through an everlasting covenant (16:60).

Jeremiah used much the same analogy in an extended manner through Jeremiah 2–5. In an especially vivid section he depicted Israel as a harlot giving in to lovers while engaged in worship at the Baal shrines on the high places (Jer. 2:20-22). He considered Israel's passion so strong for Baal that he depicted her as a female animal in heat (2:24). "Who can restrain her lust?" Jeremiah saw God as continually seeking to bring his bride back, since he was a God of mercy (3:11-14; 4:1-4).

So strong did the prophets feel about depicting God's relationship with his people in covenant form that they even anticipated that a change of the ages would necessitate a new covenant. The problem, as they saw it, was not so much the covenant, but man the covenant breaker. The era of the new covenant would be days in which God would revamp man. Hosea was one of the earliest to offer such a vision. In that day, according to Hosea, God will betroth his people to himself in faithfulness (Hos. 2:20). The covenant God will make is not a revision of the law, but a revision of life on earth (2:18). Jeremiah also saw the problem as Israel's inability or unwillingness to keep the law of God. In the new day the law of God will be written on the heart (Jer. 31:33), implying not so much a new law, but a new manner in which the law is incorporated into the life of man. Ezekiel likewise speaks of a new covenant (Ezek. 34:25). In the day of the new covenant man himself will be redone so he will be able to keep it. Man will have a new heart (36:26) and a new spirit, which will be God's spirit (36:27).

The covenant has many different forms in the OT, but through these shine certain theological foundations. First of all, God is the one who initiates the covenant out of love. Man is in no position to force a covenant from God. Second, God is always the superior in the covenant, determining its terms. Man can only accept or reject the covenant offered. Third, in some covenants it is only God who binds himself. In the Mosaic covenant the people accept the covenant and are bound to keep it. But God's covenants are never in force because humans keep them. They are in force because God has given them and sustains them. Failure to keep the stipulations of the covenant on man's part will exclude him from the covenant and its community, but law keeping has nothing to do with why one is in a covenant with God. He is there because God has loved him and called him into covenant relationship.

God Who Cares by Giving Law

The law of God in the OT is ensconced in the rest of the activity of God and receives its theological thrust therefrom. The law is not an independent entity standing above and beyond both God and man. It is not impersonal, but intensely personal, because it is the law of God. God selected Abraham and his descendants as the avenue through which he would share his goodness with the nations. The people of God were subdued in Egypt so that they no longer had a chance to bless, so God, out of his love and concern and in order to fulfill his plans for the rest of mankind, brought them out with a mighty hand. Because of his great love he protected and trained them in the wilderness. He entered into a covenant relationship with them because he desired a permanent love relationship, just as is the marriage relationship. The laws of God (and this is significant) are given by God so man can relate himself to God and be a continual recipient of God's love. The law of God itself, therefore, is an outcropping of the loving activity of God. God has given it so that man may enjoy continual fellowship with him and be blessed by the prolific fruits of the land which he has given him to enjoy. The covenant is extended by God out of love. The law set forth the requirements of the covenant. The law, therefore, reflects not the wrath and hardness of God, but his love. The manner in which the loving action of God, the covenant, and the law (precepts) are seen as holding together is found in a Psalm of praise:

> He has caused his wonderful works to be remembered;
>> the Lord is gracious and merciful.
> He provides food for those who fear him;
>> he is ever mindful of his covenant.
> He has shown his people the power of his works,
>> in giving them the heritage of the nations.
> The works of his hands are faithful and just;
>> all his precepts are trustworthy,
> They are established for ever and ever,
>> to be performed with faithfulness and uprightness.
> He sent redemption to his people;
>> he has commanded his covenant for ever.

> Psalm 111:4-9

From an examination of OT materials it is apparent that the law serves at least two functions. First, it establishes the means whereby Israel knows what to do in order to enjoy fellowship with the holy God. Second, it lays the ground rules through which Israel may retain the land given by Yahweh and enjoy its produce.

In the latter part of Exodus, rules are set forth for the construction and furnishing of the tabernacle. The workmanship must be quality; the instructions are detailed. But all this serves a purpose. When the work is complete, then God in his glory is able to tabernacle with men.

> Then the cloud covered the tent of meeting, and the glory of the Lord filled the tabernacle. And Moses was not able to enter the tent of meeting, because the cloud abode upon it, and the glory of the Lord filled the tabernacle. . . . For throughout all their journeys the cloud of the Lord was upon the tabernacle by day, and fire was in it by night, in the sight of all the house of Israel.

> Exodus 40:34-35, 38

Man, through keeping the law of God, enables God, who desires to dwell with him in love, to enter his presence and enjoy fellowship with him. Keeping the law has nothing to do with forcing God's presence. God desires to descend and be in fellowship with man. Rather, doing the law enables God's entry, for by so doing, a sanctified and holy place is provided, which is suitable for the dwelling place of a holy God.

But requisite to divine-human fellowship is not only a holy place, but a holy people. The law as given in Leviticus especially emphasizes the requirement that a holy God demands a holy people with whom to enter into fellowship. "And the Lord said to Moses, 'Say to all the congregation of the people of Israel, You shall be holy; for I the Lord your God am holy'" (Lev. 19:2). How is Israel to know the requisites for holiness? That is what the law does. It sets forth the demands. When Israel follows the demands, she is that holy people required by God, and as the result she enjoys the spiritual benefits of fellowship with him. This understanding is clear in that immediately following the demand for holiness, certain actions are set forth.

> Every one of you shall revere his mother and his father, and you shall keep my sabbaths: I am the Lord your God. Do not turn to idols or make for yourselves molten gods; I am the Lord your God.
>
> Leviticus 19:3

Earlier in Leviticus, laws are spelled out which enhance holiness. The laws of sacrifice are provided so that sins may be removed (Lev. 4:26). Rules are set out for the priests who facilitate the sacrifice arrangements (Lev. 8–9). Rules are listed concerning the animals that are acceptable and those that are abominable. Should one eat meat from an unclean animal, he is deprived of fellowship with God (Lev. 11:43-45). There are also laws for purification of women (ch. 13), of lepers (chs. 13–14), and other infirmities (ch. 15).

The law is thus not an arbitrary set of rules which God gives so that when he speaks man jumps. The law enables man to present himself holy before a holy God so that he may enjoy fellowship with him. As Paul affirms, the law is a pedagogue (RSV "custodian," KJV "schoolmaster"), but a pedagogue need not be harsh and unloving. One can look back on some of his teachers as very helpful and loving. Paul's point is that once one comes to a certain age he can make it on his own and no longer needs the guidance and protection of the pedagogue. As presented in Leviticus, the law is given by a loving and holy God to guide and protect man so that he can share the life of God.

In Deuteronomy the point is made over and over that God gave the law so that man would know what to do in the land God gave him. If man does what is proper, then God will ward off the enemies and provide rain for the crops:

> And because you hearken to these ordinances, and keep and do them, the Lord your God will keep with you the covenant and the steadfast love which he swore to your fathers to keep; he will love you, bless you, and multiply you; he will also bless the fruit of your body and the fruit of your ground, your grain and your wine and your oil, the increase of your cattle and the young of your flock, in the land which he swore to your fathers to give you. . . . And the Lord will take away from you all sickness; and none of the evil diseases of Egypt, which you knew, will he inflict upon you. . . . And you shall destroy all the peoples that the Lord your God will give over to you, your eye shall not pity them; neither shall you serve their gods, for that would be a snare to you.
>
> Deuteronomy 7:12-16 (cf. 6:20-24; 11:8-17)

In contrast, if the Israelites are not faithful to the law, they will lose all they have received:

> And if you forget the Lord your God and go after other gods and serve them and worship them, I solemnly warn you this day that you shall surely perish. Like the nations that the Lord makes to perish before you, so shall you perish, because you would not obey the voice of the Lord your God.
>
> Deuteronomy 8:19-20

Failure to keep the law will bring parsimonious harvest (28:15-19), disease and pestilence (28:20-24), the enemy will successfully overrun the land (28:25-26), and all manner of trouble will befall the people (28:27-35).

Yahweh gives the law out of love. He reveals to man what man cannot learn by his own efforts so that he will enjoy abundantly God's good gifts. Man does not force the love of God by keeping the law. God gives it freely. Israel keeps the law so that she will not be cut off from the gifts which God always wishes to bestow upon man made in his image. The law does not stand apart from God. It is his. He does with it what he pleases. When he desires, he waives punishment for law breaking (2 Chron. 30:13-22). But man has not the prerogative of taking liberty with it. Yahweh is the God who seasons justice with mercy. "I will heal their faithlessness; I will love them freely, for my anger has turned from them. I will be as the dew to Israel; he shall blossom as the lily" (Hos. 14:4-5).

Even the nations other than Israel were subject to the law of God (Amos 1:3–2:3). But it is not the law which God thundered from Sinai. It is the law which God built into the world when he created it. God was wise in his creation and in the principles by which he brought forth the worlds. Therefore, wisdom is personified as assisting God when he set out on his work. "The Lord created me at the beginning of his work, the first of his acts of old" (Prov. 8:22). The wise man is the one who searches experience and nature to learn the ways of God through and in them (Prov. 2:1-5). Since these principles are built into creation itself, they are valid for all men at all times. God thus gives his law to his covenant community. The rest of mankind, however, is subject to the law of God as discovered in nature. These rules are found in Proverbs and the other wisdom literature.

God Who Commands the Heavenly Armies

The God who gave victory at the sea received this notice: "The Lord is a man of war; the Lord is his name" (Exod. 15:3). Yahweh fought and won battles for his people, not because he relished blood and slaughter or continually sought vengeance but for the sake of his name. Through people who know and respect Yahweh, he is able to bring about his blessings (Exod. 15:13-18).

Yahweh won a number of other battles for his people as

Lord of the heavenly hosts (in Hebrew *Yahweh Seva'oth* or general of the heavenly armies. The conquest of Canaan is especially seen from this standpoint. The conquest of the land fulfilled the promise of God to Abraham. It was to bring to fruition the mighty works of God. The story of Joshua at Jericho reflects the conviction that the victory in Canaan did not depend on the strategic prowess of Israel, her implements of war, or her mighty men of valor. Rather it depended on the presence of the heavenly armies with Yahweh himself as general. Before the battle of Jericho, Joshua stood before the city (Josh. 5:13-15). A man appeared before him with sword drawn. When Joshua asked who he was, he replied, "as commander of the army of the Lord I have now come." It is not clear who this was, whether an angel or Yahweh himself. But the point is that Yahweh with his heavenly armies stood prepared to enter into the fray against the enemy, thus assuring victory. Jericho fell without battle. It fell because the armies of Israel followed Yahweh's bidding (Josh. 6:1-21). In the phrase "commander of the army of the Lord" the word army in Hebrew is *Seva'oth*, in other places often translated "hosts," Yahweh is Yahweh *Seva'oth*, Lord of Hosts. It is clear that this is a military term from the statement of David to Goliath. "You come to me with a sword and with a spear and with a javelin; but I come to you in the name of the Lord of hosts, the God of the armies of Israel" (1 Sam. 17:45).

Israel fights battles on earth; but, when she is victorious, it is because of the heavenly armies doing their work behind the scenes. This view is expressed in the strange phrase uttered as both the life of Elijah (2 Kings 2:21) and Elisha (2 Kings 13:14) ended: "My father, my father! The chariots of Israel and its horsemen!" This utterance was made as Elijah was taken into heaven by a chariot of fire and horses of fire. But it was also made about Elisha at his death. The reason apparently is that when these prophets were present there also the heavenly armies gathered, so that earthly victory was assured—no contest.

In an incident at Dothan, Elisha and his servant were

surrounded by the armies of Ben-hadad (2 Kings 6:15-19). When the servant feared, Elisha prayed that his eyes might be opened so he could see the heavenly armies at their disposal. Then the young man looked and "the mountain was full of horses and chariots of fire around about Elisha." Israel was not left to victory by her own resources. When she was faithful to Yahweh, his heavenly armies were available at her beck and call. All she needed to do was trust in Yahweh rather than in her own resources or those of her allies. But often she was not given to such trust:

> Woe to those who go down to Egypt for help
>   and rely on horses,
> who trust in chariots because they are many
>   and in horsemen because they are very strong,
> but do not look to the holy one of Israel
>   or consult the Lord!
>
> Isaiah 31:1

The wars of Israel were also Yahweh's wars when they fulfilled his purposes and when his people were obedient. The rules and theology for such warfare are found in Deuteronomy 20. When Israel goes forth to war, she is not to be afraid, for the God who brought her out of Egypt is with her. The army is first of all addressed by the priest as an indication that the outcome depends on God, not human strategy (Deut. 20:2-4). Afterward the officers address the troops. Not everyone is to be taken into battle. Those excluded have a new house (vs. 5), vineyard (vs. 6), a new wife (vs. 7), or are fearful and fainthearted. Not everyone needs to be mustered, since the outcome depends on the heavenly armies, not on the number of Israelites. (Recall that Gideon won with 300 God-picked men, Judg. 7:4-8.)

There were also rules about destroying populations, which should be scrutinized carefully in view of centuries of objections to the cruelty of the OT God. The destruction of populations depended on whether the people were outside the land promised or within. If they lived outside, terms of peace could be offered (Deut. 20:10). Only if these were refused were males to be put to the sword and women, children, and cattle taken as spoil (vss. 12-14). In the land of promise, however, everything was to be utterly destroyed (vs. 16). But there was a reason. Throughout both the OT and the NT, something is more important than life, namely, righteousness or life acceptable to God. The people of the land are to be destroyed,

> . . . that they may not teach you to do according to all their abominable practices which they have done in the service of their gods, and so to sin against the Lord your God.
>
> Deuteronomy 20:18

These people are to be destroyed, not because Israel is perfect, but because the inhabitants of the land had male and female cult prostitutes (Deut. 23:17-18), child sacrifice (Lev. 20:1-5), mediums and wizards (Lev. 20:6), as well as many other iniquities.

> Do not say in your heart, after the Lord your God has thrust them out before you, "It is because of my righteousness that the Lord has brought me in to possess this land; whereas it is because of the wickedness of these nations that the Lord is driving them out before you."
>
> Deuteronomy 9:4

Yahweh did not command this destruction on sudden impulse. In fact, according to a statement in Genesis, God waited until the stench became unbearable. "And they shall come back here in the fourth generation; for the iniquity of the Amorites is not yet complete" (Gen. 15:16).

Certain observations should be made concerning the wars of Yahweh. First, they were for the purpose of bringing his goodness, righteousness, and justice. Second, they were not for imperialistic purposes, beyond the initial conquest. God's people, after securing Palestine, did not take other territories. They only protected those of the initial promise. Third, the people so involved were to trust in God rather than their might or strategy. Fourth, wars in the NT age lost the OT purpose because, as the result of the coming of Christ, no longer were territories to be protected. All peoples now, regardless of continent, race, or time, were the people of God through Jesus Christ. But Yahweh fought for his people. He was the general of the armies. Israel remembered the victories of Yahweh down through the centuries and because of them expected future victories.

> "Therefore, as I live," says the Lord of hosts,
>   the God of Israel,
> "Moab shall become like Sodom,
>   and the Ammonites like Gomorrah,
> a land possessed by nettles and salt pits,
>   and a waste for ever.
> The remnant of my people shall plunder them,
>   and the survivors of my nation shall possess them."
>
> Zephaniah 2:9

God Who Gives His Son an Inheritance

In order to bless the nations through his son Yahweh promised him a land. "And I will give to you, and to your descendants after you, the land of your sojournings, all the land of Canaan, for an everlasting possession; and I will be their God" (Gen. 17:8). It was to fulfill this promise that the grand events in Egypt and at the sea transpired (Exod. 6:8). God adopted Israel as his son (Deut. 26:5-6; cf. Ezek. 16:3-5) ". . . in the wilderness, where you have seen how the Lord your God bore you, as a man bears his son, in all the way that you went until you came to this place" (Deut. 1:31). God is Lord of the nations. He makes arrangements for all people. But in a unique way he becomes father to Israel:

> When the Most High gave to the nations their
>   inheritance,
>   when he separated the sons of men,
> he fixed the bounds of the peoples
>   according to the number of the sons of God.
> For the Lord's portion is his people,
>   Jacob his allotted heritage.
>
> Deuteronomy 32:8-9

The other nations were assigned to the sons of God (angels? see Job 1:6). But Israel God took as his own special responsibility. "You only have I known of all the families of the earth . . ." (Amos 3:2). Israel was the oldest son of God. "Israel is my first-born son . . ." (Exod. 4:22). Therefore, according to inheritance procedures, Israel was in line to receive the estate of Yahweh. In this case the estate received was Canaan, the land of promise (Deut. 4:38).

Israel received the land as a gift from the gracious God. He neither earned nor deserved it. He received it not to be used for his purposes but for the purposes of Yahweh. This was so because he had received it as a gift. God warned:

> Beware lest you say in your heart, "My power and the might of my hand have gotten me this wealth." You shall remember the Lord your God, for it is he who gives you power to get wealth; that he may confirm his covenant which he swore to your fathers, as at this day.

> Deuteronomy 8:17-18

God's intent was that all men be benefited by these land gifts he provided. The land did not belong to Israel, but to Yahweh. It was Israel's by inheritance. "The land shall not be sold in perpetuity, for the land is mine; for you are strangers and sojourners with me" (Lev. 25:23). Because the land is God's, each person has a right to sustenance. Man is a property holder, but he holds it for the one who gave it to him as a gift. In turn he is to share with those who are needy. "And if your brother becomes poor, and cannot maintain himself with you, you shall maintain him; as a stranger and a sojourner he shall live with you" (Lev. 25:35).

The gift of the land was not simply so that God's son would prosper. The purpose, continually obvious, is that God set out to bless the nations through his people and through the land which he had given them:

> And he said to me, "You are my servant,
>   Israel, in whom I will be glorified."
> . . . .
> It is too light a thing that you should be my servant
>   to raise up the tribes of Jacob
>   and to restore the preserved of Israel;
> I will give you as a light to the nations,
>   that my salvation may reach to the end of the earth.

> Isaiah 49:3, 6

The land is not an end in itself. Its purpose is to be a distribution warehouse from which God transports his good gifts to the peoples of the earth.

If God's son is responsible and behaves as God desires, he will continually enjoy the produce of the land and the wealth therefrom. He did not receive it as the result of his righteousness or his works. He does not continue in it because he worked to earn the right. But if his life is foreign to the ways of God, God will cast him out of the land; he will disinherit his son. "And how long will they not believe in me, in spite of all the signs which I have wrought among them? I will strike them with the pestilence and disinherit them . . ." (Num. 14:11-12). It is the conviction of those who wrote the great histories of Israel that the sons of Jacob are evicted from the land because they have proved faithless to Yahweh. The Assyrians and the Babylonians are Yahweh's instruments to prosecute his people for failure in covenant keeping:

> I will cast off the remnant of my heritage, and give them into the hand of their enemies, and they shall become a prey and a spoil to all their enemies, because they have done what is evil in my sight and have provoked me to anger, since the day their fathers came out of Egypt, even to this day.
>
> 2 Kings 21:14-15

(See the extended statement about the reasons for the downfall of Israel and Judah in 2 Kings 17.)

The disinheritance of God is not something which results from a sudden, grand fit of anger on the part of Yahweh. He is "a gracious God and merciful, slow to anger, and abounding in steadfast love . . ." (Jon. 4:2). He tried many ways to get his people to return to him. He sent drought (Amos 4:6-8), blight and mildew (4:9), pestilence (4:10), and the enemy (4:10-11) in an effort to get his people to return. When all failed, however, Yahweh had no recourse but to cut his son adrift, to disinherit him. "Prepare to meet your God, O Israel!" (Amos 4:12)

But disinheritance is not forever. Yahweh is a God loyal to his people. Despite their sin, following a time of punishment he will bring them back to the land and once again they shall serve him as his people:

"Sing aloud, O daughter of Zion;
  shout, O Israel!
Rejoice and exult with all your heart,
  O daughter of Jerusalem!
The Lord has taken away the judgments against you,
he has cast out your enemies.

. . . .

At that time I will bring you home,
  at the time when I gather you together;
yea, I will make you renowned and praised
  among all the peoples of the earth,
when I restore your fortunes
  before your eyes," says the Lord.
                              Zephaniah 3:14-15, 20

The hope of Israel lies not in her works. It lies not in a bootstrap operation whereby she makes herself holy to God. It lies in the expectation that God will break into the events of history, retrieve his people, and enter anew into a relationship of love and grace.

God Who Makes a Promise to David

Yahweh's intentions in the gift of the land are related to Israel's being faithful and continuing to occupy the assigned territory. If Israel is faithful, she needs no assigned human rulers. God will provide leadership as crises arise. This is obvious in the period of the Judges. The words of Gideon serve as the theology of these times. "I will not rule over you, and my son will not rule over you; the Lord will rule over you" (Judg. 8:23). Despite Yahweh's protection and rule, Israel aspired to be like the nations and have a king (1 Sam. 8). Yahweh is seen as reticent, but finally went along, for he is always willing for man, made in his image, to bend his ear (Exod. 32:11-14). The first king, Saul, did not please God (1 Sam. 16:14). To David and his descendants Yahweh made a promise. Through this promise Yahweh took up in a new way the commitment he had already made with Abraham. A promise of continual support of a dynasty was not evident in the commitment to Abraham, yet not inconsistent with it. Yahweh is the one who fulfills his commitments in creative and often surprising ways. "I will be what I will be" (Exod. 3:14). Now it was through the dynasty of David that the families of the earth would be blessed.

The covenant of God with David contained two parts. First was the promise that God would sustain the household of David in the kingship forever:

> Yea, does not my house stand so with God?
>   For he has made with me an everlasting covenant,
>   ordered in all things and secure.
> For will he not cause to prosper
>   all my help and my desire?
>
> 2 Samuel 23:5

The second part of the promise affirms that God is not committed to any particular descendants except those who are faithful. Those who commit iniquity will be punished.

> "He shall build a house for my name, and I will establish the throne of his kingdom for ever. I will be his father, and he shall be my son. When he commits iniquity, I will chasten him with the rod of men, with the stripes of the sons of men; but I will not take my steadfast love from him, as I took it from Saul, whom I put away from before you. And your house and your kingdom shall be made sure for ever before me; your throne shall be established for ever."
>
> 2 Samuel 7:13-17 (cf. Ps. 89:28-37)

The covenant with David in one sense is like those with Abraham and Noah in that its longevity depends upon God. Regardless of what the descendants of David do, the promise remains intact. But unlike those covenants, demands are made upon the humans involved in the promise. They are to receive the love of God as long as they are worthy. But when they turn their back on God, they will be judged and punished. On what basis? No list of rules is given anywhere. The language of Psalm 89, however, makes the grounds of punishment explicit:

> If his children forsake my law
>   and do not walk according to my ordinances,
> if they violate my statutes
>   and do not keep my commandments,

then I will punish their transgression with the rod
and their iniquity with scourges.

Psalm 89:30-32

Here the language is that connected with the Mosaic covenant as given in Deuteronomy (4:40, 44; 6:1-3). God's promise to David therefore consists of the old, the Mosaic
covenant, and the new, the commitment to a lasting dynasty.
God in his freedom fulfills his promises as he wills, but
always consistently with his prior promises.

The great histories of Israel as well as the prophets interpret events in Israel in light of the covenant with David. On
the one hand, it is the ground of the hope that in some way
or another Judah is indestructible. On the other, it means
that catastrophic defeat may occur due to Israel's ingratitude and infidelity. The result is that whatever happens an
explanation is forthcoming. There is always anticipation of
the new day of God, grounded in the commitment to David.
The manner in which the theology of the Davidic covenant
throws light upon situations in the kingdoms sometimes
takes surprising turns. But history is not arbitrary. It is the
realm where God is winning his ways.

God promised the kingdom to David, but not necessarily
all the kingdom. The day came, after David and Solomon,
when the ten northern tribes broke off from the south. The
divided kingdom became Israel in the north, with Samaria
as the capital, and Judah in the south, with Jerusalem as the
capital. But why did this split come about? How should it be
interpreted in the light of the covenants of God? Clearly the
author of 1 Kings understands these developments according to the clause in the Davidic covenant that God would
punish the sons of David for faithlessness:

> Therefore the Lord said to Solomon, "Since this has been your
> mind and you have not kept my covenant and my statutes
> which I have commanded you, I will surely tear the kingdom
> from you and will give it to your servant.... However I will not
> tear away all the kingdom; but I will give one tribe to your son,
> for the sake of David my servant and for the sake of Jerusalem
> which I have chosen."

1 Kings 11:11, 13

At times, in the view of the prophets, the promise to David made Israel overconfident. During the rule of Hezekiah the Assyrians laid siege to Jerusalem and her fall seemed inevitable; but miraculously, due to the work of the angel of the Lord, the Assyrians were forced to withdraw (2 Kings 19:35-37). As the reason for the withdrawal, the promise to David was cited (2 Kings 19:34). Because of this dramatic escape, a century later Jerusalem was claimed to be impregnable. After all, it was the place of the temple of God and he would not permit his temple to be destroyed. Jeremiah condemned such thinking as false. God need not preserve Jerusalem in order to maintain the dynasty of David.

> Do not trust in these deceptive words: "This is the temple of the Lord, the temple of the Lord, the temple of the Lord." . . . For if you truly amend your ways and your doings . . . , then I will let you dwell in this place, in the land that I gave of old to your fathers forever."
>
> Jeremiah 7:4, 5, 7

Thus, even by the promise, the sons of David might sin so as to lose the very country itself. Nevertheless, it would not be forever:

> Behold, the days are coming, says the Lord, when I will fulfil the promise I made to the house of Israel and the house of Judah. In those days and at that time I will cause a righteous Branch to spring forth for David; and he shall execute justice and righteousness in the land.
>
> Jeremiah 33:14-15 (cf. Isa. 11:1-9; Mic. 5:2-4)

The importance of the promise to David is particularly obvious in the writings of the Chronicler (1 and 2 Chronicles, Ezra, Nehemiah). Little is given by way of details about the north. The focus is on the south and the descendants of David. The covenant is presented there (1 Chron. 17:10-15). In this history David is remembered not only as king, but also as the founder of rules pertaining to temple worship. He took the city of Jerusalem from the Jebusites and established it as his capital. He brought the ark of the Lord into the city (16:1-3). To him was the site of the temple on the threshing floor of Ornan the Jebusite revealed (21:18–22:1). Furthermore, he set up the arrangements for the temple worship, especially for the music of the temple and those conducting it (1 Chron. 24–27). Because of the importance of all of this, David, as well as Solomon, is looked upon as a lawgiver in the manner of Moses. The placing of these two together in this manner is obvious in 2 Chronicles 8. Moses is remembered for his legislation concerning the sacrifices and the feasts, David for his concerning the temple service and music.

> Then Solomon offered up burnt offerings to the Lord upon the altar of the Lord which he had built before the vestibule, as the duty of each day required, offering according to the commandment of Moses for the sabbaths, the new moons, and the three annual feasts. . . . According to the ordinance of David his father, he appointed the divisions of the priests for their service, and the Levites for their offices of praise and ministry before the priests as the duty of each day required, and the gatekeepers in their divisions for the several gates; for so David the man of God had commanded.
>
> 2 Chronicles 8:12-14 (cf. 29:25-28; Neh. 12:45)

So David was especially significant in the manner in which the work of God to bring his goodness to the nations was interpreted. As Ezra directed the people to taking up once again the ways of God after almost total destruction by the Babylonians, he interpreted what had happened in the light of the covenant with David (Neh. 9:32-37).

Even in the midst of sure destruction, the great prophets never lost hope. Not that they believed Judah indestructible. They were well aware that faithlessness in the sons of David would result in defeat and exile. But at the same time they believed in the promise of God that he had established the house of David forever. They did not know how Yahweh would rebuild his nation from ruins and ashes. But they had confidence that he could and would.

> In that day I will raise up
>   the booth of David that is fallen
> and repair its breaches,
>   and raise up its ruins,
>   and rebuild it as in the days of old;

that they may possess the remnant of Edom
and all the nations who are called by my name.

Amos 9:11-12

The promise to David interjected both uncertainty and permanence into the history of Israel. The permanence depended on the confidence that Yahweh is the God who keeps his promises.

Afterward the children of Israel shall return and seek the Lord their God, and David their king; and they shall come in fear to the Lord and to his goodness in the latter days.

Hosea 3:5

The theology of the OT focuses upon the mighty acts of God. He defines himself to his people through his loving actions in their history. Certain of the acts are fundamental, and they become the grounds out of which the rest of the actions of God are interpreted. All of these actions are open-ended. The later interpreters of the ways of God, the historians and prophets, saw the new actions of God as repeating and going beyond the ancient acts. But the work of God was never completed in their days. The fulfilling of the promises of God was never culminated. God is always what he will be. The future is in his hand. History will take surprising turns. But the man faithful to God looks to the future in anticipation. The future is no accident. It is the arena in which God is fulfilling his promises of old. The route Yahweh takes will be consistent with his promises and the manner in which he has related to his people in the past.

Old Testament Theology and the Church Today

The OT is not complete in itself. It is open-ended. It points beyond itself. It was not accidental that Christians found the answers to the promises of God in Jesus of Nazareth. At the same time, it is not surprising that they searched the OT Scriptures in order to make sense out of who Jesus was and what he was about (Luke 24:44-49). For these reasons the OT and the NT are inextricably interlaced. The NT cannot be understood without the OT. It is the Christian conviction that the open-endedness of the OT is taken up in Jesus. But whether one follows this path, obviously the OT is incomplete. It anticipates future action of God.

The OT, however, is more than the factual base out of which the NT is to be understood. The earliest Christians understood the OT as the very basis for achieving a proper relationship with God. "For whatever was written in former days was written for our instruction, that by steadfastness and by the encouragement of the scriptures we might have hope" (Rom. 15:4). When Paul and other Christians spoke of the Scriptures, they had in mind the OT. "All scripture is inspired by God and profitable for teaching, for reproof, for correction, and for training in righteousness, that the man of God may be complete, equipped for every good work" (2 Tim. 3:16-17). Paul can even speak of the OT as being authoritative for the Christian. "Do I say this on human authority? Does not the law say the same?" (1 Cor. 9:8; read on through vs. 12 for the point) The OT, of course, does not have authority over the Christian in respect to the institutions which Christ replaced. Jesus Christ as high priest has replaced the priesthood of Aaron and Levi (Heb. 4–5). The sacrifice of Jesus Christ has replaced the animal sacrifices (Heb. 9–10). The earthly temple has been replaced by a heavenly temple (Heb. 9:1-5). The earthly Jerusalem has been replaced by a heavenly one (Heb. 12:22).

Though the institutions of the OT have passed away, the theology of the OT remains. In fact, on it is built the theology of the NT. Beginning with Jesus Christ the acts of God are different. But the reasons remain the same. The Testaments are one in their theology. God is still defined by his action, this time in Jesus Christ. "No one has ever seen God; the only Son, who is in the bosom of the Father, he has made him known" (John 1:18). Jesus made God known through what he did and said. God still acts out of love for man made in his image. He still calls man to obedience. In the NT, therefore, Yahweh is defined as the Father of our Lord Jesus Christ (Phil. 1:2). The prodigal son story of Luke 15:11-32 has the same theology of the mercy and forgiveness of God as does Hosea in his analogy of God as father and Israel as son (Hos. 11:1-9).

The church today suffers malnutrition if a part of its diet is not the theology of the OT. In that theology are found the presuppositions for the Christian faith. From that theological base the apostles and teachers understood Jesus Christ and the response of God's people to him. The one committed to Jesus Christ, of course, ultimately asks the question as to how the action of God in the OT throws light upon Jesus. If these concluding remarks ring clear, then the reader should discover in this presentation of the theology of the OT not only the way of God with Israel, but also the way of God with each Christian as a servant of Jesus Christ.

BIBLIOGRAPHY

For the major contemporary OT theologies, see those listed at the first of this chapter. For the history of OT theology and analyses of the current scene, see:

Childs, Brevard S. *Biblical Theology in Crisis*. Philadelphia: The Westminster Press, 1970.

Dentan, Robert C. *Preface to Old Testament Theology*. New Haven: Yale University Press, 1963.

Hasel, Gerhard. *Old Testament Theology: Basic Issues in the Current Debate*. Grand Rapids: Wm. B. Eerdmans, 1972.

Laurin, Robert B. *Contemporary Old Testament Theologians*. Valley Forge: Judson Press, 1970.

Stendahl, Krister, "Biblical Theology," *Interpreter's Dictionary of the Bible*. Vol. I. Nashville: Abingdon, 1962, pp. 418-32.

X

Christian Use of the Old Testament

Everett Ferguson

There has often been an ambiguity, if not tension, in the attitude of Christians toward the OT. It is in their Bible, they read it, and they employ it for various purposes; but at the same time they recognize in it much which does not measure up to the standards of Jesus' teaching, and they feel its institutions and regulations are not binding for their lives. What, then, is the authority of the OT for the Christian? What is the proper use to be made of the OT by Christians? This article will consider the views of the OT expressed by early Christian authors, then will present aspects of the NT use of the OT: the removal of the Mosaic system of religion, the values found in the OT and problems in the NT use of the Old.

EARLY CHRISTIAN VIEWPOINTS

The Christian's relation to the OT has been a recurring problem in Christian history. In the century and a half after the writing of the NT, many different viewpoints toward the OT were expressed. These represent, often in extreme forms, the range of alternatives which have been explored in later periods of Christian history.

Marcion, in the middle of the second century, rejected entirely the Old Testament from his Bible. Marcion's own writings are lost, but we know his viewpoint from Tertullian's five-book refutation, *Against Marcion*, written in the early third century. Setting the law and the gospel against each other in his book entitled *Antitheses*, Marcion concluded that the God of the OT could not be the God of the New.

> Marcion's special and principal work is the separation of the law and the gospel. . . . These are Marcion's *Antitheses*, or contradictory propositions, which aim at committing the gospel to a variance with the law, in order that from the diversity of the two documents which contain them, they may contend for a diversity of gods also.
>
> *Against Marcion* I.19

> For it is certain that the whole aim at which he has strenuously labored, even in the drawing up of his *Antitheses*, centers in this, that he may establish a diversity between the Old and the New Testaments, so that his own Christ may be separate from the Creator . . . and as alien from the law and the prophets.
>
> *Against Marcion* IV.6

Marcion saw the OT God as a God of justice; the Christ he prophesied was the warrior Messiah expected by the Jews. Jesus, on the other hand, revealed the Father who is love and grace and was previously unknown to man. Marcion "devised different dispensations for two Gods" (ibid. III.15). His Christ came not to fulfill but to destroy the law. The consequence of this radical separation was a total rejection of the OT in favor of the New on the view that the two were so incompatible that they must come from different Gods and could not both be espoused by man. "The whole of the Old Testament, the heretic, to the best of my belief, holds in derision" (ibid. V.5). Tertullian admits a difference and declares a superiority of the gospel to the law, but he denies Marcion's explanations and conclusions. "It is the office of Christ's gospel to call men from the law to grace, not from the Creator to another god" (ibid. V.2). The differences are not so great as Marcion makes out, for there is law in the NT and grace in the Old. Moreover, book III of Tertullian's refutation presents OT predictions of Jesus and argues the connection of Jesus Christ with the Creator God of the OT. So, although the old dispensation has been abolished by something superior, even this was predicted by the OT, and the differences are consistent with the same God having planned the whole (ibid. IV.1). Marcion represents an extreme solution to the problem of the NT's relation to the Old. Few have followed him, but his very extremes help us to recognize tendencies which have recurred in Christian history.

The second-century Gnostics generally shared Marcion's negative evaluation of the OT, but there was a variety of positions. An interesting, and individual, view is that of the Valentinian Gnostic **Ptolemy** (about A.D. 160). His *Letter to Flora* (preserved in Epiphanius, *Heresies* XXXIII.3-7) presents an early example of "source criticism" applied to the OT. There are those, Ptolemy says, who teach that the law was ordained by God the Father (the orthodox Christians) and those who teach that it was given by the devil (Gnostics more extreme than Ptolemy). By way of contrast he takes a middle position that the law was given by the creator of the world (the Demiurge), who is different from the perfect God. Not all of the law, however, comes from this creator. The NT attributes some parts of the OT to God, some to Moses (not what was given by God through him but as legislating from his own understanding), and some to the elders of the people. The legislation of Moses and of the elders is without lasting authority. Even that part which came from the creator God may be divided into three parts. There is the pure legislation, free from evil, which the Savior "came not to destroy but to fulfill," identified by Ptolemy as the Ten Commandments. There is a second part bound up with wrongdoing and concerned with vengeance (such as "an eye for an eye and a tooth for a tooth"), which the Savior abrogated as alien to his nature. Finally, there is the typical and symbolical part (such as the sabbath, circumcision, sacrifices), which the Savior transformed from material and bodily things into spiritual (abstaining from evil, circumcising the heart, praise and thanksgiving).

So two parts of the OT did not come from God, and of the part that did some is still valid; some has been abolished;

and some has been transformed. Ptolemy shows his Gnostic bias in distinguishing the Creator from the Father of Christ and not allowing any of the OT to be derived from the Father. (Against the Gnostics the Orthodox church writers emphasized the continuity between the Old and the New as both given by the same God.) Otherwise, Ptolemy's view is highly original; it is nonetheless similar to other (later) efforts to make levels or distinctions within the OT, some of which is valid for Christians and some of which is not.

Another view which made distinctions within the OT, but from the very opposite premises, was that of the second-century Jewish Christians known as **Ebionites**. They represent a survival of those Jewish Christians who were "zealous for the law" and opposed Paul (Acts 15:1, 5; 21:20; Gal. 2:45). In contrast to Marcion, the Ebionites impressed the mainstream of the church with their adherence to the law. Irenaeus (ca. A.D. 180) says of them:

> They use the Gospel according to Matthew only, and repudiate the Apostle Paul, maintaining that he was an apostate from the law. As to the prophetical writings they endeavor to expound them in a peculiar manner. They practice circumcision, persevere in the observance of those customs which are enjoined by the law, and are so Judaic in their style of life, that they even adore Jerusalem as if it were the house of God.
>
> *Against Heresies* I.xxvi.1

Actually the Ebionites made distinctions within the OT, for not all of the law was considered binding. Their views in detail must be reconstructed from their teachings included in the Pseudo-Clementine *Homilies* and *Recognitions*. Jesus appears as the teacher of a kind of "reform Judaism." Some passages now found in the Torah are not original but are later falsifications (*Homilies* III.47). Jesus as the True Prophet restored the proper law of God. Among the things rejected were "the sacrifices, the monarchy, and the female (false) prophecy and other such things" (*Homilies* III.52). The real point of Jesus' mission was annulling the sacrificial law (*Recognitions* I.35ff.). The bloodshed of war seems to have been a principal reason for rejecting the monarchy, but there was OT basis for not considering it a divine ordinance. For reasons which seem complicated now, prophecy was disparaged or even rejected. Finally, offensive passages in Scripture (anthropomorphisms about God and immoral deeds recorded of OT heroes—the very things which Marcion and the Gnostics used against the OT) were rejected as false, later additions to the Scriptures. On the other hand, following and going beyond Jesus, the Ebionites intensified certain features of the law: prohibiting meat, emphasizing poverty, and increasing the purification ceremonies (ritual immersion-baths).

Jewish Christians took varying attitudes toward Gentile observance of the law: some (Ebionites proper) insisting that their law was binding on Gentiles and others saying that Jews must continue to keep it while exempting Gentiles from its ritual requirements (Justin, *Dialogue with Trypho* 47). The effort to be both Jews and Christians is reflected in the statement included in Eusebius' description of the Ebionites: "Like the Jews they used to observe the sabbath and the rest of the Jewish ceremonial, but on Sundays celebrated rites like ours in commemoration of the Saviour's resurrection" (*Church History* III.xxvii.5). Their view was largely lost to the church, as it became overwhelmingly Gentile in membership and considered such combinations heretical. After the Ebionites died out, few Jews who were converted kept the law. Conversion to Christianity meant a break with the Jewish life-style, something which was not true for the majority of Jewish Christians in the early days of the church.

The unknown author of the so-called **Epistle of Barnabas** (ca. 135, but possibly much earlier) also claimed the OT as the Christians' Bible but in a radically different way from the Ebionites. In one sense he is the very opposite of Marcion: the OT is altogether Christian. In another sense he accomplished what Marcion did without severing the church's ties with its OT heritage: the OT is not to be taken literally but only spiritually. The author used the OT against its own requirements, for example in quoting Isaiah 1:11-14, Jeremiah 7:22-23, and Psalm 51:19 to argue that God did not intend the animal sacrifices but desired a sacrifice of the heart and in quoting Isaiah 58:4-10 to argue that God did not want literal fasting but service to others.

There were those who were saying that "the covenant is both theirs [Jews] and ours [Christians]." "Barnabas" replies with an emphatic, "It is ours." The covenant was offered to Israel, but the sin of the golden calf represented Israel's rejection of the covenant (Exod. 32). The covenant then was given to Christians. Moses broke the tablets of stone, "and their covenant was broken, in order that the covenant of Jesus the Beloved should be sealed in our hearts" (*Ep. Barnabas* 4:6-9; cf. 13–14). The renewed statement of the covenant given to Moses was never intended to be kept literally, not even by Jews. God intended it to be understood spiritually, and in that way it is observed by Christians. Most of the *Epistle of Barnabas* is a spiritual or allegorical interpretation of the characteristic features of the Mosaic religion. The ritual of the atonement was fulfilled in the sacrifice of Christ (chs. 5–8); fleshly circumcision is abolished and the real circumcision is that of the heart and ears (ch. 9); the food laws refer to types of men whose immorality is to be avoided (ch. 10); the ceremonial washings of the OT have been replaced by baptism (ch. 11); the sabbath of the Jews is displeasing to God, and Christians keep Sunday (ch. 15); the temple was in vain, for God truly dwells in the Christian people whose sin he forgives (ch. 16). "Barnabas" seems not to have had direct heirs to his novel and extreme interpretations, but the idea of reading the OT spiritually as an allegory of the Christian dispensation and preserving it as a Christian book in this way was a widely influential approach in the ancient church.

It was especially the school of interpretation associated with the great city and center of learning in Egypt, Alexandria, where the **allegorical interpretation** of the OT flourished. The earliest orthodox writer at Alexandria from whom extensive writings survive is Clement (died before A.D. 215). Clement of Alexandria reflects a common early Christian teaching that the law "was only temporary" (*Instructor* I.7; cf. *Miscellanies* VI. 5-7, 17). Its purposes were to "show sin" (*Miscellanies* II. 7), to "train in piety, prescribe what is to be done, and restrain from sins by imposing penalties" (ibid. I.27). It prepared the chosen people for Christ's teaching (ibid. II.18). The "Mosaic philosophy" contains four parts: history, legislation (these two constituting ethics), sacrifice (knowledge of the physical world), and theology (metaphysics). The law has three meanings of value to the Christian: "exhibiting a symbol, or laying down a precept for right conduct, or as uttering a prophecy" (ibid. I.28). The symbols of the OT have three purposes: to arouse curiosity so men will study, to hide true doctrine from the profane, to make it possible to speak of God who is incomprehensible in his nature (ibid. VI.15). Clement shows especially the influence of Philo, the first-century Jewish philosopher from Alexandria, in finding allegories of the moral life and of the physical universe in the OT. Instructive is his treatment of the Ten Commandments in *Miscellanies* VI.16. The sabbath meant a rest from evil (not an uncommon interpretation in the early church); honor father and mother refers to God the Father and the divine knowledge and wisdom; adultery is abandoning the true knowledge of God; murder is extirpating true doctrine of God in order to introduce falsehood. The tabernacle was allegorized as the universe, for instance, the seven-branched lampstand representing the seven planets, but this Philonic interpretation is Christianized at several points, as in referring the lamp also to Christ, who gives light to the world (ibid. V.6).

Origen (185–253) systematized the Alexandrian interpretation of the Bible and carried through a massive amount of work in application of his methods. Origen found a triple sense in Scripture: the literal or historical sense, a moral or spiritual sense applying to the soul, and a mystical or typical sense referring to Christ, the church and the faith, or sometimes eternal life (*On First Principles* IV.xi-xxiii). Each passage may have all of these meanings, and every passage has a spiritual meaning even if no literal meaning. Origen applies the scheme to the NT as well as to the Old. He relates the two testaments to each other as letter and spirit. Both are necessary, because one would not have the spirit without the letter, but the more important is the spirit which gives the true meaning. So it is Jesus who interprets the law to the church (*In Joshua, Homily* ix.8). After Christ the historical has passed, and Scripture has now acquired its spiritual sense. The law itself has a literal and a spiritual element. It is always impossible to keep according to the letter—Origen cites the sabbath command as his illustration—but spiritual obedience gives life (*Commentary on Romans* vi.12). Origen appeals to Paul as a justification for his spiritual reading of the OT, for example, his use of the Exodus in 1 Corinthians 10:1ff. (*In Exodus, Homily* v.1). There is the difference, however, that for Paul the basis is a similar situation between Israel in the wilderness and the Corinthian Christians (see the treatment below), whereas for Origen the real meaning of the OT text is the spiritual reference.

Whereas some, especially at Antioch, explained what were, from the Christian standpoint, imperfections in the OT by God's accommodations to the needs and capacities of man in preparation for a truly spiritual religion, Origen is one of the purest advocates of allegorism as the way of overcoming the imperfections while holding onto the OT as a sacred book. Origen reflects many of the common interpretations of the OT to be found in the early church which are not allegorical and on occasion can use the OT as ecclesiastical law in the manner of Cyprian (see below). His own preference, however, was obviously for the form of exegesis that interpreted Scripture with reference to the inner life. This became the distinctive mark of the Alexandrian school—to put the stress on the spiritual and mystical side. Thus Origen, in interpreting the tabernacle, can refer to the older interpretation that the tabernacle is the world, but he develops an allegory first in reference to the church, and then in keeping with his primary interest he passes to the soul. "Each may construct in his own soul a tabernacle to God" (*In Exodus, Homily* ix.4). This way of dealing with the OT may be seen in the widely influential treatment of the stations in Israel's wilderness wandering as an allegory of the journey of the Christian soul towards perfection. An allegory of the religious life is combined with a statement of his principle of interpretation in the comment on the sweetening of the bitter waters of Marah, "The bitterness of the letter of the law is changed into the sweetness of spiritual understanding" (*In Exodus, Homily* vii.1). That is what Origen sought to do in his interpretation of the Bible.

By way of contrast with the Alexandrian way of using the OT allegorically as teaching spiritual lessons for the Christian life, Latin authors read the OT more literally and found in it legal requirements for Christians. The animal sacrifices were replaced by the nonbloody (spiritual) sacrifice of the eucharist, the Levitical priesthood was replaced by Christian ministers, the sabbath was replaced by Sunday, the tabernacle was replaced by the church, and so through all of the institutions of the OT, but the regulations stated for the Mosaical institutions could be applied to their Christian equivalent. The earliest expression of this tendency may be found in Clement of Rome (ca. A.D. 96), who used the OT regulations about who offered sacrifice, when, and where as an argument for the need of similar good order in the church (*Epistle to the Corinthians* 40, 41).

Tertullian reflects the two sides of the Christian attitude toward the OT when in his *Answer to the Jews* he affirms the contrast, "the old law has ceased [he has specifically mentioned circumcision, the sabbath, and sacrifices] and . . . the promised new law is now in operation" (ch. 6); but in his polemic *Against Marcion* he can affirm the continuity, "the whole Mosaic system was a figure of Christ, of whom the Jews indeed were ignorant, but who is known to us Christians" (V.11). Most of Tertullian's discussion of OT passages occurs in answers to Marcion's criticisms of them. There are hints of the legalistic reading of the OT that was to give a very Jewish cast to the developing catholic church. Thus Tertullian can cite Deuteronomy's prohibition of "the reception of the Ammonites and the Moabites into the church" [the Jewish church—the use of the Christian term is significant] as supporting the gospel's command to shake the dust of the feet off against a disobedient people (*Against Marcion* IV.24). Or again, since no idolater was found in the ark, the type of the church, "let not that be in the church which was not in the ark" (*On Idolatry* xxiv).

A clearer reflection in the early centuries of the move in the direction of the use of the OT as a legal guide for Christian institutions is to be found in the writings of Cyprian, bishop of Carthage (248–258). He argues that the clergy should not engage in secular work. His basis is that the Levites did not share in the division of the land of Canaan and so (which is incorrect) were not compelled to transact secular business, but received tithes from the other tribes. This "plan and rule is now maintained in respect of the clergy, that they who are promoted by clerical ordination in the church of the Lord may be distracted in no respect from the divine administration" but are supported by the contributions of the brethren (*Epistle* i.1). In a similar vein, on the basis of Numbers 20:25-26, where the appointment of Aaron as priest was made "in the presence of all the assembly," Cyprian concludes:

> God commands a [Christian] priest to be appointed in the presence of all the assembly; that is, he instructs and shows that the ordination of priests ought not to be solemnized except with the knowledge of the people standing near, . . . and the ordination . . . may be just and legitimate.

> *Epistle* lxvii.4

Many examples of this type of argument can be found in Western writers, as when bishop Callistus of Rome (217–222) justified his laxer policies on church discipline with the argument that the ark of Noah, the symbol of the church, contained both unclean and clean animals (to the horror of Hippolytus, who supplies the information, *Refutation of All Heresies* IX.7).

The allegorical and legalistic interpretations were not the only alternatives within the mainstream of the ancient church. Tertullian spoke of the law "as preparatory to the gospel," training men gradually by stages for the "perfect light of the Christian discipline" (*Against Marcion* IV.17).

He, Cyprian, Clement, and Origen all employ prophecies and types from the OT as pointing toward the New. The **typological**, in contrast to allegorical, use of the OT became in the fourth century characteristic of the interpretation practiced at Antioch, whose scholars were rivals in the Greek church to those at Alexandria. This historical way of looking at the Bible in terms of successive covenants and progressive revelation had important roots in the early days of the church.

Justin Martyr, in his debate with the Jew Trypho about A.D 150, gave expression to the **covenantal** or dispensational way of looking at biblical history:

> As, then, circumcision began with Abraham, and the sabbath and sacrifices and offerings and feasts with Moses, and it has been proved they were enjoined on account of the hardness of your people's heart, so it was necessary, in accordance with the Father's will, that they should have an end in him who was born of a virgin . . . who was proclaimed as about to come to all the world, to be the everlasting law and the everlasting covenant.

Dialogue with Trypho 43 (cf. also 23)

Justin also says, "Some injunctions were laid on (the Jews) in reference to the worship of God and practice of righteousness; but some injunctions and acts were likewise mentioned in reference to the mystery of Christ" (ibid. 44). Because the OT comes from the Father of Jesus Christ and because of their prophecies of him, Justin can argue from what is contained in "your (Jewish) Scriptures, or rather not yours, but ours" (ibid. 29). "The law promulgated on Horeb is now old, and belongs to (Jews) alone," but Jesus is "the new law and the new covenant" and his law "is for all universally," so that Christians are "the true spiritual Israel" (ibid. 11).

Irenaeus (ca. 180) gives the fullest exposition to this view, which allows full historical validity to the OT, but sees it as fulfilled in Christ and superseded in the Christian age. Apart from specific interpretations of prophecies, his doctrine of the **history of revelation** has perhaps more to commend itself to modern views than anything found in other postapostolic authors. Irenaeus suggests that there "were four principal covenants given to the human race": those under Adam, Noah, Moses, and Christ (*Against Heresies* III.xi.8). More frequently he speaks simply of two covenants, the law and the gospel (ibid. IV.ix.1; xxxii.2). The Mosaic law and the grace of the New Covenant were fitted for the times; they are different, but (against Marcion) they have unity and harmony because they come from one and the same God (ibid. III.xii.12; cf. IV.ix-x). God first gave the natural law (enshrined in the decalogue), then the Mosaic law to discipline the Jews and by means of types to teach them the real service of God; and Christ has now fulfilled, extended, and given fuller scope to the law (ibid. IV.xiii-xv). Christians have no need for the law as a pedagogue, for they have a new covenant in the spirit (*Demonstration of the Apostolic Preaching* 87; 89; 90; 96). Irenaeus makes much of the prophecies of the OT, but he insists that they can be understood only from the standpoint of their fulfillment in the Christian age (*Against Heresies* IV.xxvi.1).

With this review of the varied attitudes toward the relation of the Old and New Testaments in the postapostolic period as a background, we will now examine the NT attitude toward the Jewish Bible in both its negative and positive aspects.

OLD TESTAMENT REMOVED

No teaching is written more plainly across the pages of the NT than that the Old Covenant as a system of religion has been removed. A brief examination of particular passages demonstrates this teaching.

The whole argument of **Galatians 3-5** is germane. Judaizing teachers, themselves perhaps Gentiles, were insisting that Gentile converts to Jesus Christ must receive circumcision in order to become a part of God's covenant people and so heirs to the salvation promised in Abraham. The issue was this: Who are the sons of Abraham and the heirs of the promises? Paul argues the case on the level of competing systems of religion—works of law versus faith in Christ.

Paul gives three arguments in **Galatians 3:1-14:** (1) The argument from the religious experience of the Galatian converts—whether they received the Holy Spirit by doing the works of the law of Moses or through faith in the preaching of the gospel (3:1-5); (2) The scriptural argument from the case of Abraham—faith was what made Abraham acceptable to God and faith marks his sons, not fleshly descent or a fleshly sign (3:6-9); and (3) the argument from the nature of the law itself—condemnation for not keeping its demands and life by keeping them (Deut. 27:26; Lev. 18:5)—in contrast to another principle of justification, namely, life by faith (Gal. 3:10-14; cf. Hab. 2:4). Verses 13 and 14 sum up in reverse order the three arguments: "the curse of the law," "the blessing of Abraham," and "the promise of the Spirit," climaxing with the key concept of this section—faith. "In Christ Jesus" the curse is removed and the blessings come upon the Gentiles.

Paul then illustrates the promise of God to Abraham by a will (Gal. 3:15-18). The basis of the illustration is the double meaning of the Greek word *diathēkē*. The ordinary secular meaning of the word was a man's last will or "testament." The Greek translation of the OT used the word to translate the Hebrew *berith*, "covenant." Since the word which might have been expected, *sunthēkē*, implied an agreement between equals, the Jews preferred *diathēkē*, which preserved the idea of God's determination of the stipulations in the covenant. The giving of the law "four hundred and thirty years" later did not annul the earlier promises (testament) to Abraham.

Paul's arguments and illustration required him to consider the objection "Why then the law?" The answer is that it was added because of man's sins (3:19-22). It was a moral guide and disciplinarian ("custodian" or "pedagogue"). The law was temporary. Now that Christ has overcome sin, the law is obsolete (3:23-25). For the purposes of this study these verses are explicit. Now that Christ has come, now that a faith system has been instituted, the law has served its function. The Christian is "no longer under" the law. He is "in Christ" (3:26-27). The question about the recipients of the promise is answered. Christians are the offspring of Abraham, but not the fleshly offspring. Christ and all those who are in Christ—whether Jew or Gentile—are the spiritual seed of Abraham (3:28-29). The word for "offspring" in Galatians 3:16 (cf. Gen 12:7; 15:5; 17:7, 10; 22:17, 18) is a collective noun but grammatically singular, so Paul can interpret it literally of Christ, but he brings in the collective feature at the end (3:29).

Chapter 4 continues the theme of sonship from chapter 3, employing it now as an illustration (4:1-11). The essential doctrinal argument having been made, Paul turns to a personal appeal (4:12-19). Then he seeks to clinch his case for his readers by an allegory drawn from the law (4:21-31). It probably carried much weight with his readers but has only illustrative value to modern readers. The doctrinal position which is being illustrated, however, does have substantive value for the study at hand. When we remember that the issue with Judaizers concerned identifying the true sons of Abraham, or in other words, how one received the promises given to him, the story is aptly chosen and the allegory pointedly made. Abraham had children by two women, Hagar the slave and Sarah the free wife. Ishmael was born according to the ordinary course of nature. Isaac was the child of promise, born by the power of God long after Abraham and Sarah had passed the normal age of conception. There was a real hook for the Jews in Paul's application. The Arabs were descendants of Ishmael. If one wanted to make the promises depend on physical descent, then Arabs would have to be included. Moreover, Mount Sinai, where the law was given, was in the territory of the Arabs. But the true sons of God are those born according to promise, not according to the flesh. Once this is recognized, there is no objection to including uncircumcised Christians among the sons of Abraham. Paul draws several parallels between the relations of Ishmael with Isaac and the relations of Jews with Christians. For the present purposes, however, note the forceful conclusion: "Cast out the slave [the covenant at Sinai]."

The practical conclusion of the arguments in relation to the issue at hand is stated in 5:1-12. To accept circumcision as a religious rite is to obligate one's self to keep the whole law of which it was an integral part (5:3). And that is to cut one's self off from Christ (5:2,4). To seek to be justified by the law is to depart from and reject the system of grace. Circumcision is nothing; the law is nothing; to be in Christ is everything (5:6). The rejection of the law as a system of religion might seem to leave men without the moral guidance which the law provided. Paul offers an alternative basis for ethics (5:13-25). The removal of the law does not mean that any kind of conduct is acceptable. The choice is not between law and following the desires of the flesh. There is a third kind of life, that lived under the direction of the Holy Spirit. The personal activity of the Holy Spirit in the whole Christian people is frequently seen in the NT as the distinctive advance of the New Covenant over the Old (Acts 2:38f.; Heb. 6:4).

The New Covenant in Christ, therefore, is founded on the promise to Abraham, not on the Old Covenant through Moses. Behind Paul's argument for justification by faith instead of by law is his universalism. Only in Galatians and Romans, where Judaizing was a problem, does Paul make much of justification by faith. The law was given to Jews, and one was born into relation with it. There had to be another principle of justification, available to all men, in the new age that welcomed Gentiles. The answer was a spiritual principle: the faith principle, not the flesh principle. Under the Christian Age one has the privilege "to choose his own ancestors." He can become a part of the people of Abraham, Isaac, Jacob, et al.

Other passages may now be examined more summarily. **Romans 7:1-7** declares the Christian's freedom from the law. Paul employs an illustration from marriage (vss. 2-3). As often happens in an illustration, not every point matches what is being illustrated, but that does not weaken the force of the illustration. In the present illustration the woman's husband dies, so she is free from his law and may marry another man. In the application (vss. 4-6) the person himself dies and so is free from the law and marries Christ. The parallel to the marriage illustration is kept to an extent in the allusion of verse 4 to the death of Christ as the means through which the Christian dies to the law. The point is that death frees one from law (vs. 1—a good rabbinic principle), so it does not matter who is said to die. Paul may be influenced in the way he words his application by his teaching in chapter 6 that baptism is a death (vss. lff.). As the Christian is dead to sin (6:11), so he is dead to law (7:4, 6). The law to which the Christian died is specifically the Mosaic law, centered in the Ten Commandments. This is clear from verse 7, "You shall not covet," as part of the law under consideration. Freedom from sin (Romans 6) and freedom from law (Romans 7) do not mean freedom from moral guidance but (as in Galatians) is followed by freedom in the Spirit (Romans 8; note especially verse 2). With the coming of the Messiah and the gift of his Spirit the law is rendered inoperative (cf. Rom. 10:4).

The contrast between the written code of the law and the Spirit in the Christian dispensation is stated strongly in **2 Corinthians 3:6-18.** The written code kills, but the Spirit gives life (vs. 6). The theme of the New Covenant comes to the fore. The Old Covenant was a "ministry of death." This is strong language, but there is no doubt what is intended, for it was "carved in letters of stone" (vs.7). Nevertheless it came with splendor, and Paul's following verses are a commentary on Exodus 34:29-35 with its account of glory which surrounded Moses when he came down from the mount of the giving of the law. For our purposes we note the contrasts which Paul makes: dispensation of death and dispensation of the Spirit; dispensation of condemnation and dispensation of righteousness; what faded and what is permanent. No wonder the splendor of the New Covenant far surpasses that of the Old. The glory of the old was fading, transitory (vss. 7,12). Paul interprets the veil which Moses put over his face as hiding the fact that the glory was fading, so Paul the preacher of the New Covenant does not veil himself as did Moses, the giver of the Old Covenant (vs.13). The veil on Moses was seen by Paul as symbolic of a veil which lay over the law and over the Jews when they read the law (vss. 14-15). According to the Exodus narrative, when Moses turned to the Lord, he removed the veil.

Similarly when one turns to the Lord (Christ) now, the veil is removed and he can understand the OT properly (vs. 16). Some have understood verse 14 as saying that in Christ the Old Covenant is "taken away" or "made inoperative." The RSV takes the "it" which is removed as the veil. The verb for "taken away" is the same as that translated "faded away" in verses 11 and 13 and "fading" in verse 7, and it is possible that the reference here also is to the splendor of the Old that fades away in Christ. That the Old Covenant itself is removed is correct to the passage as a whole. Such is implicit in the reference to a New Covenant (vs. 6) and to the fading glory of the Old (vs. 7) and is explicit in the declaration that the New abides but the Old is abolished or "fading away" (vs.11). Moreover, the word for "taken away" is that used in other passages for the abolition of the law (Rom. 7:2; Gal. 5:4; Eph. 2:15).

Colossians 2:13-17 employs the forgiveness by God and new life in Christ as the basis for rejecting ritualistic and ascetic practices advocated by certain false teachers. There are difficulties in interpreting the details of the passage, but the application which is made by Paul is clear. God "cancelled" or erased the "bond" or debt owed by man (vs. 14). That "bond" consists in "legal demands" or decrees, a word which suggests some connection with the law (cf. Eph. 2:15—"ordinances"), although the metaphor is wider in its application. Not only did God cancel the debt, but he also won a victory over "principalities and powers" in the death of Christ (vs. 15). The guilt and power of sin are destroyed. The conclusion which Paul draws shows that one of the things from which man is freed by the death of Christ is the legal requirements of the Mosaic law (human regulations as well are included—vss. 20-21). No one is to judge the Christian in the matter of the annual festivals, monthly new moon, and weekly sabbath prescribed in the law (vs. 16; 1 Chron. 23:31; 2 Chron. 2:4; Ezek. 45:17; Hos. 2:11). These laws were a "shadow"; the reality is Christ. When one has the reality, he does not follow the shadow. The connection of thought may be something like this : Law is the result of sin (Gal. 3:19); by reason of it one is in bondage to principalities and powers (cf. Gal. 4:8-9); when sin is cancelled and the powers overcome, law is no longer binding. Legal demands are set aside, and one is not to be judged by them.

Ephesians 2:11-18 utilizes the abolition of the law to confirm the uniting of Jews and Gentiles in one new people of God. The religious condition of the Gentile world in relation to the Jews is painted in somber tones in verses 11 and 12. The change accomplished by the coming of Jesus is boldly stated in verse 13. What he did is elaborated in verses 14-18, developed around the theme of peace replacing hostility. Note especially verse 15. Jesus abolished the "law of commandments" in the ordinances of the OT. The language employs the terminology which is normal in the Bible for the OT laws. The Jewish law was a barrier between Jews and Gentiles. It had to be removed, not only in order to open the blessings of salvation to all men (as noted in the above texts), but also in order to create a new spiritual community (vss. 19-22).

The most comprehensive statement of the superiority of the New Covenant over the Old is **Hebrews 7:1–10:18**. The whole section is pertinent, but "of these things we cannot now speak in detail" (9:5) but can only sketch some of the main points. The superiority of the priesthood of Christ to the Levitical priesthood is emphasized in chapter 7. Christ was of the tribe of Judah, but the priests of the OT were drawn from the tribe of Levi (vs. 14). Christ's priesthood, therefore, must be of a different order (vss. 11, 15-17). A change in priesthood has occurred, "For when there is a change in the priesthood, there is necessarily a change in the law as well" (vs. 12). No Christian rejects the high priesthood of Christ or seeks to continue the literal Levitical priesthood. Yet so integral was the priesthood to the law that if one accepts the priesthood of Christ he must reject the law. If one is to keep the law, he must keep the Levitical priesthood.

Connected with the priesthood are the covenant, sanctuary, and sacrifice (8:1-6). The discussion of these is interwoven in chapters 8–10. The change in priesthood necessitated a change in the law on which it was predicated and to which it was central. A change in law meant a change in covenant (8:6-13). The New Covenant is better because it contains better promises (8:6). Jeremiah's prophecy of a New Covenant (Jer. 31:31-34, quoted in 8:8-12) implied the deficiency of the Old (8:7) and the replacement of the Old, and the author can declare that Old Covenant in his time ready to vanish away (8:13).

The better promises of this better covenant are due to the superior sacrifice of the new priest. This priest offers his sacrifice in a different sanctuary—heavenly rather than earthly (9:1-12, 23-25). Employing the double meaning of the word *diathēkē*—covenant and will, the author connects the beginning of the New Covenant with the death of Christ (9:15-17). This death is the sacrifice offered by Christ, both priest and victim (9:12-14, 26-27). The sacrifices of the Old were imperfect because they could not touch the conscience (9:9), had to be repeated (9:25), and brought a reminder of sins rather than taking them away (10:1-4). The sacrifice of Christ does purify the conscience, was once for all (9:26-28; 10:10), and effects an eternal redemption (9:12, 14, 15; 10:12, 14, 18). The first sacrifices are abolished by the perfect sacrifice of Christ (10:5-10). The themes of priesthood, sanctuary, sacrifice, and covenant are caught up in a summary of the whole argument in 10:11-18. Therefore, the law was a shadow (10:1), not the substance, a rough outline without details. It has been replaced by the Christian reality.

The truth of the matter is that no one follows the OT completely, or even tries to do so. Christians who appeal to the OT do so when they cannot find NT authority for what they want to do. They employ a pick-and-choose method. On that basis almost anything can be legitimatized from the OT, for all stages of man's religious history are reflected in it. But the method is illegitimate. As Galatians 5:3; Colossians 2:16; and Hebrews 7:12 indicate, it is all or nothing. There are two different covenants, two different systems of religion. If one takes Christ, he has chosen a different kind of relationship with God.

VALUES OF THE OLD TESTAMENT

The above passages may seem very negative. They do make a strong case. But they are not the whole story. There is a very positive assessment made of the OT by NT writers. The OT is not binding upon Christians. As a system of religion it has been superseded. Nevertheless, that does not mean that the OT is valueless or can be dispensed with by Christians. Let us notice the positive values of the OT for Christians.

Points to Christ

"You search the scriptures, because you think that in them you have eternal life; and it is they that bear witness to me" (John 5:39). The OT points to Christ. It continues to bear witness to him (5:46-47). This is the reason that Christians can never give it up and the reason that it is not authoritative. As road signs are very valuable in directing a person to his destination but are passed by when the destination is reached (cf. Gal. 3:24-25), so the OT provides road signs pointing to Christ. But Christ is the goal and the authority. One no longer depends on the witnesses when he has the object of their testimony to examine. The Jews studied the law as an end in itself, but instead of being lifegiving in itself it points away from itself.

New Testament and early Christian authors found Christ everywhere in the OT. The gospel of John itself shows this, when it understands the heavenly vision of Isaiah 6:1ff. as referring to the glory of Christ (John 12:41). Another example is Hebrews 2:11-15, which quotes three different passages from the Psalms as words of Jesus himself. Christian preachers preached Jesus from the OT, as Philip did to the Ethiopian in Acts 8:27-35.

This interpretation of the OT is precisely the issue between Jews and Christians. Do the prophecies speak of Jesus, point to another yet to come, or refer to the Jewish people itself? The decision on this question is the decision of faith and is a part of the total response to the Christian message.

Shows the Unfolding Purpose of God

> The prophets who prophesied of the grace that was to be yours searched and inquired about this salvation; they inquired what person or time was indicated by the Spirit of Christ within them when predicting the sufferings of Christ and the subsequent glory. It was revealed to them that they were serving not themselves but you, in the things which have now been announced to you by those who preached the good news to you through the Holy Spirit sent from heaven.
>
> 1 Peter 1:10-12

The OT gives the grand sweep of the history of salvation. Without it Jesus would seem to have come suddenly. The Christian, in looking at the OT, has an advantage over the Jews, or even the prophets themselves. There is a meaning and pattern in the OT that can be seen in the light of the NT fulfillment which could not previously be seen. The prophets spoke of the grace of salvation which now has come in Christ and is proclaimed in the gospel (Rom. 1:2; 16:26). They were able to do so because the Spirit which inspired them was the very Spirit of Christ. But they did not know of what they were speaking. They were seeking and searching concerning a truth still hidden to them. They did not know the person or the time and circumstances to which their words referred. Especially perplexing was the paradox of suffering and glory to which they testified. Their words had special reference to Christ. Thus the prophets minister to Christians. They have received the gospel through the same Spirit that had spoken through the prophets. The Spirit of Christ spoke in OT prophets and in Christian evangelists. Both have words of salvation for Christians. God all along had a purpose and a plan; there was a fuller meaning in the prophetic messages which can be discerned only from the standpoint of the Gospel of Christ. Of this, more later.

Instructs in Salvation

With the viewpoint of the above verses, even bolder claims for the Christian value of the OT can be understood:

> From childhood you have been acquainted with the sacred

writings which are able to instruct you for salvation through faith in Christ Jesus. All scripture is inspired by God and profitable for teaching, for reproof, for correction, and for training in righteousness, that the man of God may be complete, equipped for every good work.

2 Timothy 3:15-17

Whatever wider reference the passage may have, the "sacred writings" in this context refer to the OT. They are able to make one wise to salvation when accompanied by faith in Jesus Christ. The Scriptures instruct one for or toward salvation. The salvation itself is by means of faith, but not any kind of faith—the faith which is placed in Christ. Once more, there is the implication that Christian faith gives a fuller meaning to the OT Scriptures. Whether the statement in 2 Timothy 3:16 means that every passage of Scripture or Scripture as a whole is God-breathed is much debated but inconsequential for its statement of the value of the OT. The Scriptures can be used profitably for instruction or teaching, for refuting error, for correcting behavior, and for discipline or training in right conduct. They equip the preacher or teacher for every good work.

This bold statement reminds us that "the Bible" of the early church was the OT. It was the basis of preaching and teaching, understood in the light of the coming of Christ and supplemented by his teaching and that of his apostles. We now have that supplement and interpretation in the NT Scriptures. They form the norm of Christian faith and practice.

But they rest upon the foundation of the OT, which, taken along with faith in Christ, instructed men and women in salvation. Although we now ordinarily come to the Bible by way of the NT, the OT can still serve these valuable functions for us. We hold in common with the early disciples that the Christian faith is the key and standard for understanding the old Scriptures.

Provides Examples of Righteousness

A specific illustration of the way in which OT instructs in salvation may be seen in the way the NT appeals to examples of virtuous living in the OT. Hebrews 11 and 12 may serve to document the point. Hebrews 11 is an imposing roll call of men and women whose faithfulness commended them to God. Faith enabled them to do the things for which they are remembered:

> Therefore, since we are surrounded by so great a cloud of witnesses, let us lay aside every weight, and sin which clings so closely, and let us run with perseverance the race that is set before us.
>
> Hebrews 12:1

And so much the more so because God has better promises reserved for the Christian (Heb. 11:40). The person who looks to Jesus (Heb. 12:2) has every reason for steadfastness in the struggle against sin (Heb. 12:4ff.). The OT heroes of faith remain a perennial source of encouragement to God's people. The most interesting study in the world is people. The characteristics of being human come out clearly in the OT narratives. The customs may be different, but in the attitudes and behavior we can see ourselves and our acquaintances in the marvelously told stories of the OT. The narratives may in fact have first taken shape as separate stories told and repeated in the oral tradition of the Hebrews. Perhaps that is why the stories of the OT remain favorites with children. But they have a power for persons of every age because of their reflection of human nature. A respected psychology professor in a state university in his introduction course to psychology includes a lecture on "Why I Believe the Bible." The point of the lecture has to do with the way in which the Bible is true to human nature. All great literature would partake of this quality to some degree. But the Bible is especially effective in bringing out man's motives, his faults, and his moments of greatness. When such men "of like nature with ourselves" demonstrate loyalty to God, it helps us to do the same in our circumstances.

Warns of Disobedience

The same book of Hebrews, which appeals to the examples of righteousness in the OT also uses its examples of disobedience as a warning to Christians:

> Therefore we must pay the closer attention to what we have heard, lest we drift away from it. For if the message declared by

angels was valid and every transgression of disobedience
received a just retribution, how shall we escape if we neglect
such a great salvation? It was declared at first by the Lord, and
it was attested to us by those who heard him, while God also
bore witness by signs and wonders and various miracles and by
gifts of the Holy Spirit distributed according to his own will.

Hebrews 2:1-4

The author has demonstrated the superiority of the Son of
God to angels (1:4-14). They minister to those who receive
salvation, but the Son brings salvation. Angels mediated the
OT revelation, as several passages affirm (Gal. 3:19; Acts
7:53; cf. Deut. 33:2). This partial revelation (Heb. 1:1) is
inferior to the complete revelation brought by God's Son
(1:2; 2:3). Yet disobedience to God in OT times was
severely punished. The OT is replete with instances of
man's transgression and its consequences. How much more
careful, then, must man be who has the benefit of a message
spoken by the Son himself, confirmed by those who heard
him and approved by God's miraculous gifts (cf. 1 Pet. 1:12,
above).

Specific instances of retribution for transgression are
cited in 1 Corinthians 10:1-11. The Israelites of the exodus
generation knew a great salvation in their deliverance from
Egyptian bondage. They had counterparts of a baptism and
a Lord's supper. Yet they fell into sin. They were guilty of
idolatry, fornication, and grumbling. Hence, God was not
pleased with them and destroyed them in the wilderness.
"Now these things are warnings for us" (1 Cor. 10:6). The
word translated "warnings" is literally "types," which
makes the connection between Israel's history and Christian
experience even closer. The Christians at Corinth were
faced with temptations to the same sins. They seemed to
trust in the power of sacraments to save them regardless of
what they did. The experience of Israel could serve as a
warning of what might happen to them: "Now these things
happened to them as a warning (typically), but they were
written down for our instruction, upon whom the end of the
ages has come" (1 Cor. 10:11). The fulfillment of the OT has
come upon Christians. They live in the overlap of the

present evil age (Gal. 1:4) and the powers of the age to come (Heb. 6:5). So, although living in the last dispensation, Christians can still profit from experiences of men in their dealings with God in earlier dispensations. Indeed those experiences were written down specifically for their instruction (1 Cor. 10:11). The principles of God's dealings with men remain the same, and so not only the Christians at Corinth but Christians of all time need to take heed to the OT Scriptures and the lessons they teach.

Gives Hope

"For whatever was written in former days was written for our instruction, that by steadfastness and by the encouragement of the scriptures we might have hope" (Rom. 15:4). Paul has referred in the preceding verse to Christ as an example of self-giving love which rather than pleasing self accepts others in their weaknesses. He cites Psalm 69:9 as the words of Christ, as is also done in John 2:17. In a parenthetical statement Paul enlarges on his citation to affirm that all of the old Scriptures were written for Christian instruction. The Scriptures serve Christians, as our preceding citations have also affirmed. God is a God of steadfastness and encouragement, a God of hope (15:13); and, if Christians have the self-effacing and forbearing attitude of Christ, this God will enable them to live and worship together in unity (15:5-6).

God has endowed his Scriptures with the same qualities which he possesses—steadfastness and encouragement. Because God and his word are faithful and consoling, his people may have hope. Biblical religion is a religion of hope. I well remember a fellow graduate student who had grown up in Burma as the son of missionaries describing the gloomier outlook among people who did not have a Bible background. Although its modern offshoot in the Western world is a secularized version, the progressive attitude toward the future is in no small measure due to the Judeo-Christian heritage. The OT is characterized by the note of hope, yet biblical religion is quite realistic about the world and life. Few if any peoples have suffered as did Israel.

Nonetheless, there is a positive, forward-looking emphasis in the OT.

Hope, in the Bible, does not refer to what one wishes for or only desires. It involves the idea of expectation and is associated with the words for endurance and faith. What gives the character of expectation to the anticipations for the future is the nature of the God who is served. His control of the world and history gives certainty about the outcome of the human processes.

Reveals the Nature of God

What was true in OT times is true now. There is much biblical doctrine—about God, creation, covenant, etc.— which is simply taken for granted or assumed without being detailed again in the NT. Revelation of the nature of God did not have to be repeated. It is the God revealed in the OT and proclaimed in the New, whose son Jesus is. There are many references in the NT to God, but most of these depend on the OT for their content. There are new emphases and corrections of misunderstandings, but the premises about God remain the same. The Christian doctrine of God goes beyond the OT but does not contradict its teaching. Certainly more is known about God now; the Christian knows God primarily as he sees him in Jesus. The coming of Jesus has brought a new revelation of God's love. The OT, too, had declared God's love (Deut. 7:7-8, 13). But the depth and extent of that love have been shown most fully in Jesus—his coming, life, teachings, actions, and especially his death (John 3:16; 1 John 3:16; 4:7-10). The Christian God is the God of Abraham, Isaac, and Jacob, now better known because of Jesus.

Provides a Philosophy of History and Nature

There is a biblical philosophy of history. It is not stated as such, nor is it presented as modern philosophy of history might be. Because of the longer time span covered and the special nature of the OT contents, this biblical understanding of human events may best be seen from the OT. Those who have cut themselves off from the OT (as the ancient

Gnostics) have lost a historical perspective. Briefly stated, the biblical view of history is that God is active in human affairs, that he ultimately is in control, and that he accomplishes his purposes through human processes. Men and nations preserve their freedom, but God can still overrule and use their free choices for his larger designs. All human history is potentially open to God. He is not necessarily present in all events and in all nations, at least not to an equal degree. But all nations and all events are within his perception and providence. And he is particularly active at certain times among certain peoples. This does not violate the human and "secular" character of history. It is only by revelation on the one side and by faith on the other that God's actions in history may be known by men.

Human and world history had a point of beginning— creation. The biblical view of history is based on the doctrine of creation. The God who overrules history is the God who started the whole process in the first place. The Christian view of the natural order finds its fullest exposition in the doctrine of creation in the OT. God made the world, and all the earth is his (Ps. 24:1 and frequently). God has given dominion over the created order to man (Gen. 1:28). There is therefore full scriptural warrant for the scientific enterprise. Since the world remains the Lord's, man's dominion is that of a steward. Hence, there is no excuse for abuse or misuse of the natural order. Man is accountable to the Creator for what he does with the natural world.

Shows the Pattern of God's Revelatory Activity

There is a "pattern of correspondence" in God's revelations and saving activities. Because it is the same God acting in the arena of his own history and for men whom he has created, there are similarities running through the two Testaments. One of the recurring motifs of the Bible is that of the exodus (Exod. 12–15; Ps. 106:6-12, 47; Isa. 43:16-21; 63:7–64:7; Matt. 2:15; Rev. 15–16). Another common pattern is that of suffering followed by exaltation (1 Pet. 1:11; Isa. 52:13–53:12). The scope of OT history once more gives one the possibility of discerning recurring correlations.

The NT attaches itself firmly to the hopes and expectations of the OT. Perhaps one of the best ways of expressing the relationship between the Old and the New is in terms of promise and fulfillment. The OT is incomplete by itself. It is looking in promise to the future. Where does one find the completeness which fulfills the OT? The Talmud or the Gospels? The Jews, realizing the incompleteness of the OT, have sought to make the law applicable to ever new situations through the accumulated rabbinic traditions of interpretation. Jesus stepped into the prophetic tradition of the OT, and Christians have attached themselves primarily to the prophets and Psalms. This has continued the note of hope and given the further sense of fulfillment which characterizes Christianity.

PROBLEMS IN THE NEW TESTAMENT USE OF THE OLD TESTAMENT

According to one count, there are 239 acknowledged quotations of the OT, introduced by some kind of formula, in the NT; there are 198 quotations not introduced by any formula; there are 1,167 instances of OT passages reworded or directly mentioned. This makes a total of 1,604 NT citations of 1,276 different OT passages. There are many more allusions to the OT and borrowings of its phrases. Most of these passages represent a straightforward, literary use of the OT. The NT uses the Old in many ways: for vocabulary and phraseology to express its own ideas, for illustration, for proof of its statements, for moral instruction, for predictions of the new situation. Each of these and other uses could be discussed, but suffice it to say that problems in the NT use of the Old should not obscure the tremendous indebtedness of the later canon to the older, nor should they make that entire usage more problematic than it is.

An adequate treatment of the problems would involve looking at all the passages about which questions are raised, a task which must be left to the commentaries. Some of the principles applicable to a solution, however, may be seen by looking at three different types of problems: quotations in the New which do not agree with the OT text, statements in the Gospels of the fulfillment of OT passages which in their context have another meaning, and arguments drawn by Paul from the OT.

Variant text forms of the OT circulated in the first century, both in the Hebrew texts and in the various translations into other languages. Differences between the wording of OT verses and their quotations in the New Testament are often due to the latter's following a different version from that which later became standardized by the Jews. The NT authors, writing in Greek for Greek-speaking readers, most often quote the OT according to the existing Greek translation of the OT (the Septuagint) rather than making their own translation direct from the Hebrew. Usually the Greek translation is so close to the Hebrew in meaning that the English reader is not aware of any difference. Sometimes, however, the Greek version gives a different nuance to the text (as in the Matt. 3:3 quotation of Isa. 40:3). Variations from the Hebrew OT in the NT quotations are often, therefore, due to the use of the form of the text with which the author and his readers were familiar.

A few times a NT writer appears to follow the Aramaic paraphrases of the OT (the Targums) in use in the Jewish synagogues (as appears to be the case with the Eph. 4:8 use of Ps. 68:18). Christianity inherited not only a Bible, but an interpreted Bible, from Judaism. When an existing interpretation of a text fits the purposes of the author, he employs it. Sometimes the NT writers make their own interpretations of the OT and cite it according to its meaning (an interpretative quotation) rather than according to its exact wording (such may be the case in the Rom. 11:26-27 departures from Isa. 59:20-21). Or variations may simply be due in part to a free rendering as well as to an interpretive purpose (as in the Mark 7:6-7 use of Isa. 29:13). The interpretation may be effected by combining two texts from different places in the OT according to a common key word or according to a common subject matter. This Mark 1:2-3 quotes as from Isaiah a conflation of Malachi 3:1 and Isaiah 40:3. The explanation for Matthew 27:9-10, where a passage which seems to be closest to Zechariah 11:12-13 is ascribed to Jeremiah, may be that the quotation is a composite of ideas drawn from Jeremiah (cf. Jer. 18:1-3; 32:6-15). Although not covering all the problems, these practices provide an explanation for most of the instances where some have thought that the NT "misquotes" the OT.

Not all NT quotations of ancient writings are from the OT, and such quotation does not confer authority on anything beyond the idea quoted with approval (as Paul's quotation of Aratus in Acts 17:28 and the quotation of Enoch in Jude 14). The source of some quotations is unknown (James 4:5), and for the explanation to some problems we must simply confess our ignorance and await further information.

A different kind of problem is presented when a NT author assigns a different meaning to an OT text from what it apparently had in its context. The more that is learned about the exegetical practices of Jews in NT times, however, the more understandable the NT interpretation of the OT becomes. The Jewish interpretations of their Scriptures are known from the apocryphal and pseudepigraphical writings, rabbinic literature, the Targums, the Dead Sea Scrolls, and the writings of Josephus and Philo. The types of interpretation practiced in these sources were varied: literal, legal and edifying reapplication, prophetic-fulfillment, and allegorical. The NT authors' use of the Old is often parallel to the kinds of interpretation to be found in the Dead Sea Scrolls (especially in the "this is that" understanding of prophecy) and in the rabbinic literature (reinterpretation of OT texts for new situations, especially notable in Paul). Rarely, if ever, does the Hellenistic type of allegory represented by Philo enter into the NT. These various Jewish methods of treating the OT text supplied the techniques for the Christian writers in their exegesis of the OT. Such were a part of the Bible study and the communication process of the time. It would be far beyond the scope of this chapter, both in technicality and space required, to discuss these methods, but the bibliography will direct the interested reader to fuller treatments. It is sufficient for the present purpose to note that what may seem strange to the modern reader is often not so strange, or even is right at home, in the setting of first-century Jewish interpretation.

If Jewish exegesis supplied the methods, Jesus Christ supplied the formal principle for Christian interpretation of the OT. His coming and his work were seen as the key which unlocked the secrets of the OT. The problem of the NT interpreting the OT in a new sense occurs frequently in citations of events as fulfilling "prophecy." It is in these situations particularly that the revelation of Jesus Christ became normative for the Christian reading of the OT. Various theories have been put forward to explain the phenomenon: typology (an OT practice or event foreshadowed the NT counterpart), the "fuller sense" of Scripture (God had in mind a meaning or reference beyond what was described at the time), or "double fulfillment" (the prophet spoke of an immediate event which fulfilled his words, but a later event also fulfilled them). More important than labeling an explanation is to describe the reality. One passage may be selected to illustrate the nature of the problem and to suggest principles which may be helpful in a solution.

Matthew 2:13-15 says that the flight of Joseph and Mary with the infant Jesus to Egypt and their residence there until the death of Herod occurred in order "to fulfil what the Lord had spoken by the prophet, 'Out of Egypt have I called my son.'" The quotation is from Hosea 11:1. There is no element of prediction in the Hosea passage. It is a historical reference to the exodus of the nation of Israel, God's "first-born son," from Egypt (Exod. 4:22-23). One looks in vain for anything in Hosea's context which would suggest the life of Jesus or a prophecy of his time. A superficial view, therefore, might dismiss Matthew's statement as a misuse of Scripture, a pulling of a statement out of context and making it mean something which apparently was not intended. A deeper look, however, would suggest that this is a premature judgment. Matthew presents Jesus as the founder of the new Israel. His characteristic title for Jesus is "Son of God." Whether it be viewed as typology or "fuller sense" or whatever, there is a correspondence presented between what happened to the old Israel and the new salvation accomplished by Jesus. On this deeper level, the exodus of salvation for Israel found its counterpart in the experience of God's true Son. Jesus embodied and personified the nation, the true Israel; as such he was the beginning point of a new people of God. Jesus as the "beloved Son of God" "fulfilled" the experience of the people who were "typically" called God's "sons." In such a situation, instead of understanding "fulfilled" to refer to a prediction which comes to pass at a later time in history, we should think in terms of "this is the way God acts," "this is the pattern which is now accomplished," or "in this way the covenant promises are completely realized." When a Christian of the first century read the OT in the light of Christ's coming and activities, he could not help seeing parallels (patterns of correspondence) and so understand the OT in the light of the new developments. Very often, then, the presumed difficulties are of our own making when we impose our thought forms, or what we think ought to be the meaning, on the biblical texts. When we come to the Bible on its own terms and let the intentions and thought forms of the writer (which may be alien to us) determine his language and usage, then the problems or "discrepancies" either vanish or at least appear in a more understandable light.

Yet another way in which different (enlarged) meanings of the OT are found may be seen in the way Paul argues from it. Galatians 3–4, surveyed above, well illustrates the complex of freedom and faithfulness with which Paul dealt with the OT. There is a freedom which seems at times almost to abuse, if not ignore, the meaning of the OT, which on closer look is seen to be an obedient freedom derived from the standpoint of the coming of Christ. Looking at the law through Christ can mean a faithfulness to the law that at times makes him a stickler for literalism. Thus he insists on the grammatical singular of "offspring" instead of the proper meaning of the word (Gal. 3:16). He gives a literal application to Christ of the curse upon one who hangs on a tree (Deut. 21:23; Gal. 3:13). On a closer look, however,

Paul's use is faithfulness on a deeper level to the spiritual intent of the OT. It points to faith and a life of faith (Gal. 3:7, 9); it points to Christ (Gal. 3:22, 26).

The tension between an attentive listening to the text of the OT combined with a sovereign freedom in its use exemplified in the NT authors has remained a creative source of Christian theology throughout history. Maintaining the proper balance in the use of the OT remains important for the Christian today.

BIBLIOGRAPHY

Atkinson, Basil F. C. *The Christian's Use of the Old Testament*. Chicago: Intervarsity Christian Fellowship, 1952.

Bruce, F. F. *New Testament Development of Old Testament Themes*. Grand Rapids: Wm. B. Eerdmans, 1968.

Von Campenhausen, Hans. *The Formation of the Christian Bible*. Philadelphia: Fortress Press, 1972. (The first part of this study of the canon considers in depth the place of the OT in the church.)

Dodd, C. H. *According to the Scriptures*. New York: Scribner's, 1953.

Ellis, E. Earle. *Paul's Use of the Old Testament*. Edinburgh: Oliver and Boyd, 1957.

Grant, Robert M. *The Bible in the Church: A Short History of Interpretation*. New York: Macmillan, 1948.

Hanson, R. P. C. *Allegory and Event*. Richmond, Va.: John Knox Press, 1959. (Although primarily devoted to Origen's interpretation of the Bible, the first part of this book is a thorough study of the history of interpretation before his time.)

Longenecker, Richard. *Biblical Exegesis in the Apostolic Period*. Grand Rapids: Wm. B. Eerdmans, 1975.

Shires, Henry M. *Finding the Old Testament in the New*. Philadelphia: Westminster, 1974.

Tasker, R.V.G. *The Old Testament in the New Testament*. Philadelphia: Westminster, 1947.